Cafe Society

MUSIC IN AMERICAN LIFE

A list of books in the series appears at the end of this book.

Cafe ❧ Society

The wrong place for the Right people

Barney Josephson with
Terry Trilling-Josephson

Foreword by
Dan Morgenstern

University of Illinois Press
Urbana and Chicago

∞ This book is printed on acid-free paper.

Library of Congress Cataloging-in-Publication Data
Josephson, Barney.
Cafe Society : the wrong place for the right people /
Barney Josephson with Terry Trilling-Josephson.
p.   cm. — (Music in American life)
Includes bibliographical references and index.
ISBN-13 978-0-252-03413-8 (cloth : alk. paper)
ISBN-10 0-252-03413-9 (cloth : alk. paper)
1. Josephson, Barney.
2. Impresarios—United States—Biography.
3. Cafe Society (Nightclub)
4. Greenwich Village (New York, N.Y.)—
Social life and customs—20th century.
I. Trilling-Josephson, Terry. II. Title.
ML429.J65A3   2009
792.7092—dc22 [B]   2008027205

To Barney
1902–1988
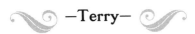 —Terry—

Contents

Illustrations follow pages 44, 102, 202, 252, and 336.

Foreword

Dan Morgenstern

Once upon a time, in Manhattan's Greenwich Village, there was a nightclub like no other before or since. Dubbed Cafe Society—an ironic touch provided by, of all people, Clare Boothe Luce (not yet a Republican member of Congress)—and adopting the slogan "the wrong place for the Right people," it was the brainchild of Barney Josephson, who had no professional experience in show business (he sold shoes). What he did have was abiding love for jazz and cabaret and profound admiration and respect for black performers, not just as artists but as human beings.

"I wanted a club," he said years after the December 28, 1938, opening of Cafe Society, "where blacks and whites worked together behind the footlights and sat together out front. There wasn't, so far as I knew, a place like it in New York or in the country."

Barney was right about that and just about everything else involving Cafe Society and then its sibling, Cafe Society Uptown, which opened on 58th Street between Park and Lexington Avenues in October 1940. The two clubs were different in layout and ambience, but the entertainment frequently involved the same cast of what Barney called a "floating company of musicians and comedians and dancers and singers."

And what a company it was! From a jazz perspective alone, the list is staggering, starting with the opening bill of trumpeter Frankie Newton's fine little band; the stellar boogie-woogie pianists Albert Ammons, Pete Johnson, and Meade Lux Lewis; blues shouter Joe Turner; and a young singer named Billie Holiday. The emcee was a then-unknown comic, Jack Gilford. The pianists and Turner were fresh from Carnegie Hall, where on Christmas Eve the enterprising talent scout and record producer John Hammond had presented his Spirituals to Swing concert, a paean to African American music. Newton was then a Hammond protege, and Holiday, of course, had been "discovered" by him.

In the early days of Cafe Society, Hammond was a key adviser to Barney and reserved Monday nights for jam sessions and showcases. The two men shared a strong commitment to the cause of black talent and what was not yet called civil rights, but Barney had his own ideas. He called the shots. Their first disagreement involved Holiday and the song "Strange Fruit," which she introduced at Cafe Society and which garnered both singer and club considerable publicity. Hammond thought the song, a searing protest against lynching, a wrong choice for Holiday—and so, at first, did she. Barney was persuasive, however, and the song remained in her repertoire for the rest of her life.

Barney's press agent, Ivan Black, was a friend from high school, and I came to know him well during my journalist days; suitably for this task, he was an original, almost as much of a maverick as Barney.

Barney also had a hand in the career of another, very different singer, Lena Horne, whose Cafe Society experience was a big step forward in her artistic maturation. The pianist and singer Hazel Scott was a third beautiful and talented discovery. She and Barney worked together on and off for seven years, and the reception at Cafe Society Uptown that followed her marriage to Adam Clayton Powell Jr. (Barney gave away the bride) tied up traffic for hours. Another great social event was a birthday party for Paul Robeson, a loyal Cafe Society patron.

A partial listing of the jazz names who appeared at the two cafes would include three pianists who led fine small bands there for long stints, Teddy Wilson, Joe Sullivan, and Eddie Heywood; the great James P. Johnson, Mary Lou Williams, Ellis Larkins, and Cliff Jackson also reigned at the keyboard. In addition, the club featured trumpeters Newton, Red Allen, Bill Coleman, and Joe Thomas; Lester Young in his first New York engagement as a leader, sharing the engagement with his kid brother and drummer, Lee; John Kirby's unique sextet; Django Reinhardt in his only American night club appearance, three weeks at Uptown; clarinetist Edmond Hall; and Big Sid Catlett, one of the greatest drummers in jazz history. Among the singers other than Holiday and Horne were Mildred Bailey, Kay Starr, and the young Sarah Vaughan.

And Barney was no stranger to the blues. Josh White became a star, and Big Bill Broonzy and Leadbelly and Sonny Terry took care of the basics. Another soulful style was presented by the Golden Gate Quartet, among Barney's favorites; he also had the bright idea of showcasing the dancer Pearl Primus.

As for the equally impressive list of folk and cabaret singers (Susan Reed, Burl Ives, and Lucienne Boyer) and comedians (Zero Mostel, Imogene Coca, and Jimmy Savo), I must leave some surprises for the reader to discover from Barney's own words, lovingly edited and expanded by his widow Terry Trilling-Josephson, and the many wonderful and evocative photographs that accompany them.

I did not experience the Uptown club, which Barney closed at the end of 1947, nor Downtown under his ownership, which ended in 1950. I did get to know Barney in 1971, when Mary Lou Williams approached him about bringing music to his Greenwich Village restaurant, The Cookery.

Thus began another great Josephson relationship with the music and people he loved. There were new faces, perhaps most notably that of eighty-two-year-old Alberta Hunter, making a celebrated comeback that emboldened other returns by vintage troopers. For jazz fans, there was the New York night club debut of the singular pianist and occasional singer Jimmy Rowles and reunions with such old friends as Teddy Wilson, Nellie Lutcher, Joe Turner, Helen Humes, Eddie Heywood, Rose Murphy, and Ellis Larkins. In all, it was a most welcome respite from then—alas, still—dominant trends in popular music. The Cookery was an intimate place, and Barney was a warm and welcoming host. I loved to watch his expression when something special was happening with the music. He knew! I'm sure that this book would elicit that same look.

Preface

Terry Trilling-Josephson

Alberta Hunter, an eighty-two-year-old blues singer, opened to rave reviews at a club in Greenwich Village, The Cookery, in 1977. I was eager to hear her, but two years went by. Then a friend invited my daughter and me to join her party for an evening at The Cookery. The proprietor of the club, Barney Josephson, was someone I had known casually years earlier. As Barney relates that evening in Part 5, he knew from our hostess that I was coming and was waiting for me. That evening in June 1979, I walked into The Cookery and into his life. It was an instantaneous romance.

During our first months together I was impressed with what seemed to be Barney's lifestyle. His apartment on Mercer Street in Greenwich Village was elegantly but simply furnished, a bachelor's apartment. Occasionally, early on, Barney would remark, "You know, Terry, I'm a poor man," without any explanation. Gradually, as our relationship grew, I learned the story behind those words. It is here in these pages.

Of more bearing during our years together were his joyous reminiscences of his cabarets in the late 1930s and 1940s, Cafe Society Downtown and Cafe Society Uptown. His face would light up. Barney was a marvelous raconteur, as you will discover as you travel along with him in his memories. The words are his from our taped recordings and from pieces of paper on which I would jot down a remembrance when the tape recorder was not handy.

I transcribed the tapes before Barney passed. He read the pages, and we worked together to clarify some of the stories on those pages. With Barney gone, the tapes and pages lay in my file cabinet for almost two years before I turned to them. I had transcribed the tapes in random fashion, picking a tape here, a tape there from the boxes. In front of me now was page upon page of unorganized, sometimes repetitive stories. How to proceed?

This was now a posthumous memoir, and I wanted to give Barney's story continuity and context. I had read a book by Maurice Isserman, the eminent American historian, in which he blended a first-person narrative with documentary material. That helped to give direction to my research into the social and political currents that swirled around and throughout Barney's life.

As I began to order my pages I found I had questions for Barney, but Barney wasn't here to answer them. I hadn't known then how much I didn't know about the world of jazz. I also encountered another, more trenchant, obstacle. Because of events over which Barney had no control, he had saved practically nothing from his Cafe Society days. There were a few press clippings and magazine stories, some photographs, and a letter answering a woman in the armed forces who had written objecting to African Americans being patrons at Cafe Society. There was no art.

I needed to fill in the gaps. My college library provided all manner of resources. I viewed a century of microfilm, from the 1900s to the 1990s, of daily newspapers. I also viewed microfilm of the entertainment publications *Variety* and *The Billboard* and "Goings on about Town" in *The New Yorker,* with their commentary on, and listings and dates of, weekly lineups of musicians and performers who appeared in New York nightclubs.

Another concern was photographs. I knew Barney employed a Cafe Society photographer, Albert Freeman, but where were all the photos? Then, one day, Al Freeman brought to Barney all the photographs he still had. When I asked about the negatives, Barney suggested that I telephone Al. Too late. Al had destroyed them to clear out his basement.

Of an evening, Barney would reminisce about the famous satiric murals that had covered the walls of Cafe Society Downtown at 2 Sheridan Square in Greenwich Village. Now 1 Sheridan Square, this 1834 building has been designated a landmark. All traces of its legendary occupant in the basement had long, long since disappeared—any remaining art painted over. I found two Cafe Society Downtown and Uptown matchbook covers, the art in color and the satiric logo, "Cafe Society: The wrong place for the Right people"— the uppercase *R*—another witty touch.

In the years since Barney's passing I have met—sometimes through sheer serendipity—and interviewed some of the musicians and performing and visual artists from the Cafe Society days. There were others whom I regret not interviewing. Now they are gone. Barney's friends and family were gracious in adding their memories as well.

As Barney's wife, I wondered whether the artists—legends now—might be reluctant to speak candidly. But what came through was their delight in sharing memories of a moment in time that meant so much to them. I was amazed at their impeccable and gleeful recollections that were, for some, more than seventy years ago. I have presented their recollections as a kind of conversation between the artists and Barney, picking up each other's memory and providing a choral quality to the story. The interviews were sometimes quite lengthy, and I cut them with great difficulty.

There are many interviews throughout. Although this is Barney's story, in his words, I felt it important to present a more transparent portrait of Barney and what transpired in his clubs from those who were there. Their recollections tell stories from a perspective which, obviously, Barney could not. I was unable to obtain an interview with Lena Horne after several requests. Therefore, I have selected relevant quotations from her various media interviews and speeches over the years. The reviews of the nightclub editors who covered the clubs also provide an added dimension to happenings.

Because of the many facets of Barney Josephson's life, his story must be considered as much in the larger context of a cultural history of the eras which his life spanned—1902 to late 1988—as the story of a legendary cabaret impresario. In these pages Barney relives that world and its values—*as it was then*—within the context of those times and without imposing contemporary values on history.

Barney was not an ordinary nightclub proprietor, engaged as he was throughout his life with the social and political issues of the day. He suffered the consequences of such engagement during the shameful McCarthy Era. Family, artists, and friends also were caught in the web of that time of fear and pain. The tales are here.

Barney's remarkable life was hallmarked by his integrity and belief in humankind—principles he brought to his work. He was a trailblazer in many ways. More than seventy years ago, Barney's policy of having blacks and whites work together on the same stage and inviting black people into his clubs as patrons was groundbreaking, even in the cosmopolitan northern city of New York.

It would be thirty years away from entertainment before Barney returned to the cabaret world in the 1970s and 1980s. That story and its accidental beginning is in Part 5, "Beginning Again: The Cookery, 1955–82." There, readers will meet some of Barney's artists of yore and his newer discoveries too.

Cafe Society was a concept before its time, acclaimed then and now for its revolutionary innovations, for its uniqueness, and for its creativity, inspired by the vision of one man. Barney Josephson's life, distilled through the prism of his words and through the observations of those who knew and worked with him, is very much alive and relevant today.

Acknowledgments

Terry Trilling-Josephson

Three men came into my life bearing gifts of encouragement, wisdom, and artistry—all because of Barney.

Ted Coons, Professor Edgar Coons, was always there for me with myriad kinds of help. He listened with compassion and understanding, always providing words of reason and reassurance whenever I needed to rail or my computer skills defeated me. I cannot count the untold number of hours that Ted unhesitatingly gave to ease insurmountable (to me) technical formating difficulties. I am ever grateful.

Jean-Claude Baker came to my rescue when publisher contracts were a bafflement; his warmth, exuberance of spirit, and book publishing knowledge were unbounded.

Tad Hershorn, media archivist at the Institute of Jazz Studies at Rutgers University, never knew Barney, but he lent his genius to my photographs and gave of his time beyond time to transforming the images—a feast for the eyes.

At the beginning, when these pages were only transcriptions of tapes, Don Congdon, my literary agent, had confidence that the pages could become a book and took me on until his retirement. I am everlastingly in Don's debt for giving me the courage to proceed. For the same reason, I will always be grateful to Peter Keepnews, jazz connoisseur for *The New York Times,* for believing that the disorganized pages he read had the potential to be an important story. Marilyn Stasio, the *Times*'s book reviewer, also was kind in offering advice.

My research was immeasurably facilitated by the awesome skills and courteous assistance of Florence Houser, Josephine Murphy, Adele Schneider, and Jeanne Galvin, librarians at my college (one of twenty-three colleges of the City University of New York), where I was a professor in the Department of Communications and Performing Arts, who located obsolete articles and out-of-print books with ease. My colleagues Norah Chase and Susan O'Malley in the English department willingly gave of their time and expertise.

At the impressive International Center of Photography in New York I met Erin Barnett, assistant curator of collections, and Chris George, an archivist, both of whom took special interest in searching the ICP's collections. Janet Kostrevski at Getty Images effected not one but two "deep searches" for pictures of Cafe Society artists.

Equally helpful were librarians in the Dance, Music, Theatre Divisions on the third floor of the New York Public Library for the Performing Arts at Lincoln Center.

Rob Hudson, associate archivist at Carnegie Hall, found unknown Cafe Society programs, the existence of which was a welcome surprise.

My friend Mikie Harris, assistant to the late John Hammond, brought me in her faithful 1986 Mercedes to Milt Gabler in New Rochelle and to Ira Tucker of the Dixie Hummingbirds at his recording sessions somewhere in Pennsylvania. The Dixie Hummingbirds's biographer, Jerry Zolten, always responded graciously to questions and provided the initial formating of my manuscript.

Ken Bloom, generous with his literary skills and contacts in publishing, led me to editor Richard Carlin, who led me to Judy McCulloh, then the executive editor at the University of Illinois Press; she, in turn, introduced me to my editor, Laurie Matheson. When an editor inspires you to believe that she loves your book, what higher praise? Laurie gave me that gift. Her guidance, patience, and support were there to bolster my (sometimes) flagging spirits. I rejoice that Laurie so well understood the story Barney had to tell.

Mary Giles, my copy editor, came late to this book and constantly amazes me with her uncanny keen eye as I abide by her expertise. I am appreciative of her care. Rebecca Crist, managing editor, never failed to respond with alacrity to requests born of my inexperience. I value associate editor Dawn McIlvain's grace, good humor, and unflagging optimism, which served to allay my many misgivings. Copenhaver Cumpston, art director, was gracious in resolving design differences.

I save special thanks for Dan Morgenstern, author, editor, and chronicler of jazz history. His prodigious harvest of work on behalf of jazz has been vital in helping keep that music alive.

I salute those photographers who freely donated their work in tribute to Barney, images that enhance these pages. Along the way were my friends to cheer me on and acquaintances I never met personally but who proffered good offices.

Above all else, the quiet love and unfailing support of my daughter, Kathe, allowed me the luxury of knowing I had someone on whom to call any time.

PART 1

A
Nightclub
Like
No Other

Prelude

Terry Trilling-Josephson

T he gale-force winds of a howling northwester had struck New York the day before, suddenly plunging the city, which had enjoyed unseasonably mild temperatures throughout the Christmas weekend just past, into the freezing depths of winter. Now, icy blasts still swept the streets and made passage difficult for the few bundled pedestrians who ventured outdoors. Some, shivering in cloth coats, could be seen hurrying along the narrow, windswept lanes of Greenwich Village. There, on the sidewalk in front of the doorway of Number 2 Sheridan Square, they were greeted by the strange sight of a doorman, directing folks through the door and down to the cellar below. A doorman may have been a rare sight in the Village; New York, like the rest of the nation, was mired in the Great Depression.

This was no ordinary doorman. True, he wore white gloves, but their fingertips had been cut off. His long doorman's livery coat was as ragged, dirty, and ill-fitting as that of any of the thousands of homeless unemployed who roamed the city. His elegant top hat was battered and discolored. But instead of asking for a handout when a couple approached, he bowed them in with a flourish, "Welcome to Cafe Society, the wrong place for the right people."

If the doorman's ironic dress and satiric greeting didn't tip off the patrons that they had arrived at a unique kind of nightclub, then the "Hitler monkey" may have foreshadowed that something different was waiting downstairs. The clay sculpture dangling in the stairwell leading to the room below sported the Führer's head on a monkey's torso, a noose around the neck. Soon, of course, it would be Hitler who had the free world by the neck.

In New York, a world war, although only nine months away, was unimaginable that night. Downstairs, patrons were shoehorned into every available space. They surrounded small tables and stood three deep at the bar. Everywhere you looked there was art—paintings and cartoons decorated all available space, on the walls, behind the bar, even in the restrooms.

Perhaps only a handful of those present had ever heard of the performers scheduled to appear. Jack Gilford, a comedian, was to emcee the show; Big Joe Turner, a blues shouter, would sing, with piano accompaniment from Pete Johnson, who hailed from Kansas City and who would join fellow pianists Albert Ammons and Meade Lux Lewis in a rousing jam session to showcase a new jazz novelty called boogie-woogie. Heading the program was a singer known only to hard-core jazz buffs, Billie Holiday. Even without big-name entertainment—you could go uptown to the Copacobana, the Versailles, La Martinique, the Latin Quarter, or the Savoy Plaza for that—an air of opening-night excitement filled the basement.

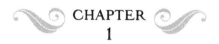

CHAPTER
1

"'Take my advice, go back to Trenton and open a shoe store that sells health shoes.'"

It was Wednesday, December 28, 1938, the opening night of my cabaret and the realization of a long-held dream. We were all set to open, everything ready—musicians, singers, comedian, waiters, bartender, hat check girl, food, liquor license nicely framed hanging on the wall, and such art as never was seen in nightclubs in this country. The room was packed with friends and relatives and friends of friends and their relatives. We were jammed with more than the legal 210 seating capacity.

Syd Hoff: *There were so many celebrities there, either from the theater or from politics. In those days there were at least a half-dozen senators and congressmen who were like-minded. I don't even recall if the customers danced at all.[1]*

Jack Gilford: *The whole dance floor was covered with tables. All the artists who had painted the murals were on due bills. The place was very crowded. Before I went on, Barney and his brother, Leon, called me into the office and said, "We must ask you not to get laughs tonight." "Why?" "Well, we forgot to get a cabaret license." So I went out and I got laughs because my routine was designed to get laughs. It was a funny routine. So they got a ticket from whoever was in charge of checking licenses.[2]*

I had forgotten to obtain a cabaret license. No entertainment in New York was possible without it. We had to do the show. So Jack Gilford went out anyway and opened the show. Every year on the anniversary of the opening of Cafe Society, no matter where he is, wherever he is working, be it on a movie location, television, stage, Jack sends a funny, nostalgic letter of those long-gone days, timed to arrive on December 28:

Dear Barney,

I keep telling you if you open a nightclub in New York City three days before New Year's Eve you will fail. I warn you three fat piano players will not attract business. Also a female black singer with a gardenia in her hair, a blues shouter singing about a sheik in any key, and a curly haired white comedian trying to convince audiences he looks and acts like a golf ball, will get you run out of town on a rail. Take my advice and go back to Trenton and open a shoe store that sells health shoes.

Yours, Jack. December 28, 1977

After I had graduated from high school in 1919, I didn't go to college. I went into the shoe business with my oldest brother, David. We were six children, two girls and four boys. Our mother had been left a widow at the age of thirty-seven when I was about six months old. She was a talented dressmaker and slaved long, long hours to feed, clothe, and house her children. Over the years the family had managed to save enough money to buy a house. Mother bought one with two mortgages. As soon as one mortgage was lifted, Dave got another mortgage to start what was to become the most elegant shoe store in Trenton, New Jersey.

Dave spoke to me, "Look, Barney, you know you're not the greatest student. We have two lawyers in the family now. I don't think you're quite smart enough to make it in medicine. But you're one hell of a good businessman and I need you in my business. Come in. When you're twenty-one I'll give you a third interest in the place."

The year when Dave made that proposition to me our shoe business showed a profit of $75,000. That was an awful lot of money at that time. And I would have a third interest, $25,000 a year, plus my living expenses. I would not have to touch the $25,000. I could save the entire amount each year. There was no income tax. I figured that by the time I would be thirty, I would be in a position to retire, I would have so much money.

I took over part of the buying. There was a shoe building in New York City on 34th Street and 6th Avenue known as the Marbridge Building. Manufacturers from all over the country had sample showrooms for shoe buyers who would come in to look over their lines, going from showroom to showroom. I would come over from Trenton because we used to do our buying almost weekly. We'd do our heavy buying from season to season, but there would always be fill-ins and new styles coming out. I would select the styles and sizes, but not from stock. The shoes were all made with our specifications. I would look at a sample shoe made in patent leather, "Well, I want that style, but I don't want that 'last,' meaning the shape. I want a rounder toe. I don't want a French heel. It's not for my clientele. I want a Cuban heel." I would pick from their swatches the exact shade of brown, blue, whatever, that I wanted. Dave relied on my taste, on my judgment.

I loved jazz. We were not a musical family in that we played any musical instruments. We didn't have money to buy them or pay for lessons. But we did have a record player. No radio. Mother played songs of famous Yiddish singers. I listened to jazz. Dave and Leon would bring me records, presents for their baby brother. They weren't interested. As a youngster I had become involved in what was then known as Negro liberation, and from that I got to jazz.

Being an out-of-town buyer, the salesmen would entertain me. "Where would you like to go?" "I wouldn't mind hearing Duke Ellington," who was playing at the Cotton Club on 142nd Street and Lenox Avenue in Harlem. He was about my age and already a big band leader. Ethel Waters was a star singer at the Cotton Club. There was a chorus line and variety and tap dance acts. We'd go to Small's Paradise or Connie's Inn at 131st Street and Seventh Avenue, owned by the mobster Connie Immerman. These were the three most popular clubs in Harlem.

During the thirteen years of Prohibition [1920–33], speakeasies, established and controlled by organized crime, sprang up, selling their bootleg booze to any and all, effectively breaking down existing social barriers. The so-called social register set mingled not only with the hoi polloi but with people of color. Rules were rewritten. Issues of race and class were obscured for booze and a good time.

The years after World War I saw a flowering of African American literature, music, dance, and the arts. Known as the Harlem Renaissance, it lasted through the middle of the 1930s' depression. In 1903 a book, *The Souls of*

Black Folks by W. E. B. Du Bois, had laid the foundation for the renaissance. Dr. Du Bois wrote that black equality could be achieved led by an educated black elite teaching pride in their African cultural heritage. African Americans brought their jazz and blues to the speakeasies and jazz clubs.

Prohibition ended in 1933 and so did speakeasies when Congress passed the Twenty-first Amendment. Some took on new faces and became fashionable nightclubs, like the Cotton Club, owned by a mobster, Owney "The Killer" Madden. In his early twenties he had served nine years of a twenty-year sentence in Sing Sing for killing another mobster over a woman. He had a deserved reputation for ruthlessness. It was known he rarely appeared at the club—had an unholy fear of publicity.

The Cotton Club was an enormous horseshoe-shaped room on two levels, seating over six hundred people, with small tables surrounding the dance floor and banquettes along the walls. The name *Cotton Club* alluded to the slaves toiling in the cotton fields down South; its jungle decor with artificial palm trees, a travesty. All their entertainers were Negro, but no Negro customers were allowed in the place. Duke Ellington couldn't have his mother come in to hear him play, in a manner of speaking. The greatest black celebrity could not enter as a patron. Or the exception was carefully screened before being allowed in and then only to be seated in the back near the kitchen or given the worst seating behind the columns—kept separate. To keep out the "undesirables," prices were exorbitant. A fifth of Scotch cost $18. To dance in the chorus line you had to be "high yaller"—"tall, tan and terrific" as the girls were advertised. The bandstand remained segregated. Black and white musicians were not allowed to perform together. Well, all this outraged me.

I would go to a club midtown called the Kit-Kat Club somewhere on the East Side in the Fifties, which stayed open until seven or eight in the morning and featured Negro talent. But the entertainment, if it was black, was all black. No mixing. The only time black and white musicians would play together in public would be in some small Harlem night spot. As more and more clubs began offering jazz in midtown they were not permitted legally to bar black patrons. But they could make it so uncomfortable that black people simply stayed away.

Colin Allen: *This was before Barney started Cafe Society. A friend of mine was a bartender at the Venetian Bar on Lexington Avenue a few* *blocks from 42nd Street. The policy there was that they would serve a black person at the bar. But when he finished his drink they would break the glass to let him know he wasn't welcome.*[3]

Wherever I went there was no Negro patronage. I thought, "Look what they're doing to these people. The only unique thing that we possess culturally in this country is the music the Negro people have given to us, our only indigenous art form. Gospel, blues, jazz, rock and roll, all originated from the spirituals and slave songs down South. Everything else was brought over from Europe."

Well, I knew what I wanted to do. I wanted a club where blacks and whites worked together behind the footlights and sat together out front, a club whose *stated advertised* policy would be just that. There wasn't, so far as I know, a place like that in New York, or in the whole country for that matter.

And—above all—I wanted a political cabaret. When I had started thinking in terms of a cabaret here, one of the most important reasons I wanted to open one, which I kept secret, was to have a political cabaret such as I had seen in Europe. This was my true purpose. Yes, I wanted a club that would be a showcase for our uniquely American music. But it wasn't that I wanted only jazz. I wanted to make a statement, to make a social and political commentary. So I dreamed I would come to this big city and open my own kind of cabaret.

Then there was another thing about it all. I was a young businessman. I saw the way the clubs were operated. They were all run by the mob. I don't know of one that wasn't. The Copacabana, El Morocco on East 44th Street, the Versailles, La Martinique, all racketeer-financed and controlled. Sherman Billingsley, proprietor of that society hangout, the Stork Club on East 53rd Street, was a terrible snob, an anti-Semite and anti-Negro. He had started out as a bootlegger and could never have made it without his gangster affiliations.

As soon as you would enter these places and looked around you could pick out the bouncers. They would have these great big brutes standing there, ready to toss you out first thing if you got out of line, drank too much, said anything that created a disturbance. They used all kinds of gimmicks to cheat their customers, trick glasses that looked big and roomy but really held maybe half a jigger of whiskey. Those things would happen often enough.

I said to myself, "The nightclub is a business like every business, why can't it be run like a business? Instead they run it like any racket in which they have an interest. They don't give you a decent drink of whiskey. They don't serve decent food. They push you around. One of these days I'd like to open one of these places and run it like a business." So I had the notion.

But our shoe business was very successful and I was making a lot of money for a kid of my age, so I didn't do anything then. We had *the* quality shoe store in the town. My brother, Dave, opened a second shop and leased a department in a ready-to-wear shop as well. There were now three places in which we were selling shoes in this small town. And I was part of this with my brother.

The Great Depression, and Dave got caught—forced into bankruptcy, forced to close our shoe store. After Mother passed away in 1935 there was nothing to keep me in Trenton. I became a clerk and buyer in a shoe store in Atlantic City, living in a $4 a week room, eating in Bayliss's drug store across the street from the store. I trimmed the windows, did the buying, sold the shoes, fitted them. If there was a complaint, I handled it. I did all the orthopedic corrections, metatarsal pads, arch supports, wedges on heels for our shoemaker to put on. I had gone to orthopedic school to learn all about feet when I was with Dave.

It was coming on spring 1937 when my brother, Leon, telephoned me in Atlantic City. "Kid, quit your job. You're coming to New York. You're going to open your nightclub that you've been dying to open." "With what?" "I've got with what for you."

I quit my job. Leon knew my dream. We were very, very close brothers. My boss, who had been a shoe clerk in our store in Trenton, had opened his own shop in Atlantic City. I'm working for him now where he used to work for us. Our roles were reversed.

"Barney," he said. "You'll regret the day you walked out on me. You'll be sorry. You'll be wanting this job back. You're making a big mistake to leave." He was so angry. I walked out, and I took a train to New York. I had seven dollars and sixty-odd cents in my pocket. The country was still deep in the Great Depression. I never went back to Atlantic City.

Leon had a couple of friends in New York who had a little money, businessmen. Leon had borrowed $3,000 from each of them, a total of $6,000. He handed the money to me. "Go, open your nightclub."

Cheap as things were then, prices were low, incredibly so by today's standards, still, to open a cabaret in New York for $6,000, I don't know what Leon was thinking. A liquor license alone was twelve hundred dollars a year. With Leon's borrowed $6,000 I started to look for a space in Greenwich Village.

Rents were cheaper there. I found a shuttered-up cellar in a building where West 4th Street merges with Washington Place, Number 2 Sheridan Square. The cellar had been the site of speakeasies, the Four Trees Inn and later the Oliver Twist. They folded with the end of Prohibition. The space had been vacant for quite some time.

The night I opened my cabaret I was in debt for $18,000. The rent was all of $200 a month, plus a couple of hundred dollars to put up for security to Con Edison. There was construction work to be done: put up a new ceiling, install a sound system, rig lights, build a kind of bandstand, a bar to stock, a kitchen to set up, food, glasses, silverware, tables, chairs, everything to be bought. I'm in debt $12,000 for construction alone, plus Leon's original $6,000 on which I'm also living. I have no income. But I don't have to pay the staff right away. And Leon said, "Take your time paying back my friends."

While I was in Trenton working in our shoe store I had met a very nice young Czech woman, Izabel Laromada. She would come and spend weekends with me in Atlantic City or I would go to New York to her studio apartment. It was nice, and we were good together. I wouldn't say I was in love with her, but I liked her a lot. When I quit Atlantic City I couldn't afford a room. Izabel, living in New York, made to order, so I moved in with her. That started our living together. It was pleasant enough so it continued. We lived together for three years. She stayed at her job in Stern's Department Store on West 34th Street. I presented her to everyone as my wife even though we weren't legally married.

I am now from shoes to booze and food and entertainment and I don't know the nightclub business. I have to learn it. I was thirty-six years old. This was the time to open a nightclub. Fiorello H. LaGuardia, mayor of New York since 1934, was giving the tinhorns and underworld a hard time. He had spent his boyhood in Arizona where tinhorns were professional gamblers. He cracked down hard on all kinds of gambling—bookmaking, cards, lotteries, craps games. He went after the slot machine empire under the "protection" of one-time bootlegger Frank Costello. Some thirty thousand slot machines had been placed by the racketeer in candy shops, restaurants, pool rooms, all over. You didn't dare refuse. Your business or your life would be wiped out. The photos in the newspapers of the mayor, sledgehammer in hand, personally smashing confiscated slot machines, were great publicity—not for the mobsters.

When the country went wet again the bootleggers found other avenues of crime. They didn't miss much—loan sharking, prostitution, importing heroin, the numbers racket, the garment and fur industries, the Fulton Fish Market in lower Manhattan, the Longshoremen's Union. Restaurants and nightclubs were Dutch Schultz's domain. He would later be killed by his Murder, Inc. partners, the dreaded crime syndicate. Chairman of that board was Lepke Buchalter, who, together with his childhood friend Gurrah (so-called for growling "gurrah-a-here") Shapiro, were the most feared mobsters of their time. Lepke would eventually end up in Sing Sing's electric chair [on March 4, 1944] courtesy of U.S. District Attorney Thomas E. Dewey.

From his first day in office, LaGuardia made war on the racketeers. He had an unrelenting hatred of them. He did his best to run them out of New York. He called them by name, so and so and so, get out of town or I'll run you out. He got a lot of them out. They went to Florida for a sun bath. This was a corrupt enough city with too many of the politicians, the police, and the courts on the take. But for whatever he was, a Republican, elected on a Fusion reform ticket to clean up the mess left by the dapper and corrupt Mayor Jimmy Walker, the "Little Flower," as LaGuardia was affectionately called—he was five feet two and rotund—was an honest man. He made New York a little more of an honest and humane city. He talked to New Yorkers on the city's radio station, WNYC; read the comic strips for the kids, taking on all the characters.

Colin Allen: *I admired Barney. He was a cool manager. Opening a club, he was the target of the mob who tried to move in. He was the target of the cops who were on the take. He also had the problem of customers who objected to—well some of them were just plain drunk—but some objected to the integration of the club. Harold Johnson, his manager, was very effective in escorting them out.*[4]

The way the mobsters operated in the clubs and restaurants was to come into a newly opened place and declare themselves partners. They'd let anybody open up, then they would walk in and tell the owner, "We're in for a third, for a half. The cloak room is ours." Whatever they wanted they would take. That would be their share for their "protection." With Fiorello LaGuardia in office it seemed safe for me to come in, and I did.

CHAPTER
2

"'I've got Billie Holiday. . . .'
'Who is she?' I asked."

When I came to New York, I had been introduced to Sam Shaw, an artist and photographer who had a feel for show biz. Sammy was a young man about town who turned out to be my guardian angel. When I told him my ideas for my cabaret, he was very enthusiastic.

"There's a guy around named John Hammond. You should meet him because he feels the way you do about the Negro people. And he knows more about jazz than anybody in the world." One of John's first jobs was writing for a newspaper, the *Brooklyn Eagle*. Sam and John had met when John had been a delegate to the first Newspaper Guild convention in 1935.

Sam didn't waste any time. "We're going to see John Hammond." In those days John was supporting and publishing something called the *Labor Press,* a newspaper of sorts. This was his interest then, among other things. He had a little broken-down office somewhere Midtown Manhattan. John was tall, with a dazzling smile.

"Sam tells me you're going to open a nightclub. What kind of a place is it going to be?"

"Well, first it's going to be a nightclub that has something to say, and we're going to have Negro and white talent working together. The talent and musicians will be integrated. I want fresh, unknown talent. In addition to that, I will invite the Negro public in as patrons."

John shook my hand. "I can help you. Leave it to me. I've got Billie Holiday. I'll bring her in for you as your first singer."

"Who is she?" I asked.

This was the time when John was producing a concert at the venerable Carnegie Hall, From Spirituals to Swing, with backing by the *New Masses,* a left-wing, highly esteemed cultural magazine. John had gotten talent he discovered traveling all over the country, from North Carolina, from Chicago, from Arkansas, from Kansas City, all kinds of places.

"Barney, why don't you come up to Carnegie Hall and take a look at some of the rehearsals?" I went up and was bowled over by the talent John was presenting. "Well John, I don't have to look any further. This is it. It's all here."

From Spirituals to Swing opened December 23, 1938, five days before my own opening. John's concert was a huge success, knocked the music critics off their seats. Nothing like this had ever been done before. His program notes referred to the southern spirituals, blues, boogie-woogie, and jazz being performed as "the music nobody knows." Billie Holiday wasn't in John's concert.

John Hammond: *I wanted to present a concert in New York which would bring together for the first time, before a musically sophisticated audience, Negro music from its raw beginnings to the latest jazz. The concert should include primitive and sophisticated performers. I wanted to include gospel music as well as country blues singers and shouters . . . artists whose music had never been heard by most of the New York public.*[1]

It was an education for this Trenton boy. John had turned over the hallowed Carnegie stage to three boogie-woogie piano players to open the program. It was quite a moment when the lights went up on an old upright boardinghouse piano with Albert Ammons seated at it. John told me he had searched to find this particular one, a Wing and Son make. Meade Lux Lewis and Pete Johnson were on a Steinway, the three playing together this unknown jazz form, boogie-woogie, which swept the country in the forties.

In his teens, John had in his record collection Clarence "Pinetop" Smith, the original boogie-woogie pianist. A few years later when he heard Meade Lux Lewis on a record playing boogie-woogie blues, he tried to locate him but couldn't find him. He was in the Club De Lisa in Chicago in 1935 where

Albert Ammons was playing and asked him if he happened to know Meade Lux Lewis.

"Sure I know him. He's around the corner working in a car wash."

John discovered Pete Johnson playing at the Sunset Club on the main drag in Kansas City, with Joe Turner working bar and shouting the blues.

Mary Lou Williams: *While Joe was serving drinks he would suddenly pick up a cue for a blues and sing it right where he stood, with Pete playing piano for him. I don't think I'll ever forget the thrill of listening to Big Joe Turner shouting and sending everybody night after night while mixing drinks.*[2]

At its height, Kansas City had some five hundred nightclubs with live music, gambling, numbers, and whorehouses. The city's political machine was controlled by a notorious bootlegger, Tom Pendergast. Besides controlling the liquor trade, he controlled the city police, the courts, clubs like the Sunset Club. Pendergast was indicted for tax evasion in 1938, same as Al Capone, and so his reign ended.

Onstage that historic night at Carnegie Hall, "Big Joe Turner shoved the mike out of the way, as though flicking lint from a lapel and started shouting the blues in an open-throated tone that carried to the far reaches of the Hall."[3] The legendary gospel singer Sister Rosetta Tharpe and her guitar and the gospel quartet Mitchell's Christian Brothers thrilled me to my bones. There were blues harmonica great Blind Sonny Terry and Count Basie's band with singers Helen Humes and Jimmy Rushing and James P. Johnson on piano with Sidney Bechet on soprano sax, jamming with Bill Basie. I heard for the first time Big Bill Broonzy, the blues singer and former farmhand from Arkansas, and the Kansas City Six with Buck Clayton and Lester Young. At one time or another most all of these artists played at Cafe Society.

I had already hired Albert Ammons and Meade Lux Lewis to open Cafe Society. Just before our opening, John comes over to me. "Barney, I'd like you to put on Pete Johnson."

I protested. "John, I have two boogie-woogie piano players now. I've got a budget. I can't just put everybody to work. I've got seven men in the band. I've got a relief piano player in between. I've got Billie Holiday and Jack Gilford. Where am I going to get the money?"

"Well, I could take him to work any place on 52nd Street, but I want you to have him. I don't want him on 52nd Street. You should have them all, get a monopoly on boogie-woogie pianists. You've got to have him. They'll all play together." I gave in. John gave me his broad smile.

A little while later he comes back. "By the way, there's a guy who sings the blues, Joe Turner. He goes with Pete." He gives me one at a time.

So I left the music to John Hammond. With his influence the emphasis in my cafe was on the music. I now had the greatest jazz connoisseur and talent scout at my elbow pushing me in that direction. I didn't need much pushing.

When I met John he was making his name as a discoverer and nurturer of unknown talent, and as a record producer. He had already produced blues legend Bessie Smith's final recordings in 1933. Three days later he made Billie Holiday's very first recording session with Benny Goodman and then again, in 1935, with Benny sitting in as sideman; Teddy Wilson, piano; Roy Eldridge, trumpet; Cozy Cole, drums; Ben Webster, tenor sax; John Kirby, bass; John Truehart, guitar.[4]

My original plan, before meeting John, had been to go around to the places where the musicians played and engage them there. I knew where to go for such talent from my days as a shoe buyer coming to New York. I certainly never could have found the unknown and remarkable talent John discovered traveling around this country. It was Sam Shaw's inspiration to introduce me to John Hammond. He recognized kindred souls.

John's upbringing gave no inkling to what was to become his all-abiding interest and life's work. He was a young millionaire whose father was a big corporation lawyer on Wall Street. His mother was Emily Vanderbilt Sloane. His maternal grandmother was a Vanderbilt who had married one of the Sloanes of the W. and J. Sloane's high-priced furniture store. He was born into a mansion at 9 East 91st Street, which had a ballroom seating 250 people, a household staff of sixteen servants. When he was twenty-one he inherited a lump sum of money in addition to an income of $12,000 a year from a trust, "ample but not princely," John's words.

He went to all the fancy schools, Hotchkiss, Yale, and yet he became a champion for Negro rights. This man, who played classical viola, was committed to jazz, to helping Negro musicians. He would scout out the talent, bring them to New York at his own expense, record them, and then have to send them back because he'd not been able to get them work—until I came along.

One time John had wanted to put the trombonist Benny Morton into Teddy Wilson's band at Cafe Society. Benny, at that time, was with Count Basie. "John, I can't afford to pay Benny what he's getting with Basie." "Barney, just pay him the usual salary and don't worry." I learned much later that John had been making up the rest out of his own pocket.

I had often wondered how John came to all this. One evening several years after Cafe Society had opened John came in with a very distinguished gray-haired gentleman. As I passed their table John reached out and stopped me.

"Barney, I'd like you to meet someone. I'd like you to meet John McChesney. Mr. McChesney was one of my teachers at Hotchkiss. He's the man who began to change my social and political opinions."

This gentleman was a socialist and an agnostic. His Sunday philosophy class would meet in his house after chapel "to undo the harm of the Sunday services" he would tell his students half-seriously.[5]

So here in this fancy boys' school, a Vanderbilt gets these ideas. I got them coming from a poverty-stricken family who had taken a boarder into their house who instilled one brother with these ideas which were handed down from brother to brother, ending up with me.

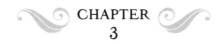
"I saw Gypsy Rose Lee do a political striptease."

S ome years earlier, in 1931, I had visited Europe and was impressed by the cabarets I went to in Paris, Berlin, Prague, Vienna. These were cafes where performers satirized the contemporary political and cultural scene in songs and poetry, comedy sketches and monologues, dance and mime. The stages were small so that there was a sense of intimacy between those onstage and the audience. You could even engage in repartee with the performers.

In Paris I visited a cabaret for the avant-garde, Lapin Agile in Montmartre. I well remember my first visit, walking up the steep, sloped, unpaved street to a little two-story house. Hanging outside the house was a hand-painted sign of a large rabbit jumping out of a frying pan, a wine bottle on an extended paw. And inside! Forget the smoke-filled room with wooden tables and chairs. On the walls hung art—a Picasso harlequin, a Utrillo, Cubist art, African art. Artists' paintings and sculpture were all around—their art in exchange for drink. This was a meeting place for artists, poets, and writers, bohemian characters then, some world-renowned years later.

It was in Berlin that I was most taken with the German cabarets where the performers presented biting satirical comment in intimate settings. Inflation was rampant. The rates on the German mark changed every hour it seemed. Millions were unemployed. The people were desperate. Thousands upon thousands of small businesses had gone under; poverty and misery everywhere. Outside of my hotel on the streets of the Potsdamer Platz, it was just terrible. People were begging for food. There could be maybe ten girls fighting over who would get the next john. These were turbulent years for Germany's first experiment with democracy under the Weimar Republic.

With Germany's World War I humiliating defeat, a demagogue had appeared on the scene promising prosperity and the restoration of German glory. In time, he would tear up the Treaty of Versailles; Jews and communists would be dealt with later. His National Socialist German Workers Party received over 18 percent of the vote and won 107 seats in the German Reichstag in the September 1930 elections. The Nazis had become the second-largest party in Germany.

During the years of the Weimar Republic the intelligentsia, the writers, artists, cartoonists, composers, poets, left-wing intellectuals, the avant-garde, were free to satirize social conditions and comment on the reactionary political forces gathering in the country. Performers worked on small stages in close surroundings. They said what they wanted to say and weren't affiliated with any political party. All this, for me, was exhilarating. I soaked it up.

The permissiveness of postwar Berlin after the Armistice in 1918 provided other kinds of entertainment, too. In these types of clubs everything went, nude dancing, erotic performances, lesbians, gays, transvestites, prostitutes, drugs.

I visited the most famous entertainment palace, Haus Vaterland on the Potsdamer Platz, something out of a De Mille extravaganza. I don't know how many rooms there were. Each room had its own special setting representing different countries, with entertainment to match. There would be an American nightclub with really good jazz and dancing for the patrons, or you could visit an American burlesque show. There was a Turkish cafe serving sweet, strong coffee, complete with belly dancers; a Wild West bar with a band of black musicians dressed up as cowboys; a Spanish room with flamenco dancers and singers; many more such rooms.

In Berlin, I saw the cabaret revues of Friedrich Hollander. He had introduced into the cabaret world the idea of musical revues which were socially satiric and political. In his time, he wrote and produced scores of these revues, with jazzy, catchy music. He wrote, too, for the German movies. One of his most enduring songs, "Falling in Love Again," introduced Marlene Dietrich in the German film *The Blue Angel*. He fled Nazi Germany in 1933. Hollywood welcomed him, where he wrote many film scores and directed any number of movies. He was one of the luckier ones. Many—so many—of the cabaret artists were brutally murdered in the Nazi concentration camps.

In Prague, I visited the Liberated Theatre, where Jiri Voskovec and Jan Werich wrote and performed their own political, biting revues. They, too, fled when the Nazis overran Czechoslovakia and found work here as actors.

From the very beginning I was always searching for political satire. I didn't want the typical vaudevillian burlesque, slapstick styles of comedy that had made the Copacabana nightclub comedian Joe E. Lewis and others of his ilk so popular. I wanted comedy with a real satiric sting. I didn't think the agit-prop shows I saw in Europe would be appropriate in New York. Agitating and propaganda were popular in the 1930s in many European cabarets to expose the rising tide of fascism. You have to present your material in a form that's palatable to your particular audience, that's amusing yet still says something. One of my ideas, inspired by the cabarets I had visited, was to have a comedian "play off" the day's newspaper headlines for satire and laughs, timing and delivery being essential.

Determined to open a European-style political cabaret, I knew where I might find this kind of talent. There was a group of wonderfully talented well-known Broadway actors who performed with a company called the Theatre Arts Committee, or TAC as they were familiarly known. They performed in a rundown building on East 55th Street called Chez Firehouse because it had once been a firehouse. The performances were on Sunday afternoons. There was Phil Loeb, who would later star as Jake, Mollie's husband in *The Goldbergs*, the first-ever television sitcom. There was Sam Jaffe, the ancient, two-hundred-year-old high lama in the 1937 movie *Lost Horizon*.

And I saw Gypsy Rose Lee do a political striptease there. "You might think my mind is on lifting my skirts. You're wrong; it's on lifting the Embargo." President Roosevelt had approved a ban on exporting arms to aid the Spanish Loyalists who were fighting a desperate battle against the fascist forces of Generalissimo Franco.[1]

> **Theodore Strauss:** *The Cabaret TAC doesn't like Herr Hitler, an attitude which can hardly be termed unique. . . . this hardy band of troupers has arrived with a topical revue which is imaginative, sharp, twice as funny as the routine gags of the Broadway bistros and almost as amusing as the gowns and other decor displayed by the glittering so-*

ciety which populates fashionable emporia also in the East Fifties. . . .
let us give a special cheer for Philip Loeb, the wittiest M.C. in town. . . .
In a season of anemic night club entertainment it is good to welcome
the actors back. They have something to say and they say it pungently.
El Morocco, choose your weapons.[2]

At one of these shows I watched Jack Gilford doing a comedy routine. I
offered him a job to open my new cabaret. I had been looking for a comedian who had satirical material. I wasn't interested in presenting just a funny
guy with worn-out jokes. Jack's satirical humor was very funny for me. His
artistry was not typical nightclub comedy. That's what attracted me. While
John Hammond was taking care of the jazz end, someone like Jack was my
doing entirely.

Jack was about twenty-nine at the time. He had been working as a straight
man for Milton Berle in burlesque, sitting in the audience throwing insults
to Berle onstage. That was Jack's first paid acting job. When I offered him the
opportunity to perform his own material, this was most appealing to him.

Jack Gilford: *The master of ceremonies at TAC was Heywood Broun, a*
friend of mine whom I had worked with in the summer. He had asked
me to get something together that would be appropriate entertainment.
It was something I'd never done before publicly, and it went very well.
The Shuberts [Broadway theater owners and producers] were there, and
they wanted me to do that act in Hellzapoppin, *which was running on*
Broadway. I didn't think it was right for their show, but I said, "Sure."
Then Barney came over, and he said, "We're opening a cafe called
Cafe Society down in the Village, and I wonder if you're interested."
"Well, the Shuberts just asked me if I wanted to go into their show," I
told Barney, "and I said yes." I don't know whether I said, "We'll see how
it goes." Anyway, I did go into Hellzapoppin *for one show, and it didn't*
do well, as I knew it wouldn't. Then I called Barney and said, "Okay."
This was in September. Barney engaged me for the great sum of $50 a
week. Nobody had any money, and $50 a week was something.

There was a writer, but I can't remember who it was. We used to meet
every day at the club while they were building it and write opening-night
material. My problem was that my material was not like the average ma-
terial of nightclub comedians in those days. For some reason I was cursed
with doing something different than the others, which made it very hard
for me.[3]

Jack had progressive instincts and feelings and was willing enough but, like most comedians, not able to write the kind of satirical material which I had hoped to present. Jack wrote some of his routines, but for some we had writers writing for him. The problem was getting writers who could write for comedians like Jack to perform in my cafe. It was easier to get performers than to get routines which at the same time would be suitable for a comedian's special brand of comedy.

"'Tell your friend to call it Cafe Society.'"

W e were going to be unlike all other nightclubs. Cigarette girls would not sell little stuffed doggies and gardenias for the ladies. No one would be taking photographs at the tables.

I had ideas about decor. Most nightclubs then were decorated with plush velour draperies and mirrors on the walls. If there were columns, as many of the clubs had because they were generally large places, the columns were made into fake palm trees, like the Copacabana. I abhorred this kind of decoration. If it was the Cotton Club or Smalls Paradise in Harlem, the decor's themes would reflect their version of exotic "primitive" African jungles. When I first visited those clubs, before I was in the business, it was Duke Ellington's "Jungle Band," playing songs such as "Jungle Nights in Harlem," "Echoes of the Jungle."

Well, I would have none of that. I wanted a place with art. No matter what I ever did in my time, as poor as I ever was, I had a picture on my wall. It could be a 25 cent print, but I had a picture on my wall. I wanted that in my club. I wanted fine art. When I told Sam Shaw that I wanted fine art on my walls, "I know the guys for you."

Syd Hoff: *It was a cold winter day in the Village. I just happened to be walking in that area. Along came Sam Shaw, whom I knew, and he had* *this guy with him who was dressed much nicer than Sam. Sam introduced me to Barney. We walked over to Sheridan Square, to this empty store, down the stairs. The chairs were on the tables. It was just nothing. Apparently there had been some kind of club there before. Barney described roughly the club he had in mind. In a second I had agreed to do a mural.*[1]

Sam called a group of artists together. We met in a place on MacDougal and Eighth Street, the Jumble Shop. I told them about my project, what I wanted to do. It was quite a group that day.

There was Adolph Dehn, whose innovative lithographs opened a whole new approach to print-making. He was considered one of America's greatest watercolorists. There was Sam Berman, who originated the original trademark for the cover of *Esquire* magazine, that little man with the bulging eyes and white handlebar mustache.

Syd Hoff: *Berman actually sculpted the* Esquire *figure called "Esky." He would make them out of clay. "Esky" was supposed to be a wealthy man, a club man.*[2]

There was Ad Reinhardt, who even then was an important talent in abstract art and was hired to head the Easel Division of the WPA Federal Art Project. The mural he painted for Cafe Society, like his *New Yorker* cartoons, lampooned the currently fashionable. "Art is a weapon," he said.

There was Alice Stander, a really good artist who was married to the gravelly voiced Hollywood actor Lionel Stander. Earl Kerkam was actually from the world of fine arts, painting still life, portraits, and figures. In his youth he had drawn political cartoons for the *Washington Post*.

There was Abe Birnbaum, a discovery of the legendary *New Yorker* editor Harold Ross. Abe drew over two hundred covers for the magazine during the forty years he was on staff there. He was versatile. He drew portraits for their "Profiles" and drawings for their "Reporter at Large." His last cover appeared three weeks before he passed away.[3]

There was the brilliant Syd Hoff, who signed his *New Yorker* cartoons of working-class folks "hoff," always with a small *h*. In the years to come Syd became even more famous as a storyteller in the delightful children's books he wrote and illustrated.

Syd Hoff: *I probably have done maybe 250 children's books. My most important ones are the ones I did for Harper [and Row] in 1958. Harper* *published my book* Danny and the Dinosaur, *which will probably be a best-seller forever. Since then I've done about a half-dozen sequels to that book.*

In 1936, when Franco led the fascists against the elected Republican government of Spain, artists here took it upon themselves to appear in public to enlist support for a ship that was called the Relief Ship, bringing medical supplies to Spain for the Republican side. Abe Birnbaum and I stood on the street at Columbus Circle in New York City. A crowd would gather around, and we would do a "chalk-talk," drawing figures. The point of it really was to create morale.[4]

There was John Groth, who was art editor and cartoonist for the newly founded *Esquire* magazine in 1933. He drew gag cartoons and illustrations for the *New Yorker* and political cartoons for the afternoon New York newspaper, *PM*. During World War II, as a correspondent for the *Chicago Sun*, he scooped all the other journalists by riding the first jeep into Paris at its liberation from the Nazis. He covered five other wars, including Vietnam.[5]

There was Gregor Duncan, a very young artist, a wonderful painter, whose life was sadly cut short, killed on the Anzio beachhead when we invaded Italy in World War II.

There was William Gropper, whose paintings and cartoons have been likened to Daumier. His cartoon in *Vogue* magazine satirizing the Japanese emperor, Hirohito, was front-page news in 1935 when Tokyo called the U.S. State Department to suppress it.

Anton Refregier had fled the Russian Revolution with his parents when he was a teenager. Years later, in 1957, he was honored with a retrospective of his work at The Hermitage in Leningrad.

There was Christina Malman, who in her too-short life drew over thirty-five covers and more than five hundred drawings for the *New Yorker*. She died [in January 1959] of some rare disease at the age of forty-six.

Talented and modest, Colin Allen captured Cafe Society in his witty newspaper ads and designed our equally witty matchbook covers in five colors.

Colin Allen: *I was a struggling cartoonist in those days, doing what they call "gag panels" for* Colliers *and the* Saturday Evening Post *and illustrating columns and articles for King Features. Very little of my work for the* New Yorker *was published. They bought ideas from me and other cartoonists. They would farm them out to the regular staff.*

I had been doing some work for the Journal-American *for their Saturday or Sunday magazine section. They had run some articles ridiculing the nightclub situation in the Stork Club, the Club 21, and others as being arrogant and snobbish. I illustrated them. They were more or less the same attitude we had at Cafe Society, ridiculing the arrogant and the snobs.*[6]

I had never met any of the artists before. It was all Sam Shaw's doing. The basement room had spaces with columns coming down the walls. I told the artists, "You're free to paint what you like, absolute freedom. I do not want you to submit any sketches. Choose your spaces. This is your panel, your space. Paint." Sam made a deal for me with the artists. I would supply the panels, the canvases, all the materials to paint with. Everyone was to be paid the same, $125 each. In addition, I would give them due bills of a like amount for food and liquor. Sam worked that out with them.

Syd Hoff: *The wonderful thing about the due bill is that my wife and I became visitors at a nightclub. For that $200 we were there almost all the time. Barney had a wonderful cook. This was a fellow who had a small store on University Place, and Barney put him in charge of the kitchen. And so the meals were wonderful. We were there supposedly eating up our due bill, but I'm sure we went all the way over that. At the time, Sam Shaw was working for Irving Hoffman who was sort of a Walter Winchell.*[7]

Colin Allen: *Sam Shaw told me that he and Irving Hoffman, a publicist who had Coney Island as one of his accounts, cooked up the idea in the Fun House of ejecting a stream of air, and when a woman walked over it, it would blow her skirt up. It was Marilyn Monroe who originally was at Coney Island with them. Sam did the same thing for a movie with Marilyn Monroe over a subway grate in Manhattan.*[8]

One of the people I hired was a young antifascist seaman, Harold Johnson, a member of the National Maritime Union, Joe Curran's union. Harold was hired as my manager. I gave people of this persuasion jobs in my establishment because that's how I felt too.

We hadn't opened yet. I was just hiring staff. Harold was married to Reni Kittle, one of the smart gals writing copy and developing ideas and stories for *Vanity Fair* magazine. There was another very bright woman, Helen Brown Norden, and a third, Clare Boothe. Clare was married to

Henry Luce, the publishing magnate. At this time she had a big hit play running on Broadway, *Kiss the Boys Goodbye.* These were three smart, chic gals from the Condé Nast publishing empire. I got to know them all, Reni and Helen in particular. Helen was a close friend of Clare's, who had gotten her a job at *Vanity Fair.*

Reni and Helen were kicking names around for me. One day at lunch with Clare, Helen mentioned that she had a friend who was opening a nightclub in the Village, explained the kind of club it was going to be and that he was trying to find a name for it. Helen called me, excited, after that lunch. "I've got it! I've got a name for you! I've just had lunch with Clare Boothe and she said, 'Tell your friend to call it Cafe Society.'"

At that time there was a society gossip columnist, Cholly Knickerbocker, not his real name, on the Hearst paper, the *Journal-American.* He would often write about "café society" to characterize the moneyed crowd, not in any disparaging sense mind you. They were the people he adored. When Clare heard that I wanted not only political but social satire she came up with the name, and I jumped on it. I told the artists who had been waiting for the name. "We're calling this place Cafe Society. You guys can do anything you want to satirize that crowd and politics." I had told the same thing to Jack Gilford, whom I had already engaged.

Six weeks before I was to open my club, an unthinkable event took place in Germany that shook the civilized world—Kristallnacht, the Night of the Broken Glass, the savage, Nazi-orchestrated pogrom against Jews on the night of November 9 and into the next day, November 10.

> *Beginning systematically in the early morning hours in almost every town and city in the country, the wrecking, looting and burning continued all day. The main shopping districts as well as the side streets of Berlin . . . resounded to the shattering of [Jewish] shop windows falling to the pavement, the dull thuds of furniture and fittings being pounded to pieces . . .*
>
> *All Vienna's synagogues [are] attacked: fires and bombs wreck eighteen of twenty-one. Jews are beaten, furniture and goods flung from homes and shops.*[9]

The *Bremen,* a German ship, had docked at one of our piers on 12th Avenue and 46th Street. There was a scuffle on the pier with the Nazi seamen. Harold Johnson was involved in that.

Colin Allen: *I was there. I was on the dock. I had been a member of the Maritime Workers Industrial Union. I went to sea for several years as a merchant seaman, but I couldn't go very far because of my poor vision. I once paid someone to take a vision test for me. That's how I got my able-bodied seaman's.*

This day, the ship's company, North German Lloyd, had invited the public to visit, and a group of people went on board. One man, and I regret that I don't remember his name, ran up to the fo'c'sle of the ship and ripped down the Nazi flag. He was shot in the testicles by one of the Nazis. He's a very brave man and should be remembered.[10]

The day the *Bremen* was due to leave, November 15, 1938, more than five thousand people demonstrated on the pier, shouting, waving signs, "Down with Hitler—Up with Democracy," "No Nazi Ships in American Ports." The whistle blew, the ship departed, the demonstrators sang the *Star-Spangled Banner*.

It was not the best of times to open a nightclub "unlike any other club." The nation's jobless [number] was listed at over nine million, and the world was in turmoil. The news from Europe was surreal. Jews fleeing the Nazis were shunted back and forth across frontiers. The Spanish Civil War was in its thirtieth month, with Franco's fascists and Nazi Germany's planes bombing unprotected civilians from the air. On the other side of the world the Japanese army had invaded China, raping and murdering millions of Chinese. A world gone mad.

On the home front, a Catholic priest, Charles Edward Coughlin, the "Father of Hate Radio," spewed forth venomous attacks on President Franklin Roosevelt and the Jews. His weekly Sunday radio broadcasts, *The Hour of Power*, attracted millions of Americans. In a speech [on December 18, 1939], Secretary of the Interior Harold L. Ickes asked how any American, specifically naming Henry Ford and Col. Charles A. Lindbergh, could "accept a decoration at the hand of a brutal dictator who, with the same hand is robbing and torturing thousands of fellow human beings."

The oppressive news from abroad did not deter those New Yorkers who could afford it from celebrating the holiday season; others would be less able. On Times Square, four hundred artists held a demonstration to protest WPA layoffs. Broadway theaters reported they had their biggest matinee, Wednesday, December 28, since 1929. the *New York Times* reported 681 [using] standing room at the Broadway theaters. You could celebrate New Year's Eve with dinner, entertainment, souvenirs, and noise makers all included in the price, taxes extra, with Tommy Dorsey and orchestra in the Terrace Room, Hotel New Yorker, $10 tab; Eddy Duchin and orchestra in the Persian Room, Plaza Hotel, $15; Cabaret TAC at Chez Firehouse, $3.50 (minimum).

CHAPTER
5

"There we were, occupying six windows of the elegant Bergdorf-Goodman."

We found an empty store on Twelfth Street that we used for a studio. The artists stretched their canvases on the floor and painted. Some of the murals would be painted onto the canvas, and some painted directly on the walls.

We had the jazz. John Hammond was taking care of that. We had our slogan, "The wrong place for the *Right* people." I don't recall who came up with it. Those ladies had ideas. Helen Norden suggested that we have a doorman garbed in an outfit in keeping with these depression times. Our doorman was a veteran of the Abraham Lincoln Brigade, those dedicated Americans who volunteered to go to Spain to fight in the Spanish civil war. We found a mangy winter coat with a fur collar, the kind the well-known theater critic George Jean Nathan was famous for wearing. That was the idea. The fur was worn bare; you could see the skin of the fur, the backing. We cut off all the buttons and took a rope, tied it around the coat.

As soon as we became famous limousines would pull up in front. A fancy party, "real" cafe society–type people so to speak, would come downtown wanting to see what this thing was that was being called Cafe Society. You think our doorman opened the limousine door for them? No. They had to open their own door. He just stood there. When this "upper-clahs" party walked down the entrance stairs he followed them to a table, sat down with them. Of course he got up soon after. This was all rehearsed, part of the gag. I had wonderful people creating all these kinds of crazy ideas.

The artists had their theme. Their murals would mostly satirize Manhattan's well-heeled supper club patrons. Such a contrast, their carefree, luxury-filled world with the tragic events taking place in the world around them.

Being in a basement you had to go down a somewhat steep set of stairs to reach the room. As you descended, you saw Sam Berman's Hitler monkey in front of you, dangling from a pipe. Sam was a marvelous caricaturist who not only painted but modeled in clay and papier-mâché and all sorts of other materials

Along the stairwell was a mural by Anton Refregier, a lovely, sylphlike woman with a corsage at her waist. She seemed a fetching figure until you noticed that her neck was the armature of a gramophone, the old-fashioned kind. In place of her head was the gramophone's head with its needle pressed into the groove of the record on the turntable, which was held by her long-gloved arm. This represented the society gals who never stopped gossiping. This was a known fact.

At the bottom of the stairs was another Refregier mural, a fat dowager type. In place of her head was a good-sized wooden knob with lovely material draped around her torso, such as you see in dressmaking establishments. This was Ref's clothes horse.

I had told the artists that I was not going to have the typical mirror behind my bar. Instead I wanted a painting. When you're drinking and you see yourself blotto, especially if you're a lady, you don't look so good. I always thought people looked just awful when they had too many under their belt. Why should they have to look at themselves at their worst? When people would be at the bar drinking they would be looking at my back-bar mural, the bottles of liquor below it.

Sam Berman took that idea a step further. He was noted for his drawings of animals. Sam designed a wondrous mural for the wall behind the bar. His mural became, in effect, a mirror of the people drinking at the bar but reflecting them in the form of animals. He drew a walrus, a bear, a monkey, a pig, a dog, an orangutan, lizards, whatever, all dressed like humans, holding their glasses, drinking, bending each other's ears, talkative as drunks get. All of them blotto. So there they were, my customers, on the back wall.

Sam was somewhat smitten with Christina Malman I think. He wanted her to do a panel, but I had no more space for one. Gentleman that he was, he found a solution. "Christina can do the upper portion of my panel." All his figures were below at standing bar level, so there was space above his mural.

Christina painted various kinds of clouds, storks floating around, pulling them through the air by their tails, women holding them up. Other people were in all kinds of fantastic poses, wild stuff but beautiful. One of the clouds was a little dark one with women sitting over the edge, their legs dangling on the edge, about to dive off; one woman, having dived, [was] floating in space.

"What's that, Christina?"

"That's my suicide cloud."

Wonderful surrealist things that Christina did.

The artists and Jack Gilford knew about my loathing of the typical night-club atmosphere. Alice Stander picked up on that and did a panel satirizing nightclubs. There was a lone, perplexed man sitting at a table in a nightclub, his collar sticking out unevenly from his tuxedo, his bowtie untied, a bottle of wine and a wine glass on his table. He's clutching a handful of money. A female fortune teller has grabbed one hand and is reading his palm. A woman is singing, playing an accordion. A cigarette girl with the tray around her neck is trying to sell him a stuffed doggie and cigarettes. A waiter is standing by trying to take his order. Another man, crouched down, is taking his photograph to sell. A sketch artist is sitting on a low stool beside his table, drawing his portrait, and a hat-check girl has his silk top hat on her head, his coat over her arm. All are soliciting at the same time. All those petty annoyances to make a buck.

> **Jack Gilford's routine:** *We're different from other nightclubs. You go to these places, I won't mention names, but the initials are Stork Club and El Morocco. The cigarette girls come around and sell you little doggies, gardenias and other insults. Well, we don't have anything like that. We have a cigarette girl too. She just sells cigarettes. But we have something they don't have. We have another girl following our cigarette girl.*[1]

At this point Jack picks up an ashtray off one of the tables and mimicking a girl's walk, approaches a table, calling out, "ashes, ashes."

The social event of the year in New York for the bluebloods was a debutante ball which introduced wealthy young girls of correct pedigree to society. In 1938 the debutante of the year was Brenda Frazier. Her photograph and goings-on were in all the gossip columns, newspapers, magazines, on radio. The next year's debutante of the year was Esmé O'Brien, later John Hammond's second wife and a dear friend. We kidded the obese Elsa Maxwell, the party-thrower, without whom no society function could take place. We immortalized her. Gregor Duncan painted a panel of the debutantes' coming-out ball. The young ladies are tied together with blue ribbons as if they were horses, held from behind by Elsa Maxwell with her big rear end.

> *It was the largest debutante dance of the season thus far. . . . Miss Frazier wore a gown of heavy white duchess satin made with a hoop skirt and trimmed with a cascade of white ostrich plumes from waistline to the bottom of the skirt.*[2]

No one had heard of Cafe Society so Jack's opening routine was designed to tell people something about us.

> **Jack Gilford's routine:** *We were just a few boys who were trying to hide from Brenda. One of the fellas found this little place here in the Village. So he took us down and we said, "This is just perfect. Now we can hide from Brenda." We called some artist friends that we knew. "We found a little place where we can hide from Brenda and we'd like some pictures on the walls. Would you come and paint some?" So they did.*
>
> *[Gilford grows dramatic]: The place started to be built. Down came a wall, up went a Birnbaum. Down came another wall, up went a Reinhardt. Down went another wall, up went a Hoff. Then we found a little hole in the wall. Now everybody knows that you can't hide from Brenda with a hole in the wall. We called Gropper. "Bill, we've got a little hole in the wall and we're trying to hide from Brenda. Would you paint a little picture over that hole?" Gropper came down and painted a picture over that hole. Ladies and Gentlemen.* It covered the whole damn wall!

Gropper's panel was the largest of all the artwork done, running fifteen to twenty feet across. Placed behind the banquette he had painted a series of different dancing figures jitterbugging, very humorous.

Colin Allen's mural showed a group of society figures, all blotto, drinking. One of the figures is playing on the cash register labeled "Social Register." The Social Register was a book of the names and addresses of those considered sufficiently prominent in high society to be listed.

> **Colin Allen:** *I didn't paint on the wall. I was pretty much alone when I*

did it. Sam Shaw was there. He was the art editor of a magazine called
Friday, I believe. He was of great encouragement to me. I had been
frustrated trying to draw something that just didn't work for me. I just
didn't have any ideas of what to do. It seemed that every time I'd put a
paint brush on canvas, Sam would rave about it and tell me how good
it was. That really picked me up.[3]

John Groth painted two phrenology heads sectioned with lines. One was a female whose head is filled with race horses and a cocktail glass with a cherry pit in it. That was what was on her mind. In the male's mind were cocktails and torsos of nude women without heads.

Ad Reinhardt painted a headless female torso leading a bluenosed society figure with a chain through her nose, the chain over her thumb. A champagne bucket and glasses are on the floor nearby. Three other characters, one with tongue wagging, one with ears extended, one looking through a lorgnette—speak no evil, hear no evil, see no evil.

The mural at the far end, going down the West 4th Street side was another Refregier. Seated at a nightclub table is this big butter-and-egg man with his big cigar, one arm round a very small, frizzy-hair blond, leering at her covetously. In the center of the table is an old-fashion wooden butter tub with a knife to cut into the butter, which was sold that way before the days of packaged butter. Texas Guinan ("Hello, sucker"), the legendary nightclub mistress of ceremonies, described her well-heeled customers as "big butter and egg men." In the 1920s, her club, El Fay, funded by underworld taxi czar Larry Fay, was packed with politicos, movie stars, millionaires, whomever.

Syd Hoff did a painting of one of his working-class characters, a big man with a walrus mustache, in red underwear from neck to ankles doing a fan dance. Some dowager society ladies sitting at their tables are haughtily surveying him through their lorgnettes. Syd has just finished signing his name on the lower righthand corner: a small *h*, a little *o*, and two little *f*s.

He steps back, looks at his work, looks at the other work around him. "Well, I'll be goddamned. What the hell, I'm as good as any of these guys." Now he dips his brush in his palette, walks forward, and in large capital letters paints *N* period, *A* period beside his name. "That's what goes next to my name—National Academy." Wonderful things like that happened.

"You know, Barney, now that I've finished my mural, I've always wanted to decorate restrooms." Here was Syd Hoff wanting to paint in such rooms. "They're yours, Syd."

In the ladies lounge Syd drew a white line-drawing on the black wall of an old-fashion bathtub. Seated in the tub is a dowager character with water up to her bosom, her lorgnette with her even in the tub. Beside her is her butler, the one Syd always drew with the turned-up nose, one sleeve rolled up, ready to go into the water with his hand. As the butler is about to fish for the soap, the dowager exclaims, "I thought the ad said 'it floats.'" This was the famous advertising slogan for Ivory Soap.

There was a narrow strip of wall on the left. Syd drew the same dowager leading an overgrown boy of about thirteen by the hand into the room. The boy is wearing a Little Lord Fauntleroy outfit, Buster Brown collar, flowing tie, pants cut off just above the knees, buttons on the side, silk stockings, and patent leather shoes. Mama is saying, "It's time you went by yourself already."

In the men's room Syd drew a urinal. Alongside he painted a twelve-inch ruler. His dowager is peering into the urinal through her lorgnette, exclaiming, "Ooooh . . . soooo big." That was the only cartoon in the men's room.

Abe Birnbaum's mural was titled *The Four Seasons,* and it became very famous. He painted the same French poodle with four different hairstyles, one for each season. This was Abe's comment on society dogs with their fancy haircuts. That was all, but in beautiful colors. When he finished, he signed A. Birnbaum, stepped back, brush in hand, looked, paused, then announced, "My colors vibrate."

The department store, Bergdorf-Goodman on 5th Avenue, decided to use Abe's four dogs, duplicated in papier-mâché with false hair. In four different windows beside each dog was a chic mannequin wearing a gown depicting each season, with the dogs on their leashes. In each window were printed cards: "From a Mural Entitled 'The Four Seasons' by Abe Birnbaum at Cafe Society."

Adolph Dehn had done a mural showing a group of potbellied elderly men in full dress, white tie, top hat, and tails, and three bald-headed men carrying their top hats. They're gathered around a snooty looking gorgeous blond society debutante, a cigarette dangling from her lips, in a fur coat with an enormous white fur collar, trimmed at the bottom with white fur. The men are eyeing her lecherously.

Bergdorf-Goodman had two more windows. In each was a mannequin, copies from Adolph's debutante in her evening gown and fur coat and one of the potbellied gentlemen with his pince-nez, standing alongside her. The cards in those windows read, "From a Mural by Adolph Dehn at Cafe Society."

We had just arrived on the New York scene and there we were, occupying six windows of the elegant Bergdorf-Goodman on 5th Avenue and on East 58th Street, the side facing the Plaza Hotel.

We made all the magazines, *Harpers Bazaar, Town and Country, Vogue, Vanity Fair, Look, Life, Time, Click*—we were in everything. We were launched.

And when my customers came into the cafe there wasn't a piece of velour to be seen.

CHAPTER
6

"'What he should have is
six goils and one guy.'"

It had all happened so quickly—Sam Shaw introducing me to John
Hammond who engaged the musicians and Billie Holiday, my finding Jack Gilford, Sam Shaw bringing in the artists. It's no wonder I
neglected to obtain the cabaret license opening night.

The show went on. Jack, as emcee, introduced the boogie-woogie piano
players, Albert Ammons on the old upright boardinghouse piano from John's
Carnegie Hall concert, Meade Lux Lewis and Pete Johnson on a Steinway. There
they were, the three greatest boogie-woogie pianists ever—on my stage.

That old piano was something, an upright made of solid oak. It had a
fourth pedal which controlled a metal bar about a half inch in width. This
bar had little red tapes about a quarter of an inch wide to which were fas-
tened little tin disks smaller than a dime. When you touched the fourth
pedal, this bar would drop just enough. As you held the fourth pedal down,
the hammers came forward to hit the strings. As the keys were played, the
bar hit the little tin disk first against the string. This gave it that honky-tonk
sound. I've never seen one before or since. We removed the front board
so that the audience could see the hammers hitting the strings, they were
going so fast.

Then Big Joe Turner came out to shout the blues. Jack introduced Frankie Newton and his swing band. Then Billie Holiday.

John had first heard Billie singing in Monette Moore's supper club in Harlem, which had only a brief existence. Prohibition was still the law, and the speakeasies were all selling illegal booze. They didn't need visits from the enforcers of the law, so a singer couldn't use a microphone for fear the sounds would penetrate into the streets. Billie would move from table to table, singing the same song but improvising on it differently at each table. It was 1933. Billie was eighteen and John was twenty-two. "She was completely beautiful, with a look and a bearing that were, indeed, lady-like and never deserted her."[1]

John followed her wherever she was singing, the Hot-Cha Bar, Pod's and Jerry's, the Alhambra Grill, Dickie Wells, and other Harlem speakeasies. He brought Benny Goodman to hear her.

Before John introduced me to Billie she had toured for almost two years, a year with Count Basie, then with Artie Shaw, and had recorded at least two dozen records, getting good reviews: "You should hear the buxom lass go to town with two very fine recordings, 'Miss Brown to You' and 'Painting the Town Red.'"[2]

Artie Shaw was engaged to open in the Blue Room of the Lincoln Hotel in October 1938. In addition to Billie, he hired another singer, Helen Forest. Singers with bands sing only one chorus of a song. They sit to the side of the band, try to look animated, wait for their chorus, get up in time to get to the mike, sing the chorus, then retire to their chair. Billie was not permitted to sit onstage with the band although Helen Forest did. She had to make her entrances from the wings, finish her chorus, and then retreat to a small room to which she was assigned. To get to the stage she was forced to ride up and down in the freight elevators because the hotel management said their guests complained about a colored person riding in the passenger elevators—in the *Lincoln* Hotel!

Billie Holiday: *I would stay up there, all by myself, reading everything I could get my hands on, from ten o'clock to nearly two in morning, going downstairs to sing just one or two numbers. Then one night we had an air shot, [a radio broadcast not emanating from a studio], and Artie said he couldn't let me sing.*[3]

I was billed next to Artie himself, but was never allowed to visit the bar or dining room as the other members of the band. . . . I was made to

enter and leave the hotel through the kitchen and had to remain in a
little dark room all evening until I was called on to do my numbers.[4]

To add insult to injury, the September issue of *Metronome* featured the
Shaw band on its cover with one girl singer, the white Helen Forest, seated
in front of the band. Billie quit.[5]

Now she would be working in a setting where discrimination would not
be tolerated. She would not sing just the chorus of a song. I had the idea I
wanted to feature all of my singers, stars in their own right.

Opening night Jack introduced Billie. She knew how to command her
audience. She walked slowly up to the microphone, waited. Then with Sonny
White as her accompanist, the band behind her, Billie sang. On my little stage
that night I had the greatest jazz singer in history.

Almost from the night we opened Cafe Society became the talk of the
town. We were written up in all the newspapers and magazines:

> *A lively and highly diverting addition to Manhattan's night spots is Cafe*
> *Society which opened recently in the redecorated basement at 2 Sheridan*
> *Square. . . . The walls of the main salon are covered with the gaily impu-*
> *dent fancies of Colin Allen, Adolph Dehn, Sidney Hoff and others—in*
> *short, as distinguished a collection of artists as ever besmeared the walls*
> *of a lowly bistro. The entertainment includes enough top-notch Negro*
> *purveyors of swing to rival the 52nd Street clubs. Frankie Newton trum-*
> *pets like mad; . . . Billie Holiday, whose legato renditions . . . places her*
> *near the top of present day "blues" singers. Jack Gilford serves as M.C.,*
> *and for those who have not yet seen his impressions of the emotional*
> *frustrations of a golf ball at Cabaret TAC, it should be added that he is*
> *one of the funniest entertainers to have bobbed up this season.*[6]

52nd Street is the big jazz street. The nightclub boys there were puzzled.
The guys would come down to see what my place is about. A new joint opens,
they all come to take a look. Two mob characters, partners in the Famous
Door on 52nd Street, come down to case the joint. We're jammed. The stairwell was full of people, and the line of patrons waiting to get in stretched
out the door onto the sidewalk. The mobsters are talking to my head waiter,
who used to work in the clubs on 52nd Street. I was standing nearby within
hearing distance. They didn't know me.

"Can't figga dis joint," one of them says. "Here's dis shoe guy from Noo
Joisey comes into Noo Yawk. He's doin' dis big business, and he don't know
what goes. He's doin' everyting backwards."

"What's he doing that's so wrong?" my headwaiter asks. "Well, he's got six guys in his show and one goil. What he should have is six goils and one guy."

The six guys were Albert Ammons, Meade Lux Lewis, Pete Johnson, Big Joe Turner, trumpeter Frankie Newton, Jack Gilford—six guys. Billie Holiday, the one goil. There were times when I didn't have a girl in my show at all. It just happened that way.

The boogie-woogie pianists and Big Joe Turner worked in Cafe Society off and on for over five years. Pete has said of his years at Cafe Society, "I count them as the happiest years of my life."[7]

So many memorable stories. One morning after four, when the place had closed and everybody was gone, just Paul Robeson and a few others were still around. Lennie Bernstein came down with Marc Blitzstein. Lennie had just accompanied Marc in a concert performance at Harvard, of Marc's marvelous depression-era opera *The Cradle Will Rock*. Someone asked Lennie to play it.

He sat down at the old boardinghouse piano. At some point during the score he hit the keys so hard that five or six hammers broke off and went flying on the dance floor. These wonderful things that happened in those days. Imagine Leonard Bernstein playing *The Cradle Will Rock* in Cafe Society at five o'clock in the morning.

CHAPTER
7

"'You'll be a big star.'"

When we opened, the big excitement was the jazz band, the boogie-woogie pianists, Big Joe Turner and Billie Holiday. With this kind of line-up, Jack Gilford found it very difficult to get the attention of the audience, and he became very discouraged. Night after night he would beg me, "Let me out. These people don't want to listen to what I'm doing."

And night after night I'd plead with him, "Jack, you're not going out. You are the funniest comedian in this country. There's no one like you. You're going to remain here until the people who come here understand this. You go out there and just keep being funny."

Jack Gilford: *Right in the beginning, Barney said, "I want you to come and you'll stay forever." Then two weeks after we'd opened, he told me, "I have to let you go." I said, "Whatever happened to 'forever?'" "Well, people tell me that a show shouldn't stay in a cabaret too long. You gotta keep changing," he said. Okay. I went to the William Morris office, and they got me a job in New Orleans. Next day I told Barney I was leaving. He said, "I changed my mind." Now his change of mind was the very important step as to why that club became the huge success it was and why Barney's method turned out better than any of his advisors. In those days shows ran two to four weeks. Barney kept us on months, years.*[1]

You might wonder how a shoe salesman had the courage of his convictions. Well, I knew I had a good eye and a good ear. When I was a buyer for our shoe store in Trenton, I never bought a lemon. Everything I bought was in good taste. My brother Dave, similarly. Mother had exquisite taste. I would say it's a family trait. I felt I was right about Jack. I knew what I wanted in a comedian in my cabaret. That's why I stayed with Jack.

Jack Gilford: *Barney would stand by the door, smoking, and he would laugh at me, which gave me a hook into making fun of him. I'd say, "Can you imagine? I do this routine every night and this man laughs at me." And he, of course, would laugh at that, too. I can say that in the fifteen months that I worked for him he was around almost every night.*

Aside from everything else, I had my own personal problems. I had a thing with a girl, and I just wanted to go somewhere, and Barney kept saying, "You'll be a big star." He just would not let me leave. I was never a big star. People came in and went and they became big stars, Susan Reed, Hazel Scott, Lena, Zero. Nobody heard of me.[2]

Jack was there three, four months, and nothing was happening for him. Then it was just like everybody in New York had a gigantic rally somewhere and the slogan was "Jack Gilford for President." Suddenly, overnight, everybody began to recognize this great talent at Cafe Society. Everybody's copying his routines, his slow-motion golf ball, his movie scenes. Jack Gilford became the byword in entertainment.

Jack Gilford: *My double-feature movie got to be so famous that Sid Caesar said he used it when he was still a saxophone player in the Catskills. He's a very strange man, and I don't know him well. One night he came to the Cafe Uptown during one of my reengagements in 1948. By that time Sid was getting to be a pretty big star. He asked me to sit with him. He made a very bold statement: "You're responsible for my being in show business." "Really? How?" "I did your movie routine for a couple of years up in the Catskills." In his book, which is one of such torment it's very hard to read, he never mentions about what started him in show business. I would like to tell him, "You never paid me for the use of my routines."*[3]

The punch line to Jack's movie routine has become a classic, still quoted today. It goes like this: "The Rialto Theater plays mystery movies all night long. You can walk into the theater any time. The first scene, a dark castle on a hill, the moon shining through heavy clouds, bats flying all over. The handsome hero presses the doorbell. The door squeaks open slowly. The butler opens the door. The audience yells out, *'The butler did it'*—and the movie hasn't even started yet!"

Double-features, two movies for the price of one, were common in movie houses. Together with his mystery movie, there was Jack's gangster movie. "The gangsters are all waiting for da stoolie pigeon. The door opens, da stoolie is standing there, and the camera pans from one gangster's face, moves over to a guy who has a scar from his ear all the way over to the next guy's ear." As Jack is describing this scene, he's pantomiming all the action. What he was able to do with his face! In his hospital movie Jack is the patient. "Don't touch me nurse. I'm sterile. Wash your hands."

When Jack, as emcee, introduced the musicians and Billie, Cafe Society became the first nightclub in New York, and as far as I know in the United States, that placed a white performer and black performer together on the same stage as a matter of deliberate house policy. This did not go unnoticed. Sometime after we had opened a customer remarked to Jack, "Why you're the only white person in the show."

"I am? I hadn't noticed."

One night Billie, the boogie-woogie pianists, and Big Joe Turner are out doing a benefit between shows. I had told the people running the benefit, "You have to put them on at a certain time because they have a twelve o'clock show here." These people don't know what the hell they're doing. It's time to put on our show. They're not back. Jack comes to me.

"What am I gonna do?"

"It's time and the show has to go on." I was always a stickler about starting on time.

"There aren't many people here for the show."

"It's not their fault, Jack, that we aren't crowded. They're entitled to a full show."

"But I can't give them a full show. We haven't got one, and I have to go out and be funny without a warm-up before I come on?"

Jack doesn't know what he's going to do. "Good evening ladies and gentlemen. Welcome to Cafe Society." He starts his opening routine as emcee introducing Meade Lux Lewis "who is not here." Now he imitates Meade Lux's facial expressions, what he does with his mouth and his eyes, how he plays the piano slowly. He was a slow blues player, how he would almost fall asleep at the piano. His head would go down almost to the keyboard. Everybody's laughing.

"I would like to introduce Albert Ammons, but he is not here." Then Jack sat down at the piano and with his marvelous rubber face puckered his lips like a fish as Ammons would do. The way he scrunched up the back of his neck, you actually saw Ammons's rolls of fat. The audience is roaring. He introduces Billie Holiday, "who isn't here," and pantomimes her.

"And don't ask for anything to eat because the chef isn't here." The chef thought Jack was so funny he would come out of the kitchen and was seen in full view of the audience.

"The bartender's gone, and here I am all alone, and I have to be funny." Then Jack finished with his own act.

You never know who's in the house. I've always told that to performers. If there are two people in the audience you've got to do a show. A young man who had four smash hits on Broadway at the age of twenty-five, all within eighteen months [1925–27], something unheard of, happened to come in. I had heard of the Broadway boy wonder, Jed Harris, but had never met him. He had been spending a lot of time in Hollywood, writing and directing. He catches this performance of Jack's. He's very impressed. After the show he introduces himself to me.

"There's a show in Hollywood called *Meet the People.* Jack Gilford has to be in that show." He talked to Jack, then asked to use my phone. I take him into my office. He calls Hollywood and tells them about Jack. "You can't come into New York without Jack Gilford."

I was happy for Jack, but at the same time I didn't have anybody to replace him. Jack knew someone. "Barney, don't worry. I know a very funny guy. I worked with him in the mountains at the Green Mansions Hotel. If you think I'm great, you'll like him. I'll get him down for an audition."

"Jack, if you like him and you say he's good, I already like him. Tell him he's got a job. He doesn't have to audition. If you say he can follow you, that's okay with me. What's his name?"

"Danny Kaye."

Jack goes to Danny. "You've got a job."

"Oh, I can't follow you. You've been in that joint since it opened. It's your room. I go in there and I'll die."

He wouldn't take the job. This was before Danny opened at La Martinique on West 57th Street, where Moss Hart caught his act and put him into his show *Lady in the Dark* with Gertrude Lawrence, where he was a smash. So I missed my chance to introduce Danny Kaye, to make another star.

Bertha Josephson with her family about 1906. Front row (left to right): Leon, Louis, four-year-old Barney, Bertha, Lillie. Back row: Ethel and David. (Author's Collection)

Barney in knickers with Mother around 1917. (Author's Collection)

(top) Barney in his mid-
twenties, outside of his
Trenton, N.J., home.
(Author's Collection)

(bottom left) Leon and Lucy
Josephson at The Cookery
about 1958. (Author's
Collection)

(bottom right) A young
Jimmie Josephson, wife of
Barney's brother, David,
mid-1940s. (Author's
Collection)

(top) Terry and Barney at Barney's favorite Chinese restaurant, 1981. (Author's Collection)

(bottom) Honored by the National Urban League Guild at the forty-second annual Beaux Arts Ball, Grand Ballroom of the Waldorf-Astoria, February 26, 1982, Barney holds his award. In the background are Mollie Moon, the Guild's president, and Lena Horne, who presented the plaque. (John Spaulding photo, Author's Collection)

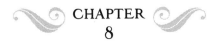

"Billie looked at me. 'What do you want me to do with that, man?'"

The notion that black Americans should enjoy equal rights was regarded as a radical, even subversive idea in this country, even seventy-five years after the Civil War. In 1938, when I opened Cafe Society, though segregation was illegal it was all too real in New York. Actually, slavery had lasted over two hundred years in New York before it was abolished by passage of the Thirteenth Amendment in 1863. Its heritage would continue to taint every aspect of society in the North as well as the South. The Fifteenth Amendment declared that no U.S. citizen can be denied the right to vote "on account of race, color, or previous condition of servitude."[1] To circumvent the law every southern state instituted the convention of literacy tests, poll taxes—and violence—to restrict Negroes as well as poor whites from voting.

While the Great Depression had depressed the membership of the Ku Klux Klan, there seemed to be enough of them active. In 1939, Tuskegee Institute, an industrial education college for Negroes, issued statistics on lynchings still occurring in southern states. In 1930, twenty-one persons were lynched; in 1931, thirteen persons; in 1932, eight persons; in 1934, fifteen persons; in 1935, twenty persons; in 1936, eight persons; in 1937, eight persons; in 1938, six persons; in 1939, three persons; in 1940, five persons; in 1941, four persons; and in 1942, six persons.[2] A year before, in 1938, an antilynching bill had been introduced on the Senate floor by Robert Wagner of New York and was derailed by a filibuster of southern senators.

One early evening soon after we had opened, a young man walked into the cafe and introduced himself as Lewis Allan. His real name was Abel Meerepol, a teacher in the New York City public high school system. Fifteen years later, at the height of the cold war, Abel Meerepol and his wife, Anne, would adopt two young boys. They were the children of Ethel and Julius Rosenberg, who were unjustly convicted of handing over atomic bomb secrets to the Soviet Union. In June 1953 the Rosenbergs would die in the electric chair despite worldwide appeals for clemency, including one from the pope. President Eisenhower refused to intervene. The boys were left orphans.

This day Allan had brought a sheet of music in his briefcase and asked if I would look at his song, perhaps have someone in the show sing it.

"Let's see it." Now everyone thinks from my history with jazz and music that I can read music. They're astonished when I say I can't tell one note from another. But I sure can read words, and I read lyrics on that sheet which brought tears to my eyes. The title was "Strange Fruit."

"Stick around. I have a singer whom I would like to sing this if she will, Billie Holiday. There are two pianos in the rear. As soon as Billie comes in I'll have you play the song for her. Sing it to her and we'll see what she says."

"That's fine," he agreed.

"However, I must warn you that I do direct the shows, the performances, and check on the material. I will tell the performers if I feel the material is a reflection upon the Negro people or if it's anti-Semitic. I'm very adamant about that. But this kind of material you've shown me, I cannot impose upon an artist to do. This is very special, and they have to want to do it. But I'll encourage it. I must caution you, though, when Billie listens to this song and says no. That's it. You may not try to persuade her. I won't allow that. If there's any persuasion to be done, I'll do it—or none."

Billie came in. I introduced them. Lew played and sang the song for her. Billie looked at me, "What do you want me to do with that, man?"

"Billie, I think it's a wonderful song. It would be just great if you would be interested in doing it. But you have to want to do it. I will not tell you that you have to sing it."

She shrugged. "If you want me to sing it, I'll sing it."

While I never told Billie what to sing and she was always careful about her program, I did check it. She instinctively knew how to balance her program, the faster rhythm with the slower. I always looked upon Billie as a finished artist. You don't tell a professional how to work. I felt the same way about Mildred Bailey. You'd be out of your mind to try.

At that time I had four acts. I couldn't leave time for Billie to sing for forty-five minutes because what of the acts before her. What was Jack Gilford going to do? And the boogie-woogie piano players and Big Joe Turner, not to mention the guys in the band? They were all scheduled to perform, and I couldn't let the show go on for two hours three times a night. I wouldn't get any turnover. So I would limit them.

When Billie would come out the rule was, "You do three songs. That's your show. But you honor all encores." So she would do her three songs and go off, come back and bow. Go off to applause, come back, do an encore. Again go off, come back, do an encore. She would wind up singing six or seven songs. If she had sung six songs originally, she would be on doing ten. With three songs and four encores, that satisfied the audience. Jack would be on for twenty, twenty-five minutes, then the boogie-woogie pianists. I didn't want my show to run more than an hour and fifteen minutes. That's quite a show, four different acts. Nowadays clubs can't afford anything near four acts. We have one performer who can do three-quarters of an hour show, an hour tops.

Normally, singers come out, open with a swing tune, a rhythm number, then they may go into a slow ballad, then another, contrasts in their performance, different types of songs. Then their encores. With "Strange Fruit" I staged it to give it full impact.

I told Billie, "This is such a dynamic piece of material that nothing can follow. This is the last song you sing. You've done your encores, and this is going to be your last encore. Nothing can follow this song. What are you going to do after this? Your feeling would be not to want to leave people with this kind of taste in their mouths, to want to sweeten it up with something nice to walk out on. You can't do that. I don't want that. You're the closing act. Nothing follows you anyway." My idea was that when people walked out of Cafe Society, I wanted them to remember every word of the song or at least to go out thinking about it. Or what would be the purpose?

I stopped all service in the place. All the lights went off. The waiters were not allowed to move, had to freeze wherever they were in the room with a tray of drinks or food. The cashier can't ring the register. The bartender can't shake a drink. The head waiter may not seat anyone during the performance of that song. Everything stops. Nobody must even strike a match. This is it. All attention.

We had a very low ceiling, with one little pin spot just illuminating Billie's face and maybe five or six inches to her bosom. Billie knew how to get under it exactly right. No other lights. Complete darkness. The spot came up on Billie. She never moved, her arms down at her side. She didn't even touch the microphone. Billie sang:

> Southern trees bear a strange fruit
> Blood on the leaves and blood at the root
> Black bodies swinging in the southern breeze
> Strange fruit hanging from the poplar trees.

The lyrics of the next two verses describe the lynched body, juxtaposing those words with irony—the "pastoral scene" and the "gallant" South and "scent of magnolia" with "smell of burning flesh."

Now you go to a club, you want to dance, you want to drink, you want to have fun, you want to enjoy yourself. You want to laugh. The first time Billie sang, part of it was this staging in a nightclub, it was like a bomb is dropped from some height. Before it can burst there's a slight split second. That's what happened the first time. Silence. Absolute silence. And then—boom! This big explosion. The audience really exploded, to the point where they rose to applaud. It was a terrific thing.

Then the publicity started. The columnists took it up. There were so many entertainment columnists, gossip columnists, they all wrote about this song. People started to come to hear it. Cafe Society and Billie Holiday were the big, big event in the nightclub world.

I was never quite sure how much this song touched Billie. I witnessed every show. I watched everything so closely. At the beginning, to me, Billie sang it in a very matter-of-fact manner. When she sang anything her facial expressions were never a studied thing. If she sang a happy song, her face took on that expression. It just came that way with Billie. Some singers simply sing words with no feeling at all. Or they can sing a sad song with a smile. Not Billie. Everything moved in her face in response to what she was singing. They weren't just words to her.

But when she first sang "Strange Fruit" she didn't have that feeling a black person would have singing these lyrics. Until one night. I was in my usual spot, watching her. As she came to the words "the bulging eyes and the twisted mouth" her face was twisted, contorted, as if she just saw it. It had happened in her view. A tear came down one cheek. And I almost wept, "Now she knows what this song is all about. Just now she knows." And that's the way she sang it after that. In retrospect these many years later, it's possible that Billie tried to keep her feelings out of the song because it was so painful. Being the great artist she was, finally she couldn't distance herself from it. Just a passing thought.

One night the music critic for *Time* magazine, whose name I don't know now, came in and heard Billie. A few days later he called on the phone. He would like to come down one evening with a staff cameraman to take photographs of Billie singing "Strange Fruit." They came, Gjon Mili, with his stroboscopic camera, taking fast, fast pictures, what seemed like hundreds.

Oftentimes the entire music column of *Time* magazine featured two or three different stories in one column. This time it was all Billie Holiday. There was Billie, a narrow, full-length photograph at the microphone in an evening gown, her gardenia in her hair, singing the song. The caption read, "The most unusual song ever to be heard in a night club." And the entire lyrics of each verse were printed. With her skin color, beautiful face, black hair, and white gardenia she was very striking.

To my knowledge, photographs of Negro performers were not used in the top publications, magazines like *Time, Town and Country, Life, Vogue, Vanity Fair, Look,* et cetera. They would review a black performer, instrumentalist, but not with pictures, always identifying them by color. The attitude was that a picture of a Negro was a defacement of the publication. I believe this was pretty much the attitude.

With that photograph of Billie it seemed to me that *Time* magazine had broken down the color barrier. Photographs of black artists started to appear in all the fine publications. There was no longer a restriction. That's what that song did in that regard.

When Billie appeared in *Time,* that gave her such prestige. No matter how much Billie was knowledgeable about things, I don't know yes or no, this made Billie a black performer who had something to say and was saying it, had the nerve to say it, to sing it. It gave her tremendous stature for all that she was the most unique stylist in her singing. No one has ever been able to duplicate that. Many singers have tried to copy her. Nobody can do what Billie did with a song. John was critical: "I never liked 'Strange Fruit' myself and I urged Columbia to have it recorded elsewhere. In many ways the song hurt Billie as an artist, although there is no doubt that its shock value helped her career."[3]

Columbia Records did not want Billie to record the song even though she was under contract to them. Milt Gabler, owner of the legendary Commodore Music Shop, stepped in. Milt's record label, Commodore Records, so-named from the days he worked in his father's radio shop on 42nd Street opposite the Commodore Hotel. Milt had started by reissuing out-of-print records he'd been collecting.

> **Milt Gabler:** *I first met Billie when she would come into my shop on 42nd Street with Teddy Wilson. John Hammond liked to come to my shop because I had bought all the old Okeh records when Charlie Stinson was the contact. I went up to Bridgeport where Charlie warehoused records he picked up from dealers around the country and cherry-picked the ones I wanted for the store.*[4]

Milt began to record jazz artists under his own label when he moved to his famous 52nd Street location in 1938. He did something then that had never been done before: He gave credit to the musicians and the instruments they played on his record labels.

> **Milt Gabler:** *I got to know Barney by going to Cafe Society to hear the music. I didn't spend much time with Barney. I went there to be in the audience, maybe to have a drink. I went there pretty often. We would close the store at nine, nine-thirty, and I would take the subway downtown to Sheridan Square. Barney had such great musicians working there as sidemen just to accompany Billie, whomever.*[5]

Billie very much wanted to record "Strange Fruit." She and Milt Gabler worked on Columbia Records to allow them to record the song on Milt's Commodore label.

> **Milt Gabler:** *When I did the record date, Tab Smith, the famous alto sax player, set the riff that was used as an intro. We call them head arrangements. The musicians get together, set the harmonies. They know the chord changes. They do it by ear. They memorize it enough to do twelve or fifteen seconds to get the record started. I wanted an introduction to Billie because you just can't sing "Strange Fruit" without setting a picture, a framework, background for it, for the artist to perform it. On that record I had to have more than a four-bar or eight-bar intro to set the mood. That's what a producer does. When Tab Smith set that*

riff the other sax players rounded out the harmony in it. Then they set it. It wasn't written. It was copied later and written. The day we did the record there was no music. When they set the riff, I said, "Okay, that's it. Let's do it, and Billie will take it after Sonny White plays the piano," which has part of the harmonies in the song.[6]

I got involved with a lawsuit because Lewis Allan said he wrote the music. Evidently he did. He has the copyright license from Washington. As far as I know I already had put his name on the label. I wanted to get a copyright license for "Strange Fruit." The law called for two cents copyright or they could get triple damages. Abel Meeropol or Lewis Allan wanted to charge me triple damages. He had a lawyer call me. Someone told him to ease up on Milt Gabler. He's a good guy. He's a right-thinking guy. I didn't have to pay triple damages. Eventually I got my license. Lewis Allan didn't like the fact that Leonard Feather, when he did the liner notes for my reissue, said he [Lewis Allan] didn't write the music. I don't know who he said wrote it.[7]

For the other side, Milt wanted Billie to write a twelve-bar blues. The night before they were to record, Milt came down to the cafe, and they sat at a deuce table in front of her dressing room to work on the words. Billie had jotted some down. Okay. But Milt wanted some more original wording. Batting around ideas he came up with

He wears high-draped pants,
Stripes are really yellow.
But when he starts in to love me
He's so fine and mellow.

The record is out. Some jukebox dealer from Chicago calls Milt, wants "Fine and Mellow." The guy drives in from Chicago, takes all the records, puts them in his jukeboxes. He's the only one in Chicago with the record. Suddenly "Fine and Mellow" is a big hit. Now Milt gets a call from Decca Records. They want "Fine and Mellow." But it's not copyrighted, and he's afraid Decca will put it out cheaper than what he's selling it for. So he tells Decca he's cleaned out.

He asks a musician who had come into his store if he knows how to copy music from a record. The guy says yes. Milt now has the song on a sheet of music. He writes on top "Composer: Words and Music by Billie Holiday," sends it off to the Copyright Office in Washington, D.C. And for the rest of Billie's life she received all the royalties. Milt is a gentleman.

Milt Gabler: *When the "Strange Fruit" and "Fine and Mellow" record was such a big hit, the big hit was really "Fine and Mellow." "Strange Fruit" was the most famous song. When we did the "Fine and Mellow" for a coupling, I credited Billie with the whole thing. I even mailed the copyright card in to Washington, D.C. I wanted Billie to make the money on it. . . . I never pushed to make a million dollars, I was just satisfied with it [the Commodore Music Store] being the most important jazz store.*[8]

I have said that nothing really happened for Billie until Cafe Society. I'm talking stardom. True, she was popular above 133rd Street but hardly known below it. Although she had sung with Count Basie and Artie Shaw, when she was with them they had not yet made the big time.

Ella Fitzgerald and Maxine Sullivan were now ahead of Billie Holiday in popularity stakes. Somehow she just seems to miss receiving the build-up and public appreciation that would put her in the top niche where she really belongs.[9]

At no time would Billie compromise with her style of singing. John has said, "We tend to forget what a shocking impact Billie's sound and style had at the time, once she was on records."[10]

Billie Holiday: *I don't think I'm singing. I feel like I am playing a horn. I try to improvise like Les Young, like Louie Armstrong, or someone else I admire. What comes out is what I feel. I hate straight singing. I have to change a tune to my own way of doing it. That's all I know.*[11]

With "Strange Fruit" Billie became a star. This was a turning point in her career as a popular artist. That song, Billie knew, made her. No matter where she was afterward, even when she was on heroin and had served time in prison in 1947 at the Federal Reformatory for Women in Virginia and was out, wherever she worked, joints, well-known clubs, she sang that song. She was that important a singer that she could say, "I sing this song or I don't work here." She kept my staging always. She would not follow "Strange Fruit" with any encores.

Milt Gabler: *You can't sing "Strange Fruit" and go back to the middle and do the last half over again, because once you sing it, its done. You can't sing two choruses, you can't sing one and a half. You've just got to sing it one time and go out.*[12]

Billie was very possessive of the song. It was hers: "Years after me at Cafe

Society, Josh White came on with his guitar and his shirt front split down to here and did it. The audience shouted for him to leave the song alone."[13]

Ballad singer Josh White sang "Strange Fruit" on his program, not in every show but often enough. He did it quite well to his own accompaniment on his guitar. Billie was long out of Cafe Society.

> **Josh White:** *For a time she [Billie] wanted to cut my throat for using that song which was written for her. One night she called by the cafe to bawl me out. We talked and finally came downstairs peaceably together, and to everyone's surprise had a nice little dancing session. I loved her interpretation of the song, but I wanted to do "Strange Fruit" my way. After that, she often came in the cafe, more often than not for the late show around 2:30 in the morning. Sometimes she was real late and wouldn't even come in. She'd drive down to 2 Sheridan Square and sit outside listening to the car radio with her big boxer dog, Mister.*[14]

Teddy Wilson, who had worked with Billie for so many years since 1935, surprised me with his feelings about Billie's singing.

> **Teddy Wilson:** *I was never too fond of Billie's singing. I liked the other girl she was singing with, Beverly White, the two of them working in this little club in Harlem. John Hammond introduced me to them, but John never said anything about Beverly. Billie to me wasn't a real singer. Beverly had style. I had just left Chicago working with Louis Armstrong, and Billie sounded like a girl imitating Louis. That made her sound different from anyone else. No one was doing that. A lot of singers like Billie. She had no range. She could get a good note and sing it. She had good rhythm though, excellent sense of rhythm. A lot of girls in the nightclubs in those days could sing a whole chorus with two notes. They'd get a note that fit the chord and shout one or two notes. But real singers like Sarah Vaughan, Ella, and Dinah Washington, there are really not singers like those people.*
>
> *I listen to a Sarah Vaughan record, but I wouldn't bother listening to a Billie Holiday record. That whole concept of singing, Hammond thought Billie Holiday, Bessie Smith, and Mildred Bailey, outside of them all women singers you could flush down the toilet.*[15]

I didn't feel comfortable asking Teddy whether he had always felt that way about Billie's singing, even in his young days, or whether this was some kind of hindsight. We'll never know.

"You don't keep anybody working
for you under contract.
That's slavery."

My relationship with Billie was friendly but not close. To put it in context for those years, there was such racial discrimination and segregation of Negroes in our society, North and South, where Negroes worked for whites, there was quite a cleavage. There usually was very little communication between a Negro artist and a white boss.

John Williams: *Working with Billie all those months, it was a pleasure to come to work. No one bothered you. You had to make time and be a gentleman, that's all. Billie was a lovely person to work for, and Barney treated everyone the same.*[1]

Billie was meticulous about her work. Every few weeks she would rehearse with the band around three in the afternoon. She was tough and could raise hell if she didn't think a note was right. At night when she'd hang around the club she spent her time with the musicians, playing cards, blackjack, kidding around with them, sometimes with me.

John Williams: *Billie and Newton would kid around with each other about the band. It was Frankie's band but Billie would say, "This is my band," and would go to Barney and say, "Newton don't need a raise but* *give my band one." Her dressing room was always open to us and I've never known her to hurt anyone but herself.*[2]

As far as the boss, me, was concerned, with Billie mostly it was in and out, hello, good night, goodbye. Oh, we had our tiffs, and she could tell you off with some choice words.

Colin Allen: *Of course she was a wonderful singer and a beautiful person. But she also had a temper. I was in the club once when the musicians had all left their dressing room because she was having a temper tantrum. You could hear her breaking up things.*[3]

She never went up to Harlem with us. Billie went her own way. She was proud, a free soul who did what she liked. If a man she was attracted to came along, she went with him, a woman, the same. If you offered Billie a drink, she'd drink it; same with pot. There were many occasions when a patron would invite her to their table. She didn't always accept, only when she wanted to. But she had that kind of social contact with the patrons in my cafe, white and black.

In 1935, before I opened, Billie had been hired to sing at the Famous Door on 52nd Street, at that time a new nightclub, mob-backed. It was run by a syndicate of white musicians, Jimmy Dorsey, Glen Miller, and Lennie Hayton, who later married Lena Horne. Billie was not allowed to sit with the customers, even at the bar, not permitted to mingle. She had to sit outside of the toilets during her break. Billie resented the treatment, naturally, and made it known. Less than a week into her gig she was let go.

Colin Allen: *On a number of occasions I sat with Billie Holiday and Jack Gilford at the cafe. The three of us were at the table and had supper together. Memories of Billie: on the positive side, she wasn't talkative. Gilford would talk about his act and things he was going to work on. He'd try out jokes on us and see if he'd get a response from us. Billie was a good audience who laughed at his jokes.*

She was very popular. There were occasions, I recall one in particular, where some nut objected to her singing "Strange Fruit." He tried to start a disturbance, and Harold Johnson and a friend escorted him out. He went out and came back with the police. He may have been part of a plan to disrupt the place. Billie was cool. She just kept on singing.[4]

There are many patrons in a club who are taken by performers, certain musicians. They become friendly with them, invite them out, buy them drinks, entertain them in many ways. It came to my notice there was a lovely young woman, white, who seemed very interested in Billie. This young lady was from a noted family. Her father was a prominent industrialist having to do with bathroom equipment, by the name of Crane. There was some buzz-buzz about this lady being a lesbian, gossip about what's going on between them. She would come in two or three times a week. They would spend time sitting at her table, often going out between performances, bringing Billie back in time for the next show. I never knew more except that they were very friendly. Just as long as Billie was back for her performance, not my business.

Many of my patrons would come two, three times a week, practically lived in Cafe Society. They saw the show over and over and over and were never satisfied. They just loved it. That's how I could keep Jack Gilford for his first engagement for sixty-five weeks. It's unknown that a comic could perform pretty much the same material for over a year and people wanting to see him again and again. And shouting out, they knew all his routines, "Jack, slow-motion golf ball." He couldn't get off without doing it. That's the kind of place it was.

I would run the whole show. I would go to the back where the performers came off. If I didn't want them to do any more encores I'd say, "Take another bow. No more. I have a line going up the stairs waiting for the next show."

One night Billie came out to sing. The women singers always wore evening gowns and slippers. Generally, they had nothing on underneath. This night, as always, Billie is introduced by Jack Gilford. She came out, sang one song, finishes it, turns her back to the audience, bends far over, picks up her gown, way up, shows her behind to the audience, and walks off. She would not come back. That was her performance for that show. What she was saying was "kiss my black ass." I didn't know why. I was not aware that anyone had offended her by any remark. I went to her dressing room.

"What do you mean by that?"

"Fuck 'em. I'm not going back."

I was really angry. "How dare you do that? Don't you ever do that again because you know what the customers will say to me? 'Fuck you.' They're not going to take this from you or me. You do that once more. You walk off the stage, keep walking. Just don't come back."

She never did anything like that again. But she did it once. Sure she was high. She was high all the time, just on hash. In those days Billie was not on heroin. That happened long after she left me. On the other hand, I really don't know what triggered that incident. I had warned Billie and all of the musicians that if I ever caught any one of them smoking marijuana in my place they would all get fired.

"I won't ask who was smoking, and I don't want anyone to snitch on whoever is because the most abhorrent thing to me is a stool-pigeon. If I smell this stuff around here and I know it's coming from you guys, I'll put you all on notice. I'll put in an all new show and new musicians."

When they wanted to drag on weed they would go out on their break. They'd go upstairs through the back entrance onto West 4th Street near Miss Douglass's little bakery shop and smoke.

There was a hack stand, a big, open space in the center of Sheridan Square. There were cabarets around the entire square. On the other side of Sheridan Square was the Greenwich Village Casino. Around the corner on 7th Avenue was Jack Delaney's. Next door to Delaney's was the Village Nut Club, a crazy kind of place for tourists. To the right on Grove Street was a wonderful Spanish club, El Chico. It was run by a Latin guy, Benito Collado, who brought a lot of good talent from South America, such as Argentinita, an exciting, marvelous flamenco dancer. Fats Waller was playing at the mob-run Nineteenth Hole on Barrow Street, the corner of 4th where it comes into Sheridan Square.

Cabs would line up there, and as people came out of the clubs, the doormen would blow their whistles and the cabs would drive up to the front of the club to pick up their passengers. The same cab drivers always came back. They worked an area where there was business for them, where the sports were, where they would get good tips. They liked to work the nightclubs. So instead of cruising they would come back and park on Sheridan Square.

Billie got to know one of these guys, and she became a steady customer. She had this deal. He would take her into Central Park. She would sit like a queen in the back of his cab, drag on one weed after another as they would drive through the park, around and around until it was time to come back for the next show. But she didn't smoke in my place. Perhaps it was one of those times when she was high and someone in her audience did or said something that she showed them her behind.

One afternoon, Billie's mother, Sadie Fagan, phoned, asked if she could come and see me. I had known her mother was alive and that was all. I didn't know what she looked like or what she did. I knew Billie's father, Clarence Holiday, was a jazz guitarist with the Fletcher Henderson band. I never met him. Sadie was short, plump, rounded nicely, matronly, not very old, the same coloration as Billie, plainly dressed. There was a definite resemblance. She told me that she was working nights in an office building, cleaning offices.

Billie had promised to give her $5 a week. She couldn't make enough from her cleaning job, hadn't seen Billie in a long time. She asked me, if I would be good enough, when the opportune moment came and I could manage to get it in, would I, could I, somehow mention in some way to get Billie to start sending the $5 she had promised? She was trying to tell me how to speak to Billie. "But remember, be sure you don't give her any idea that I came to see you about this. You might say, 'By the way, how is your mother?' just to remind her that I'm around. Nothing more. She would kill me if she knew I came to see you."

"All right. I'll handle it discreetly."

She was such a sweet, nice woman. Anyway, I don't remember exactly how the hell I handled it. I got around to "Billie, how's your mother?" Something like that, to remind her. Billie just passed it off. There wasn't anything more I could do without eliciting a strong reaction according to her mother's warning.

Billie was with me pretty much a year. She could have stayed on. It wasn't my choice. An agent, Joe Glaser, for whom she'd worked before, took hold of her. Because of "Strange Fruit" and all the publicity, Billie was becoming very popular, a draw. She had no contract with me so she was free to go with Glaser and presumably a great deal more money than I could afford, although she never spoke of that. Joe would be getting his agent's cut. So Billie just announced she's leaving, going out with Joe Glaser, had enough of the joint, wants to go somewhere else, had a long gig here.

I wouldn't try to keep anybody. I never signed artists to contracts unless they wanted one. That was our understanding. I always believed that you don't keep anybody working for you under contract. That's slavery. You're unhappy with me—go. That's Barney.

When Billie left me she was getting one hundred and a quarter a week, which was good money in those depression years. And she was living at home, not touring on the road with all kinds of touring expenses, room, food, not to mention the agent's cut, all of which came out of her salary.

John Chilton: *Overall, Cafe Society was probably the happiest booking of Billie's life. It did wonders for her confidence on stage, enabling her* *to project a more sophisticated act. Barney Josephson encouraged and advised Billie; later he was to do the same thing for Lena Horne.*[5]

For a man who became rich largely handling black artists and musicians, Joe Glaser was a crude, uncouth man. Before he came to New York he had been involved with Chicago bootleggers, the likes of Al Capone; had managed boxers, a mob-dominated sport; pimped for prostitutes; and married a woman who managed a whorehouse. He was a horrible chauvinist. What he would say about black women, and he had some very pretty black singers he booked around, good young singers. Well, Joe's dead now so I guess I can tell this story.[6]

He came down to the cafe one night. Now he knew the kind of place it was. He'd been in many times before, always looking around for talent to take over and handle. This night I was sitting at a table with him. He looks around the place.

"Why do you have so many jigs in here, Barney?" Jig is a derogatory term for blacks that whites would use who wouldn't want to use "nigger," although that never stopped Joe.

"Well, Joe, this is the kind of joint I'm running."

"Now don't get me wrong, Barney. I have no prejudices. Nobody likes a little nigger pussy better than Joe Glaser."

This is the kind of man who's representing black artists. Louis Armstrong was one of the many artists Joe managed. He practically owned Louis. It's true he got Louis the gigs that led to his fame. He completely managed Louis's finances and bookings. Well, maybe there was a kind of trade-off. Louis and Joe were together for over thirty years. Louis has said, "I never cared to become a band leader; there was too much quarreling over petty money matters. I just want to blow my horn peacefully."[7]

Billie stayed on through the first week in November. From the South, for his second Carnegie Hall, From Spirituals to Swing Concert, Christmas Eve 1939, John brought up one of the great blues queens of the 1920s, Ida Cox. When he heard about Billie's leaving, John quickly suggested Ida as a replacement. "Who is she, John?"

She had worked the southern tent shows and the TOBA circuit.[8] The theater owners of the circuit were notorious for exploiting the performers, paying pitifully small salaries with horrible working conditions and tough schedules. Among the cognoscenti, TOBA was known as "Tough on Black Asses." The greatest of the black artists played the circuit, Ma Rainey, Bessie Smith, King Oliver, Ethel Waters, Louis Armstrong, Sippie Wallace, Bert Williams, Buck and Bubbles, Bill Robinson, Bennie Moten. They got them all.

John said Ida had recorded over seventy-five songs for Paramount Records from 1923 on. "John, I'm just not sure she's for me. How old is she now?"

"Barney, you know she's worked with some of the greats in jazz, King Oliver, Jelly Roll Morton, Lovie Austin, Louis Armstrong." Okay, I was ready to bring her in.

Downtown Cafe Society, Joe Sullivan; Boogie-Woogie Pianists; Ida Cox; Ed Hall (clarinet) joined Joe Sullivan. Ida Cox rediscovered. Contemporary of Bessie Smith. Had been touring the South with a unit, "Darktown Scandals." To cut an album for Columbia Records.[9]

Ida was to open November 3. She postponed; she was appearing in a black burlesque show in New Jersey and would not be free until the twenty-first of December. This would be a week before she was to appear in John's Carnegie Hall concert.

John Hammond: *Ida Cox, a better singer than Ruby Smith, appeared in heavy make-up and false eyelashes, not exactly what I thought a blues singer should look like, but she was a hit.*[10]

Jack Gilford knew I was stuck for a female singer. "I heard a little girl play a piano at a bar in a joint in Harlem [he told Barney]. I think she'd be good for you. Her name is Hazel Scott."

I went to the phone book and found a Hazel Scott at a Harlem address. I called, told her who I am, that I'd like to hear her play. She auditioned, and I hired her right off for three weeks until Ida would come in. The three weeks turned into seven and a half years.

Ida opened. She did not work out. But now I had become excited about the potential of her temporary replacement. Hazel was nineteen and legally a minor. Her mother signed the contracts for her. She was born in Trinidad, where her father was a well-known Negro scholar and teacher; her mother, a talented musician. They came to New York when Hazel was four. Her father had gotten a teaching position in a Negro college. He died when she was a teenager, and her mother, Alma, then organized her own woman's orchestra. Hazel, who was a child prodigy on the piano, played in the band. When it broke up she landed a singing role in a Broadway show, *Sing Out the News.*

When that closed she worked in various small, dingy, smoke-filled clubs until I hired her.

Our press releases touted Hazel's specialty, "swinging the classics." She would begin by playing Chopin, Bach, Liszt, the classical composers as the music had been written. Then gradually she would shift into a swing tempo with a little boogie thrown in. She was a sensation.

> If somebody should ask me the name of the best-natured night-club enter-tainer in town, I'd say Hazel Scott. Miss Scott is the dark and handsome young lady who went downtown to Cafe Society on Sheridan Square a few months ago as a fill-in singer and stayed on to become mistress of ceremonies. Her singing and piano-playing haven't suffered because of her additional duties.[11]

Hazel was not, however, for my friend John Hammond.

> **John Hammond:** *I couldn't stand her. When she would perform, I would read the newspapers. She was a good enough musician but she didn't have anything to say musically. Barney realized she would go over. She was Barney's discovery.*[12]

> **Teddy Wilson:** *Oh, he [John] hated Hazel. He used to sit, right down front, with the lights on Hazel. He'd have a newspaper,* The New York Times, *reading while she was playing. . . . That was aggressive action to read a newspaper when Hazel was performing, you know. He's there with his newspaper, and he always got a ringside seat.*[13]

John was in the club practically every night.

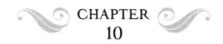

CHAPTER
10

"'Never borrow a week's salary from the M.C. to pay other bills.'"

For his first Spirituals to Swing concert John had brought a gospel quartet, Mitchell's Christian Singers, to New York from Kingston, North Carolina. He had found them in a backwoods shack with no electricity or running water.

"They're the finest gospel group I ever heard, Barney." John booked them into Downtown. They were a flop. I let them go without telling him; gave them their two weeks notice. They went to John.

John Hammond: *I told them I don't own the place and there's not much I can do. They weren't commercial, and they didn't pretend to be. Nobody knew what was happening because they didn't slap their thighs. I thought Barney would defer to me. Everything else I had brought in was so good.*[1]

Meanwhile, I hired another act. John was furious. He came flying down the stairs to my little office under the stairwell. Now John never ever uttered a profane word, but he was so outraged he began to stutter "you—you—you," and then the only profanity he could come up with, "You *stinker!*" After all, John was my mentor and guide in all things musical. How did I handle it? What did I do? I kept both acts for a while.

John Hammond: *They made some great records for Vocalion. I told them that history would vindicate their greatness and that their records would live long after this little incident is over.*[2]

I was the first nightclub owner to sign with the American Guild of Variety Artists (AGVA). Jack Gilford was a member. With my orientation I was hardly antiunion. Would you believe that Jack's membership caused two picket lines to appear in front of Downtown at the end of the summer of 1939? The American Federation of Actors was involved in a jurisdictional dispute with AGVA, and we got in the middle. The actors' union was protesting the employment of entertainers who had been wooed away from their union to AGVA. They threw a picket line in front of Downtown. To protect us, AGVA placed their own picket line out front with placards proclaiming that management was fair to organized labor.

Before I opened I had gone to the Musicians Union, Local 802, to find out what the salary scales were. I was told that the scale for musicians was $40 for six nights, hours from seven P.M. to four A.M., three shows a night. The musicians were to be available for rehearsals to play the music for any performer who required it, a singer, a dancer, a comedian. They would play intermission for dancing. When they were to take their breaks was set, too. Orchestra leaders got 50 percent over $60 a week. This was on the theory that they had to hire arrangers for their music and had extra expenses. This was depression time, and there were loads of union musicians playing in nightclubs and joints around which did not have union contracts and getting less than union scale.

John told me what to pay. "You give Frankie Newton, the leader, $75," which was over scale. Nobody was doing this. Depending on who the other musicians were, he'd say, "Give this one fifty, this one fifty-five." That's the way the salaries were set for Cafe Society musicians. John was always free with somebody else's money. That's a joke. John was generous with his money for the musicians.

Jack's annual letter, December 29, 1986:

Dear Barney: Here are a few tips to remember if you are looking to open a nite-club, be sure to make your bartenders your partners. If you don't, they will. Be sure to get some of their take. How can they steal from themselves. I changed my mind. They can steal from themselves.

Love again, Jack

I had bartenders who were stealing, and I couldn't control it. I thought I was a businessman, right? Well, I discovered that nightclubs are not shoe stores. I sold Scotch an ounce-and-three-quarter drink for 40 cents; a bottle of beer for a quarter; Coca-Cola for 15 cents. I served a full-course dinner for a $1.75 to $3. I was, in fact, giving my merchandise away to the public, and they were having a grand time. It was ridiculous. In every club on 52nd Street, the jazz street, all drinks were the same price across the board, 75 cents. I really didn't know what I should get, didn't know the merchandising of it, what my percentages should be. I ran out of money.

Jack's annual greeting, December 28, 1981:

I hope you learned a lesson in 1938. When you open a nightclub never borrow a week's salary from the M.C. to pay other bills.

Love, Jack
P.S. This did happen.

It looked as if I would have to close not too many months after I had opened. I told John Hammond about my plight, and he talked to Benny Goodman. Benny was already a big-time band leader. Years later he married John's sister, Alice, who had been married to Lord George Arthur Duckworth, a Tory member of the British Parliament. John and Benny loaned me $6,000, which in those days was a goodly sum.

John Hammond: *Although Barney invested $16,000 [Leon's loan was $6,000, not $16,000] to open the club, by the second week he was out of money. Benny Goodman, Willard Alexander and I each put up $5,000 to keep it going, and from then on it made money. We all got our investment back.*[3]

John's and Benny's money just about enabled me to continue—barely. I was able to pay off my most pressing debts, so some of the pressure was off for the time-being.

Jack Gilford: *When we were Downtown things were so bad that there were weeks when I didn't get paid. My mother, whose politics were never developed very much, used to say, "A boss is a boss is a boss. You should never do that." I'd tell her, "Well, he's a different kind of boss," which he was.*[4]

Although John's and Benny's loan kept the place open during the early months, I wound up losing $10,500 on my first nine months' operation. Plus I owed $12,000 for the original opening. I was in debt to the builders for all kinds of construction and other furnishings. Plus I owed $6,000 to Leon's friends, who hadn't seen their money either. Plus I owed John and Benny. Plus I hadn't paid the city sales tax. I had been using that money to pay the creditors. I would give this creditor $100, this one $50, this one $200, pacifying them all. Somehow they played along with me. I wasn't the mob. They figured, here's a legitimate businessman and he isn't going to take us. They all felt that way about me. So they let me take my time paying. They didn't threaten me. When I had some money to give to them, I gave to them.

John Hammond: *Why did I do it? I thought this was a wonderful place in New York where I could bring my friends; where talent was properly presented; where Negro talent was not exploited, as they were, utterly, in those days. And Barney was a straight, decent man. That's what attracted me to him.*[5]

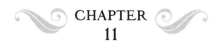

CHAPTER
11

""There will be no craps-shooting Negroes in my place.""

For his second Spirituals to Swing concert, December 24, 1939, John brought up a gospel quartet from Charlotte, North Carolina, the Golden Gate Jubilee Quartet. They were fantastic; Willie Johnson, narrator and baritone; Clyde Riddick, second tenor; Henry Owen, first tenor; Orlandus Wilson, bass. Five months after Hazel came in they were added to the program.[1]

> **Orlandus Wilson:** *After the concert at Carnegie Hall, John Hammond invited us to go and have a drink at Cafe Society to look around. When we did, they asked us to sing a few songs. That's when we first met Barney Josephson. He said, "These boys are good. They got a job here."*[2]

> **John Hammond:** *They had all the jive that people wanted, and they were a smash hit.*[3]

But their costumes, for that's what they were, I didn't like. They wore identical suits, styled like full-dress suits made of purple cloth with purple silk lapels, a purple bow tie and brown-buckled shoes. For a change of costume they wore white flannel tails with black silk lapels with a black stripe running down the side of the trousers. Both outfits looked like they belonged in a minstrel show.

I spoke to them about their clothes, about white people's concept of what Negroes wear. I didn't want that in Cafe Society. I made a suggestion. "Please take this money and go to Bond's clothing store." Bond's store took up the entire second floor of the Criterion Theater building on Broadway between 44th and 45th Streets. F. W. Woolworth occupied almost three-quarters of the ground floor, with a Whelan's Drug Store next to it on the corner. Atop the building was an almost block-long waterfall covered by a huge neon sign, BOND, and below it, "Two Trouser Suits." On the left was a huge figure of a man dressed in a toga, the sign below, "Clothes for Men"; on the right, a huge figure of a woman in a toga, "Apparel for Women."

I told them, "Buy four blue serge suits, all alike, white shirts and any kind of blue tie you like that would go with the suits, and four pairs of black shoes." And when they came out onstage they looked terrific.

Next we had the matter of their material. Their main format was the spirituals. They sang about Noah and the flood, Jonah and the whale, and other biblical tales with characters like Shadrack, Daniel, Nicodemus. Occasionally I discovered they would throw in something humorous, a song they called "The Preacher and the Bear." It went like this: "The preacher, though he was a Christian gent, went hunting on a Sunday morn. And though he was a Christian gent, he took his gun along." The chorus after each verse was the popular "give me that ole time religion, that ole time religion, that religion's good enough for me." Came the next verse: "The preacher meets up face to face with a big black grizzly bear and the preacher went splittin' through the wind."

The way the quartet slapped their four pairs of hands, as if they were running, you got the picture common in movie cartoons, where a Negro gets scared, his face turns white, and he goes "splittin'," done by speeding up the camera. He runs so fast because of the myth then that Negroes were scared of ghosts and animals. This was the image that came across from the way the quartet sang this song.

I thought, "Oh, Jesus, the scared Negro." The song continues: "He comes to a tree, climbs way up out on a limb, with the bear looking up, licking his chops. But along about morn, that old limb broke and that preacher came tumblin' down. He took his razor and he cut the bear six times before the bear struck the ground. Give me that ole time religion," and so forth. And I'm screaming to myself, "Christ, now with a razor."

After that show I asked them to come to my office under the stairwell. I explained that there are some white people who think Negroes always carry razors. "You can shave with a razor, but you can't sing about it in this particular story. I understand the preacher should have been in church as the song signifies instead of hunting on a Sunday morn with his gun. Every hunter, Negro or white, takes his gun to go hunting, and he may take a knife if he skins a rabbit, a bear, a fox, not a razor. There are no razors in Cafe Society."

One night they sang another song, "Ain't it a shame to beat your wife on Sunday when you got Monday, Tuesday, Wednesday, Thursday, Friday and Saturday, ain't it a shame?" Well I kind of let that verse pass until they came to one "ain't it a shame to" and as they sang "to" they dropped to their knees. With their four pairs of hands they snapped their fingers as if they were shooting craps and made a whack-sound with their voices. They don't sing the rest but act it out and then continue "when you got Monday, Tuesday" et cetera. So now I've got craps-shooting Negroes. I had to tell them, "No dice. There will be no craps-shooting Negroes in my place and no razor-wielding preachers."

They became one of the finest acts in show business. It was fascinating to watch their microphone technique. They would address it as if it were a musical instrument. When they sang "John De Revelator" about the crucifixion of Christ, "They nailed him high, they stretched him wide," slapping their thighs with their beat, you could hear the ringing of the hammers in Jerusalem streets as they drove in the nails. They made my blood tingle, I, an atheist. They were the first to sing spirituals and tales from the Bible in a nightclub.

They sang a topical spiritual "Stalin Wasn't Stallin" for the *March of Time* newsreel, "one of the great songs to come out of the war."[4] Willie Johnson, the founder of the quartet, was their gifted story writer and narrator.

> Well, now, Stalin wasn't stallin'
> when he told the beast of Berlin
> that they never would rest contented
> 'til driven from the land.

The narrator describes how the devil gives birth to "Adolph" [Hitler]. The devil was jealous of the Lord for creating Adam, and he swore to create one of his own. So he packed two suitcases, containing misery and grief, and traveled with them to Germany. The story goes on for many more verses, the lyrics in rhyme. Willie Johnson narrated the entire story as the others sang rhythmic gospel behind his narration:

Ira Tucker: *People say rappin. Hell, rap was here back then. We was doing harmony with rap back then. Willie Johnson, with the Golden Gate Quartet, he started it all.*[5]

One New Year's Eve we had a crowd trying hard to raise hell. When the Golden Gate Quartet took the floor they didn't sing "Chattanooga Choo Choo" but Negro spirituals. After the first eight bars you could have heard a pin drop.

Orlandus Wilson: *It was fantastic because the club was full every night. They were turning away people. Barney was very happy, and we were very happy because it was the first time we had a chance to work like that. Barney did a lot of good things.*

When we first opened the religious ministers thought it was scandalous doing spirituals in a nightclub. They didn't realize what was happening. Barney had a great idea. When we went on at night, the bar was closed. You couldn't get served a drink. If you called one of the waiters he didn't even pay you any attention. When they started to scandal about us singing spirituals there, Barney invited the ministers, the different religious ministers. "If you want to come in, you can see what is happening here." Finally they came in. They saw that everybody was still. You could hear a pin drop. This was the thing that changed the mind for a lot of people.

We used to go over to Brooklyn because they had one of the priests at one of the Catholic churches. Barney, he would let us go over there some nights. We would do a show for the kids in their recreation center in the basement.

It was fantastic the things that went on at Cafe Society that was really great. One thing Barney was very concerned about the Golden Gate Quartet because he knew that the name dealt with religious music and he was very touchy about that. He didn't want us getting into anything that would be detrimental to that.

Nights we came in, and we met the other musicians, and we had jokes. Everybody was happy. It was more or less like a family club. Barney was very quiet, but he always joked with us. Fats Waller would come in and say, "Where are those four ministers you got here?" He called us the preacher boys. This was always a big joke for Barney.

Then we signed a contract for three years with CBS to broadcast six days a week. We were one of the busy acts at Cafe Society, doing our radio shows every day plus Cafe Society every night. And from time to time we were doing the Paramount Theater, Loewe's State Theater, or Radio City Music Hall. Once when we were at the Paramount we were sleeping at the theater because we had to be at CBS in the morning.

I remember once, well—this happened to us quite a few times. We did a benefit at the Hotel New Yorker. Barney, he sent us for the benefit. Ivan Black was with us, and we went in to the bar to have a drink. They refused to serve us. That was always a problem we had. This became a big issue because the papers wrote about it the next day and everything.

This was one of the things that Barney was very touchy about. He didn't like this type of thing because this was about the only club that you found in New York that was open to black artists. They did their jobs there, and they were treated like artists. And it was no problem whatsoever. I don't think any of them made problems for him. If they started to make problems, he would say, "Look, let's be reasonable about it. We know what the situation is. We just check it out together, and we work it out together." And he kept it that way.

We used to have drinks together at the bar, the musicians and us. I was the youngster in the group. There was one incident that Barney didn't like. I was drinking with the guys and then we went uptown. I got out of the taxi. There was snow everywhere, and I just slid under the taxi. They pulled me out and got me into the room. The next day I opened my mouth and nothing came out. I had lost my voice completely. It was like that for a whole week. When Barney found out what had happened, well, the bar was closed to me after that. I was aggravated with him about that, but it was nothing I could do. I still found a way to have drinks anyway. We had a trumpet player, Emmett Berry, who used to bring his flask of whiskey every night. He would wave it at me. "Will you have a drink of Doctor Berry's rootin' tootin' oil?" because he blew the trumpet. Him and I was having our drinks together anyway. Barney knew.

All of these things going on at Cafe Society. It was a fantastic thing for us, for all the artists who worked there. Sometimes he came uptown with us. It was surprising to see Barney come uptown, but he was used to it because most of the musicians that were in the after-hour places were all musicians he knew anyway, that had worked for him one time or another. There was one place, Monroe's uptown house, that we used to go to after hours. All the gang you would see them there having fun, having jam sessions. He would really enjoy himself, coming to the up-town houses.[6]

The quartet was leaving for a while to go on tour in 1942. John and I wanted another gospel group to take over. Willie Johnson told John about a group, the Swanee Quintet, singing at a radio station in Philadelphia with much success. They auditioned for us.

Ira Tucker: *Barney said to John, "Look, you take care of them." We did a lot of polished-up numbers. John said, "Don't you have some other songs? I want some down, real down." We said, "Oh, yeah," and we came up with that. He said, "Now that's what I'm lookin' for." So we got the job. When we got to Cafe Society, John Hammond and [Barney] said, "We rather have your name the Jericho Quintet." In Philadelphia at the radio station WCAU they had switched us from the Dixie Humming-birds to the Swanee Quintet.*

We had worked school auditoriums and churches, but this was our very, very first time in a nightclub. There was Helen Humes, Connie Berry, Pete Johnson, Albert Ammons, Prez [Lester Young], and Lee Young. Oh, it was the end, I'm tellin' you. It wasn't nothing to compare with it.

We had a way that we would run out and slide, then we would stop, and Prez would start the music. We had good choreography. We had good rapport with Prez. When we opened—oh god—we were hot! It was nothing like it. It was just a beautiful thing every night. I just lived for that.

That's why when my wife said, "Ms. Josephson's called," I said, "You know, that's one of the best things that ever happened to me to know that she was still here and wanted to see me."[7] Oh, it tore me up because I thought he didn't have anyone livin'. It's a real thrill to me because that was my first love, Cafe Society.

It was a beautiful system Barney had. Some people came in there one night with a little prejudice because they saw a black guy come in with a white lady. Barney said, "Look, I have nothing to do with nobody's choice. When you come in my place, you're jus' whoever you are. We're not supporting any prejudice." We felt good behind it. Barney would come and stick his head in the door, "Hey guys, everybody okay?" "Yeah, man, we doin' fine."

Pete Johnson told me, "Look, try to keep John clappin' fast, because if he ever slow up like this [claps slowly] start packin' your clothes." That's what happened. The army got our bass singer, and we didn't have a chance to train nobody that quick. We had to come out of there one month earlier than we would have. We had five months there. Barney said, "Ira, I hate to see you leave like this." When we left we went back into the name Dixie Hummingbirds."[8]

Not only was I concerned with the nature of the material on my stage but how to reach out to the Negro people as audience. Well, I invited them by taking out ads in, and sending press releases to, the major Negro press all over the country, the *Amsterdam News* in Harlem, the *Pittsburgh Courier,* the *Chicago Defender,* and so forth. The ads urged their readers to come to Cafe Society when they came to New York. But it wasn't easy to overcome their justified suspicions. If you've been turned away often enough you don't try anymore. Now I was inviting Negro people to come to my cafe. They were not used to this. But then word began to get around. When they did begin to come, they were given choice seats. I told my maitre d' to always give them the best tables, never behind columns or in a corner. He and my waiters were also instructed that if people objected to sitting next to Negroes, being in the same room with them, "Check those people out." I wouldn't hear of any such talk in my clubs.

Mollie Moon: *I knew Barney Josephson as a man who changed a long-standing custom in American nightclubs. I can well remember visiting Cafe Society Downtown at Sheridan Square and Cafe Society Uptown on East 58th Street. On one occasion when I was at Cafe Society Downtown there was a long line waiting to be seated. Mine was the only black face in the line, as was my escort's. The maitre d' came out and beckoned to us to come forward and be seated. Because we were near the end of the line we stepped forward. There were cries of protest. One woman turned livid and said, "You see," she said to her friend, "You have to be a Negro to get good seats around here." Today this would be called discrimination in reverse. Because Barney held fast to his beliefs, both clubs flourished. I can think back to the dates during those days when being a civil rights activist was neither possible nor socially acceptable.*[9]

Downtown was also the college place. Came the weekend with the college boys from Yale, Princeton, Columbia, and their dates. I had a long bar. They'd stand three and four deep, buy a bottle of beer for a quarter to share with the girl friend. One beer, turn their backs so as not to look the bartender in the face, and watch the entire show. My bartender had a sawed-off broomstick. He'd reach out and tap them on the shoulders, "What are you going to have, bud?" "Okay, give me another beer."

I had certain business principles then that still hold. I told my manager, "These kids who are coming from the colleges around, treat them nicely. You don't know who their parents might be. That boy over there, his father could be chairman of American Cyanamide Corporation. Now he gets an allowance. When he gets out of college he'll go into the company, someday become a big executive, whatever." For years as these kids came out of college they'd come in and recall those days. They never forgot.

Herbert L. Schultz: *Dear Barney, Here's a photo . . . me with the boogie-woogie piano players. I'm sure I should have been studying at Princeton at the moment it was taken, instead of studying the piano technique of Albert Ammons.*[10]

All the black intellectuals, artists, businessmen, politicians were our patrons. That's how I met them. Paul Robeson, Langston Hughes, Duke Ellington's physician Dr. Arthur Logan and his wife Marion, Richard Wright, actress Fredi Washington, Henry Lee Moon and his wife Mollie, Billy Rowe, Ernest Johnson, Mr. and Mrs. de Passe, Canada Lee.[11]

Fredi Washington: *In '45 when the end of the war came, a couple of fliers that were in the mission over Italy, came by the* People's Voice *to see me. I made a reservation to take them to the Copacabana. Lena was working there, and I thought that would be a treat for them. I gave the guard my name, told him we had a reservation for three. He looked at us and the boys were of a color. "Wait a minute, let me check the book." He came back, "I'm sorry, there's nothing here for Washington." "It's got to be. I made the reservation at noon." I asked where the manager was. "He's not here yet"—conveniently. I'm getting more embarrassed all the time; here are two soldiers in uniform. I said, "Look boys, we'll go where we're appreciated." I got a cab. "Take us to the Village, Cafe Society." And Barney was so pleased that I'd brought them down, and they enjoyed it.*[12]

They all came. They couldn't go anywhere else. Here was a place that welcomed them.

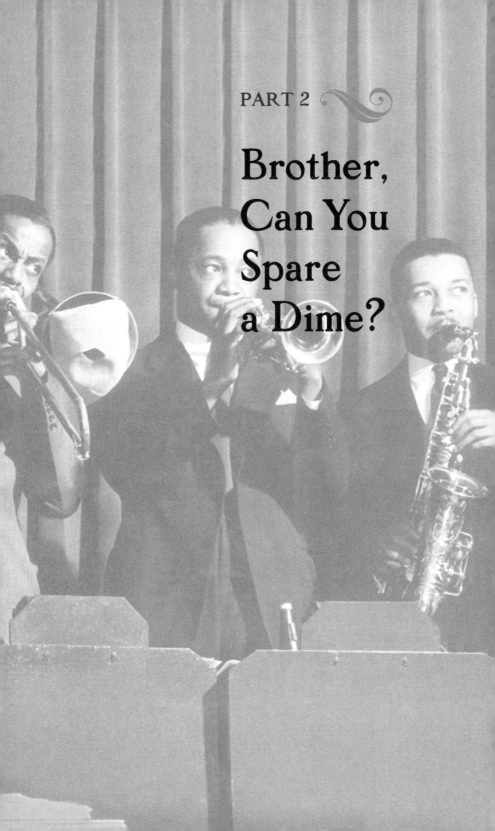

PART 2

Brother, Can You Spare a Dime?

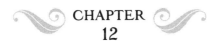
"Always hand-me-downs like that, but I had beautiful clothes."

Many people, some time in their lives, have made an estimate of their talents and their abilities. There are those, of course, who are credited with something more than they are. But you yourself know who you are. In my case I always felt I had a taste for good things, for art, for literature, for talent, for quality. I knew how I wanted to conduct my cabaret. I didn't want a line of half-naked girls. I didn't have that taste. I didn't want Negro comics. I felt their acts were derogatory, playing on the white stereotype of the Negro, a put-down of themselves.

How did I arrive at such a certainty? My family were not the Vanderbilts. I was not privy to the financial or cultural advantage of my long-time friend John Hammond. Our growing-up years were worlds apart. In fact, if records be our defining mortality, then I wasn't born. When I went for my first passport in 1931 I discovered I was uncreated. I had been delivered by a midwife at home, and the midwife knew nothing about reporting the birth of anyone.

At the Department of Vital Statistics in the State House in Trenton, New Jersey, I was told, "We have no record."

"Well, here I am. I was born here. I have all my school records."

They searched and found a 1905 census, the official census record for Mercer County. It stated: "Ward 4, 556 Warren Street. The household there: Bertha Josephson, widow, thirty-nine; Ethel Josephson, single, seventeen, seamstress; David, fifteen, clerk; Louis, thirteen, clerk; Lillie, ten, at school; Leon, seven, at school; Barney, three, no school."

Then I was given an affidavit for my mother to sign affirming that I was born February 1, 1902. This became my birth certificate.

The port of entry to America, the "Golden Door," was Ellis Island when my family came from Russia. As an immigration station, it was located on an island because it was difficult to escape from it. Ostensibly this conformed with the intent of the Immigration Act of 1882, which excluded convicts, idiots, lunatics and any persons not able to take care of themselves.

My family, like most immigrants, came over steerage, so they were down in the hold with the cattle and horses that were being shipped. My brother Leon was just a baby carried in my mother's arms. I was the only one born in this country. When my mother came with her brood of five from Latvia in the spring of 1900, she had bribed a Czarist guard and in that way managed to escape. My father had come over before to settle the family.

In Latvia, my mother, Briena Hirschfield, had been left an orphan. An uncle and aunt immediately invited her to move in with them and their family of six, to share their meager resources. They lived in the village of Talsen in Kurland, now Latvia. We are what are known as Kurlanders. Latvia was originally a German-speaking territory ruled by a German lord subservient to the Prussian king. At the turn of the nineteenth century Latvia was conquered by Peter the Great and made part of the Russian empire. While the language of the peasants was Latvian, the official language was German. Even a hundred years after it was conquered the educated people still spoke German. In the Gentile schools the language was German. Russian, the required language, was taught as a foreign language.

There lived in Talsen a German lady descended from the lesser Baltic nobility. She selected a few attractive little Jewish girls from the neighboring ghetto and tried to give them the secular education considered appropriate for young ladies at that time. In this unconventional way, in the attractive surroundings of this lady's estate, my mother learned to read, write, and speak German. She learned to sew and to embroider as well.

My father, Joseph Josephson, was a cobbler by trade. He learned his trade in Russia. What did a Jew do in those days in Russia? They didn't take to farming. The peasants were non-Jews. The Jews lived in ghettos in the small cities. The large cosmopolitan cities didn't permit Jews. As a Jew, you couldn't go to Moscow or to St. Petersburg or to any of the large cities. You had to have a special permit as an artisan or an intellectual or a teacher. If you were a merchant of note you might be permitted to trade.

So my father learned to be a cobbler in the little shtetl where he had to live. He would repair shoes, make shoes, beautiful shoes. Many a time my brothers and sisters had no shoes to wear, and their father was a shoemaker. He earned enough so that they had enough to eat. When he was able he would buy enough leather to make a pair of uppers for one of his children's shoes. Then a week or two later he might have saved up enough to buy leather for a pair of soles to attach to those uppers to finish the shoes.

Mother had two brothers. One emigrated to Canada, and the other, a tailor from Trenton, met them at the boat. That's how we got to Trenton. Mother brought few possessions, but they were prized. The worldly possessions were a down-feather bedding that all those immigrants schlepped over here. How? They did it. They were bulky things. She brought a pair of brass candlesticks, a mortar and pestle made of brass, an iron which I've never seen anywhere since. It was hollow inside. On the wide part in back was an iron handle and something like a shutter that lifted up to put hot coals inside to heat the iron. That fascinated me always when I watched her iron.

She brought a picture, maybe three feet square, with a gilt rococo frame, a picture of a man who had a beautifully trimmed, Van Dyck–shaped white beard six or eight inches long. The picture showed him with phylacteries, which are two small leather boxes that contain prayers on parchment. Narrow leather straps were wrapped around his left arm and around the boxes on his forehead. This is used in morning prayers by Orthodox men.

This picture always hung on the wall of our house over a black leather couch which was against a wall in the dining room—the everything room. When I was old enough I got to wondering who was this picture. I thought maybe there was a grandpa somewhere. I never knew a grandfather or a grandmother. I asked Mother, "Who is this, a grandpa?"

"No, he is not a grandpa. You may wonder why I brought this picture because this man was a rabbi. He was the chief rabbi of Vilna, the Vilna *gaon*, a man of great learning, who lived in the early nineteenth century. It is said he slept only two hours a day and the other hours were spent with his books."[1]

Mother explained, "Vilna was the capital of Lithuania and the seat of Jewish learning. We are Jews, and we are proud of being Jews even though we are not religious." None of my brothers were bar mitzvahed. We didn't go to synagogue. Mother would light the candles Friday night for the Sabbath, just out of habit really. Well, the Vilna gaon's dedication to learning made a tremendous impression on me. To this day I have such admiration for educators.

The family settled in Trenton on Mill Street, a section in what was then called the "Valley of the Israelites" near the Mercer County Courthouse. One day my father stepped on a rusty nail, and gangrene set in. His leg was amputated to try to save his life. Those were the days before penicillin. The poison had already spread into other regions of his body and that ended his life. He was in his early forties. He died when I was an infant, about six months old. There are no photographs of him so I never knew what he looked like. I don't know anything about my father except that he was a shoemaker.

Mother was now a widow of thirty-seven with six children and no money. She was a very wonderful, talented seamstress. In those years we had ladies' tailors—men tailors who specialized in making women's clothing. They did not make men's suits. Women wore lots of suits and coats that came down in three-quarter length. When I was too young to be left alone at home Mother would go to the ladies' tailor, pick up shirtwaists, whatever, from his shop, bring the bundles home, and sew there. Ready-to-wear clothes were just in their infancy. It was great for the employer. Mother would sew well into the night for that man.

My earliest memory is when I was two. The house on South Warren Street in which we lived was a house in back of a house. The front house was occupied by a family named Harris. Mr. Harris was a blacksmith, the only Jewish blacksmith I ever heard of. He used to shoe horses. There was an alleyway with a yard. Where the yard once was, a house had been built, our house. I don't know how many rooms we had, but they were few enough. Everybody had to double up. There was a large closet you could walk into. My sister Lillie, the younger of the two girls, slept on a shelf in this closet. A mattress was put on the shelf, and she slept there. That was her bed.

I don't know where I usually slept. I probably slept with my mother because I have a recollection of an uncle of mine kidding me about sleeping with my mother. I told him, "I can sleep with my mother because my mother is my sweetheart." After that I had a nickname in my family. They would say,

"Here comes sweetheart." When I was asked who I was going to marry when I grew up I'd say, "I'm going to marry my sweetheart." I must have been about three or four.

Mother had a stepsister living in Trenton who was getting married. The only place for this wedding to take place was in this small household of ours, this house behind the main house. Mother's brother, the Trenton tailor, had a son and daughter. His son was a year younger than I, named after the same grandfather. They called him Bernie and me Barney. I have some recollection of the festivities, but what I remember most is that Bernie and I were put in one bed together to sleep.

We had a few rich Jewish families in the area who lived in big houses. One of these families, the Wolfs, had a son and daughter. Mrs. Wolf was a sister to the Guggenheims who founded among other businesses Anaconda Copper. These were the German Jews who came to this country in the 1800s. The Wolfs' son was a classmate of my nephew Joseph Kline. The two boys were in each other's homes very often. Joe would describe the Wolf home to his mother, my sister Ethel. The furniture, obviously good furniture at one time, was worn absolutely threadbare; the Oriental rugs, also threadbare. This didn't trouble the Wolfs at all. The way of the rich.

The daughters of many of these rich Jewish families didn't know how to sew. When they needed an evening gown to go to a dance, Mother made gowns for them. She made the most gorgeous evening gowns with designs sewn with sequins and little rhinestones. She was known for that kind of work.

Every department store had a notions and patterns department. People who wanted their clothes made would buy their material—yard goods—buy all the findings, which are all kinds of small objects used in making garments such as buttons, buckles, clasps, and so forth. They would bring the material and the Butterick patterns which they had picked out. It was such a long name for me to know—Butterick; it seemed a mile long. Those patterns were all over our house.

Mother would sew at night at the kitchen table after the rest of us were put to bed. We had no electricity in our house, just candle light, or an oil lamp, or a gas mantle with a 25 cent meter. Sometimes I would stay up to keep her company, trying to help.

So Mother had day work, night work, and not having enough sewing work she made every dress, every blouse for my two sisters, every pair of pants, every shirt for all the boys. When my sisters' skirts went out of style or they outgrew the size and she couldn't let out the hem anymore, or a pair of pants of the suits my older brothers were now buying was too worn out, Mother would rip the skirt or pants apart and make a pair of knickers for me. Not a pair of pants, knickers. Always hand-me-downs like that, but I had beautiful clothes.

On our block was a shirt factory, a sweatshop where all the immigrant Jewish and Italian girls worked. Italians were moving in on the other side of the railroad tracks. When they cut material for shirts, often at the end of the bolt there would be a piece left over, not enough to make a whole shirt. This left-over material was thrown into a pile.

Mother would go to the shirt factory and pick out material from these remnants. It was fashionable then to wear pure silk shirts in very gaudy, colorful stripes. So we would have a shirt, the front part only, not enough to make a full tail, but there was enough material to get inside the belt far enough down. She would sew together odd pieces of material so the back would be green or yellow or white, it didn't matter. We'd protest, "But Ma." She'd say, "Who can see it?"

We always wore jackets and ties. We didn't know what it was to buy a shirt, and we had beautiful ones. Our shirts were ironed so that there was never a wrinkle. The collars and cuffs starched just enough to be comfortable. My sisters were always dressed elegantly. The only article of clothing they ever bought was a hat. Shoes, well, my brother David was an errand boy in a shoe store, so he would get shoes at cost or at a discount.

By the time I went to school I was sharing the same bed with my brother Leon, one with metal springs. Those spring beds somehow were breeding places for bed bugs. Mother would buy a can made of flexible metal with a nozzle which stuck out. When you squeezed the can in the middle, powder would spray out in puffs. I can still smell the powder. She was after those bed bugs all the time. She would take the mattress off, spray all the joints where the springs were welded together, spraying into the seams of the mattress.

In those years there was no aid of any kind for the poor, for the widows. You had to rely on the charity of neighbors. The neighborhood had been predominately Irish, and then the Jewish immigrants moved in. Mrs. O'Brien, who lived on our block, offered to take care of me because Mother would never ask anyone to do anything like that for her. Mrs. O'Brien had sixteen children, one boy and the rest, girls, all stunning, especially Kathleen, whom I liked the most. Mother would leave me with Mrs. O'Brien and her brood while she went to work for the ladies' tailor in his shop instead of working at home. Mother told me Mrs. O'Brien took care of me until I went to school. I have no recollection of that. It's strange because I can remember all the important and not so important events in my life.

Mother was never one who coddled or babied me in any way. A kissing-or-hugging me kind of momma she wasn't. She was very warm and sweet and thoughtful, all of that, but she never gushed over me. I had two older sisters who loved their little Barney, but there wasn't any hugging and kissing in my family. Yet they always made me feel that they loved me. I was the baby.

One day I overheard Mother talking to one of the women in the neighbor-hood. They were speaking about their children. "My Berele is a little angel." I must have been about four, and those words have never even been in my consciousness until now, as if I just heard her voice. I was such a good child, Mother said, because I knew how hard she had it, losing her husband, speak-ing of my father's death. That's how I found out. I had always been told that he was not home because he was traveling, working to make money to support his family. Somehow I sensed I should not give her any trouble. I just started thinking about the father I never knew and now I'm crying.

When my brother Dave's son was born on June 3, 1933, there was a bris of course. In Judaism this is the religious rite of circumcision which takes place the eighth day after birth. The baby was named after my father, Joseph Josephson. After the ceremony I broke down and began to cry hysterically, unable to stop myself, "My father has returned. My father has returned." I was twenty-one years old.

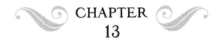

CHAPTER
13

"'She was a remarkable woman,
way ahead of her time.'"

Young though she was when my father died, Mother never re-married. I had heard her say on several occasions when she was asked by neighbors that she had opportunities enough. There were men, strangely enough, she said, who wanted to take her on with her six children. But no, she had made up her mind when my father passed away no one would ever be a stepfather to her children.

I wasn't always an angel although everyone used to say I looked and behaved like one. When I wasn't an angel and did something naughty Mother would scold me in her quiet way. "Now, my boy, a Josephson doesn't behave in this manner. A Josephson boy does not do so and so. You're not behaving like a little boy from South Warren Street, you're behaving like one from Decatur Street," which was a very depressed street a block away where the poorest of the Jews lived. She would shame you and give you the sense that you were hurting the great name of the family so that I would almost beg for a whack.

"Why don't you slap me, Ma? Then it would be over with. The next time I do something wrong you'll recall all the things I ever did wrong." I was getting a little bigger now and could speak up to her. But no, no. I would get the whole life story rehearsed, all spoken very quietly. I'd get all the punishment from her tongue, a litany of wrongs from day one.

Jimmie Josephson [David's wife]: *When I was a child the Josephson family lived across the street from us. Mrs. Josephson was a very capable woman. She cooked and sewed and was the head of the household in every sense. The children accounted to her. I think she was a no-nonsense lady. Her husband died when Barney was about six months old. They were all very industrious, and they were very independent and very proud, very proud. They weren't people that anybody thought of, you know in the Jewish community there are always some people who are needy, especially those who are widows, but nobody would ever think of her as being anything like that. She held her head high. She supported the children, ran the household, and everybody was well-kept, well-dressed. I really think they all worshiped her. She was certainly an unusual woman, talented in many ways. She learned to speak English well. She wanted to read everything, and she wanted to hear all kinds of music. She was a remarkable woman, way ahead of her time. She was born at the wrong time.*

I knew Dave as a child, as I was growing up. I never paid any attention to him then. He was about sixteen when I became more or less aware of him. He would ride his bike to where he worked in a shoe store. They all worked at something.

My girls, her grandchildren, are almost the same age, so I used to dress them alike. She got such pleasure out of making clothes for them. One was a pink duvetyne coat and hat with a little cape on the coat edged in narrow fur. They looked so beautiful in them.[1]

My oldest sister Ethel was really an angel, always very quiet. She had learned to sew from my mother. She was about fifteen when she went to work, slaving as a seamstress in a sweatshop sewing silk kimonos. To complete her high school education she had to attend night school.

A nice Jewish boy like my brother David went to the YMCA night school. He became a rather good basketball player on their team. It was quite a thing for a Jewish kid. I don't even know why they took him in, there was so much anti-Semitism.

My sister Lillie had the temper. One time she was down on the floor, scrubbing the linoleum with a hand brush. Leon came in from having played ball and walked on the wet floor. Lillie screamed at him, "Don't you walk on my wet floor!" and threw the brush at him.

In order to better make ends meet Mother took in a boarder. It wasn't enough that she had six children, sewed for a ladies' tailor during the day and for her family and others at night, she took in Mr. Kneppler. I've never forgotten this man. He had a game leg which he couldn't straighten. I'm not sure whether it was the right or left. It was always in a knee-bend position. He walked that way, up and down, up and down. He moved into our attic room. He rigged a trapeze into the ceiling to which he attached a couple of rings. He would get his legs through them and go swinging, doing all sorts of acrobatics up there.

And he was a socialist. There was no such thing dreamed of in our family until then. He would talk to my oldest brother Dave, selling him on this idea, giving him pamphlets to read. Dave would have none of it. At this early age he was already a rugged individualist, working as a clerk in a shoe store, fitting people with shoes, dreaming of the day when he would own his own shoe store, a chain of them. He was going to make it. He wasn't interested in this socialist stuff. He just rejected Mr. Kneppler.

Not to give up, Mr. Kneppler went after the second-oldest brother, Louis. Here he found a ready ear. Lou got the bug from Mr. Kneppler. He became a very ardent socialist. Every night he was on a public soap box on a corner, the main stem in Trenton, haranguing crowds of people about socialism, espousing such "radical" ideas as social security, unemployment compensation, fair labor laws, government housing. So Mr. Kneppler has Lou, and Leon got the bug from his next-oldest brother, and I get it from Lou and Leon. I was about eight years old. Now the three of us are infected with this disease.

I wonder if our lives would have been different but for Mr. Kneppler. Lou might have been named to the New Jersey Supreme Court, a proposition which was actually dangled in front of him many years later. He had become so well known that political bigwig Frank "I Am the Boss" Hague sent his emissaries to Lou, promising him such an appointment in return for his support of Hague's party's ticket. Lou declined, refusing to be part of Hague's corrupt and antilabor political machine. He never regretted that decision.

Lou became a lawyer although he never went beyond the fourth grade. He believed the working class needed lawyers to defend them with authority. Each night after coming home from working as the manager of a delicatessen store at State and Stockton Streets he did his school lessons to get his high school equivalency.

We had this four-story house with no heat except for the coal stove, and Lou used to sit way up into the night studying with the LaSalle Extension University in Chicago, a small mail-order law school. He couldn't make it—too tough. Leon, who was in Trenton High School, would tutor him each night. Lou got his law degree from the old New Jersey Law School in Newark, now part of Rutgers University. Leon went on to New York University Law School because our family's fortunes had improved by then.

Lou became a prominent labor lawyer for the AFL and the CIO, separate unions then. He also had a general practice, most of it free for poor clients. He made a living but never became a rich man, never was interested in that. In 1939 the city commissioners of Trenton offered him the post of city counsel, an office he held until his death, July 29, 1960. Lou was so beloved that the Trenton Housing Authority's first public housing project for elderly citizens was named in his honor, the Louis Josephson Apartments on Oakland Street.

Jimmie Josephson: *The apartment complex was one of the earliest attempts to do something in housing for senior citizens. It was designed beautifully. You never had to stand on a ladder to reach anything. It was done with good social consciousness of the needs of older people who live alone. This is the city's memorial to Lou. The apartments are still there although Lou never knew about them.*[2]

A bronze bust of City Counsel Louis Josephson is permanently displayed in the City Council Chambers at City Hall in Trenton.

CHAPTER
14

"As natural to me as drinking a glass of milk."

When I was in grade school I worked in the corner drug store. Mother made me a white coat of piqué with white buttons. I was a fountain boy, a delivery boy, and a porter, everything in Mr. Stretch's Drug Store. Mother made this coat for the fountain, this beautiful fountain made of lovely marble with all the fittings. The spigots with all of the flavors were silver-plated. I used to polish them with silver polish to make them gleam. Oh—that was my fountain.

All the little girls in my neighborhood would come around on their roller skates when I was behind the fountain. You'd hear their skates because they were metal with ballbearings. They'd skate by the store and yell, "Baaaarrneee, Baaaarrneee," and scoot away, bashful-like. All the little girls were in love with me. I was twelve, thirteen, and really cute then.

They would come in for their sodas, great big ice cream sodas for a nickel. We made our own chocolate syrup. Mr. Stretch bought lump chocolate, and we'd cook it on a gas stove in back of the store. Mr. Stretch had those eyes. When I opened the little spigot for the syrup to run out into the glass, if he saw that it was for one of my friends he'd stand a few feet away, look, tilting his head to make sure I didn't put in too much syrup. Son-of-a-bitch.

This was my first job. I worked from five to eleven o'clock behind the fountain. I'd sell other things, too, anything that didn't need to be dispensed by a druggist. Every day after school I would deliver prescriptions. I had Leon's bike. Mr. Stretch had me come in the nights the two other druggists had off. He was afraid to be alone. My pay was 50 cents a night.

Saturday morning I'd come in at eight o'clock, scrub and mop the tile floors, wash and clean all the show cases, polish the fountain, and run errands for which I was paid an extra 50 cents. All told, it came to $2.50 a week. Mr. Stretch would pay me in nickels, dimes, and a few quarters. He would stack them up in denominations. "Here you are, Barney. What are you going to do with all that money?" "I'm going to give it to my mother." He paid me off that way so that it would look like a lot. He had it all figured out. If he gave me two $1 bills and a 50 cent piece it wouldn't look like as much money. Not that he thought he was underpaying me.

We all came home with the money we earned. It was all given to Mother, every penny went on the table. No one ever took a dollar or a penny. If I wanted a penny for candy I would ask for it. Everything went into the kitty. And when my sister Ethel married Harry Kline she had a dowry of $500.

The neighborhood where I went to grade school was largely Jewish, some few Irish, and a good sprinkling of Italians. Everyone went to the neighborhood school, the Charles Skelton School on Center Street. I vividly remember my first-grade teacher. I was very much in love with her.

I went to junior high school on Princeton Avenue in another area of the city. It was the first junior high school in Trenton, Junior High Number One, just built. It included all students from all parts of the city. It was here that I met my first black classmate. There were no black people in my neighborhood. I never knew a black person.

I was not the best of students, and I don't think I was too happy about going to school ever. So I wasn't the first kid to walk into the classroom that first day. Half the room was already occupied. The system was that you were never assigned to a seat. You came in, first come, first take. You sat where you wanted to sit. If you wanted to be in the corner where the teacher couldn't see you to call on you, you'd take a corner seat.

I walked into the classroom and saw this young black boy sitting at a desk in the center of the room. He apparently was the first one to be there. I remember how well-dressed he was. I was the kind of kid who always wore a starched collar, shirt, and tie. In those days boys went to school dressed that way. And a black boy, going to junior high school in those times, his mother really dressed him carefully. He had a white, starched shirt, a tie, and a part cut into his hair. He was a handsome-looking young fellow. There he was on a little island in the middle of the room. Everyone sat everywhere else away from him.

I encompassed the room at a glance. I always had this ability to quickly take in a room, see it all. So I got the picture. I unhesitatingly walked over to this youngster and put out my hand. "My name is Barney Josephson. What's yours?"

"Rudolph Dunston."

"Can I sit next to you?" I'm asking him if I can sit next to him.

"Sure."

So I sat next to him. I was a little socialist boy then, a member of the "Yipsels," the Young People's Socialist League. This was when the only radical party in the country was the Socialist Party, with Eugene Victor Debs its perennial presidential candidate every four years.

Having ideas about equality and socialist principles was largely a question of morals. Capitalism breeds war. So it was an antiwar movement. Women are exploited, so we were for the vote for women. I remember Leon showing me a picture in a newspaper of the tens of thousands of women marching in New York City demanding the right to vote. I was fifteen.

Three years later the Nineteenth Amendment was ratified in Congress [on August 18, 1920], giving all citizens, regardless of gender, the right to vote. We were for trade unionism. We believed in equal rights for all people, that included the Negro people. I had these ideas as a youngster of nine. So when I walked into the classroom, what I did was as natural to me as drinking a glass of milk at breakfast time.

Our English teacher, Miss MacDonough, decided we should have a debating team as part of our classwork. She appointed me a captain and asked me to select a couple of boys for my team. She asked a blond-haired crew-cut boy to be the other captain. I picked Rudolph Dunston because he was smart, and a nice Italian youngster, Paul Plumieri, who was also smart. The other captain picked two more like him. I was asked to select a topic for our first debate.

I spoke to Leon, who told me about a book in the library, *Topics for a Debate*. The book had a list of a couple of hundred topics. I picked out one: "Resolved: Military training should not be in the public school system." With

Leon's help I wrote all three speeches because the other boys didn't have any feeling for the subject.

I made my speech, then the other captain, then each of the two boys alternating. I presented my rebuttal. My point was that the nature of military training is not to think but to obey. Therefore you can't have nonthinking military training in an educational institution where you are taught to think. I waxed very emotional, as I can get. Here was this Jewish boy saying, "I don't know how we can go to church on Sunday and learn 'turn thy swords into plowshares' and then come to school on Monday and shoulder a gun for military training. Either give up your Christianity or give up military training in the schools."

Well, they took this as a "goddamn kike" attacking their religion, and I didn't mean that at all. In addition, I've got a nigger and a wop on my team. We lost.

The next period is gym. I get into my gym clothes. Three of the opposing debating team and some others work me into a corner on the gym floor and start roughing me up, "You nigger lover, wop lover." I just happened to catch a view of the gym teacher observing all of this from his office just off the gym floor and not doing anything. I was a kid who would speak up. I yelled, "Mr. Smith, you're seeing this whole performance and you're not doing anything to stop it and I hold you responsible." He had to come out and break it up. I was about fourteen at the time.

Every day after school I worked in Dave's shoe store. I had quit my job with Mr. Stretch. Dave wanted me in the store. I worked not only after school, I worked before school. I would ride my bike to the store at seven-thirty in the morning. We opened at nine. The store had copper trim around the window frames. I'd buy oxalic acid in the drug store. It came in crystals, very strong stuff. The crystals were put in an old citric of magnesia bottle which had a secure top. I'd shake up the bottle, dissolving the crystals, and, with a rag, go around polishing all that copper. I'd wash the windows, mop the tile lobby between the display windows, clean up the store, sweep the carpet, set out the empty cartons, mash them down for the garbage men to take away. By this time the help would start to arrive, and I'd ride off to school.

Jimmie Josephson: *They built a store that was beautiful. It was a show place; so unusual. They spent so much money. They didn't save on anything. Dave had wonderful taste. It had a Circassian walnut entrance.*

That's very beautiful walnut that you don't see anymore. You got a feeling when you approached the store that you were entering something elegant. People would come from all over Princeton to buy shoes there. Dave was very particular about the help. Nobody ever waited on a customer with a jacket off. There was a decorum in the store that I haven't seen in any store. Everybody working there was supposed to look a certain way and act a certain way. Dave had a way of sitting down and fitting his customers and talking to them.

Dave had a wonderful name for the social things that he did for other people. Any Jewish kid who wanted to go to college knew he had a job at Josephson's. They worked there summers, weekends, part-time. Every once in a while I hear from someone who became a doctor or a lawyer who worked for Dave.[1]

In the afternoon there was a first gong at three-fifteen and a second gong at the end of school at three-thirty. Working boys could get out at the first gong. As soon as that first gong rang I'd run to get my bike, get down to the store and work. If we were busy, I'd sell shoes. The shoes had to be delivered. Who was the delivery boy? I was a salesman, and I was the porter.

One Saturday morning I was in the lobby, mopping the tile, wringing out the mop, the dirty water running up my arms. A woman came tip-toeing up, "Pardon me, I hate to walk on your clean tile," and tip-toed into the store. We got busy early, and all of the help were with customers. Dave called, "Barney, come in and take a customer." I rolled down my sleeves on my soiled, streaked arms and waited on this same lady. I sold her the shoes. When she said she would take them, I told her, "We'll deliver them to you." I was always willing to oblige. "You'll have your shoes late this afternoon."

It was early summer, a nice day, and my customer was sitting rocking on her front porch. I drove up on my bicycle with the package in my basket. She looked at me astonished, "My goodness, you're everything in that place, aren't you?" She didn't know I was family. I was very proud, you know, when she said I was everything.

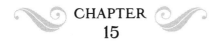

"Leon set up that kind of thing, share and share alike."

My older brothers and sisters were so busy working they didn't have much time for me. When I would ask my mother what my father looked like, because there were no photos of him, she would say, "Leon is the only one." So Leon, the next youngest in our family, was the picture of my father. Being too young to work, Leon was in school. I was in school. Leon was my big brother, my father, my mentor, and a tremendous influence on my life. He taught me everything I knew and watched over me and guided me. He taught me how to ride his bike. I was so proud when I learned to ride with no hands. "Look, Leon, no hands!"

There was this wonderful thing between Leon and me. We would be walking down the street toward our house, and he would ask, "How much money have you got, kid?" He always called me kid. It was a term of endearment. I'd dig into my pants pocket and pull out 13 cents. He would take out his money. He's got 15 cents. He'd give me a penny. It had to be even-steven. Leon set up that kind of thing, share and share alike. We always had to have the same.

He was the kind of guy who would always take me along. If he was going some place with his friends, he'd say, "Come on, kid, you're going with us," Three and a half years older is quite a difference when you're young, fourteen, fifteen. Usually the big brother doesn't want the kid brother around. I was never left out. I was always introduced as Leon Josephson's kid brother. I was not Barney Josephson, just the kid brother. Leon read more than I. He was reading everything. My feeling was that Leon could express everything so well, he was expressing it for me, too. For years we would be together at political gatherings. I hardly ever spoke.

"A woman is a human being like a man. A woman isn't a screwing machine, and you shouldn't have sex with a woman unless you feel a love for her." Leon had a sense of morality on his own, and he imparted that to me. Our mother never discussed such things with us. One of the first things Leon had taught me was that one must not masturbate, that it leads to softening of the brain and you wind up in an insane asylum. I don't know where he got that information, but he was so well-read that I accepted anything he told me as gospel.

One day, with a young man's curiosity, I walked into a burlesque show on West 42nd Street in New York City. While the women were doing their striptease, you couldn't see a damn thing. They were very careful about that. When they were completely disrobed, there were G-strings which covered just enough. Three men are sitting in the first, second, and third rows. The lights coming off the stage illuminated them, too. While the women are stripping these men are masturbating. It revolted me, and I walked out. Burlesque was for degenerates. Such was my brother's upbringing.

By the time I was sixteen all the boys in my gang already had gonorrhea two or three times. There was always some little girl around who was promiscuous, would pick up something and pass it on. The boys used to scoff at me, "What the hell, you've never been laid. You're not a man until you have the gonorrhea at least three times." That was an expression. But I didn't feel abnormal. I felt so fucking superior—that's the word to use—without fucking. They couldn't bring me down and make me feel less a man.

Leon always had a big library. Shakespeare, that's what we had all over the house, and I would read the plays. I never thought consciously that I wanted to be an actor, but when I was thirteen, fourteen, fifteen I would close the door to my room and act out scenes from Shakespeare. Particularly, I'd do *Hamlet* and declaim, "Get thee to a nunnery: why wouldst thou be a breeder of sinners?" I'd go through it all. I would do death scenes and stab myself very dramatically. All by myself I'd go through all the tragedies. Nobody in my family knew I ever did such a thing.

I was sixteen when I began to go to the theater in New York. I saw all the shows. I'd go mostly week nights because Saturday nights I worked late until ten in Dave's store. After the play I'd catch the milk train from Penn Station, so-called because it delivered milk. It was a long, slow ride, stopped at every station. I'd get back home two in the morning.

Walter Hampden was a great favorite of mine. When I saw him as Cyrano, oh, I wept as he sat under a huge tree, the autumn leaves falling as he died and the curtain slowly, slowly came down. *The Jest* was one of my favorites. John and Lionel Barrymore were the stars. How exciting those brothers were. It was the sensation of the season, sold out all the time. I saw it three times at the Plymouth Theatre in 1919. If I liked a play I'd go back again and again. The other Barrymore, sister Ethel, was in her own big hit, *Déclassé*, written by a woman, Zoë Atkins.

I was aware of the actors strike in August 1919 because something like twenty-one theaters closed. Not only actors but chorus girls, stagehands, and musicians all joined the walkout demanding recognition for the union, Actors Equity. John, Lionel, Ethel, and their uncle John Drew supported the strike and closed their shows. That "Yankee Doodle Dandy" George M. Cohan said he would spend his last dollar to fight the strike.

Ethel Barrymore: *A good many managers appear to think they are simply merchants and the actors are their stock in trade. . . . They are behaving exactly like the Kaiser and the whole Prussian military crowd. Their argument is that of force. . . . Actors don't need managers; managers can do nothing without actors. All we are working for is democracy in the theatre, justice, equality, truth. . . . I never thought of leaving the cause. I believe with my whole heart that it is right. They are my people.*[1]

This was not the only strike in 1919. Countrywide, strikes abounded. Workers were demanding better working conditions and higher wages. Across the nation, twenty-four race riots, which had started in Chicago in late July, were counted. Seventy-six Negroes were lynched down south. The Justice Department rounded up 249 "radical aliens," including Emma Goldman, for immediate deportation to the Soviet Union.

On October 28 the nation would enter a prolonged dry spell, ushering in the age of Prohibition and illegal hooch. And in November the United States Senate rejected President Wilson's dream of global peace, the League of Nations.

"I had never dated a girl."

After graduating from high school in 1919 I began to work full time in our shoe store. I liked to arrange the displays for our store window. We sold silk stockings of various shades, and I would fashion them into roses, arranging them with our shoes so that the colors of the stockings and shoes complemented each other. I would change these displays, creating different arrangements. People would stop by our store just to marvel at our windows.

I was making a lot of money then, $150 a week. I supported my mother by myself. No one had to contribute. I took care of her. All my brothers and sisters were married except Leon. He was living in New York or traveling around.

We had a lovely home on Greenwood Avenue in a nice residential section of the city. As our financial status improved we had moved a couple of times. We were the first Jewish family on that block. The family on one side of our house moved out because Jews moved in. Then another Jewish family took that house. Then another family adjoining that house moved out and a rabbi came in with his whole family. That ended that block. They all moved out. One Protestant family remained. They wouldn't move come what may.

Mother had developed angina for all the years she had worked like a slave.

The house was getting too much for her to take care of, so we sold it. I took an apartment in the best area in Trenton, West State Street, a quiet residential area not far from the city park. I lived with Mother until her death in 1935.

Kitty MacGregor, a lovely little Scotch girl, was working in our store as a salesgirl. I was a young man in my early twenties. Kitty took a shine to me, made it apparent she liked me. Our main stock room was on the second floor of our store. Sometimes sales people had to go up to get a box of shoes from that reserve. Whenever I went up there Kitty would find a way to come up there for something, too. She would brush up against me, rub against me.

I had never dated a girl until that time. One day, I don't know how it happened, but this young lady pretty well let me know that she wanted to be with me, wanted a date with me. I had to explain, "We have a rule in our family business that we do not go out with anyone working in the store. I like you very much, and I would love to take you out but not while you're working here."

Dave had cautioned me, "Barney, you never give a girl a pair of shoes, a pair of stockings from stock. If you want to buy a girl a pair of shoes or give her stockings, give her the money and let her come in and buy them. Once you start that they'll own the goddamn place." Now I was getting sex instructions from my oldest brother.

Well that Saturday night was pay night, and Kitty MacGregor gave my brother notice that she was quitting. She had already gotten another job at Vorhees Department Store in their shoe department. I made a date with her. I had never touched her, but this first date I made was to take her to New York for the weekend. I was twenty-two now, and I thought, it's about time.

I called the McAlpine Hotel, which was a good, decent hotel on 34th Street, and reserved a room for Mr. and Mrs. Barney Josephson. We walked in. The bellhop took us up to our room, put our bags down, and we were alone. Imagine how I felt. How she felt I don't know except for what she did. We had come to New York after work, having met at the railroad station. It was rather late. "Kitty, you must be hungry. Let's go out and find a restaurant." She was very reluctant to leave the room, said she wasn't hungry. So I knew that answer to mean that she wanted to go to bed now.

She went into the bathroom and undressed. I undressed in the bedroom and got under the covers with the lights out. She came out of the bathroom and got into bed. Before I could enter her I already had an orgasm on her. It wasn't a minute later that I was hard again. At that age and for the first time I was erect immediately. And I screwed and screwed and screwed like I was never going to get it again.

I took her home Sunday night and had sex with her again in her house in the parlor. I had used eleven condoms. I had eleven ejaculations in twenty-four hours.

Kitty and I had an affair for about two years. Where do you go in Trenton? It was not very convenient in her aunt's house. I lived with my mother. Where could I take Kitty but to my brother Lou's law office in Trenton. I had a key. We'd get on the carpeted floor. I don't think I had sex with her less than three or four times in an evening, I was that active. I guess that's pretty much normal for a man that age.

Then Kitty moved away from Trenton and got married. I didn't want to get married. I was living with my mother. I wasn't interested in marriage.

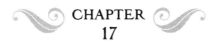

CHAPTER
17

"The workers sleeps in a old straw bed and shivers from the cold."

One day in early September 1929 I received a letter from Leon postmarked North Carolina. He was writing from a little town there, Gastonia. At this time Leon was a young lawyer working for the International Labor Defense, which was defending a group of mill workers who were charged with the murder of the chief of police in Gastonia, Orville F. Aderholt.

To avoid union organizing, and attracted by cheap white labor, the American textile industry had moved from New England to the hill country of North and South Carolina in the early 1900s. Typical of all company towns, they built housing for their workers. The houses had no sanitation facilities, not even running water. Rent was 50 cents a room for four rooms. Workers toiled in twelve-hour shifts with a half hour for lunch. You can imagine the inside of the mills, hot, poor lighting, filled with fiber dust, conditions ripe for accidents which occurred all too frequently. Workmen's compensation was not even a dream.

Finally, by the late 1920s the mill workers, fed up, began to strike in town after town in the hills of the Carolinas. A union, the militant National Textile Workers Union, had been recruiting workers in one of the mills in the little town of Loray, North Carolina, near Gastonia.

A strike was called April 1, and 1,700 workers walked out of the Loray mill. The owners brought in strikebreakers. One day [June 7, 1929] the strikers had gathered, preparing to go to the Loray mill to talk to the scab workers. Suddenly the Gastonia police descended on them. Shots were fired, and the chief of police, Aderholt, fell wounded, shot in the back. He died the next day. The strikers were all facing him, his deputies were behind him, so one of them must have fired that shot. Seventy strikers were arrested. They were released, but the union organizer, Fred Beal, and six others were charged with conspiracy to commit murder. This story would make the front page of the *New York Times*.[1]

The letter I received from Leon contained a list of shoe sizes. Many of the seventy arrested strikers were too poor to buy shoes, barefoot hillbillies. I sent a case of shoes without telling my brother Dave. He was a Republican, and I wasn't so sure he would have approved. I don't think I pulled the wool over his eyes, but he never said anything.

One of the strikers was Ella May Wiggins, a mother of five, with a gift for singing and writing new words to old mountain ballads.

> The boss man sleeps in a big fine bed
> And dreams of his silver and gold.
> The workers sleeps in a old straw bed
> And shivers in the cold.[2]

Ella May was on her way to a union meeting with a group of other cotton mill workers, September 14, 1929. Their truck was ambushed. They were fired upon. A bullet found Ella May Wiggins in the left breast, shot dead. She was thirty-five years old. On a rainy September 18, Ella May was buried as the hundreds of mourners sang one of her songs:

> How it grieves the heart of a mother,
> You every one must know,
> But we can't buy for our children
> Our wages are too low.[3]

Nine men, employees of the Loray mill, were accused of killing Mrs. Wiggins. The Gastonia County grand jury listened to seventy-five witnesses for three days. They refused to indict the nine, "no grounds for true bills." The men were freed. No one was ever charged again.[4]

Up north this same October, prices crashed on the Wall Street Stock

Exchange, Black Thursday. Four days later, Black Tuesday, October 28, 1929, crowds stood before the ticker tapes watching their fortune disappear. The Great Depression was ushered in. Banks failed across the country. Industrial production declined. Republican President Herbert Hoover refused to adopt any economic measures, "prosperity is just around the corner." By 1933, 25 percent of the nation's workforce was unemployed. Apple sellers appearing on street corners with surplus apples for sale, 5 cents each, was a sight to forever symbolize that time.

David had become an active member of the Republican Club in Mercer County and a big wheel in the Young Men's Hebrew Association, on the board of directors. By now he was married, with two daughters and the youngest, Joe. Dave was a strong supporter of Herbert Hoover; he'd quote the Republican slogan, telling me, "No need to worry, Barney." As the depression deepened Dave refused to heed the warning signs. While he hadn't invested in the stock market, he had another investment.

We sold only expensive shoes. Dave had a keen sense of style. If he picked a hundred pairs of shoes, they were all good. But he over-bought. He loved to buy. Grey is the color for the next season. Dave has grey suede and grey kid and grey calf and grey satin. Then he has this kind of strap and another kind and so on. Sometimes we would go to buy together.

I'd tell him, "Dave, you're buying too much. You can't."

"But I like this one."

"If you like this one, eliminate another one. You have three too many now."

We had fights about that all the time. There he was with all those expensive shoes and $75,000 in accounts receivable. He showed a profit, but in inventory not cash. Like so many businessmen during the depression Dave lost his business.

Jimmie Josephson: *When things were hard for Dave, Barney tried awfully hard to help Dave to get out of the jam that he was in. . . . I don't know how Barney is, but Dave was not anybody that you could direct to do things. He had a mind of his own. I was always taught to stay out of my husband's business. I knew what was going on.*

Dave was always very optimistic. He always thought that things would work out. Actually, when Dave lost his business, my brothers and my father came in and set him up in a business of his own like theirs, yard goods, materials. My father was a wholesaler, a jobber. They do exporting and importing. Dave opened a store on Johns Street in New York, a retail store, selling all kinds of materials. He did very well. He worked there until the end.[5]

With our shoe store gone and Mother no longer alive I left Trenton. Leon's phone call to me in Atlantic City would change my life. I would leave the shoes behind. I would enter another world.

(top) Comedienne Paula Lawrence; Claudia, Barney's stepdaughter; Barney; and movie star Bonita Granville at Cafe Society Uptown, about 1945. (Albert Freeman photo, Barney Josephson Collection)

(bottom) Barney chatting with violinist Eddie South, Cafe Society Uptown bar, 1940. (Collection of the Institute of Jazz Studies, Rutgers University)

Barney at his desk, Cafe Society Uptown, about 1943. (Albert Freeman photo, Barney Josephson Collection)

Paul Robeson, then on Broadway in *Othello,* Hazel Scott, and Barney celebrate her birthday, 1943. (Harold Stein photo)

(top) Jacques Pils, Lucienne Boyer, their daughter Jacqueline Pils, and Lena Horne at Cafe Society Uptown, 1947. (Albert Freeman photo, Barney Josephson Collection)

(bottom) Lucienne Boyer in performance, Cafe Society Uptown. (Albert Freeman photo, Barney Josephson Collection)

(top) Lucienne Boyer looks on as Charlie Chaplin signs the guest book at Cafe Society Uptown, 1947. (Albert Freeman photo, Barney Josephson Collection)

(bottom) Jimmy Savo juggling lightbulbs, 1943, Cafe Society Uptown. (Roman Vishniac photo © Mara Vishniac Kohn, courtesy the International Center of Photography)

(top) Jimmy Savo and First Lady Eleanor Roosevelt during Franklin D. Roosevelt's fourth-term reelection campaign, 1944. (Albert Freeman photo, Barney Josephson Collection)

(bottom) Program cover for Hazel Scott's concert at Carnegie Hall, November 26, 1945. (Courtesy Carnegie Hall Archives)

(top) Mary Lou Williams entertaining soldiers about 1945 at Cafe Society Downtown. (Mary Lou Williams Collection, Institute of Jazz Studies, Rutgers University)

(bottom) Factotum Johnnie Garry assisting Mary Lou Williams in the artists' dressing room at Cafe Society Downtown, around 1946. (Mary Lou Williams Collection, Institute of Jazz Studies, Rutgers University)

(top) The Count Basie band at Cafe Society Downtown, around 1943. Left to right: Dickie Wells, trombone; Freddie Green, guitar; Harry "Sweets" Edison, trumpet; Lester Young, saxophone; Ed Lewis (behind Young), second trumpet. Mural by hoff [Syd Hoff] is in the background. (Collection of the Institute of Jazz Studies, Rutgers University)

(bottom) Helen Humes with Count Basie, 1938. (Collection of the Institute of Jazz Studies, Rutgers University)

(top) Josephine Baker at forty-five, always elegant, 1951. (Courtesy Jean-Claude Baker Foundation)

(bottom) Billie Holiday at Cafe Society Downtown, 1939. The writer and humorist S. J. Perlman is among those seated at the center of the table in the foreground. William Gropper mural in the background. (Collection of the Institute of Jazz Studies, Rutgers University)

(top) Billie Holiday recording "Strange Fruit" for Commodore Records on April 20, 1939. Left to right: Johnny Williams, bass; Frankie Newton, trumpet; Stan Payne, alto sax; Ken Hollen, tenor sax. (Charles Peterson photo, courtesy of Don Peterson)

(bottom) Albert Ammons on an old boardinghouse piano. Left to right: Pete Johnson, Princeton University student Herb Schultz, Big Joe Turner at. Cafe Society Downtown, early 1939. (Author's Collection)

(top) Albert Ammons and Meade "Lux" Lewis, Cafe Society Downtown, 1939. (Charles Peterson photo, courtesy of Don Peterson)

(bottom) The Phil Moore Band. Moore on piano. Left to right: Art Trappier, drums; Doles Dickens, bass; Remo Palmieri, guitar; Gene Sedric, tenor sax; Johnny Letman, trumpet. Cafe Society Uptown, mid-1940s. (Albert Freeman photo, Barney Josephson Collection)

(top) The Golden Gate Quartet rehearses in Coolidge Auditorium at the Library of Congress for an appearance in the American Folk Song Concert at the White House. Left to right: Alan Lomax, Folk Lore archivist, Library of Congress; Harold Spivacke, Music Division, Library of Congress; Archibald McLeish, Librarian of Congress; Golden Gate Quartet members Willie Johnson, Orlandus Wilson, Clyde Riddick, Henry Owen. (Author's Collection)

(bottom) Beatrice Kraft of the Kraft Sisters performing their Javanese Temple dance, 1943, Cafe Society Uptown. (Author's Collection)

PART 3

Riding the Crest

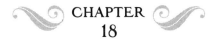

CHAPTER
18

"I'm the right man in the wrong place."

Cafe Society had been open about nine months. I was still heavily in debt when I made up my mind that I'm the right man in the wrong place. Barney Josephson is not for Greenwich Village. I never should have opened in the Village. I don't belong in the Village. It's not for me. I'm not a Village character. I should have opened Uptown on the East Side. I'm for the chic, smart crowd Uptown. They want a guy like me. I was now a celebrity of sorts, and it was heady.

I told myself before anything happens to this place, I'm going to recoup, close the cafe. But before I do, I'm going to open another club. I figured based on Downtown's success artistically, if not financially, I would open a place Uptown. I'll use Downtown to promote a club Uptown, get it going and close Downtown, put the key in the door.

I started to look for a location and found a four-story building with a basement at 128 East 58th Street between Park and Lexington Avenues. In the early 1900s it had housed the New York College of Music. A gentleman by the name of Alexander Lambert had been its head. I possess a drawing of Mr. Lambert sketched and autographed by Enrico Caruso, dated 1908, which had been found in one of the rooms. Caruso, Paderewski, Misha Elman, Josef Hofmann had given concerts at this college. A photograph shows a group of musicians seated on two broad, low steps with pillars behind them. The building looked then much like the small college it was.

By the time I came upon it, it had been a nightclub for many years, exterior and interior completely changed. One mobster after another going back to Prohibition days had run clubs there. Recently, there had been a fire in the building. The fire had a cloud over it, so to speak, and the people who had the club last never got their insurance money.

I looked over the building. The kitchen was intact. Everything was there. There wasn't too much damage actually from the fire except for the wiring. The Dry Dock Savings Bank owned the property, having taken it on a mortgage default. They had permitted the former occupants to leave everything there so that if someone wanted to lease it they could have a place that was set up and could make a deal with them on the equipment.

I met the mob characters who were the former lessees and worked out a deal to buy what was in there for $6,000. I didn't have a cent, but I had contacts of my own. I had some good friends by this time. People liked me somehow. I didn't need Leon's friends. I borrowed $7,000. I could pay back the loans over a period of time.

The bank gave me a two-year lease. It was as if I had two properties for the price of one, so large was the building. The rent was $650 a month with the lease assigned for the first month's rent. No rent security. Today landlords want a year's rent as security. Then they were glad to get an occupant. Half the places were empty.

I'm broke but I've got a nightclub uptown. My press agent, Ivan Black, sent out a press release. "Blah, blah, big success, Cafe Society. Such a huge success that Barney Josephson is opening a branch on East 58th Street to be called Cafe Society Uptown." As soon as the release hit the papers the Uptown crowd started to flood Downtown. They came to see what this nightclub in the Village is that's so great they're expanding uptown to Park Avenue.

Downtown was now a big smash, and I'm stuck with two nightclubs. I was making money. I had finally caught on to some of the tricks of the business and how to control the stealing. I paid off John Hammond and Benny Goodman and the loans from Leon's friends.

When I opened Uptown, Tuesday, October 8, 1940, there were no office buildings on Park Avenue, only fancy, upper-class, floor-through apartments. So I figured all the residents in that area were my potential customers, all those who lived in the town houses in the forties, fifties, and sixties. The only office building on Park Avenue at that time was the New York Central built to house the sumptuous offices of the railroad barons whose companies used Grand Central Terminal. It's now the Helmsley Building, with its exterior all gilded. The only other buildings not residences were the Racquet and Tennis Club and St. Bartholomew's Church, both still there. It wasn't until after World War II, when the Tishmans built their first office building on Park Avenue and 57th Street, that the office building boom began on Park Avenue.

With the $6,000 I gave for the effects, Uptown cost me $28,000 to open, which was nothing really. All the smart boys on 52nd Street from the jazz clubs predicted, "Now he'll get it, this guy who brought the niggers into the Village is bringing them to Park Avenue. They'll never let him do that. Park Avenue will go slumming downtown and they'll accept what he's doing there, but they don't want it in their neighborhood. They'll run him out of New York."

The 52nd Street boys weren't the only ones who didn't expect me to make it. The owners of the swank uptown spots thought I was crazy to dream of succeeding on Park Avenue with my philosophy. When they heard that our new place was at 128 East 58th Street, then they knew I was out of my mind. This particular location was supposed to be jinxed. A whole parade of failures, Mother Kelly's, Zelli's, El Rio, the Surf Club to mention a few that had opened and closed there.

Just at this time a friend who knew Marc Chagall arranged for me to meet the great artist at his home on Riverside Drive. My idea was to ask Chagall if he would be interested in painting some murals for my new place. While my friend and Chagall were engaged in conversation I wandered over to look at the paintings hanging on the walls. Most of them were signed and dated 1903, 1905. Apparently, Chagall had been watching me. "I saw tears in your eyes, my friend." Thereupon, he agreed to decorate Uptown for a reasonable sum. He was only worried that the smoke from the cigarettes would damage his work. Then Chagall's daughter suddenly decided to move to Paris with him. I don't think she was too happy about his agreeing to paint a nightclub.

I commissioned Anton Refregier to do the entire room. I selected Ref because I liked his surrealism. He was more advanced in that sense, at that time, than my other artists. There were huge walls in the place, and Ref, more than the others, was a mural painter. The walls were just large, flat spaces. Ref painted huge murals that were highly satirical, approximately fifty feet long and almost two stories high. The main dining room had a high, arched ceiling, and the height from floor to ceiling was easily two and a half stories high. Ref did all the areas, the powder room area, the lounge area upstairs, all in a surrealistic fashion. It was a show place.

The boys from the press came to see what was going on. Malcolm Johnson, the *New York Sun*'s nightclub editor, was impressed: "Barney Josephson has turned loose a crew of inspired contractors, carpenters and brush wielders on the premises and evolved a layout that is remarkably attractive and eye filling."[1]

Ref deferred payment. All I had to give him was the money for the paint and canvas. "When you can, you'll pay me." I suppose every court throughout the ages had its painter. I don't fancy myself a connoisseur of the arts, but I know a little and I know what I like. People used to kid me and say Refregier was the artist to the court of Josephson. I thought that would be good for a laugh.

> *It looks like a joint out of a Hollywood production, with all the fancy trimmings from a wild exhibit at the Museum of Modern Art.*[2]

When Ref explained what he planned for the art I asked, "How will you be able to do all the work by yourself?" After all, there were huge spaces to paint. He didn't plan to. He would hire one of his art students as his assistant.

Paul Petroff: *Ref was one of the best art teachers at the American Artists School where I had a scholarship. He wouldn't allow you to get into any groove. If you were sitting on a chair, he would sit you on the floor or on a table, make you a little uncomfortable at first. But then you realized you began to see new things. As a friend, he was absolutely marvelous. Such consideration. At the time, hard times, I didn't have any money whatsoever, living from meal to meal. He knew I was modest about asking, so he would always suggest that I come over to his house. But he always made it sound as if it just so happened. He did this to several students.*

I was with Ref at Uptown from the very beginning. He would give me sort of an outline of what I should do for the little murals. The big murals he had pretty well set. He would make cartouches, large paper drawings, and then we transferred them. And the big thing, which I was really surprised Barney wanted me to do, was that big mobile hanging from the ceiling in the main room. It was a big undertaking for me and for the place.

Barney gave me a studio space upstairs, a large enough room to as-semble all the parts because I had no place to work. He just let me do anything I wanted to do. The mobile was made out of metal. Barney gave me money for the tools to cut it out. He was very considerate about doing that. One of the reviewers coined a new word, "stabile," station-ary mobile. I certainly had good reviews on that. I was always amazed that Barney was willing to chance somebody that didn't have a name to do these things.

The outdoor entrances, Uptown and Downtown, had the same kind of poster at the entrances. It was a huge shape, a billboard. Barney gave me the text every time there was a change of show. The lettering within that shape was sort of important, and to give it importance usually I had some kind of graphic to illustrate what the show was about.[3]

I took the entire show, orchestra and all, from Downtown and moved it right into Uptown—Hazel Scott, two of the boogie-woogie pianists, Albert Ammons and Pete Johnson, the Golden Gate Quartet, Teddy Wilson's band with clarinetist Jimmy Hamilton and drummer Yank Porter—the whole shebang.

Malcolm Johnson: *For those weary folk who have denied themselves the pleasures awaiting them at last year's night club sensation in Sheri-dan Square because of the journey to Greenwich Village, Cafe Society's board of governors has decreed the establishment of an uptown branch in East 58th Street. Since a decree is practically execution with these busy gentlemen, the place is not, to use a current catch-phrase, "on order," but in being. The swanky crowd which took in the surroundings and the music on the opening night, found itself in one of the handsomest supper rooms in town—East Side, West Side or Broadway.*[4]

Well, I opened Uptown, and they all flocked into the place. Opening night there was a special treat. Without any announcement, Benny Goodman, pale and thin from a long bout of sciatica, stepped up right out of the audience with his clarinet and sent out "Somebody Stole My Gal." Teddy Wilson's band joined in. Benny's send-off to me.

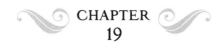

CHAPTER
19

"'A Rockefeller can afford
to wear such a coat.'"

We were well-reviewed. The *New Yorker* nightclub editor was there opening night.

A new place with the old Downtown line-up of Negro entertainers. . . . It's hard to believe, in a way, that Cafe Society has actually invaded the East Fifties, but there it is, and if it doesn't prosper, I'll be convinced that the address is really jinxed.[1]

The *New Yorker* never failed to mention color. They weren't the only press. It was common practice in those days. Often enough I would be asked why 90 percent of our talent was Negro. "You see, we specialize in jazz music, and it just so happens that Negroes are the ones who perform best in that area. It's simply a matter of talent selectivity." I had in mind all the black musicians and performers. I often wondered how Billie Holiday, for instance, who always kept one eye on the door when she sang, must feel when singing in a place where her own people were not permitted in. But if they were welcomed and seated at ringside tables, wouldn't that make a difference in Billie's performance and others also?

So much of our talent was black. I had made the decision early on with Ivan Black, who took care of all our public relations, that our press releases would extol our talent as artists, not "Negro" or "colored" or "black" or "dark."

Ivan and I had grown up together in Trenton. He went from our high school to graduate from Harvard in 1924 with degrees in renaissance art and literature and architecture. A man of many talents, he was also a published poet. It was pure coincidence that Ivan became a press agent. Leon came into Downtown one day, "I ran into Ivan Black on the street. You know, he's a brash kind of guy, he'd make a good press agent. I know you're looking for one. Why don't you ask him?" That's how Ivan became a press agent.

But persistent as Ivan was, we couldn't win. I had put in Eddie South's Trio for the serious-eating dinner crowd and late hours at Uptown. Malcolm Johnson, nightclub editor of the *New York Sun,* appreciated the trio.

Eddie South is a violinist of genuine gifts who combines a substantial fiddle with the Negro's gift for rhythm. . . . the sound the group produces is not strident enough to be an intrusion on your dinner, which is something in a contemporary night club.[2]

So I had ideas. I never had nor wanted to have the policy of other nightclubs. The mobsters, the former bootleggers and such, who went into the speakeasy and nightclub business in the 1920s and 1930s to sell their illegal hooch knew little and cared less about legitimate business. In our shoe business, when a customer walked into our store for the first time we wanted to give her such service that she would become our customer for life. A good last, on which the shoes are made, is shaped to a person's foot. The last in which she'd feel comfortable is the one we'd stick to for that customer. The pattern could change, but the last would remain.

I brought this idea to my nightclub business. Most clubs engaged an artist at most two, three weeks. Four weeks was a tremendous gig. I wanted to give my artists steady employment. Hazel Scott was with me for seven and a half years, Mary Lou Williams for over five, Jack Gilford, the boogie-woogie pianists, Billie Holiday, Imogene Coca, Mildred Bailey, Susie Reed, Teddy Wilson, the Golden Gate Quartet, Jimmy Savo, Sarah Vaughan, Lena Horne, all the many, many fabulous musicians all spent many consecutive months and years working in my cabarets. We added to our shows from time to time and moved the artists back and forth between the two clubs, which kept them working almost on a permanent basis.

This was wholly unorthodox then, a revolutionary concept for nightclubs. It gave performers an opportunity to try out new routines and certainly a sense of security. And we were unionized. Not many clubs were. We had three shows a night, with the artists performing different numbers for each show. Malcolm Johnson named us the Cafe Society Stock Company.[3] Reviewing Red Allen's band with J. C. Higginbotham on trombone, Billy Taylor on bass, Edmond Hall on clarinet, Jimmy Hoskins on drums, and Ken Kersey at the piano, Malcolm wrote he "could not recall a band in a night club that appeared to enjoy its work as much as this one."[4]

I do believe most all of the musicians and performers had good feelings about Cafe Society. I tried. One year the Harvard Club in Boston wired me, asking how much it would cost to have Albert Ammons play for their members at a smoker. I asked Ammons if he wanted to go. "Sure." "Would you go for $75 and fare both ways?" "Sure." I wired Harvard the terms. Ammons went and wowed them. The dean of Harvard, Kenneth Murdock, a hot jazz fan, invited Ammons to stay overnight as his guest. Ammons returned happy as hell, even happier when he received his full pay.

Concessionaires usually ran the hat check room in the clubs. I didn't want that. The hat check girls in my cloakrooms were paid a good salary. They had some surprises with some patrons. One evening Nelson Rockefeller came in, checked his coat. The hat check girl called me over and showed me his coat with his name inside. The fur collar and nap were worn thin, a very old but well-tailored coat. The young lady was perplexed. I explained, "A Rockefeller can afford to wear such a coat."

Once one of our waiters, at the request of a patron, called over our girl who sold cigarettes but never made the table rounds. He wanted a pack of cigarettes and gave her a dollar. "Keep the change. It's the first time I've ever been in a nightclub without being bothered."

I would not have any black waiters. Why? Well, I did not want to put black men in the position of waiting on people. Given the history of slavery, I felt it was wrong to put black Americans in what would appear to be a servile situation. Even today there's a scarcity of black waiters. Black Americans do not apply for jobs as waiters, perceiving it as a belittling job.

In most nightclubs food was also a concession, so the waiters would be instructed to push the liquor not the food. I would not treat my patrons in such a manner. I knew nothing about kitchens, so I hired Oscar Schimerman. He had been the former head waiter at Sherry's and had very successfully managed the Claremont Inn on Riverside Drive at 104th Street, noted for its cuisine and view of the Hudson River for evening dancing. Oscar planned the menus, hired the kitchen and dining-room staff, bought the food, selected the wines. Our food, especially Uptown, got high marks for our cuisine and wines. Robert Dana, nightclub editor of the *Herald-Tribune,* always in the club, "On its food alone, Cafe Society ranks with many fine restaurants. We can recommend the squab chicken casserole, served with several green vegetables and potatoes. The cream of mushroom soup is delicious and the list of imported wines is ample."[5]

Downtown, John Hammond built a new band for me, Joe Sullivan on piano; Ed Hall, baritone sax and clarinet; Murph Steinberg, trumpet; Danny Polo, tenor sax; Henry Turner on bass; and Johnny Wells, drums.

> *Cafe Society, 2 Sheridan Square ([telephone] Ch 2-2737). The whole show's changed in this crowded Village place. Billie Holiday, Sister Tharpe, Art Tatum, Meade (Lux) Lewis, and Joe Sullivan's band are there now.*[6]

Billie was to come in for a couple of months, turns up three weeks late. I was plenty aggravated and threatened to cancel her. I didn't. She stayed for five weeks.

> **Malcolm Johnson:** *The popular night club known as Cafe Society in Sheridan Square is offering a stimulating new program of entertainment. . . . It is about the finest entertainment of its kind to be found anywhere. . . . continues to attract capacity business—concrete evidence of the soundness of the idea promulgated by Barney Josephson, its proprietor. . . . he had some very definite ideas as to what he wanted and he proceeded without benefit of advice from the wise guys who know everything. [Joe] Sullivan, the leader, is white; the men in the band are all colored.*
>
> *Sister Rosetta Tharpe rates unqualified enthusiasm for the stirring quality of her songs, sung in the spiritual vein of swing tempo. At Cafe Society she is offering some new compositions of her own, but "Rock Me" is still a favorite with her audience.*[7]

Sister Rosetta Tharpe not only could sing electrifying gospel but what an acoustic guitar she could play. John explained, "She is one of the first to use it for melody-plucked lines. Her technically astonishing lead breaks invented the rock and roll guitar." In his 1938 From Spirituals to Swing concert, Sister Tharpe "was a surprise smash; knocked the people out."[8]

Rosetta Tharpe was a child star. Born in 1915 in Cotton Plant, Arkansas, she was a baby when her mother took up preaching, traveling from church to church to spread the gospel. As a four-year-old, Rosetta was already singing and playing the guitar. She was the big attraction that brought in the worshippers to her mother's services.

Rosetta Tharpe was a pioneer. When she sang gospel on a secular stage she scandalized the sanctified church. They never forgave her. Religious folk opposed singing in cabarets; it was synonymous with the Devil, God's enemy. They told Sister Tharpe that either she serve the devil or God. She would respond that the Lord knew her heart and it wouldn't lead her astray. She was the first gospel singer to sign with a major recording company and to appear in a nightclub—mine. "Her song style was filled with blues inversion. . . . She bent her notes like a horn player, and syncopated in swing band manner."[9] My secular audiences were fascinated with her blues-oriented gospel, a first for many of them.

With both clubs doing great business I was a happy man. My accountant phoned, "Barney, before the tax office gets after us, let's take some of this money and make a deal with them." We went to the New York City tax office, introduced ourselves, told them we were delinquent in our tax payments. "We'd like to make arrangements to start paying it off."

The guy goes to the files, comes back with a folder marked "Cafe Society, 2 Sheridan Square," somewhat puzzled. "You know, there's a warrant for your arrest. It's been buried in this file."

I thought, "Somebody was a friend in this office." I explained, "I don't know how that happened except I'm here now. I didn't pay because I was losing a lot of money trying to keep the club going. Now it's going. But we can't pay all the back taxes at one time."

I gave him $3,000. I owed a lot of money. I agreed to keep our current taxes paid on time and to pay off so much a month on the remainder. The tax situation was off my shoulders. I could breathe freely.

Uptown had caught on fast. The Park Avenue crowd loved the place. Celebrities from stage, film, radio, writers, columnists, diplomats, the rich, the famous, they just had to be seen there. And lovers of our great jazz continued to be our patrons.

Whitney Balliett: *I used to go to Cafe Society Uptown when I was seventeen or eighteen. We'd go right to Cafe Society Uptown on vacation. I went mainly to watch Sidney Catlett, the great drummer who was in Teddy Wilson's marvelous band. I must have gone at least half a dozen times. I don't remember Barney at that time. I remember the murals. I remember the bandstand, the curtains. No matter where you*

sat there were banquettes. There were raised levels on the sides. There
was also a balcony in the back.

I'd either go with a girl or by myself. I can remember going for some-
body's birthday party once. There must have been ten or twelve of us,
and we had a table right in front by the floor where they had the show.
There weren't any adults, just us kids. The atmosphere in that place was
so welcoming and pleasant. It was extraordinary. But Barney created
that kind of atmosphere in all his places.[10]

Uptown, I had three weeks in October, four weeks in November, four
weeks in December, in all eleven weeks to New Year's Eve. With the business
I was doing Uptown and Downtown I made enough money to pay off the
entire $28,000 investment. I don't owe anybody a nickel. I'm free and clear.

CHAPTER
20

"Everybody was making
a big fuss over me."

After I opened Uptown I would cover both clubs each night. I'd spend half of the night in one and the rest of the night in the other. One night I came to Downtown from Uptown. Big Joe Turner was at the bar with the boogie-woogie pianists. I'm the kind of fellow that if I'm upset, it shows on my face. When money wasn't a problem there were others. I walked over to the bar to say hello to the guys. Big Joe takes one look at me.

"What's the matter, Pops?"

"Oh, nothing."

He knew me better. Goes into his inside jacket, takes out his wallet, takes out a piece of paper, carefully unwraps it, removes a little brown bean about the size of a coffee bean.

"Look, Pops. In this hand is a bean and in this bean is a face, alive as you and me. You can tell it your troubles." Then Joe rubs the bean in his hand, makes a fist, opens it, slaps it down on top of the bar, covering it.

"Come on, cover my hand, Albert." Ammons puts his hand on top.

"Pops." I put my hand on top of Ammons. We all did, black and white hands piled up, pyramidlike. Then he makes a mumbo-jumbo, sasa-fasa-juba-jaba, breaks our hands apart. Takes the little bean, pulls out the piece of paper, wraps the bean back in it, puts it in his wallet, back into his breast pocket.

"Pops, now you got nothing to worry about. Your worry's over." I started to laugh. "You see, Pops? Everything's okay."

The women were all crazy over Big Joe. He was largely unschooled, unlettered; don't think he ever spent a day in school. He was tall and slim and never stopped moving while he sang. He had an endless repertoire of blues, not just the slow, sad blues of the Deep South but "pepped it up some," he would announce:

Now you can take me, baby,
Put me in your big brass bed.
Eagle rock me, baby,
Till my navel turns cherry red.

Reliving those years—indeed, your entire life—there are some things you want to forget. And then there are things that come to mind that you wouldn't tell anyone, things that keep coming forward, that suddenly appear.

The time came when I became disinterested in Izabel, the woman with whom I'd been living since I came to New York three years ago. No fault of hers. I was riding high. The clubs and I, personally, were garnering huge amounts of publicity, more than all the clubs in town put together.

Somehow I had moved on to a level where I felt Izabel was not for me now. I just lost interest. I guess I was taken by the grandeur of my being a big nightclub impresario. I was meeting Hollywood stars, political stars, theater stars, big-time artists, writers, high society so-called—everybody who was anybody. I'm this grand guy. Everybody making a big fuss over me. It must have gone to my head.

Izabel was well-liked. Billie wrote about this "really wonderful girl" in her autobiography.[1] John liked her, and I had thought Leon did, too. Many years later Leon wrote that he hadn't ever thought she was right for me, that we had so little in common. I didn't do right by her really, though I must say for myself I always introduced her as Mrs. Josephson. I believed in the legality of our relationship. Common-law marriage was legal in New York state. When I told Izabel I wanted to leave her, she was very understanding.

"But what am I going to do?"

I was incredulous that she should ask. "What do you mean, what are you going to do? You're my common-law wife. Do you think I'm just going to put you out? I'm not going to do that."

"You know, Barney, common law is not recognized here anymore." I wasn't aware that the law had changed. "I don't care. I recognize it."

By this time I was making money. "Look, Izabel, I will take you down to the vault, to my safe deposit box. I have government bonds that I've bought from time to time. I have cash put away." There was a considerable amount.

"I'm taking you to the bank. I'm going to open the deposit box and hand it to you with the key, and I will walk out. You take half of whatever is there. That's yours. When you're finished, give the box to the attendant. He'll put it back in the slot and lock it. I presume you want to stay in New York, so I will do the following. You're a beautician, and you'll want to open a beauty salon here I expect. You find a location. I will set it all up for you, all the hair-drying equipment, combs, scissors, shampoo, the shop. Whatever you'll need it will be yours."

"No, I don't want the beauty salon."

"If what I've offered is not satisfactory, tell me."

"No, Barney, you're more than generous."

Some time later she left New York. I do know she got married. That was the end of that relationship.

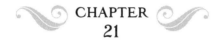

"'Lena, what do you think a song is?'"

One evening early 1941, John casually mentioned, "There's a singer who's appearing with Charlie Barnet's band at the Paramount Theater. I'd like you to catch her." The Paramount's stage shows featured big bands with their singers and big-name stars, with first-run Hollywood films on the screen. Frank Sinatra, appearing there with the Tommy Dorsey Orchestra, created pandemonium with teenage bobby-soxers screaming and dancing in the aisles. It had started out as a publicity stunt when Frank had appeared there as a supporting act with Benny Goodman's band. Wynn Nathanson, Benny's publicist, concocted the idea, and then it took on a life of its own wherever Sinatra sang. The Paramount Theater was one of those magnificent movie palaces which opened in 1926, between 43rd and 44th Streets on Broadway. Now gone, gutted, the Hard Rock Cafe at street level, offices above, its grand marquee replaced by a sleazy replica.[1]

Always eager to discover new talent, I didn't hesitate. The very next afternoon I was in the audience at the Paramount. Charlie's band was a big swing band with his singers seated to one side of the band, getting up to sing a chorus and then sitting down again. The female singer was Lena Horne. Charlie's band was all white, and you couldn't tell that Lena wasn't white. So, unlike Billie Holiday with Artie Shaw, Lena sat on stage, "sort of foot-steppin' around Charlie Barnet's orchestra. I think I sang eight bars or so."[2]

Immediately after the stage show was over I went backstage, introduced myself. "How would you like to be a singer featured on your own, not a band singer? I can offer you such a spot in my cafe, and you would have Teddy Wilson and his band accompanying you." Her eyes opened wide. Here was this guy appearing out of the blue, owner of a famous cabaret known for its great jazz, asking her to appear as a featured singer no less, something she had never done before. She was not a jazz singer, but she was beautiful, and I thought she had potential. I asked her what her commitments were with Charlie. She didn't have any. She could leave right away. She wanted to come to Cafe Society immediately, quit Charlie then and there.

"How long is Charlie's engagement here, Miss Horne?" "Another one or two weeks." "Whatever it is, you should stay with Charlie until he finishes his engagement, then you can come to work for me."

Lena Horne: *Then I got the sweetest job I ever got in my life. It was at Downtown Cafe Society here in Greenwich Village. It was operated by a man named Barney Josephson.*[3]

Lena's uncle Frank Horne was a friend of John Hammond. Uncle Frank was a member of President Franklin Roosevelt's so-called black cabinet, assistant director of the Division of Negro Affairs [in the National Youth Administration, 1936–39]. John had seen Lena when she was a teenager in the chorus line at the Cotton Club in Harlem and in a revue there in the spring of 1934, when she was given a song-and-dance duet with the talented tap dancer Avon Long. He would become famous on Broadway for his role as Sportin' Life in Gershwin's *Porgy and Bess*. Years later Avon came to dance at Cafe Society.

Lena had gotten the Cotton Club job through her mother, Edna, who knew the captain of the chorus line. Edna was ambitious for her daughter. She began pestering the mobster bosses to give Lena a chance as a solo singer and even egged on her second husband, a white Cuban, to talk to them. The result? They stuck Mike's head down the toilet and told him to shut up. Lena was watched over. Her father, Teddy, was known in some of the shadier Harlem circles. He put out the word that his teenage daughter needed to be protected, and Dutch Schultz's boys obliged.

With the advent of Prohibition, midnight, January 1, 1920, gangsters like Dutch Schultz, "the king of beer," came into their own. His South Bronx gang, a ruthless bunch, had started out supplying beer to speakeasies and restaurants from the Bronx to Harlem to the Upper West Side of Manhattan. The legendary Helen Morgan sang to big crowds in Schultz's Embassy Club. He ended up mowed down by machine guns "while coming out of the can" in a Newark cafe.[4]

John had heard Lena sing with Noble Sissle's Society Orchestra and seen her on Broadway in Lew Leslie's *Blackbirds of 1939.* The title was designed, of course, to let the public know the color of the performers in the show. The first Negro musical hit on Broadway in the 1920s, *Shuffle Along,* was a collaboration of Noble Sissle and Eubie Blake. There were songs about pickaninnies, little black children, with the singers wearing Aunt Jemima bandanas. Josephine Baker performed a comedy dance number in blackface, crossing her eyes, making "funny Negro-type" faces. In 1925 Josephine departed New York, sailed for Paris to become the toast of the Continent.

When Lena had toured with Sissle she was with an all-black band, but touring with Charlie Barnet's all-white band was a different story. The hotels were segregated. It's to Charlie's credit that he did something about it. "Our band manager would go to the desk, order the rooms, jabber to Lena in Spanish double-talk. Then he'd tell the desk clerk, 'Our Cuban singer would like a single room with bath.'"[5]

John has said that he didn't think Lena was a particularly good singer. Given that, what possessed him to send me over to the Paramount Theater? I never asked him. I did ask Teddy Wilson.

> **Teddy Wilson:** *I don't know. She was such a pretty girl. But that generally didn't influence Hammond. I could not understand him liking Lena Horne because she's not a jazz singer. She's more like Ethel Waters, a ballad singer. She can't sing jazz like Ella Fitzgerald or any people associated with the jazz world. She's not an improviser. She sings songs as they are.*[6]

For Lena's first rehearsal I asked some of the guys in the band to come in about three in the afternoon. She began with songs of her own selection. The first song she started to sing was "When It's Sleepy Time Down South." I stopped her, asking if she knew what happened to Negroes down south, like lynchings. "Do you know what this song is really about?" Lena hadn't thought about it. It was a popular song just then. I explained that it expressed the myth that Negroes down south were content with their lives and did she really think that was true? I think she realized that I was right. Anyway, she switched to some Latin numbers. Many of them were rumba numbers.

Rumba and Latin American rhythms were very popular. Most nightclubs that had more than one orchestra would have a smaller rumba unit, six or eight men, alternating with the swing band. Lena could do with the hips, rumba movements, very well. She'd sing a chorus, break away, go around the mike with more rumba movements of her body and hands. I listened to her, let her finish, and called her over. We sat at a table.

"Lena, I don't like this rumba stuff. I don't think it's good for you to do." "Why? What would you have me do?" "Throw it all out. You can't do any of it here. You know, Lena, your looks are such that you could be anything, Brazilian, Cuban, Spanish. You're not trying to pass are you?" I said this consciously because I wanted to jolt her. She was offended. "What do you mean pass?"

"I want people to know who you are. Let me present you as a Negro performer. I want you to sing the good old standards, 'The Man I Love,' 'Where or When,' 'Summertime,' other songs from *Porgy and Bess*." So we worked it out. All right. She was willing to follow my instructions. "And Lena, at one time in your program, in each performance, I want you to sing a blues song." "Oh, no," she protested. "I can't sing blues. I'm not a blues singer."

"I'm well aware of that. I want you to sing a blues number because the people sitting out front, the white people, won't be sure what you are. When you sing the blues they'll think, well, I guess she is. And that's what I want them to know." I wanted her to sing Billie's "Fine and Mellow."

> **Lena:** *I refused. He insisted. . . . So I got myself together one night and went to Kelly's Stables [on West 52nd Street] where Billie was singing. . . . She said, "You've got two babies?"*
> *I said, "Yes."*
> *"And you take care of them?"*
> *I said, "Yes."*
> *"Well," she said, "sing it. I don't care. Sing anything you want to open your mouth and try to do 'cause you've got to take care of your children. You have to live your life. I'll always be here when you want a friend."*[7]

When Lena came to Downtown, Teddy Wilson's sextet was playing Uptown. Once musicians and performers left the Village and went up to Park Avenue they didn't want to go back downtown. Now they were "playing the

Palace." It would be a comedown they felt. In the heyday of vaudeville the best and most renowned of the hoofers, singers, comics, acrobats all worked the Palace Theater on Broadway on a two-a-day performing schedule. No movies were shown. Just the acts. Appearing at the Palace carried more prestige than any vaudeville house in the country.

Hazel was Uptown. As a pianist she didn't need a band behind her. Lena hadn't developed as yet into the real singer she is today. The piano player whom I had in the band Downtown was good with the band but not good for a vocalist. Teddy Wilson was one of the greatest for singers.

John Hammond had discovered Teddy while listening to the radio one day in 1933 and heard piano playing that was unique. He called the station and got the name, Teddy Wilson. John knew Benny Carter was looking for a pianist, so he loaned Benny $150 to go to Chicago to bring Teddy back. Two years later John persuaded Benny Goodman to form a jazz trio with Teddy and drummer Gene Krupa. The Benny Goodman Trio was wildly successful and an important event. It was the first interracial group to perform publicly in this country.

Teddy Wilson: *When I was twenty-one years old in 1933 I was making Columbia Records for John Hammond. He saved me years it would have taken me, just to come up the normal way, to be heard and recognized. This guy [John] walked into the studio and sets up record dates. John was too pure. He thought that jazz was a collective improvisation rhythmically integrated. That was his definition. He was a millionaire who could indulge. I was one of his boys, me and Basie and Goodman. A lot of people he didn't like, Johnny Hodges, Roy Eldridge, Gene Krupa, Armstrong, Artie Shaw, Ben Webster, Lionel Hampton, Ellington. He only liked Buck Clayton and Bill Coleman as trumpet players, Lester Young on the tenor, Benny Goodman on the clarinet, and Ed Hall on the clarinet. Jo Jones was his favorite.[8]*

I asked Teddy, "Do you want to do a nice gal and me a good favor? Hazel doesn't need you here. Please come Downtown and play for Lena. You can help her. You can give her a push along. I believe she's going to be a big star one day. I'll put in another sextet here." "Okay, Barney, if you want me to play for her, I'll go down."

Lena Horne: *And at that time Cafe Society was the gathering place for every giant that we had in jazz. For instance, Teddy Wilson had the* *house band there. He started out by trying to teach me how to carry a tune. He had a great trombone player named J. C. Higginbotham and a great drummer named J. C. Heard. So you see, I was in the cream of everything that is wonderful in my profession.*[9]

I had another thought. "Lena, I'd like you to change your name to Helena." She was so beautiful I thought it suited her better. During her stay at Cafe Society she was known as Helena Horne.

She opened with "The Man I Love," Gershwin's "Summertime," Billie's "Fine and Mellow," "Embraceable You." Gorgeous as she was, Lena wasn't going over with my audience. When she sang she didn't have any contact with them. She wasn't putting any feeling or meaning into the songs. To make matters worse she would close her eyes when she sang or look up at the ceiling. Somehow I had learned how to shape talent. I had learned how to bring out the best in a performer.

I saw I had to do something with Lena's performance. Billie always knew just what she wanted to do with a song. But Lena needed help. I knew she had two children and was still married to a man named Louis Jones whom she had met through her father. They had lived in Pittsburgh. Her daughter, Gail, about four, and son, Teddy, just a baby, were born. They were still with him. Jones wouldn't give them up.

I started by asking, "Lena, what do you think a song is?" She was taken aback. "What do you mean? A song is a song." "No, Lena, it's a story with music. When you sing, you've got to pay attention to the words. You've got to feel every word. You have two little children whom you love, right? Well, when you sing 'Summertime,' think of Gail and little Teddy. Sing it to them."

The next night when she sang it, she heaved a big sigh right in the middle of the song. Almost before she finished the audience burst into applause. This song became one of her big hits. *PM*, a marvelous liberal afternoon New York newspaper, sadly long since gone: "'Summertime' has become a Cafe Society spécialité de la maison."[10] The knowledgeable jazz critic John S. Wilson was performing these duties for *PM* in those days. Later he would become the preeminent jazz critic for the *New York Times* and a good friend.

I had to talk with Lena about her lack of eye contact. "You're not onstage in the theater where you can't see your audience. In this small room you have to give each person the feeling that you're singing only to them. When you look up at the ceiling you draw attention away from yourself. They'll think maybe there's a cockroach up there. Is it because you can't look white people in the eye? Is it because you feel inferior?"

She bristled, but I had said that quite deliberately. "You must look your audience right in the eye, knowing that you're as good as any of them, which, of course, you are. When you sing 'Embraceable You,' let that man in the audience think you mean him. Lena, you're prettier than any white gal who's going to walk into this place and more talented than many of them."

I wanted to give her a feeling of pride in herself, who she was. It worked. When she started doing all these things, that's when she was on her way to becoming a singer. With all this encouragement, after a time when Lena ended with her blues song which I insisted she sing she had gotten to the point where people would stand up and shout.

CHAPTER
22

"Truth to tell, I was falling."

Hazel was ensconced in the grand Uptown place as the star. Lena was the female star Downtown. Hazel had her Cadillac and chauffeur. Between shows she would go around visiting all the night spots, drive up in her car, swish in. Because of her underslip there was always the sound of swishing like sand paper. She would swish in Downtown to show off, I guess, to Lena.

This night Hazel came Downtown. Lena was at the bar having a drink with a couple of the musicians, among them the incomparable Art Tatum. Some words were exchanged. Hazel called Lena a whore, and a fight ensued. Hazel had short hair very close to her scalp. Lena had beautiful long hair, shoulder length. Somehow they began pulling each other's hair. How did it end up? It ended up in Walter Winchell's column: "Hair pulling contest between Hazel Scott and Lena Horne at the bar in Cafe Society Downtown."

The night after the Winchell story appeared Alma Scott came in to see me. "It was a terrible thing that got into the papers. Hazel's embarrassed by it and hurt. When she came home she cried all night long. Wait until you see her eyes when she comes in tonight."

During the time that Teddy was Uptown I would see Hazel and Teddy walking around the place holding hands all the time, going into her dressing room holding hands. I figure it's a little affair, something's going on. Okay.

Teddy's a nice guy. Now he was Downtown, and I notice Lena and Teddy holding hands. I figured that Hazel is jealous of Lena because she was taking Teddy away from her. That was in my mind. So when Alma came to me distressed about the fight and told me how upset Hazel had been, I said, "Alma dear, what can I do? Teddy's holding Lena's hand now. What am I supposed to do?" Alma looked at me. "Man, it's not over Teddy at all. It's you!" She pointed her finger and repeated, "It's all over you."

I'm shocked. "What do you mean over me?" When Hazel told Alma what had happened, she said, "Ma, before that whore-son-of-a-bitch gets her claws into Barney, I will take a gun and shoot him."

Not Lena but me! That was the first time it came to my attention that a woman who doesn't want the man at all—me in this case—doesn't want somebody else to get him. "Barney, Hazel thinks Lena's got her claws out for you and she thinks you're falling for her." That's what was behind the fight.

Well, truth to tell I was falling. The only women who caused a great excitement within me, could we say, love, sexual attraction, whatever, were very few. Among those women was Lena. She became a very passionate thing for me. That feeling didn't come when she first started, but it grew as the months went by. I thought she was beautiful. I didn't think she was really a good singer, and I told her so. But I also told her that she certainly had enough of everything else to make her a big star with her wonderful looks and a manner of performing from her days in the Cotton Club chorus line, walking around the floor to music. The way she worked her shoulders, her arms, and body, it added a great deal of excitement to her performance. I would say I was madly in love with Lena.

She was the first black woman I ever felt that way about. It was that strong that I proposed to her. I asked her to marry me. She was still married to Jones, but I still wanted to marry her. I knew her not only from working for me but after working hours. Often enough we all would go out to after-hours clubs. We would work until four in the morning, and there were places—up in Harlem, mostly—that we would go to, Art Tatum, Teddy Wilson, Lena, Hazel, the Golden Gate Quartet, whoever wanted to join us. That was our relaxation. Waiters who worked in clubs, chorus girls who worked in clubs, they all had places to go to after work. Lindy's, Reuben's, and all those kinds of restaurants were packed with show people all night. They'd start getting full to the doors at four when the joints closed.

Lena turned me down. "I like you, Barney. You're a nice man, but I don't feel that way about you." We were just as friendly. I never had an affair with her. If I had, I might have been jealous of Teddy, marriage or not. But not having such a relationship, then I didn't pursue her for anything short of marriage. So when she was holding hands with Teddy, that didn't bother me at all. I was out of the picture.

Joe Louis, heavyweight champion of the world, however, was in the picture. I gather they had met during her Cotton Club days and had resumed their acquaintance when she was singing with Charlie Barnet. On occasion Joe would come to Downtown, and of course he was always seated at ringside, so to speak.

Joe Louis: *I remember when Barney Josephson opened Cafe Society Downtown in Greenwich Village. What was special about this club was that he not only hired black entertainers . . . he let the audience in too.*[1]

Joe would sit looking at this gorgeous creature with the expressionless face which the newspaper would comment on. How he could sit there and not show any emotion for this woman I don't know. At that time Joe was doing a lot of fighting. His training camp was in Pompton, New Jersey.

One night he gets me on the phone. "I'm at the training camp, Barney. I'd like to have Lena come up for the weekend. She tells me that the last show on Sunday night is slow." That would be the two in the morning show. "Then you're closed Monday, and Lena's next show is nine o'clock on Tuesday. If you could excuse her from the last show Sunday, I promise I'll have her back for the show Tuesday night. Can you do this for us?" "Joe, of course." "Then I'll send my car down to pick her up."

A couple of days after her return a manila envelope came addressed to Lena. I see it's from Joe. Lena shows me the photos. Joe and Lena in a rowboat on a lake at the training camp. Joe at one end, rowing. Lena at the other end, looking at him. And Joe Louis is beaming, this man who almost never had a picture taken with a smile.[2]

Another time Joe called. "Barney, I'd like to have Lena watch me fight. She'd like to be excused, if you can do it, for the early show. She'll be back for the midnight show." "Okay, Joe." I made some excuse to the audience about her absence.

In the meantime, even though I loathe prizefighting I'm making bets. I'd seen some Hollywood movies about prizefighters and the love stories around them. I don't remember who Joe's opponent was at the time. All the guys in the band, all the black help, would never bet against Joe Louis. But there were bets taken on how many rounds his opponent would last, five, ten. I don't know anything about betting. I'm giving the odds. I'm calling the round when Joe is going to take care of his opponent, when he's going to knock him out. I'm betting five to three. I'm giving the five. I find out later, I'm supposed to get the odds. The guy who calls the round is supposed to get the edge. I didn't learn this until after. They're all taking my bets.

I'm envisioning a Hollywood movie now. Lena's at ringside. Joe is in the ring, and he's sparring around with his opponent, playing with him, showing off to Lena. He also wants to give his fans something for their money. Now he's getting tired of playing around. He looks down at Lena, throws her a wink, saying, "Baby, this one's for you." He gives the other fighter a "klapp" and down he goes for a count of ten as the bell rings to end the third round. My bet was that the fighter would not last more than three rounds. That's exactly what happened. Everybody wondered, How did you figure it out? I wouldn't say anything.

Time passes and Joe's got another fight. Lena and Joe have "fuffed." They're no longer seeing each other. Joe is calling from his training camp on the pay booth phone every night, trying to talk to her. "I don't want to talk to him."

Now here's this guy, me, with Hollywood movies in his mind. I go to Lena, "What is this? You won't talk to Joe? How can you do this to this man on the eve of a fight? Couldn't you wait a couple of days? It's not right to upset him at this point." "Aaaah." She waved me off.

I start laying bets again. Joe's fight is going to last thirteen rounds before there's a knockout. I'm still giving five to three. How am I figuring out this fight? I'm writing another scenario. Joe's lost Lena, and he doesn't give a goddamn about anything. He's fighting listlessly. Finally he says to himself, "What the hell am I doing? Gonna ruin my career over this girl?" He pulls himself together and gives his opponent a klapp. Down he goes, out cold in the thirteenth round. And that's exactly what happened. They all wanted to know how did I figure out the two fights? "On love, man, on love." Wouldn't say another word.

I knew Lena was trying to get her children back from Jones in Pittsburgh. She was doing a little grieving and talking to me. He wouldn't give them up. He wanted Lena to come back to him. To Teddy Wilson and the men in the band she was crying her eyes out. I would get all the stories from them.

Lena had been Downtown a couple of months when one evening Mr. Jones appeared. She introduced him to me then absented herself from the table to get ready for the show. Jones and I sat talking.

"Mr. Jones, I can understand that you want Lena back. She does have a career as a singer you know. She misses the children very much, talks about them all the time. We're a little place, and we're like a family here. I get all the stories from the men in the band. I gather you don't want to give them up, hoping she'll come back. Is that right?" "Yes. That's why I'm here to talk to her now." "Lena doesn't discuss these things with me. After all, I'm her boss. But from what I hear tell, if you want her back what you're doing will never work. I would like to suggest something. I think if you brought the children to New York and let her have them for a while, from the way the guys talk there's a chance that you'd get her back. As long as you keep them away from her, she'll never go back."

Jones listened intently. What do you think happened? He brought the children to New York. That's when I met them. He went back to Pittsburgh without the kids. Lena couldn't go to Pittsburgh and take the kids without his consent. That would be kidnapping. Now she's got possession. If he comes to take them away without her consent, now he's kidnapping. So I got him where I wanted for Lena. To this day Lena doesn't know that I did this. I never told her. It's my little secret. We can tell it now.

Lena's father had a nice house on Chauncey Street in Brooklyn which he had inherited from his parents, Cora and Edwin Horne. Her father arranged for her to have the house. I visited the family there several times. Lena's cousin, Edwina, a widow, came from Chicago to look after the children. She was a splendid woman, even lighter than Lena, with blue eyes. Lena was a very responsible mother. She wasn't going to leave the children alone with just anybody.

Lena Horne: *That was a great period. I was at Cafe Society the best part of a year. The children were living in Brooklyn with the family and I commuted by BMT subway to the Village. I sang ballads and Barney taught me to use my love of words, my whole personality. Even my voice improved. For me it was Cole Porter, Gershwin, Arlen. I'm a Catholic and so I was never into blues or gospel.*[3]

I don't know what arrangements Lena and Jones finally made. The boy did go back to live with his father. He was three years younger than Gail. I never saw a boy so handsome. Imagine Lena at that time. He had it on Lena. Little Teddy died, tragically, when he was not quite thirty from a kidney disease. He had been on dialysis and took himself off, saying he didn't want to live like that.

I helped Lena not only in her career but in her awareness of who she was. I realized her knowledge of the world was very limited, nonexistent one might say. The great Paul Robeson was a frequent visitor, and I thought to enlist his help. Paul was acquainted with the Horne family from his college days. The story is told that Cora Horne had contributed toward his scholarship at Rutgers. "Paul, Lena is going to be one of the most important Negro performers one day. As such, she'll be important to her people. I'm the white boss here, and I can't talk to her about racial issues, but you and some of the others might want to begin to educate her. She doesn't even know what's happening in this country to her own people. If I try she may wonder, What's this guy's angle? Many Negroes think I'm strange enough to be doing all the things I'm doing."

Paul, through my urging, got interested, and he and others began talking to her. Paul usually came in with a group of friends, black and white. Lena would sit at their table, and they would all talk. It was during this period that Lena got into the habit of reading, reading African history, African American history, American history, world history, making up for her lack of education.

Lena Horne: *I want to tell you that Barney was an early equal opportunity hirer. I got my first training about being socially oriented, I guess that's the way you call it. I had my first training at Cafe Society because I didn't remember that all before that time my ancestors had known about social orientation. When I went to Cafe Society, and I found people there decent to each other. And I renewed a friendship with Paul Robeson. He and Barney taught me a great deal about what it is to be proud and to be black and how to work.*[4]

Lena never forgot. Forty years later she spoke of those days.

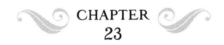

CHAPTER
23

"Nine months later
she dropped a bomb on me."

I have always liked to help out a worthy cause and to try out new ideas. Two and a half years after the opening of Downtown, and with Uptown going full blast, I had the idea to rent Carnegie Hall for one night to present my Cafe Society artists on that sacrosanct stage. It would be a first, the first concert ever presented in Carnegie Hall by a nightclub with its artists performing. Of course I was taking a leaf from my mentor, John Hammond. The worthy cause was the Musicians Union, Local 802. I donated the proceeds to their health fund.

On April 23, 1941, Carnegie Hall was host to a Cafe Society concert, From Bach to Boogie-Woogie. I picked up Lena at Downtown and Hazel at Uptown. Riding in the cab, Lena was shaking like a leaf, she was so nervous. She was going to be on a concert stage in Carnegie Hall. Hazel just tossed this off. When I told Lena she would be singing there, she wailed, "Meee? I'm not good enough."

I comforted her. "Yes, everybody performs." Truth to tell, I wasn't so sure. She was new at Cafe Society, had only been there a little over a month. But how could I exclude her? Lena used to drink Bisquit Duboushay. I took an empty Coke bottle from the bar—I didn't want to carry a whole bottle of brandy—filled it up and put it in my pocket. It just fit. On our way to

Carnegie I plied Lena with shots of the cognac. There they were, two gorgeous gals, one on each side of me, plying one with brandy from a Coca-Cola bottle. Before Lena walked out onstage I had the bottle, and she took a swig. She went out and sang with her knees knocking.

We had Teddy Wilson's sextet and Henry "Red" Allen's band. We had Eddie South's trio. Eddie was known as the "Dark Angel of the Violin." Where the name came from I have no idea. He was born in Missouri, graduated from the Chicago Conservatory of Music. He could grace any concert stage with his violin but had to go to jazz because of his color. For ten years he played with his swing band on the European continent and was so well known there that when the world famous French actor Jean Gabin came to New York he went straight to Cafe Society to look for Eddie.

We had Kenneth Spencer, a graduate of the Eastman School of Music and Julliard, equal to any singer in the Metropolitan Opera, but he couldn't get a job singing except in a nightclub—mine. He was tall, handsome, and personable. For the program he sang Negro spirituals and songs by Beethoven and Schubert.

There were the Golden Gate Quartet and the marvelous clarinetist Edmond Hall with his sextet from Downtown. We had Cliff Jackson, one of the great stride piano players of all time. We had the boogie-woogie pianists and Big Joe Turner with Pete Johnson. We had Art Tatum, nonpareil, who was Downtown on the program with Lena Horne. We had Hazel Scott to swing Bach, Liszt, and de Falla.

We ended with a jam session. Count Basie and his orchestra came onstage for the finale. John Hammond, Bill Basie's discoverer, had brought him in to play Cafe Society Uptown.

Count Basie: *The big thing for us in New York was our gig at Cafe Society Uptown for six weeks. When we went in there in September 1941, it was leaping! John Hammond still remembers that as one of the best club dates we ever played. There were two CBS radio broadcasts out of Cafe Society every week. So the actual sound of that band in live performance can be heard on a couple of records that were made years later from air checks between September and November. There is a two-volume set put out by a collector's item outfit called Jazz Unlimited.*[1]

Count Basie's men walked on one at a time and sat in with the other bands. Then Bill came onstage, pushed Meade Lux Lewis off the piano stool.

Then somebody pushed him off the stool. Another guy would come in with his horn and so on and on. We had all of Basie's fifteen men and all of my men, totaling about twenty, all onstage together, blowing the roof off. An old Chinese usher who had been there all his life walked up and down the side aisle, his hands behind him, muttering, "My god, my god, jazz at Carnegie Hall. What's happening to my Carnegie Hall?"

Lena didn't bomb that night. But nine months later she dropped a bomb on me. She was leaving Cafe Society. A nightclub owner, Felix Young, was planning to open a big, glamorous club in Hollywood with a revue featuring Duke Ellington, Ethel Waters, the Katherine Dunham Dancers, and Lena. Harold Gumm, who had gotten this spot for Lena, had gotten work for her when she was married, living in Pittsburgh. She must have signed with him while she was working for me. I know because when I hired Lena she had no agent, and with my policy of no contracts with my talent she had none with me. I couldn't believe she had signed a contract, been negotiating behind my back. But she had.

I was hurt. I was angry. I didn't want her to leave for selfish and unselfish reasons. Business was going great Downtown with Lena, and she was becoming a better singer.

John Hammond: *The help she received from Barney turned her into the fine singer she became.*[2]

Jack Gilford: *Lena didn't behave well toward Barney.*[3]

Even putting aside my justified feelings of betrayal I didn't believe Hollywood was exactly the most enlightened work setting for black performers. But she wanted to go, and go she did.

Lena Horne: *I cried when I left Cafe Society. It was family. But I'd signed with an agent who wanted me to try a black revue being produced in Hollywood.*[4]

Felix Young was having trouble raising money. Waters and Ellington dropped out of the show. The legendary dancer Katherine Dunham quit. Her company couldn't work in the too-small area. Lena sat around with no work. Finally, Young was able to open a tiny club on Sunset Strip, the Little Troc, which had gambling upstairs, typical of a mob-run operation. Lena was left as the sole attraction. Eventually she was reviewed, which led to a movie contract with MGM.

Lena was not happy in Hollywood. The contract she had signed was bad, a contract I would never have allowed her to sign. She would be getting $350 a week for forty weeks a year with a $100 a week raise each year for a total of seven years. She had twelve weeks free but wasn't permitted to take engagements in clubs and theaters not owned by MGM. I had tried to explain to her what would happen out there, but my words went unheeded.

Lena Horne: *This was beginning of a long line of films whence I was pasted to a pillar to sing my song. That was my basic screen posture for the next several years.*[5]

Months later, Lena, back from Hollywood, came to Downtown one evening with Billy Strayhorn and offered her mea culpa. I'm not one to hold grudges. Being the kind of guy I am, I thought I'd help her. I called Leonard Lyons, the gossip columnist for the *New York Post,* who was always open for a juicy tidbit. I told him about the small amount of money Lena was making and gave him the figures. I made the point that as Hazel Scott's manager I had never allowed Hazel to enter into one of those seven-year slave contracts. I explained all the stipulations I always made certain were incorporated into Hazel's contracts.

The story appears in Leonard's column. No sooner does it appear than he receives a call from Marvin Schenck in Hollywood, one of the money bigwigs at MGM. The upshot was that Lena's salary was raised to $900 a week with a $100 increase each year. Still nowhere near the money and contracts I would negotiate for Hazel for her movies.

CHAPTER
24

"'You have to be her trustee.'"

"Barney, you don't know how lucky Hazel and I are." Alma Scott and I were schmoozing at Uptown.

"What do you mean, Alma?"

"Well, just before you called Hazel to audition, Joe Glaser wanted to take her on as her agent." Hazel was still a minor, so her mother had to sign any contract. That's how Alma knew all the details.

Now there is such a thing in show business as a managerial-ownership contract. Joe offered to give Hazel $100 a week for the first two or three years and another $25 for the next few years and so on, up to $175 for the balance of a seven-year contract. Anything she made above that would be his until the end of the contract. She would pay her own touring expenses on the road.

"Barney, I was about to sign when I met a friend and told her about the great luck that had befallen us." The woman was horrified. "What? You're not going to let that child get into Joe Glaser's hands! When he travels on the road with his pretty little colored chicks he crawls into bed with all of them." Hearing that, Alma didn't sign. She didn't tell Joe why. Hazel would have been tied to that man for all those years. Who knows what would have become of her?

Uptown, Hazel Scott was big excitement for some of the biggest Hollywood stars. Franchot Tone was mad for her, Burgess Meredith, the biggest society playboys in New York—all after Hazel. All looking for this big excitement, and she was.

Franklin D. Roosevelt Jr. had a crush on her. He liked her so much that he brought his mother, the First Lady, Eleanor Roosevelt, to meet her one night. He wasn't planning to marry her, but among other things he thought she was a very exciting entertainer. He wanted his mother to hear her, and, I suspect, to show her this integrated nightclub. Mrs. Roosevelt was championing equal rights for Negroes and women, and we were presenting black and white talent to integrated audiences in honest, attractive surroundings. Without exception the nightclubs were mob-financed, with gangster types much in evidence. I was told that Mrs. Roosevelt had never been in a nightclub in her life, and as far as I know she never went to another. I have been asked whether Hazel had an affair with Franklin Jr. Well, I couldn't say because I didn't see it.

Dixie Tighe: *Eddie South, Cafe Society's swing fiddlist, wishes Mrs. Franklin D. Roosevelt would pay another visit to the night club—he was out when the First Lady, accompanied by her son, Franklin Jr., stopped in to hear the show. The reason violinist South was missing was because he had been selected by Benny Goodman as one of the entertainers he would like to hear at a party given in his honor. Night club or no night club, Mrs. Roosevelt did not depart from Cafe Society without leaving a feeling of that homey touch. Cafe Society is sending along a recipe to the White House entitled "A Boiled Dinner," but apparently it isn't the standard New England type.*[1]

In the spring of 1942 Hazel went to Hollywood to make her first movie, *Something to Shout About.* It was a Columbia Pictures production directed by Gregory Ratoff with Jack Oakie and Cyd Charisse as the stars. Ratoff had heard Hazel at Uptown and went wild for her. He was in the middle of shooting this picture. The movie was almost completed, but that's how they do it in Hollywood. They see something they want, "I gotta have it. Must have that girl."

Ratoff shot a few sequences of Hazel at the piano, took them to Hollywood to insert into his movie. The heads of Columbia were so impressed that they wanted to bring her out. "Gotta get her out here. Have her here by Friday." I made a deal with Ratoff. Not only was I Hazel's employer, I was also her manager. She went to Hollywood with these stipulations in her contract which I insisted upon. I had told Ratoff, "Otherwise you can't have her."

   a. You cannot change her color, nor make her darker than she is.

   b. She would play the piano and sing, but not as a maid in somebody's house.

   c. You cannot put a bandana on her head, nor an apron on her body.

   d. You cannot present her in any way that would be a reflection upon her people; if you do, she won't work.

I want all that written into her contract. "All right, all right, all right," Ratoff agreed.

Now a gal like Hazel could record in one day. In Hollywood they would set up a recording session. Hazel would record at the piano. They'd play the recording back. Don't like it. Play it again. They could keep her going for a whole day if necessary until they got what they wanted. In not more than two days at the most Hazel would have been recorded. The third day they would shoot the scene with Hazel at a dummy piano, no strings, dubbing the action to the sound. If they had only needed her for two, three days, they would want to pay her only for one week's work for whatever money I had negotiated, say $4,000. But not with Barney Josephson as her manager. I told them,

"If you want Hazel Scott, she must be guaranteed five weeks salary. Even if she works only three days you have to pay her for five weeks. If you use her for five weeks and a day, you must pay her pro-rated for any day's work over the five weeks."

Agreed. The contract was signed. Hazel was guaranteed $20,000 for her first movie. That was a lot of money in 1942. She did a second film for Ratoff, *The Heat's On* starring Mae West. It was to be Mae's last movie for many, many years. Essentially, she was forced out of Hollywood by the Hays office censorship.

Hazel had become very friendly with Jack Oakie and his wife during the movie. Mrs. Oakie bred Afghan dogs and gave one to Hazel. Personally, I can't abide them. By this time Hazel had accumulated an extensive wardrobe of gowns, a white fox cape, short and long silver fox coats, a beaver sports jacket. She had it all, and I had bought Alma a lovely mink coat.

Hazel's back from Hollywood after filming the Jack Oakie movie, and I met her at Grand Central Station. In those days you traveled to and from the Coast by train. Hazel disembarked with her fox coat draped over one arm, pulling the Afghan with the other. My press agent had press photographers to greet her. It was commuter time, five o'clock, and people were dashing to their trains. In that huge ballroom space it was quite a wild scene, and then this celebrity walks through and I was in the middle of it all.

The next year, 1943, Hazel was busy in Hollywood. She was signed for two pictures with MGM, *I Dood It* with Red Skelton and Eleanor Powell, directed by Vincente Minnelli, and *Broadway Rhythm*. Lena was a contract player there under a seven-year bad deal. Hazel was not a contract player. They have to hire her picture by picture at her usual salary. Hazel and Lena were cast in both movies. In *I Dood It* they each had one number. Hazel sang and played the piano, Lena sang. They were listed in the movie credits as "Herself."

Hazel and Lena were not exactly friendly, going back to Lena's Cafe Society days and the hair-pulling to-do.

Jack Gilford: *I came in one night after my stage show on Broadway,* Meet the People, *and Barney had a look of gloom on his face. So did Lena. I asked, "What happened?" Barney told me, "The pianist, Billy Kyle, didn't show up tonight, and Hazel had to play for Lena. Hazel is very jealous." "So what happened?" "Well, Hazel's fingers just wouldn't behave." It must have been a terrible show. I remember clearly, I introduced Lena that night. "I would like you to meet a performer who one day will be a big star." I think it made her feel pretty good.*[2]

The first day on the MGM set Hazel came dressed to kill, being from New York. Lena, more accustomed to the casual ways of California, came to the rehearsal in slacks. Hazel, not to be outdone, came to the next rehearsal in slacks. Lena, equally determined, came in wearing a suit from one of the studio designers.

I had cautioned Hazel, "If, in any film, they show you in any way that's derogatory, you stop working. Call me in New York. Don't get into any hassles. Just say Mr. Josephson told me what's in my contract. You can straighten it out with him."

One time it did happen. Hazel was in an MGM film playing "Herself." They were treating her all right personally, but her scene turned out to take place in Harlem. The back end of the apartment building had a clothesline strung from the window of one building over to the rear wall of the other, with raggedy clothes hanging out on the line. The inside of the apartment had dirty clothes and a dirty mattress on the floor. Hazel sat down and would not work.

Hazel had made $20,000 from her first movie, *Something to Shout About.* Some jeweler in Hollywood sold her a piece of jewelry for $22,000, a necklace and bracelet as a companion piece. Back from Hollywood, she came to work at Uptown and brought two photographs of the jewelry. Typed on the back was what these pieces contained, so many diamonds at point so-and-so carats, so many sapphires, so forth. She wanted me to get insurance for her.

"Hazel, I haven't seen this jewelry yet, but from what I see here, what did you do? I warned you when you went out there that half of the $20,000 would go to taxes. All you would have left would be $10,000. You've just spent more money than you've earned, and you still have to pay taxes on this money. For a man who knows nothing about jewelry, me, I can see there isn't one stone that's worth anything. There are hundreds of tiny stones in these two pieces. If you want to spend $22,000 you buy one great big diamond. Then if you're ever short of cash you can take it and hock it. What you've got here is a design. It comes apart. You can have two clips for your gown, one on each side, another piece for something else. Put together it all spells a necklace of no great value. And Hazel Scott, you may not ever wear this jewelry in Cafe Society."

"What do you mean I can't wear it?"

"Because when you come out and sit at the piano and the spotlight is on you, this thing starts sparkling. Your audience won't know whether it's real or not. That's distracting. Some will think it's just shiny junk. If they think it's real they might say you're just showing off. Any way you figure, it's not good for you to wear it. Please, put the jewelry in a safe deposit box and leave it there."

Well, I raised hell. She was in tears. She went home and told Alma. They were very close. The next day Hazel came in with Alma. "Barney, you're absolutely right. Hazel had no business to do this. She agrees she did the wrong thing. She's sick over it. You have to be more than her manager. You have to be her trustee so that she can't spend money like this without your approval."

A trustee agreement was drawn up, and I became her trustee, too. All the monies that she would make in the theaters through personal appearances, movies, recordings, including the money she earned at Cafe Society, were put into an account which I opened, "Barney Josephson, Special Account for Hazel Scott." I put everything away. I paid for her personal hairdresser weekly. I paid for her car, for the gasoline, for the wages for her chauffeur. I paid for her clothes, all from her account. She finally took the necklace apart and wore a piece as a clip on her gown.

One day Hazel walked into Bergdorf-Goodman's, and two pairs of shoes came COD for $35 a pair, a lot of money for evening shoes. I looked at the shoes and sent them back. When Hazel came in I told her. "Why, Barney? I have the money."

"Hazel, no one can see what's on your feet when you're sitting at the piano hitting the pedals. Your evening gown covers them. I'll buy you shoes." After all, this was my business before the cafes. I went to A. S. Beck shoe store and bought two pairs of evening slippers, $3.95 a pair. I did all those things for her.

For all that, Hazel was making a great deal of money, enough to have her own Cadillac and chauffeur; she still lived in Harlem. Hazel had been out ill for several days. I had never been to her apartment on St. Nicholas Avenue, where she lived with her mother. After her absence of a few days I thought I'd better go up and visit her. I took a cab up. When I walked in I was really taken aback to see how they were living. It was one large room that looked like a loft space. A wire was strung across the center of it with some kind of cretonne curtain separating Hazel's section from her mother's. The room was pretty bare of any furniture.

"Hazel, Alma, how can you live in a place like this? You've got a car and chauffeur, and you're living in a slum. You'll get tuberculosis in a place like this. You've got to get out of Harlem." They agreed. I went looking for a house. I found one in White Plains, 25 Monroe Place, out in the country. Lots of open space around. I bought it from her money. "Now you've got a house in the country, Hazel. You've got your car and your chauffeur. When you finish three, four o'clock, your driver will take you out there. Your mother's going to be there. You've got a room for your chauffeur. When you wake up in the afternoon you can take a walk through the woods and fill your lungs with some fresh air."

I bought her life insurance. No insurance company would give any sizable amount to a Negro. Sure, they would issue a policy, enough to buy a coffin and pay for your funeral, those $500 policies. A Negro was considered a bad risk, especially in show business. In general it was harder for show people to get insurance. I was able to buy a policy for Hazel for $50,000. I don't even know how I got it.

One night I was sitting at the bar Uptown when Hazel came in for her early show, looking radiant in a new gown, a new hair style, obviously in a very up mood. I complimented her and gave her an affectionate kiss on her cheek on her way to her dressing room. A well-dressed woman further down the bar left her stool, glared at me, and spat out, "Nigger-lover. Only a Jew could kiss a nigger." I didn't respond, just ignored her, turned to my bartender, "Give her the check and get her out of here." Hazel was out of earshot and hadn't heard the woman. I made my bartender promise not to say anything about this to Hazel. I didn't want her to be hurt.

As Hazel left the club later that evening, she very dramatically planted a kiss on my cheek, walked to the door, turned, paused a moment, then, so she could be heard by all, "Only a nigger would kiss a Jew." She had waited all evening to let me know she knew.

CHAPTER
25

"'I'm nobody's fat black mammy, but that's how I make my money.'"

Running back and forth to the West Coast negotiating Hazel's contracts was personally expensive, and I had to neglect my cafes although Leon was there. Leon and I, you might say all the boys in our family, have always been concerned with fighting, in our way, the injustices in this world as we've perceived them. For me, getting a fair and humane deal for Hazel in Hollywood was a paramount issue. I had the small hope that what I might accomplish with Hazel's contracts would chart a path for other Negro performers.

Paul Robeson came in one evening as he usually did when he was in town. He was in the midst of his record-breaking run in *Othello* on Broadway in 1943. "You know, Paul, I have Hazel on the Coast doing a film, and I don't know whether I did well for her or not. You've had experience out there. What do you think? I got her $4,000 a week for a five-week guarantee."

Paul looked at me in astonishment. "Whaaaat? You got her $4,000 a week? When I went out to Hollywood I asked for $1,000 a week. The producer looked at me, '$1,000 a week? We don't pay'—and he used the word 'we don't pay niggers a thousand a week.'" Imagine hearing a thing like that. Paul Robeson. The unmitigated gall to say that to this great artist. This is what went on in Hollywood.

It wasn't only in Hollywood. One evening John invited Paul Robeson out to dinner. Paul suggested they go to Cafe Society because he knew everyone there. John wanted to take him to a restaurant noted for its gourmet food. Paul declined, "For god's sake, John, don't try any games. You'll only be embarrassed. I'm used to it. It doesn't bother me." "It" meaning not being served in "whites only" restaurants, illegal though it was then.

It wasn't only in gourmet restaurants. It was in Cafe Society. One evening Paul, John Hammond, and his then wife Jemy came to Uptown. Jemy was a stunning blond beauty. John never dances. Paul asked Jemy to dance. When Paul was on the dance floor you couldn't miss him. He was tall, broad, and handsome.

A waiter came over to me. "The party at table forty-one want to speak to you." I looked in that direction but didn't know them. I figured it's another group from out of town who want to be able to say they've met the owner of Cafe Society. I went over and sat down at their table. One of the men asked, "Do you allow niggers to dance with white women?"

I scolded him. "We don't use such a word in Cafe Society."

"Well, we don't like it."

"You don't have to like it." I looked at my watch. It was time for this group to go, but before they did I made a speech. "We're in a war against Hitler and his hateful racial theories. This is still a democracy. You have a right not to like it, and they have a right to dance together. You don't have to remain here. No one is forcing you to stay. Besides, there's a law in New York state that makes it a crime to discriminate against anyone for race, color, or creed, punishable by a fine of $500. Anybody who is well-behaved, well-dressed, and can pay the check is welcome here."

I had just gotten started. "I don't know who you are, but I'd like to tell you who those people are. Paul Robeson is currently starring in *Othello* on Broadway. He was an all-American varsity player for Rutgers University, Phi Beta Kappa with a law degree from Columbia University, and one of this country's outstanding singers. The lady he's dancing with is Mrs. John Henry Hammond Jr. and that's Mr. Hammond sitting at the table. Mr. Robeson is their guest. Now for Mr. Hammond. His aunt is Mrs. Cornelius Vanderbilt. His father was the Wall Street counsel for twenty-odd of the largest corporations in America. He, himself, is our foremost discoverer of jazz talent and the best record producer in the business today. Now, who the hell are you?"

What does the bigot reply? "Would you want your sister to sleep with a nigger?" "Mister, I have two sisters. If one of them wants to sleep with Mr. Robeson, I would feel honored to make their bed." You never saw people rise and walk out of a place so fast. But I made sure not before they paid their entire bill even though they hadn't finished their dinner.

Negroes were not ever portrayed in films where the story would be built around a Negro family or person. They were used merely to "hypo" the stinkers, as they called movies that needed a boost. What were they going to do with them? They didn't want to throw them in the garbage. So to hypo a bad movie they would bring in some entertainment talent to create some excitement. They'd get Cab Calloway and his band, or the fabulous comedy song-and-dance team Buck and Bubbles to do a fast number, or the amazing acrobatic tap-dancing young Nicholas Brothers, or Hazel or Lena. These Negro sequences gave the movie entertainment value. When they were shown down south that segment could always be edited out.

Phil Moore, a wonderful pianist, arranger, composer, orchestra leader, who had played at Cafe Society, told this story to me. Phil is now working at MGM as a house musician, house bands that play for films that need music. They were hypoing the movie *Rhapsody in Blue* with Buck and Bubbles. They had given Bubbles one song. Phil Moore and others on the lot, white and black, did not like the song, which they felt was derogatory to the Negro people. This was during the war years and the first beginnings of standing up and saying, "This is disparaging."

A committee was formed and went to Arthur Freed. In the 1930s Freed had been a lyricist for many of the musicals. Now he was Louis B. Mayer's righthand man. The famous Arthur Freed Unit was, in fact, responsible for the golden years of the MGM musicals in the 1940s and 1950s. One of Freed's important innovations was integrating the musical numbers into the plot.[1]

The committee tell Freed that if he allows Bubbles to sing that song there'll be a lot of national protest. Negro organizations are going to scream about it; the Negro press will take it up, and there'll be a boycott of the movie, not good for box office receipts. Arthur Freed had been hearing a lot of these stories. He threw up his hands. "All right. You don't want the song? It's out." He walks out of his office to the set. Calls over Bubbles. "The boys don't like the song. Do any goddamned thing you want. What would you like to sing?" Bubbles looks at him, "Mistah Freed, ah's jes love to do 'Shine.'" If you don't get the connection, there was this common presumption that Negroes "shine" when they sweat. That's the way the story came back to me, dialect and all. Was Bubbles putting Freed on?

Joe Glaser, Louis Armstrong's long-time agent, had no such concerns for Louis. He allowed Louis to be cast in the most stereotypical roles, a servant, a garbage collector, a shabbily dressed horse groom.

> **Whitney Balliett:** *The usual Uncle Tom effects were visible . . . Armstrong's "Shine" opened with two Negroes shining a huge shoe—an unpardonable visual pun, since the title of the song is simply a pejorative term for a Negro.*[2]

In John Hammond's view, Louis's "deterioration began when he chose to think of himself as a vocalist, a showman, a soloist, rather than an ensemble musician."[3]

Owning a person, as agents did, was reminiscent to me of the days of slavery when human bodies were properties. That's why I've never taken a fee or a percentage of any entertainer's earnings whom I've managed. Nor did John Hammond. I was Hazel's manager, and she got every penny of the money she earned. The terms of Hazel's first contract that I negotiated had become known, and gradually the movie moguls began to pay more for Negro entertainers. But their agents would get the two, three thousand dollars while the performers got only a small percentage. That's how they were exploited.

These were the war years, and all performers gave freely of their talent to entertain our Armed Forces. In Hollywood, the NBC network asked a group of Negro entertainers to broadcast a radio program which would be beamed overseas to our Negro troops. Our Armed Forces were still segregated then. There were all-Negro units, and only Negro entertainers could perform for them. Here we are fighting a desperate war against fascist racist ideology and the over one million Negroes in the Armed Forces are totally segregated.

I went to the recording session with Hazel. Lena, Hattie McDaniel, and Rex Ingram, who had played Da Lawd in the movie *Green Pastures,* were also on the program. Hattie had won an Oscar in 1940 for the best supporting actress in *Gone with the Wind,* in which she played Scarlet O'Hara's mammy. This was the first time a member of her race had ever been honored by the Motion Picture Academy. The Academy Awards ceremony was held at the Coconut Grove in Hollywood. When Hattie and her escort arrived they were seated at a special table reserved for them at the rear of the room near the kitchen.

I had always resented the way they presented Hattie McDaniel in the movies, always the cheerful black servant with the big, good-natured smile. I would think, "What they've done to this woman." I knew she had once been a well-regarded singer. Actually, she had started in show business as a singer, had written more than a dozen songs, some of which she had recorded for the Okeh and Paramount labels in Chicago. Typically, she sang in small-town tents and vaudeville. Supposedly, she possessed one of the biggest voices of all the singers then, and she was compared with Ma Rainey for her ability to sing with deep feeling. She could tell it like it was. Criticized for playing the mammy roles, "I'm nobody's fat black mammy, but that's how I make my money. It's better to get $7,000 a week for playing a servant than $7 a week for being one."

The broadcast was set for late Sunday morning when there wasn't any shooting. Hazel arrived in a pair of beautiful slacks and nice blouse. Lena arrived looking beautiful, even more so than Hazel. Then Hattie McDaniel walked in wearing kelly green, but a greener green that knocks your eyes out. She wore a suit, a long, green jacket-coat, a silk blouse to match, stockings to match, green suede shoes to match, a green hankie tucked in at her wrist, and a green suede bag. If I remember correctly, she wore a green hat. This is quite a lot of green. I thought, "This the studio had nothing to do with. This was her own choice." It was embarrassing to me to see a black person dressed this way because it would be amusing to certain types of white people. That was my reaction then. In retrospect, perhaps I was overly sensitive to any possible deprecation of Negro people. But those were the times and the attitudes.

I know that during the war Hattie chaired the black section of the Hollywood Victory Committee that organized entertainment for the black troops. When she signed the contract in 1947 for her radio show *Beulah,* she could command her own terms: no southern, black dialect and total script approval. She passed in 1952 at age fifty-seven. At her funeral, fans had been lining up twelve hours before the services. One thousand crowded into the church, and four thousand more stood outside; 125 limousines brought Hattie McDaniel to her final resting place in Rosedale Cemetery. She was the first black person to be buried there.[4]

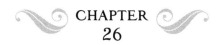

CHAPTER
26

"'Why don't you call him Zero? He's starting from nothing.'"

Although my original idea had been to open a European-style cabaret satirizing local and world events, I had difficulty finding fresh comedic commentary. I was always on the lookout for the comedian who could write his or her own material. An acquaintance, Himan Brown, a radio producer, who, I think, had a monopoly on every radio show on the air, called to tell me about a comedian he knew, Sam Mostel.

Himan Brown: *I was producing and directing on radio,* Inner Sanctum, *David Harum,* Dick Tracy, Grand Central—*the trains come in and the stories come out—among others. I must have done thirty, forty thousand plays. One of the writers, Sig Miller, who wrote an occasional script for* Inner Sanctum, *told me about this funny guy who was taking people around, explaining the paintings to groups of people at the Museum of Modern Art. Let's say he would be showing a Rousseau painting with animals, so he'd imitate the animal sounds. Sid said I should give him a job.*

But he couldn't act. After all, he was an amateur and couldn't read a script. He was totally undisciplined. On a second reading he wouldn't read the script the same way, wouldn't read the same lines. This was not for radio. But I thought he was funny, and I told him, "You belong in a nightclub." I called up the Martinique on 57th Street. I was young and brash and twenty-six years old. Well, they didn't like him. After all, he was fat and sloppily dressed. His clothes didn't fit. He wasn't for such a club.

I heard about Cafe Society and knew Barney Josephson. I said, "Let me see if I can get an audition for you there." I called Barney, and he saw what I saw in Sam Mostel, an irrepressible clown. I didn't go to Cafe Society but a few times. I had to get up at 6 A.M. I had David Harum *going on the air at 10 A.M.*[1]

Sam was an artist on the WPA Artists Project, making $22 and change a week. All the artists on the project, no matter how talented, got pretty much one salary. He had never performed professionally except for clowning around at house parties, where he had begun to develop a reputation as a funny man. Saturday nights there was always a party at somebody's house or in a rented hall to raise money for worthy progressive causes such as the Abraham Lincoln Brigade, the Joint Anti-Fascist Refugee Committee, tenant groups, whatever. They were known as the five-and-ten cent parties. If you paid a quarter, that was a big admission price. Then there would be a cash bar which could raise more money. They would call on people like Sam to entertain, and they were actually paid for performing.

Sam was getting the standard fee of $2.50 a performance. Now he has reached a point where he is a star attraction, so he decides that he should get a raise. He speaks to the committee putting on this particular affair, and it was agreed that he would get $5. The affair comes off. The hall is full to over capacity. People are lined up outside. Firemen are there to keep the crowd from overcrowding the hall. That's the kind of turn-out for this affair. After the party is over, a committee member goes to pay Sam and gives him $3.50.

Sam protests. "But you promised me five bucks. What's this $3.50?" "Well you see, Sam, we had such a big crowd. We didn't expect so many people so we had to buy more ginger ale and more ice. Because of these extra expenses we can only give you $3.50."

Some logic. They had more admissions, didn't they? They sold more booze with the ice, and I happen to know they didn't pay for the booze. They always got liquor for nothing, donations from saloonkeepers who were sympathetic to their causes. So they cut down on poor Sam. That was typical. They held up everybody they knew for this or that worthy cause. Nothing wrong when you give voluntarily. I was always asked to donate, and I did. And they always wanted free entertainment when they could get it.

For all the time that I operated the cafes, and because I was a well-known progressive, I would be asked to send talent to affairs run by such organizations. So whoever was performing in my cafes would willingly go wherever I would send them, the boogie-woogie guys, Billie Holiday, Hazel Scott, the Golden Gate Quartet, Mary Lou Williams, Jimmy Savo. They went because some of these events would be huge rallies held at the old Madison Square Garden, seating twenty thousand people, or to other affairs with hundreds of people in attendance. Cafe Society Downtown seated 210. How many nights of performing would it take to reach thousands of people and an audience kindly disposed to the artists for helping their cause? There was no television to reach vast audiences. It was invaluable publicity, and the artists knew it.

At the same time, they were exploited. These organizations just would not pay. Came the day when a few of the artists got together and formed Theater Authority with representatives from the different entertainment unions. Henceforth, organizations requesting talent, no matter what the cause, would have to get the Authority's approval before the artist could perform. If they were not to be paid, the sponsoring organization would have to pay X percent of their paid admission to the Authority, which, in turn would give part of the money to the entertainers. Then I discovered that some of the organizations had made a deal and were giving Theater Authority a percentage of their receipts, but the artists were still not getting paid. This infuriated me. From that time on, when any of the organizations called, they were informed, "My artists have told me they won't appear unless they get paid." I made that up. The performers never mentioned money. I broke the ice in that regard.

> **Mary Lou Williams:** *The only drag in New York was the many benefit shows we were expected to do, late shows which prevented me from running up on 52nd Street to see my favorite modernists. Sometimes Johnnie Garry [the factotum at Downtown] and I would dig a boogie character coming to take me on a benefit. We'd tear across the street to the 18th Hole and hide real quick under a table till the danger was past.*[2]

I had never heard of Sam Mostel until Hi Brown sent him to me. He had been auditioning for a few nightclubs around town like the Versailles on 50th Street, La Martinique, with no success, rejected by them.

Mostel came to audition at Uptown, which was where I saw talent. I had originally rented this four-story building with the basement, but now

I owned it. When my two-year lease was up in 1942 I bought the building for $87,000, practically nothing for what I got. I had so much room that each performer had a dressing room of their own. The musicians had their room. The waiters had their room. Ivan Black had his own office space.

This one afternoon Mostel was auditioning when Ivan came by on his way to his office upstairs. The room was darkened, with only a spot on Mostel, who was before the mike. I beckoned to Ivan. He came over quietly, sat down, and listened. Sam was doing a couple of his routines. He had finished his third one and was continuing when I interrupted him. "That's enough. Come over here." Auditioning is really dreadful. I was always aware of that. Go tell a guy to be funny to a bunch of chairs. Mostel sat down with us.

"How much of this stuff have you got?" I asked. "Oh, I've got lots of it." "Who writes your material?" "All mine," tapping his breast with four fingers.

Immediately I get a flash in my brain. "Am I a lucky guy. Here's a comedian who writes his own material. It's common knowledge there are comedians who can't write a line of their own. Then there are the writers who can't deliver their own comedic lines. Here is this guy who not only can deliver lines but he writes his own material. If he can keep writing, he's his own source and I'm in clover. This is what I've been looking for." All this flashed through my mind. "Okay. You're starting on Tuesday night [February 16, 1942] at Cafe Society Downtown." This was a Wednesday.

"You know, Mostel, you may not be aware of it because you're new to this business, but there's such a thing as anti-Semitism in show business in this our great country. To be a Jew is a handicap even though many of our great comedians, singers, film stars, the movie moguls themselves, are Jewish. You've got a little-bitty nose. It's not what people think of as the stereotypical Semitic nose. Your name, Mostel, could be anything. But Sam Mostel could be Jewish. Jack Gilford, one of the greatest comedians for me that ever was, changed his name from Jacob Gellman; Danny Kaye's last name was Kominski."

When Jack Gilford was the straight man for Milton Berle in vaudeville, Milton wanted him to change his name because he said it wasn't theatrical, meaning it was too Jewish. Berle himself was Jewish. They finally agreed on Guilford, but Jack insisted without the *u*. I was trying to be tactful. I did not know then that Sam's father was a respected religious consultant who made wine in their neighborhood on the East Side of Manhattan. Sam loved his pop, a gentle person with a dry sense of humor. His mother, too, was very witty; a household which appreciated learning.

"Sam, do you mind if I change your first name?" He raised his eyebrows. "I don't give a damn if you call me shit. I want to work." Ivan Black, as a gag, suggested, "Why don't you call him Zero? He's starting from nothing."

Mostel clapped his hands. "That's it. My name is Zero. People are going to ask me how'd you get that name? I'll say, 'From the marks on my report cards.'" In fact, he had graduated from City College in New York, known then as the Harvard of the working class. I've been told you had to have top grades to get in and to graduate. Zero was fast. He came up with three or four more cracks, one about that's how his bank account looked.

"Sam, what have you got for clothes? I don't like what you've got on." "I've got a brother who's an accountant, and he's kind of heavy. So for the audition I borrowed his suit so I could come here in a suit. It doesn't fit." I could see that. "We have to get you some clothes."

He didn't have any money. I took him to Bond's clothing store. I asked the salesman to fix him up with a couple of suits. Zero selected two suits, sold as "two-trouser suits," advertised as such on Bond's large electric sign on the building.

The salesman called the fitter. He came with his tape measure around his neck and his white chalk to measure Zero. Zero had a routine with sleeves. He had a way of drawing his arm up into the sleeve. To do that he would push the jacket up away from his collar. This lengthened the sleeve. He would draw his hand up into the sleeve out of sight then bring out one finger at a time to emphasize a point.

Now Zero starts doing his tricks. He withdraws his arms into the sleeves so the fitter can't measure his sleeves. He wouldn't stop. He hasn't opened yet—he's performing. Wherever he went he performed. The fitter, disgusted, "To hell with this," and walked away. The poor salesman wanted to make the sale. I had to explain. "Your fitter doesn't know it, but this is the greatest comedian who ever lived. He can't control himself. Get another fitter. I'll control him." We finally got the suits fitted. That was Zero's beginning with me.

Paul Petroff: *Oh, he was very wild, I can tell you. Crazy, because I knew him very well. On the street it was impossible to walk with him. He'd grab a branch off a tree, make a wreath around his head and dance along. On the subway one time, he said, "You want to see something?" "Okay." He put his hand in his pocket and took out a bunch of pennies and threw them on the floor of the train. It was very crowded. He got*

*down on his knees and began to pick up all the pennies, pushing women's
legs apart, crawling around.*[3]

He was a talent. He could sing, pantomime, dance, act. For one of his
routines he impersonated a jitterbug in the Roseland dance hall. Jitterbugging involves fast, acrobatic movements to swing music. One reviewer wrote,
"He looks like an elephant in pants, but was, in fact, extremely agile and a
graceful dancer." His impersonation of the movie star Charles Boyer, with his
sexy French accent, as Pepe le Moko in the movie *Algiers* with Hedy Lamarr
had everyone in New York parroting his line: "Let me run through your hair,
Hedy—barefoot."

Most important for me was Zero's political satire. His Professor Remorse
was a take-off on the British prime minister, Neville Chamberlain, whose
historic claim to fame was his appeasement of Hitler for "peace in our time"—
and the Nazis overran Czechoslovakia in 1939. Zero's Professor Remorse was
an ornithologist who gave a lecture entitled "Whither Birds; or, What the
Hell Are We Going to Do with Them?"

An organization, America First, had sprung up with an agenda to keep
America out of the war. It had a roster of members comprising a disparate
group of isolationists, Nazi sympathizers, anti-Semites, reactionaries of every
stripe. The aviation hero Charles Lindbergh, a Nazi admirer, spoke at many
of their rallies. Zero satirized this group with his creation of the isolationist
Senator Polltax Pellagra—"they call me by my first disease"—Zero's take on
the infamous southern poll tax law which disfranched southern Negroes and
poor white folk. I know all his routines:

Senator Pellagra: *Mah fellow Amuricans, ah yield to no one with
respect to 100 puhcent Amuhricanism in this great land of Dee-mah-
crah-see, where we have a past, present and the sacred principles of
[and here Zero would doubletalk]. They say no poah man can vote
in mah state. Ah wish to say that is a Red trick to besmuhch the faya
name of suthun womanhood.*

*As to the most grievous problem facing Amuricah today, that so-
called attack on Hawaii, ah'd like to ask y'all [and Zero would roar]*
What the hell was Hawaii doing in the Pacific anyway?

Zero was a smash from the first night.

*The first nighters rose nobly and generously to the occasion as they wit-
nessed another new star being born.*[4]

The media guys had a ball describing him:

Roger Butterfield: *resembles a boneless shad, a balloon, a whale.*[5]

Kyle Chrichton: *not big in an obscene and senile way; he is not even youthfully fat; he seems merely to be something loosely in burlap. His face is not only mobile, but it has a faint trace of beauty. He is moon-faced, with lugubrious brown eyes which he can control with incredible precision, rolling them back into his head in opposite directions when he chooses.*[6]

He was such a hit that less than three months later I put him into Uptown as well. He's playing both cafes, seven nights a week. Each cafe was dark one night, Downtown on Mondays and Uptown on Sundays. He had this energy. He loved it.

Everybody was after him. Radio executives from the Blue Network didn't waste any time signing him for guest appearances on a program, the *Chamber Music Society of Lower Basin Street.* The show was broadcast nationally every week and was very popular. Its format was somewhat similar to Cafe Society, combining satirical comedy with jazz. Zero was such a success that he was signed to appear regularly each week.

A Broadway producer, Clifford Fisher, signed Zero for a vaudeville-type show, *Keep 'Em Laughing,* starring Hildegarde, songs; Paul and Grace Hartman, a top ballroom dance couple; the comedy team of Victor Moore and Billy Gaxton; and Zero for comedy also.[7] Gaxton and Moore had been Broadway headliners for years. Gaxton was the straight man. They were still performing their act from their vaudeville days which had made them the big stars they became. But it was dated. They flopped. Zero, his first Broadway appearance, came out with the comedy honors. He stopped the show at every performance. The audience had come to see Zero, "whose night club clowning has become a Broadway legend."[8]

Following this he went into the Paramount Theater's stage show at $1,250 a week for a two-week engagement. When I first hired him we agreed on $50 a week, which sum rose considerably in very short order. Zero, at the Paramount, his name on the big marquee outside: *Zero Mostel—Broadway's Newest Comedy Sensation.* His name above everyone else—above Hollywood star tap dancer Ann Miller, above the popular Phil Harris and his orchestra. Zero continued performing at Cafe Society doing the late shows.

"No Zero."

T hree months in show business, that's the way this boy rose to stardom. Every Hollywood producer was burning up my telephone wires to get him out there. I was playing it very cool. I had a contract with Zero to be his personal manager. I had been burned by Lena, who had walked out on me, who, as was my wont, had no contract. My brother Leon reminded me of that. The contract with Zero stated that in consideration of being his personal manager I would get 10 percent for every engagement outside of his performances at Cafe Society. I never took any commission. I wouldn't, not my philosophy. But I have to say here that Zero never once mentioned it. Conveniently forgot.

Not only was I his manager and employer, I was his nursemaid and disciplinarian who could not discipline him. An impossible task. I made a deal with Metro-Goldwyn-Mayer for him, but I wouldn't permit any screen tests. I told them, "You want him. You saw him. You take him. Mostel does not screen-test for anybody." I was very, very independent.

And no long, seven-year contracts. The deal was that he was contracted for one film at $5,000 a week for not less than five weeks' work. If filming went on longer, the same rate. Included in the contract was an option for one more movie for that year, only two for the first year. I knew about a lot of things that go on in the moving picture industry. They take you and burn you out. You're a success for your first picture. They put you in another, then another, and in three, four, five years you're finished. Everyone would have Zero Mostel coming out of their ears. You want a long life for an artist. Zero was young, twenty-seven.

For the second picture he was to get a thousand more a week, then an option for two more pictures for the third year. If they picked up the option for the second year they must take him for the third. If they picked up the third-year option they had to pay him for two pictures even if they would only use him for one. They could not use him, however, for three. In essence, Zero was obligated to MGM for three years, not more. I figured that after the third year he would be a big star, and they would have to compete with all the other studios for him. That's the way I set him up, and I had no experience in this kind of deal, none whatsoever. With Hazel we were negotiating for one movie at a time in which she would appear, at best, in only one spot.

Zero and I went to Hollywood. When you have a contract they give you a call date, the date you are to appear at the studio to start on the picture. We went out several days before to get settled. Now I've traveled worldwide, but only in Hollywood would you find a name of a hotel where we stayed, called Garden of Allah, on Sunset Boulevard. There was a main building with a few rooms on top. Primarily you lived in the cottages, an exotic arrangement surrounding a swimming pool with palm trees all around, quite lush. I rented a cottage for Zero and myself. Humorist Robert Benchley's quip, sitting at the pool: "Gotta get out of this wet bathing suit and into a dry martini." That's the kind of place it was.

"Zero, tomorrow morning we're going out to the studio to sign you in." I took him out to the Burbank Studios. We walked into the main office. There was a young lady behind what was a sort of bank teller's arrangement. "Barney Josephson signing Zero Mostel in." The call date was for three days hence. She gave me a piece of paper. I signed it. Zero signed it. She took it. "My friend Zero, you're now on the payroll, and you're going to get a half-week's salary. That's the way they do things in Hollywood."

"You're crazy, Barney. You think they don't know what they're doing?" "They're crazy. They don't know what they're doing."

Zero's first picture was *DuBarry Was a Lady,* a musical hit on Broadway and now being made into a movie starring Lucille Ball and Red Skelton. That was pretty good company for Zero for his first vehicle. It was being made by the Arthur Freed Unit.

When we arrived they weren't ready to shoot the picture, as always. While I hadn't allowed him to be screen-tested when we were in New York, we're now on the payroll waiting to start. They would have Zero come in to make so-called screen tests. They'd tell him, "Go ahead, do your funny stuff." They'd shoot it and put it in the can. L. B. Mayer had a private screening room. When he came in and was in bad humor they would show Zero's film to him and that would set him up. He would laugh himself sick and was pleasant for the rest of the day.

One day Arthur Freed called me at the Garden of Allah. "L. B. is having a little party at his country club." When a man like Louis B. Mayer is a member, it's his club. When Hazel was making *I Dood It* she was asked to perform at a benefit for Mrs. Mayer's luncheon at the Reformed Temple in Hollywood. I went with Hazel. Mrs. Mayer introduced her as our Hazel Scott. They owned everybody who worked on the lot. Now Zero is their property. L. B. wanted Zero to entertain his friends Monday night at his club.

"Of course, Arthur." "Mr. Mayer will send his car and chauffeur at 6:30." "Fine. Zero will be there." When I saw Zero later, I told him. "Fuck 'em. I'm out here under contract to the studio. I'm not out here to entertain his fucking friends. What the hell is this?"

"Look, Zero. I'm your manager and I made the commitment. You cannot do this to me. You're not the only person I represent out here. I have Hazel, and I'm breaking my ass to get Josh White into a picture. From now on I won't make any commitments for you. If I'm asked, I'll tell them to check with me tomorrow. I'll get your approval. If you say no, I'll think up some excuse. But I don't want to be placed in this position at this moment."

"We'll see." That's the way he left it. Came Monday evening, Zero is not at the Garden of Allah. The car and chauffeur arrive. No Zero. The chauffeur waits half an hour or so. No Zero. He goes to the country club without Zero. At this point I'm tearing out my hair. No Zero. I don't know where he is, what he's doing, what happened. He had been at the studio until five o'clock and then disappeared. This was early 1943, and Metro-Goldwyn-Mayer had their own spy apparatus. They watched everybody, what they were doing. This was the most reactionary studio in Hollywood.

I had warned Zero, "Watch your *p*s and *q*s. Be a good boy. You're already being spoken of in the same breath as Charlie Chaplin. Make yourself a Charlie Chaplin, then you can thumb your nose at all of them and nobody will be able to do anything to you." No reply.

MGM had their stool pigeons in every mass organization in Hollywood. This night, Zero had appeared at a 25 cents admission party being held to raise money for the defense of Harry Bridges. Bridges was the militant CIO labor leader of the Longshoremen's Union on the West Coast. Under Bridges's leadership, the longshoremen there had broken away from the mob-controlled International Longshoremen's Association and formed their own mob-free union. I don't believe much has changed to this day. The U.S. government had been trying to deport Bridges since 1938 as an undesirable alien even though he had come to the United States from Australia in 1920.

A few days before I had been in Arthur Freed's office to chat about their plans for Zero. "Barney, I want to tell you how we feel about Zero. He is the greatest comedy property we have ever owned. We have a script for his next picture in which he'll be the star."

He pulled out some papers from his desk drawer and read to me. I was astounded at what they had in mind. Zero would be a window washer in Washington, D.C., looking in from the outside, watching all the high-level meetings, hearing what was being decided. Now the window washer was able to call all the political turns. This was made for Zero, right? At MGM? I couldn't imagine they could ever dream up a story like that, but somebody did. They didn't know what they were doing, really. This was going to be Zero's starring vehicle. I was amazed because I knew this studio didn't do stories like that.

A week later I was at the studio on this huge set. It was at least a city block square. They were shooting the picture. From afar, Arthur Freed comes onto the set with two people, showing them around. When this man would come onto a set, everything stopped. Everybody came to attention. They would practically salute him. He's about 150 feet away from Zero. He doesn't greet either Lucille Ball or Red Skelton. He only greets Zero. From this distance he raises his right arm to full length with a clenched fist, the Communist Party salute, and yelled, "Hiya, Zero."

I looked at Zero. He turned all kinds of colors from green to yellow to red. I'm sure I turned pale. Freed continued on his way, showing the people around. "Well, Zero," I told him, "that was a public demonstration against you. What you are doing in this film is now on the cutting-room floor. You're finished. Your option will not be exercised."

Not another word, but that's exactly what they did. In the film you get a fleeting glimpse of Zero walking through a room. That's what he did to himself. There was no way to control this boy. Against my wishes he had brought Katie, his girlfriend, to visit him. And he still had a wife. A Hollywood scandal he didn't need.

I hadn't known he was married when I hired him. Uptown he and Hazel were sharing the bill. Katie had come in with a young couple on their honeymoon. She was a Rockette, dancing at Radio City Music Hall. I had never met her, but apparently she knew who I was because she brought the couple over and introduced them. Well, they've met the owner of a nightclub in New York. Very impressive. I told my captain to give them a good table. Later in the evening I went over, sat with them, and bought them a drink. That's the way I am, always the grand host. I love doing that.

The show is over, and they're on their way out. Zero is in the bar lounge with some people. I wanted to give the honeymooners a good send-off, so I invited them to meet Zero Mostel. I introduced them, then I turned to the third person, "And this lady is . . . what is your name?" "Kate Harkin." Zero stretched out his two arms, threw them and himself bodily around her. "You're for me. You two"—waving his hands at them—"you two, *go!* She's for me." The honeymooners walked out and left Kate with Zero. He took her home.

His wife? In 1939 he had married a young lady, Clara, whom he'd met when they were students at City College. Clara didn't appreciate her husband's artistic pursuits which didn't bring in money. She wanted to be able to quit her job and raise a family. Sam was dedicated to his painting. Nothing could interfere with that. He rented a small room, no heat, on West 28th Street, which he shared with three other artists. He always kept this studio, even during the long run of *Fiddler on the Roof* on Broadway. Sam would stay over many nights in the studio. One day in 1941 he returned home to find Clara had left him, cleaning out the apartment, including their chandelier.

Now he's the big star at Cafe Society. He's served with an order from Domestic Relations Court by his wife, asking for separate maintenance. She claimed he's earning so and so much a week, really far in excess of what he was making then. They hadn't been living together, and he hadn't supported her all this time. Not a nickel. She wanted X percent of his salary. "Oooooo," Zero went crazy. "What'll I do? What'll I do? What'll I do? This horrible woman, now I'm making some money and she's gonna get it all!"

I didn't know her but Zero was my friend. "Look, Leon's a lawyer. We'll show him this court order." Leon read the order. "This is what we'll do. I'll draw up a new business manager's agreement that says Barney guarantees you forty weeks work at $100 a week whether you work or not. Anything beyond that is Barney's for promoting and publicizing your career, getting you bookings, etc. I will make only one copy of this agreement which you'll sign. Barney will not have a copy. This way you don't have to spend 5 cents for a lawyer. You'll answer the summons. You'll go into court. You'll show the judge this contract. The judge will award your wife $25 a week, 25 percent of your salary as stated in this contract. Do you object to your wife's getting that?" "Oh, no, no, no."

That's just what happened. Eventually he got a divorce and married Kate. They're not married long when they have a big fight. Kate orders him out of the house. He goes into the bedroom, makes loud packing noises, comes out to say goodbye, carrying a suitcase. He's completely nude except for socks and a bow tie, not around his neck but around his most intimate part.

The things that man would do. A lot of actors used to go to the Seventh Avenue Deli between 55th and 56th Streets after their shows. Zero would go there with his pals, Sam Jaffe and Phil Loeb. On the table were big baskets of bread, pickles, green tomatoes, and butter. This was not a kosher deli. Zero starts buttering his rye bread. He doesn't take a piece of bread, he takes the whole slice on the palm of his hand, smears it like cement on a brick. Now he's going up his arm, all over his face, down the other arm, taking butter off the dishes from the other tables, then over to Phil and Sam, smearing them—Zero, as the spirit moved him.

If a woman walked by in the club with a low-cut gown and her bosom showing, he'd leer and cross his eyes. When he starred on Broadway his ad-libbing onstage drove authors and directors to distraction. He wasn't a womanizer as far as I know, but he would like to tap chorines on the ass as they passed him onstage.

In my opinion, money and success went to his head. A few years later he thought nothing of dropping me as his manager, just like that, claiming I wasn't doing enough for him. Even though we did have a contract, written and signed, I just let him go. I never took a commission for all the work I did and got for him. When he was cast in *Fiddler on the Roof*, he dropped his then agent the same way, but she sued.

Yes, Zero was a prodigious talent. His end came in 1977 while he was rehearsing the part of Shylock, not Shakespeare's, a different interpretation by the British playwright Arnold Wesker. Zero collapsed suddenly, aortic aneurysm. Taken to the hospital, he never recovered.[1]

"We are on the same beam together, Barney and Mildred."

"Barney, there's a woman whom I consider to be the world's finest white jazz singer, Mildred Bailey. I've invited her to drop into Cafe Society Downtown."

I knew what John Hammond wanted. Mildred Bailey dropped in, and I persuaded her to sing a couple of songs with the band. She had not been around for some years and now she would be singing Downtown, picking up what had been a fabulous singing career.

John said "white jazz singer," but in fact Mildred was part Indian on her mother's side and proud of it. Her father was Irish-German, and she was actually born on an Indian reservation near Spokane, Washington. Mildred has said that the Indian songs, with their wide range, that she learned as a child from her mother, who was a piano teacher, were invaluable to her musical development. Her mother died when she was fourteen. Three years later she went to live with her aunt in Seattle. There she married a man, Ted Bailey, whose name she kept. Mildred was sensitive about her birth name, Rinker. She was afraid people would play around with it, Mildred Rinker, Stinker, so she changed it.

When she joined the Paul Whiteman Orchestra in 1929 she was the first important girl singer to sing with a big band. Her brother Al Rinker and Bing Crosby were two of the famous male trio, the Rhythm Boys, with Whiteman's band. Mildred left Whiteman in 1933 and married Red Norvo, who had played vibes in the band. They became phenomenally successful, touring across the country as Mr. and Mrs. Swing with their own band.[1]

Mildred was a wonderful, wonderful singer. Her style was unique, a lyricism unequaled in jazz. "Her voice was a superb swinging instrument. . . [she was] a musician of extraordinary taste and sophistication."[2] She was a skilled scat singer, too. I have told singers who have worked for me that they could learn everything about phrasing and diction and emotion if they would listen to Mildred's and Billie's records. To my mind Mildred was not far from Billie.

Opening night Downtown [May 1, 1942], the "Rockin' Chair Lady" shed a tear when the audience kept calling for her signature song, showing they'd not forgotten her. The story goes that one day Hoagy Carmichael was visiting Mildred, and she sat down in her little niece's rocking chair. When she got up the chair clung to her. Mildred, always delightfully witty, laughed, "This ol' rockin' chair's got me." A month later Hoagy sent her a song:

Ol rockin' chair's got me
Cane by my side
Fetch me that gin, son
'Fore I tan yo hide.

She was short and fat. She sang a song, I don't know how she got it, but it fit her, "Scrap Your Fat," which always tickled her audiences. What she could do with a song! She made you hear the song. To this day, my great pleasure is playing a Mildred Bailey record, a Billie Holiday record.

Mildred had the reputation of being very difficult. John told me that her well-known rages came out of her frustration. She never made it truly big commercially as she should have, and she resented it. She was good, and she knew she was good. When she opened Downtown, I know that the reviews praising her as the great singer she was made her very proud.

One night we were gabbing. "Barney, you know my reputation with everybody I work for?" "What do you mean, Mildred?" "Well, that I'm tough. I fight with everybody." "Yeah, I've heard. But we don't. We get along." "You know why?" "Why?" "Because you and I, Barney, we are on the same beam together." Then I learned about a religious sect called Unity. Mildred explained, "If you are on the same beam with the Lord, then all is right with the world, with you and everyone like you." So this is why we two never have an argument. We are on the same beam together, Barney and Mildred.

She was a great lover of dachshunds and had two or three of them. She would bring them to Cafe Society. Wherever she went she had them with her. She loved them, and they all slept with her. They were in bed with her and Red Norvo, too. This time she had an engagement Uptown, and, of course, she had her dachshunds. She would take them out for a walk on 58th Street. I had a doorman there. He was very meticulous about himself, his uniform, the frontage, which he swept all the time. A very good doorman. We had a canopy to the curb. This particular evening Mildred came out with her dogs, who used one of the canopy stanchions to eliminate. My doorman said something to the effect, "Why don't you watch where your dogs pee?"

Mildred had a mouth. Boy! She knew all the words and made some up herself. Well, she let out a stream of invectives at this poor doorman who dared to criticize her precious little darlings. Someone came in to tell me, "Mildred and the doorman are having a thing out there. You'd better go out." I went out. I just stood there, astonished, listening. That's when I learned she added to the four-letter vocabulary with about twenty I never heard before. It came out rapid-fire, one after another.

Off and on, Mildred was with me for a long time. She would come in for three or four months at a time. She had a good following. Everybody loved her. Whenever Bing Crosby would be in New York, he would always come in to see her and tell me, "Barney, this is the little lady who taught me how to sing." Always credited her. She actually coached him.

She wasn't always in the best of health, diabetes. Toward the end of 1949 she had become seriously ill with a heart condition. Bing was concerned enough to bring her out to the West Coast for better treatment. She did improve, but a couple of years later she suffered another heart attack and passed in Poughkeepsie at the too young age of forty-four.[3] She had made thousands and thousands but had almost nothing at the end.

CHAPTER
29

"'He'll never come back.'"

Y ou're only as good as your last flop—show biz humor. When I hired Jimmy Savo in 1943 he was considered washed up. He wasn't working after thirty-eight years in show business. He had not been in a hit show since *The Boys from Syracuse* in 1938, the Rodgers and Hart musical based on Shakespeare's *Comedy of Errors*. He had been in three flops in succession. Movies had passed him up although he had made a few years before. A friend told me about him, that he was terribly discouraged and broke. I knew of him and asked him to see me at Uptown. He came in one afternoon, looked around, "My, this is a concert hall nightclub."

I calculated Jimmy was about forty-seven, but in fact he was ageless. I offered him an engagement of ten weeks for $450 per, not very much for someone who had been a headliner in vaudeville and a star on Broadway. He felt he needed to get his act together in front of an audience because he hadn't worked for a long time. Didn't want to open cold. He got himself a gig in a club in Philadelphia.

I went over to catch his act. The place was a real dive, filled with mug-type characters feeling up the gals' legs. Nobody was paying any attention to Jimmy. After his act he told me sadly that he had been bombing every night. He offered to tear up the contract I had drawn up. It just hadn't seemed right to me not to offer a contract to him, especially that he hadn't worked for so long. I reassured him, "This is no place for you. You'll be a terrific hit in my club."[1]

Jimmy had begun juggling with small stones when he was a tot of six. "There were plenty of stones in the vacant lots in my neighborhood." He was adept enough when he was seven to enter amateur nights, eventually juggling his mother's pots and pans. At twelve he was touring the vaudeville circuit, billed as the Child Wonder Juggler, adding singing, pantomime, rope walking, and comedy to his juggling act.

Jimmy and I had one thing in common, not juggling. If truth be told, my coordination skills are not athletic in nature. When I was a youngster I was always the last one to be chosen for the baseball teams in the neighborhood. Both our fathers were cobblers. His had a shoe repair shop in the Bronx. I don't know if his father could make the beautiful shoes I was told that mine could, but neither of them had the money to keep much stock.

In vaudeville he had teamed up with Fred Allen, later a famous radio comedian. They wrote a revue, *The Vogues of 1924,* which played the Schubert Theater on Broadway:

> **Allen:** *What's that you got under your arm?*
> **Savo:** *Ten pounds of sugar for my coffee.*
> **Allen:** *What's that you got under your other arm?*
> **Savo:** *Ten pounds of sugar for my tea.*
> **Allen (tapping him over the head with a mallet):** *Here's a lump for your cocoa.*

Jimmy was tiny, no taller than five feet, elflike in a baggy, oversized suit, a derby hat perched on his black bangs, suspenders holding up his pants, floppy shoes. He was as graceful as a dancer and had a sort of wistful, endearing quality.

He sang lyrics to popular songs of the day, "Dancing in the Dark," "That Old Black Magic," "Those Little Things Remind Me of You," pantomiming the words, turning them into a pun or gentle satire. "As Time Goes By," he'd bring his watch near to his face, walk it across in little steps to the music, moving his head to follow the watch as time went by.

One of the all-time audience favorites was "River Stay 'Way from My Door." He would run from the mike, pleading and shooing away the water with his hands and feet as it rolled on. Then, with the audience applauding, he disappeared, slipped back under the piano, sat at the edge of the band-stand, crossed his legs, joining in the applause, beaming like a little child.

One evening I was introduced to the *World-Telegram*'s well-regarded drama critic Burton Rascoe. He wrote his own review:

> Paul Martin, the World-Telegram's *connoisseur of cuisine and appraiser of night entertainments . . . fearing that my education is being neglected, invited me . . . to do a bit of pub-crawling with him. "I'll take you only to Cafe Society Uptown, where you can catch Jimmy Savo and some other numbers in what is about the most sophisticated of the current floor shows in the tony saloons."*
>
> *So, presently, there I was, about midnight, sitting at a "ringside" table in a long, low-ceiling room that was so crowded that you had to weave and wiggle your way in and out. There is a long bar at one side of the entrance, and beyond that is the floor show. The floor is so small—just as in the old days—that the show is called "intimate" because the performers are practically in your lap.*
>
> *For twenty years I have been a Jimmy Savo fan. . . . and yet each time his performance is to me a fresh and utter delight, so like a wistful leprechaun is he, at once pathetic and mischievous, ingenuous and knowing, childlike and yet so critically wise. His satirical pantomime is always tender, but is devastating just the same. He is subtle, extremely so, but only in the points he makes; his means of making points are always broad and clear enough and so richly imaginative that he always provokes laughter. . . . It was a pleasure to see the warm response Mr. Savo's act evoked. In the speakeasy days his act would have been impossible, because of the noisy drunks whom the managements had to tolerate because they were afraid of retaliation.*[2]

This tribute from a drama critic! On Jimmy's first anniversary, May [17], 1944, we sent out a press release: "The Broadway wiseacres who said a year ago, 'He'll never come back,' will be picking crow out of their teeth."

Jimmy had been Uptown about a year and a half. I had an idea that he should change his trademark tramp outfit to smartly tailored dinner clothes. My audiences howled. Now he receives an offer to appear in the stage show in his new outfit at the Roxy Theater for $2,500. That costume laid an egg there. Jimmy changed back into his tramp clothes and laid them in the aisles. Just months before the Roxy management wouldn't consider paying him a thousand in his tramp outfit. That Roxy show, advertised as the Cafe Society Uptown Show, also featured Mildred Bailey and Pearl Primus.

We occasionally had foreign servicemen, this night British sailors. Just before Jimmy finished his act, one of the Brits jumped up, grabbed the mike, and announced he was going to sing a song about when a British sailor knocked out that "nigger Jack Johnson." In 1908 Johnson had become the first Negro heavyweight champion of the world. Can you believe that such a song was still around? Sid Catlett, our drummer, was sitting on the bandstand, his arms folded, watching the show. He immediately picked up his drumsticks and began a tremendous drum roll. The men in Teddy Wilson's orchestra joined in, drowning out the sailor who might have had too much to drink.

There was almost a riot because there was a large contingent of American servicemen in the room. I went over to the sailor to calm the atmosphere, explained the word *nigger* was offensive to me, to my guests, to my musicians, and performers. He said he didn't know it was a derogatory word.

Big Sid Catlett was one of the greatest drummers, if not the greatest, who ever lived. He was a huge man, six feet four inches tall, a sweet, gentle, funny man. He loved to tell jokes and could go on all night. When he performed his drum solos he tore down the house. What he could do with those sticks defied everything human.

> **Whitney Balliett:** *His solos had an uncluttered order and logic, a natural progression of textures and rhythms and time that made them seem predesigned. He was also a sensational show drummer. He'd spin a stick in the air, light a cigarette, and catch the stick. Or he'd get up and dance around the set.*[3]

Helen Humes, the great jazz singer, was standing beside him when he suddenly collapsed with a heart attack and died instantly in 1951. He was barely forty years old.

Jimmy, at Uptown, continued to pack the place, deserving of his $3,500 a week salary, when in September 1946 a malignant tumor was found in his leg. It had to be amputated above his knee. I visited him at Memorial Hospital and found him rehearsing new songs for his return. He showed me some of the letters he had been receiving from all manner of celebrities, Sophie Tucker, Bob Hope, Mary Martin, Bill Robinson, Stan Laurel, Phil Baker, strip-tease artist Ann Corio, Eva Tanguay, a famous vaudeville headliner in the early 1900s (known as the "I Don't Care Girl," a song she sang), and from soldier amputees. He had always been generous donating his time entertaining the men in service. There must have been fifty baskets of flowers. One came from a group, the Bench Sitters Association. The attached card said they had watched Jimmy feeding nuts to squirrels every day in Central Park.

Jimmy was on crutches when I came in. "Barney, I'll need about six weeks to learn how to use my new leg and two more weeks to rehearse my routines." "Any time you feel you're ready to work again, you can come in. How do you feel, Jimmy?" He looked down at his one leg, his crutches, and with that ingenuous smile, "Well, I won't have any trouble keeping my best foot forward."

Just about the time Jimmy came to Uptown, a group who called themselves The Revuers came to my attention. They consisted of five people, Betty Comden, Judith Tuvim, later that fine actress Judy Holiday, Adolph Green, and a wonderful comedian, Alvin Hammer, a little fellow, a Buster Keaton-type performer. With them was a young man whose last name was Emery, who played the piano and sang with them. They wrote all their own material, and I had the hope they might be able to work up some satirical political commentary. Finding writers for this kind of satire was so difficult. The Revuers, in their own way, satirized songs and films, "songs and foolishness," the New Yorker commented.

They opened at Downtown beginning of August 1942, on the program with Albert Ammons, Pete Johnson and Teddy Wilson's orchestra. They were the most amateurish performers you ever saw, but their talent was recognized. They did very well and I brought them back Uptown for several months with Hazel Scott.[4] They had been with me for a number of months off and on, and had become important performers, getting a great deal of publicity. My friend Bill Morris, owner of the famous William Morris Agency, which handled top talent, had taken them on.

They were back at Downtown for another gig when they got a booking into the Copley Plaza in Boston, a very swanky hotel. They had made it. Came opening night at the Copley, I wasn't there but I know the story—Mr. Emery blows his stack. He went nuts. The top of his head just blasted off, so to speak. He began to call all those ladies and gentlemen, their sons and daughters, Boston aristocracy, all the curse words in his vocabulary, "Fucking no-good, shitty, rotten bourgeoisie" and so forth.

The Revuers were canceled out on their opening night. Emery was incarcerated somewhere. I don't know the ending for his life, but I do know they took care of him for a long, long time.

"She took one leap."

Nearly all the nightclubs, with few exceptions, hired only name talent. They wanted box office. If they saw a talent they wouldn't know it. After a talent became a big star, then they bought it, and when they bought it they had to pay for it. They paid huge sums to stars like Sophie Tucker, Belle Baker, Carmen Miranda, Hildegard, Carl Brisson, Ruth Etting, Tony Martin, Benny Fields, Milton Berle, Olson and Johnson. But Barney got his talent from the ground and brought them up.

Two American dancers from Englewood, New Jersey, Beatrice and Evelyne Kraft, intrigued me at their audition. I decided to try them out Uptown. Ivan's press release described their act, "Oriental dancers who swing and sway in positively authentic Hindu dances to the accompaniment of such old ritual music as the 'Boogie-Woogie Temple Dance' and 'The Bombay Lindy.'"

Virginia Forbes: *Two beautiful girls who have a dance form that is unique. Their dancing is of concert style with added satirical touches. . . . Two authentic Hindu dances, "Invocation," and "Flirtation," the latter a play-dance without music. Barney Josephson's unerring judgment prevailed over advice to the contrary.*[1]

Teddy Wilson: *One of the most sensational things that ever happened*

when the Kraft Sisters first came to Cafe Society, they had no music.
They had done their choreography from recordings. They practiced with
a recording, and you know, they brought us a recording and no phono-
graph. They thought we could play the music from that record without
a phonograph; we could look at those grooves. This is the truth. That
Beatrice, couldn't she dance? Evelyn was very pretty but kind of clumsy
compared to Beatrice.[2]

"Barney, there's a lady on the phone who says she's a dancer and wants an audition. Do you want to speak to her?" Tibal, my secretary, wasn't so sure I wanted another dancer. She was protecting me as always. "I'll take it, Tibal." "Mr. Josephson, I'm a dancer, and I'd like to audition for you." "My audition days are Tuesday and Wednesday. Which day do you want to come in?" I auditioned almost everyone who called me. They didn't come through agents. I didn't want agents, those ten-percenters. Anyway, between John Hammond and myself, we did all right without them.

A spring afternoon and in walked this young black woman in her early twenties I judged. You form an opinion when someone comes looking for a job, how they come dressed, how their hair is combed, wanting to make a good impression. This woman came in not really well-groomed, as if she just had not bothered getting herself together for her audition. I was very unimpressed. I didn't know then that she was a graduate of Hunter College in biology and even then was studying for her master's degree in psychology.

"Are you the young lady who brings her own records as your accompaniment?" I thought, "Oh god, I can't present anyone who looks like this." "Yes, I am." "Well, my record player isn't working, and I don't know how I can see you perform today." I just wanted to put her off. I didn't want to audition her. Well, she was tearful. She was working, doing clerical work in the office of the National Maritime Workers Union. This was in the early days when they were organizing. She needed money desperately, had taken the day off to audition and didn't know when she could afford to take another day off. My heart melted. "I tell you what. Wait here. Give me ten, fifteen minutes. I'm going up to my office to see what I can do with the darn machine. Maybe I can tape it somehow to get it to last long enough for your audition."

So I climbed upstairs to my third-floor office and lit a cigarette. I used to be a heavy smoker. I smoked three or four cigarettes and came down carrying my portable record player. "Here it is. I hope it will last the audition."

"I have a leotard I'd like to change into." I sent her up to the ladies' lounge.

She changed, came down, gave me her record. I put it on the player. Now the dance floor was a pretty good-sized one. She took one leap, one leg behind, both arms outstretched, I thought she'd go through the wall. Her legs were very muscular, like a man's legs, strong, powerful, like iron, and bronze, her color.

I had no special feeling about dance then. I liked jazz tap dancing. I didn't care much for ballet and interpretive modern dance. But as little as I knew about dance, and that was little enough, when I saw that leap I knew it was something. This woman, whom I had been trying to get rid of, knocked me off my ass.

"I tell you what we'll do, Miss Primus. I haven't an opening here. I'm fully booked, but I can put you in Downtown. My budget will take it there. I'd like you to go there and try out that small space yourself. If you can dance in that space you can start Tuesday night."

She went down to Sheridan Square. A half hour later she's on the phone. "I can do it." At that point in her career she could dance on a dime, the size of the dance floor Downtown. I opened her in April for a ten-month engagement.[3] Ivan Black knew John Martin, the foremost dance critic we've ever had, a splendid gentleman. He had never been in a nightclub in his life. Ivan, always persuasive, convinced him to come down.

> **John Martin:** *"Rock Daniel" and "African Ceremonial" are on Miss Primus's program at Cafe Society, and even at the close range of a night club floor show, with a minimum of space and no theatrical framework, they are excellent dances. She has a magnificent team of drummers assisting her, and the threesome present just about as exciting a quarter of an hour as you are likely to find in any known nitery.[4]*

> **John Martin:** *There is no doubt that Pearl Primus is quite the most gifted artist-dancer of her race (she is Negro) yet to appear. The roots of her real quality lie in her apparent awareness of her racial heritage at its richest and truest . . . and by any standard of comparison she is an outstanding dancer without regard to race.[5]*

Three months after I brought in Pearl, the folk singer Josh White came to sing at Downtown.[6] He was a treasure. Josh played a marvelous guitar, singing the folk ballads he'd learned as a little boy traveling in the South, leading blind musicians. One day when he was seven he helped a blind Negro singer-guitarist cross the street in the town where he was born, Greenville, South Carolina. The blind singer, Joe Taggart, asked Josh's mother if Josh could lead him around every day after school. Josh once told me, "My mother believed that to lead the blind would be doing God's work." For ten years he traveled from city to city, leading different blind musicians. One was the famous singer Blind Lemon Jefferson. Josh learned the guitar and the spirituals from these blind minstrels.

Josh was sex personified, and he knew it. When he stroked his fingers across the strings of that guitar, and I knew Josh well, it was like he was stroking a beautiful vagina. Every woman watching and listening got it.

He was married with three children, but that didn't dissuade the girls who would literally line up outside waiting for him. Nor did it dissuade Josh. One of the girls, a white teenager, caught his eye, caused him some trouble. Her brother, a big guy, was the doorman at the Liederkranz Club. When he found out about the affair, Josh got roughed up. A committee of women who were against Negro violence took up the incident. When Josh was questioned he claimed, "It's not true. I'm impotent."

Irene Selznick, the daughter of Louis B. Mayer and divorced wife of movie producer David Selznick, was a Broadway producer and agent in New York. She was quite taken with Josh. I found out they were planning to go to Chicago together on a booking. I took Josh aside. "I don't think this is a very good idea, Josh, especially who her father is. It could ruin you in Hollywood." As Josh's manager I had been trying to get him into the movies. He heeded me, but that wasn't the end of that affair. I spoke to Paul Robeson about Josh's affairs with white women. "You know, Barney, every time Josh sleeps with a white woman, he's beating up on her in his mind."

I staged Josh's performance. He sat on a stool with one foot propped on one of the rungs, his shirt open. He usually had a lit cigarette behind his ear. Josh knew how to quiet his audience. If he heard a whisper, his hand would pause above the guitar and he'd shoot a cold look at the offender and wait. He'd wait until quiet reigned. The tender, tear-in-the-throat quality of his voice made quiet necessary to put over the effect he wanted.

He was not a blues shouter. He sang blues. He sang songs of social conscience, some of which he wrote. He sang of Jim Crowism, of slums, of lynchings, of chain gangs, of hunger. He wanted attention paid to the words. Josh had introduced a song, not his own, which was sweeping the country, "One Meat Ball," a true depression song. Jimmy Savo performed it Uptown. The song tells of a little man who goes into an eating place with only 15 cents in his pocket, carefully looks over the menu. He can afford just one meat ball, orders it, and politely asks the waiter for bread with his order:

The waiter's voice roared down the hall,
"You gets no bread with ONE MEAT-BALL."
The little man felt very bad,
But ONE MEAT-BALL was all he had.[7]

I had an idea for one of the songs Josh wrote, "Hard Time Blues." I asked him if he would sing this one song with Pearl dancing. I placed him against a column on one side where he wouldn't be noticed. Pearl stepped out on the floor. Josh sang, "It's hard, hard times." Pearl crouched forward. She had a way of raising her leg, this powerful limb, in slow motion. People were fascinated by the power in her legs and arms. As she slowly brought up this leg, her right hand reached out just before the knee. She touched the knee, then the full part of her thigh, then turned and swung on the other leg from left to right, all in slow motion, "It's hard, hard times." Her hand outstretched in begging fashion, she moved the hand slowly from side to side. It was affecting.

One night Pearl wanted to speak to me. We went into my two-by-four office under the stairwell. "The dance floor is much too small, Barney. I can't work in that small space." This after performing here for almost a year. I looked at her.

"My darling, this floor is exactly the size it was when I sent you down from 58th Street and asked you to try your dancing on it and that if it worked you could start on Tuesday. I expect, dear Pearl, that you have become too big for the floor. You're too big for Cafe Society Downtown. You belong on the concert stage, and that's where you should go."

Suddenly the floor had gotten so small she couldn't move. Well, I said it for her. It turned out I wasn't very far off. What I hadn't known was that she was booked to give a solo concert, her first, at the YMHA on 92nd Street in April 1944. A couple of weeks later she asked to come back and this time, I put her in Uptown.[8]

Gene Knight: *Back in starring position these nights is the scorching piano magic of Hazel Scott. Recovered from her recent illness, Hazel leads off one of the hottest variety bills in town. Added are the jam and jive artistry of Teddy Wilson's Band, the inimitable pantomime of Jimmy Savo, and the disturbing drum dances of* primitive *Pearl Primus.*[9]

Pearl had introduced a powerful dance that she called "Slave Market," which portrayed the old slave custom of singing spirituals as a secret code. I brought this kind of entertainment to Uptown.[10]

CHAPTER
31

"When Mary Lou plays
it all looks so easy."

Mary Lou Williams had come to play at Cafe Society Down-town.[1] It was her first gig as a solo performer. For twelve years she had toured with Andy Kirk and his Twelve Clouds of Joy band. Her husband then was saxophonist John Wil-liams, who was in the band.

John Williams: *Terrence Holder was the original leader of the Clouds of Joy band. One time he left town with the payroll, Christmas. The owner of the Louvre Ballroom didn't want him in the place anymore. Andy Kirk was the oldest in age and settled. The owner asked Andy would he take charge. But the way the band was run, the saxophone player calls all the numbers and all the tempos. That became my job. Andy was just a tuba player. I ran the band.*

Mary and I were married from 1925 to 1940 when she quit me. It's pretty tough for two professional people to stay together because the girls are hittin' on you and the boys is hittin' on her, and you got to have some space. Mary and I made it as long as we did because Mary was just like a kid. I mean I had to teach her a lot of things. For fifteen years old you don't know much. And space, you ride together, you sleep together, you eat together. So what we would do when we'd play a dance where we have a week's stand, she would hang out with whoever she would hang

*out with in the band, a drummer, or go to a shoe store or something.
I used to hang out with the two saxophone players. But we made it a
rule that we would both be home by three in the morning. We'd play 'til
one, so we'd give ourselves two hours' space to do whatever you want.
And if you can't do it in two hours, I'm sorry. We were never jealous,
never had a fuss about who was that girl or who was that boy. What
you don't see, you don't know. She told me if I ever saw anyone I like
better than you, I'll tell you. So she finally told me, and it happened to
be my old schoolmate Ben Webster. We still hung out together. You don't
fight with someone who don't want you. You getcha somebody else.*[2]

Touring was never easy. There were many, many one-night gigs, traveling
long distances on the road between gigs. They were often cold and hungry.

Mary Lou Williams: *I often wonder what an agent would do if he
had to travel with the band he's booking. After the release of our Decca
records in 1936, the Kirk band traveled five or six thousand miles a
week on one-nighters all through the South, repeating most of the dates
before coming West again. . . . By now I was writing for some half-
dozen bands each week. I used to write in the car by flashlight between
engagements.*[3]

The big band leaders, Benny Goodman, Tommy Dorsey, Duke Ellington,
Paul Whiteman, Glen Gray, Bob Crosby, all vied for her arrangements and
the songs she composed. Her fees ranged from $3 to $15, no royalties.

The Clouds of Joy had a gig in Washington, D.C., in 1941. When Mary
checked the piano, it had ten dead keys. She took her suitcases off the bus
and went back to her mother in Pittsburgh, where she hibernated. At some
point in 1942 the drummer, Art Blakey, persuaded her to form her own six-
piece combo. Harold "Shorty" Baker, a four-foot-ten-inch trumpeter with a
big tone, joined the band, and they married.

John Hammond had been trying to get Mary for Cafe Society for years.
When Mary came to Downtown she was apprehensive about performing solo
as a featured artist. She'd always had a band around her, and she worried that
my audiences wouldn't relate to her.

Mary Lou Williams: *Sometime in 1943, I had an offer to go into Cafe
Society. I accepted though fearing I might be shaky on solo piano since
I had been so long with Andy Kirk's band and my own combo. At my
opening people were standing upstairs, which I was glad to see. Georgia*

Gibbs, who was just starting out, was in the show with Ram Ramirez playing piano for her. Pearl Primus was also in the show and Frankie Newton had the small band. . . . He was a real great trumpet man, always easy on the ear.[4]

Mary isn't a showy performer, making with the body and hands and eyes. When Mary Lou plays it all looks so easy. I now had one of the all-time great jazz pianists, male or female, settled in Downtown. My patrons appreciated her for one of the finest musicians jazz has ever produced. Whitney Balliett's poetic description: "The grapes are others, the wine is her own."[5] "Mary Lou Williams is back with her top boogie-woogie keyboard but the gal just hasn't got it when it comes to putting over to the uninitiated. . . . [She] is greeted with acclaim by the hipsters who recognize the great talent she possesses."[6] Off and on Mary played at Downtown and Uptown for over five years.

Mary Lou Williams: *For short periods I would be out of the Cafe on concert tours and such, and then go back. I had become like one of the fixtures, and was treated like a member of the boss' family.*[7]

Susie Reed: *We all shared the same dressing room at Downtown. Mary would be sitting at her little tiny section of the dressing room table with a mirror in front, writing. I was next to her. The band would be playing loud, and she would be writing, with the band playing some entirely different jazz piece onstage, everybody coming and going.*[8]

Mary Lou: *We were kind of a family there and Barney Josephson thought of us that way . . . I used to be quiet in those days—a zombie. When people talked to me, I looked at them and nodded, but in my mind I was writing an arrangement or going over a new tune.*[9]

Susie Reed: *I learned a lot about life from Mary. She would never gossip. She spoke very little, but what she said was right on. She said what she meant. When a musician would come to Uptown Cafe Society and they weren't working that week, I've seen her hand over her pay envelope, the whole envelope, to them. Not say a word. Once we were talking about someone who did so much for others. Mary said, "Yes, and she always tells you about it."*[10]

Mary had composed a work, "Zodiac Suite," not a jazz piece. She explained to me that each of the twelve parts portrayed the characteristics of those born under each astrological sign. She was so proud of this work and wanted to hear it played with a full orchestra. I offered to present it, but not

in Cafe Society which wouldn't have been an appropriate setting. I rented
Town Hall on West 43rd Street for a late afternoon, December 30, 1945.

Ed Hall's sixteen-piece orchestra under the direction of Milton Orent
had Ben Webster on tenor sax, J. C. Heard on drums, Al Hall on bass. There
were also ten string instrumentalists, a flutist, an oboist. "Zodiac Suite" made
up the entire first half of the program, and the second half, Mary's boogie-
woogie and jazz compositions. Town Hall was packed with musicians, press,
and the public. The suite was received enthusiastically by the knowledgeable
audience, and Mary was pleased.

There were a few detractors, among whom was the music critic Paul
Bowles of the *Herald-Tribune:* "An ambitious and sometimes amusing project, it so lacks integration and style in its writing that it falls quite outside
the categories of either serious or popular music. . . . The result, despite
occasional freshness of sound, is episodic and monotonous."[11]

A few days after the concert Mary went over to Town Hall to pick up the
records of her program, which I had paid to have made. The records were
not there. Someone had taken them. They were there when we left the hall
after the concert. We had an idea who did take them. They've never surfaced.
So Mary was not ever able to hear how her music sounded that day.

One of her compositions on the program was "Gjon Mili's Jam Session,"
dedicated to her friend. Gjon was the famous photographer for *Life* magazine
and an habitué of Downtown. He had dinner there, I would say, every night
and sometimes would stay for the second and third shows. Always sat up
front. He was truly an artist, never cared about marketing his photographs
though he could have made quite a bit of money. The picture itself on the
page was what essentially mattered to Gjon.

He was born in the mountains of Albania and came to this country in
1923 when he was nineteen to study electrical engineering at MIT. He met a
Professor Edgerton when they were both speakers at an MIT symposium in
1939. Edgerton had just developed an electronic flash for taking pictures, and
Gjon began experimenting with the technique. That's how he invented his
stroboscopic flash photography. With this breakthrough he could take one
picture after another rapidly, capturing the movements of his subjects. When
he developed these pictures he could then reproduce one given moment of
the action. At that time, *Life* was developing a magazine which featured what
they called photo-journalism. Gjon's stop-movement photos fit right in.

Gjon had an enormous studio on the second floor of a five-story building on East 23rd Street, just off 5th Avenue. Once a year he threw a huge holiday party, with jazz greats like Billie Holiday entertaining his guests. One day, mid-1960s, a horrible disaster, the building caught on fire. A dozen firemen were buried beneath a caved-in floor. The building was totally destroyed. Gjon's photographic equipment was ruined, but, miraculously, two-thirds of his files were intact.

It seemed Mary was hardly settled in Downtown when the sad news came that Fats Waller had passed, December 1943. He had taken ill in Hollywood but didn't stay to get better. Instead he left for New York on the Santa Fe Chief train. He never made it back to New York. Apparently, he passed away on the train during its stop at Union Station, Kansas City.

Whenever he was in town Fats loved to pop into Downtown, kibbutz with the guys and sit in with them. We wanted to celebrate his life, so a few weeks later we honored him at a benefit for the Children's Fund of the *Amsterdam News*. Donating their talents, the many greats of piano jazz foregathered, James P. Johnson, the father of stride and Fats's teacher; Art Tatum, Count Basie, Teddy Wilson, Mary Lou Williams, Eddie Heywood, Willie "the Lion" Smith. The program was broadcast December 21, 1943 over radio station WNEW, which gave time and line costs as their contribution.

We had a different kind of celebration coming up, a fifth anniversary of Cafe Society Uptown. Ivan Black performed the duties of master of ceremonies. It was then that he announced his retirement from "this particular field of publicity." He would enter the field of public relations. I would miss my Boswell, so-named by *Variety*'s Abel Green.[12] Bob Dana, nightclub editor at the *Herald-Tribune*, wrote, "He has done a splendid job and we wish him well."[13]

Leonard Feather: *In 1939 I settled in New York from London. Ivan Black got me my job as his assistant in 1941. Even though it was not a good-paying job, it was lovely to be associated, even indirectly, with Cafe Society. Ivan was a very good press agent. He was a very enthusiastic man who really believed in what he was doing and did it most efficiently under difficult circumstances. He had to be aggressive. In those days it was pretty hard to be a press agent for a club like Cafe Society. There was so much, almost automatic, resentment against anything that smacked of integration.*

One thing happened when I was working for Ivan Black that was really important. He was able to get Hazel Scott on the cover, I think it was, of the Daily News's *illustrated section, which was an absolute* coup at that time. To get any black person anywhere except in the crime news or the sports news, you know, it was quite an achievement. Ivan worked hard on that.

He also got me a few assignments writing a piece about Louis Armstrong and a couple of other pieces for the New York Times, which was almost unheard of in those days. The daily press ignored jazz, or put it down, or made fun of it, largely because it was black. Even the white musicians got no publicity. Ivan really deserves a lot of credit for what he did because he really did have to fight every inch of the way. All those columnists that were around like Westbrook Pegler, Louella Parsons, Hedda Hopper—most of them, I would say—were very far to the right, and it was just infuriating to see how they would jump at anything that gave them a chance to attack Eleanor Roosevelt or anybody who was a little bit to the left of them.

My job with Ivan was a dual godsend, for it meant that I had regular access without payment to two clubs where I could hear Lena Horne, Hazel Scott, Teddy Wilson's band, and others of that caliber. Even when I stopped working for Ivan Black and got a slightly better job which paid $20 a week instead of $15 I still continued to go to both Downtown and Uptown. It was just marvelous. The ambience was just very pleasant, very friendly, with none of the hostility you might encounter on 52nd Street. For about the best part of 1940 I had a beautiful black girlfriend, Louise McCarroll, who was a singer. One time we went to one of the clubs on 52nd Street and they wouldn't let us in. I knew that would never happen at Cafe Society. Barney Josephson's gentle personality and liberal social attitudes were totally at odds with those of the typical club owners I had known.

I did not have a very intimate relationship with Barney. He was very kind and polite and very nice to my wife and me.

Jane Feather: Whenever I saw him, it's always like he was glad to see me. When you're someone's wife, you don't always get that treatment, like they'd go straight to Leonard, but, "Oh yeah, hi" [to me]. Barney was specially nice to me, a very warm, very generous person.[14]

Ivan Black passed away in 1979, age seventy-five, respiratory failure from emphysema. Whoever wrote his obituary in the New York Times knew Ivan well: "His own enthusiasm was the greatest tool in his publicity kit, and he was a frequent visitor to newsrooms, where he tried to and usually succeeded in persuading reporters and editors to immortalize those he mentioned."[15]

To Ivan's everlasting credit, it was his dedication and belief in what the clubs were about that got our stories and photographs into the class magazines, the big metropolitan newspapers, rotogravure sections, and syndicated columns. He understood that I wasn't bound by the convention of the nightclub business—scantily clad chorus girl lines, comedians telling off-color jokes. Above all, Ivan saw to it that our artists were treated with respect in the media.

"'I am, believe it or not, usually pretty shy.'"

Jimmy Savo left Uptown to appear in a Broadway show by Lerner and Loewe, *What's Up,* staged by George Balanchine. With such talent you'd have thought the show would be a smash. It closed two months after it opened in November 1944. Jimmy was due back for another year, but he wanted a vacation.

I found an extraordinary comedienne to pinch-hit for him, Imogene Coca.[1] The charismatic dancer Avon Long of *Porgy and Bess* fame would be on the program with her. I didn't audition Imogene. It wasn't necessary. I knew her work from Leonard Stillman's *New Faces* revues and from a supper club in the Fifties. The club was on the second floor of Theodore's Restaurant, which he would close at ten. Then Theodore would open his upstairs room as a club, which he named Reuban Bleu. He knew nothing about entertainment or music so he engaged Herbert Jacoby to run the club. Julius Monk, who had some taste for entertainment, took over and ran it for many years, which is when I saw Imogene. She was a perfect replacement for Jimmy. She, too, had a wistful quality—large, dark eyes.

Imogene Coca: *I do a lot of pantomime. I don't even realize I'm doing it. I guess Barney maybe related that to Jimmy Savo. I'm not comparing myself with Jimmy Savo, but perhaps that's why Barney thought I would be good to fill in for that month while Jimmy was vacationing.*[2]

When Jimmy returned I brought Imogene to Downtown. I asked if she would mind working Downtown. "Not at all, Barney. I'd love to."[3] One of her hilarious routines, "I. P. Wolf," was a take-off on the then-famous I. J. Fox Fur's radio commercial. To the tune "A Pretty Girl Is Like a Melody," she sang, "A pretty girl is even prettier when wrapped in gorgeous furs, in a sable or mink, she will look in the pink," wrapping herself in a ratty fur coat as she sashayed around.

> **Imogene Coca:** *The fur thing at Downtown I originally did at the Martinique. They had a line of girls all garbed in gorgeous fur coats. I'd come in and out between them with these terrible furs. But I said nothing. Then I went to a small club in Washington. I really didn't have much material then so I had to do the fur number by myself. There was just a pianist. I realized that in getting out of one coat and getting into another, all of which were piled on a chair, I had to fill in somehow. I found myself foraging for dialogue, using a lot of clichés. Suddenly I had dialogue going with the coats that evolved after I had played enough places. So by the time I got to Cafe, I had the dialogue. That was a fun number to do. I think those furs are still downstairs in the basement. The moths have probably had a ball.*[4]

Imogene had a routine, "Syncopated Sack-but," which I figured was one of her zany wordplays. No. She informed me there really was a medieval wind instrument, forerunner of the trombone.

> **Imogene Coca:** *I played—after a fashion—"Hold That Tiger" on the trombone. The number was called "I'm Slush-Pump Annie, the Girl with the Mean Trombone."*[5]

The great trumpeter Buck Clayton was in the band, playing for Imogene.

> **Buck Clayton:** *On the bill with us was Imogene Coca, who used to interest me with what she couldn't do with a trombone. She could make some odd sounds on that trombone.*[6]

> **Imogene Coca:** *My father was a conductor for the Keith-Albee vaudeville orchestra, and he was a third generation of musicians. I came from a family of musicians and actors. I'd go up with my father to the vaudeville house on Mondays before I went to school, and I'd sit in the theater. He'd rehearse the acts. Then, when I got a little bit taller and a little bit older, he'd let me hand out the music to the different musicians in his*

orchestra. Frank Black was the pianist in my father's orchestra and gave me music lessons.

The musicians at Cafe were absolutely wonderful. I had kind of complicated music, especially in the opera number. There was a lot from Puccini and a little from Debussy. Every night that show was played, and I was there a year and a half, they played so beautifully, so meticulously. And I think that reflects a lot on Barney because of his choice of people. He had a wonderful sense of theater, a sight for talent.[7]

Buck Clayton: *The audience was beautiful. There was so much spirit—in both places. I know that Cafe Society Downtown was for everybody that wanted to go, and then when they moved Uptown they wanted to go there, too. I took Rex Stewart's place. I don't think either John or Barney hired me. I think Rex hired me. He asked me if I would hold his job down 'til he got back, and he never came back so I was stuck there for two years with Edmund Hall, Cutty Cutshall, and a trumpet player, never heard much about this guy outside of the Village, Frankie Newton. We had a group Downtown, Kenny Kersey, Scoville Brown, Gus Johnson. Sometimes the memories all merge together. . . . You can pick me up on dates. They all seem to merge into one.[8]*

Imogene Coca: *To tell you how marvelous everybody was, we would all dress in the same room—this could really test everybody's nerve. Some of the musicians would come in and have something to eat. Then it would be time for the show, and you learned to undress without exposing anything. We'd go right on with our conversation and talk about happy things, sort of enjoyed it—sort of? We did enjoy it. It was sheer magic. I was very often the only off-beige person in that group, but we all loved each other. One night we were dishing some white people, and they suddenly looked at me and started to laugh. Everybody had forgotten I was white, including me.[9]*

Susie Reed: *Imogene was tiny and funny and nice. She tried to try out new material. It was the hardest thing for her because once you get secure it's very hard to bring in new material. She would schedule it, plan it, rehearse it, get all ready, and then not do it, chicken out. She's very shy, the kind of person that if she hadn't had a character to hide in she probably wouldn't have pushed herself enough to do it.[10]*

Imogene Coca: *Phil Spitalny and his All-Girl Orchestra was opening at* *the Paramount Theater, and John Hammond brought him down to the cafe. Phil wanted me to work with him. I thought, "Ah, the Paramount. They wouldn't understand what I was doing. They'd kill me." So I told him, "I don't think I'm right." "Yes, you are." "I don't really think so." "Yes, you are." So I went up to see the people at the Paramount. I'm not a very good businessperson, but the money they offered was ridiculous. I really didn't want the money. I just wanted* out *because I was afraid to get on that stage. They said, "Look, Spitalny is a very strong-willed man, and he insists that you just sign the contract and get it over with. We agree with you. You're not going to do anything here," which was a* big *help.*

I did the show and stopped it. And Phil Spitalny brought me back again and again. "Do you like her?" And the audience applauded. "You'd be shocked if you knew how little they're paying her and what they're getting away with." I did very well there. Isn't that amazing? But apparently Barney thought that I would and so did Mr. Hammond, and I did.

I doubled at the Paramount. I did five shows a day there and three at the cafe. Johnnie Garry would help me get the props up to the Paramount, and after the last show he'd get them down to cafe. He had a personality that was just bubbling all the time. He was typical of the kind of people who worked there.[11]

Buck Clayton: *Johnnie Garry'd clean up every night and have it ready for the next night. There was an Indian fellow who worked with him. We had a craps game that would go on from five o'clock in the morning 'til eight or nine o'clock. The whole band. And this Indian fellow, he was a colonel in the Indian army, whenever he started to line the shoes up like military fashion we knew it was time to go home.*[12]

Imogene Coca: *The way I'm talking today, it's like I've known you [TTJ] all my life. I am, believe it or not, usually pretty shy. Was Barney a little on the shy side? We didn't talk much, but he was always very nice to me and made me feel, somehow, silently, that everything was fine. Well, the very fact that he kept me there so long. It was like doing a show for a very established producer. Barney enhanced my career. Oh yes!*

I didn't have a contract with Barney. In a way it's a good thing because you don't feel too tied-in. Barney would have had to change my mind entirely because I knew it was time to go. That was a long run. You're very grateful for having had a job that you really thoroughly en-

joyed. I think that's an essential part of any kind of work, to be around people with whom you have fun and still be very businesslike.

Barney gave you a sense of security. If you're somebody who isn't terribly secure anyhow, they can very easily make you question whatever you're doing. If Barney ever did make a suggestion, it was done in such a way that he was giving you an idea for another number. You take two people who suffer from shyness, but somehow I think we understood each other.[13]

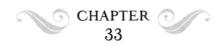

CHAPTER
33

"'Mr. Josephson, you are asexual.'"

We were still at war when news of President Franklin Delano Roosevelt's sudden death of a massive cerebral hemorrhage on April 12, 1945, in Warm Springs, Georgia, saddened the nation. His life was snatched away three weeks before the unconditional surrender of Nazi Germany.

He did not live to witness the horror and disbelief of the American GIs who helped free the skeletal survivors of the Buchenwald and Dachau concentration camps in Germany. Nor did he know that Adolph Hitler and Joseph Goebbels and his family had committed suicide in an underground bunker in Berlin. Nor did he give the command to the dropping of a single bomb on Hiroshima, Japan [August 6, 1945] and another, three days later, on Nagasaki.

Late into the war, the city had imposed a midnight curfew.[1] Because of the curfew, instead of three shows a night we had two, one at 8 and the last at 10:30. Having broken off with Izabel some years ago, been turned down by Lena, I had not found another woman who interested me sufficiently to have any committed relationship. I was living alone in a three-room apartment on East 39th Street.

One evening, friends of mine, Bobbie and Joe Weinstein, came into Uptown with another woman whom they introduce as Mrs. Hirsch. I was a single man, and I was looking to get married. I was looking at women with that thought in mind. I no longer wanted to be single. I was forty-three years old. When I heard "Mrs." I didn't pay any attention to the other woman. I didn't look at her twice.

With the curfew, places had to be closed, the people out, the premises dark by midnight. It was getting on twelve o'clock. The bartenders are closing the bar. We're finished for the night. Bobbie doesn't want to leave. "Gee, Saturday night. Go home at twelve o'clock? It's too early." They have this beautiful home, everything in the world there, but they want to stay out.

"Okay, Bobbie. I'll tell you what. Wait until everybody is gone and the place is dark. I'll take out a bottle of Scotch, and we can sit and talk as long as you like."

Everybody's gone. I still haven't looked at the other woman. I walk over to the bar. I'm not aware I'm being followed. I sling my ass onto the bar and slide around on it to jump down to the other side. I get out my keys to open the bar lock when I heard this deep voice drawl, "Mr. Josephson, you are asexual." Now what can a man say to that? So I go, "Uh huh." That was my retort. I got the bottle, went back to the table. We had some drinks. An hour or so later the three left. The next day the challenge bothered me, so I called Bobbie Weinstein. "Tell me about this Mrs. Hirsch."

"Sylvia's married, has a child with her husband and two more children that are his by a former marriage. He's in the navy. They're going to be divorced. It's all settled. He's going to take his children to California, where he lives when he comes out of the service. She's staying here with her child."

I thought. "I don't want to be involved with any husbands." Bobbie read my mind. "You want to call her? Here's her number."

I call. "This is Barney Josephson. I wasn't quite sure what you meant by that word last night so I just looked it up in *Webster's*. What time are you free this evening?"

"Well, before I get the three girls fed and bathed and put to bed it's ten o'clock."

"I'll see you at ten o'clock. What's your address?" At ten o'clock I was there, and before eleven o'clock I proved to her that I was not asexual.

I was smitten with Sylvia's little girl, Claudia. I enjoyed buying her pretty clothes, playing games with her, taking her ice-skating at the rink in Rockefeller Center. That is, I hired an instructor and sat with a drink, watching her. I melted when she put her little hand on my cheek and asked, "Are you going to be my daddy?" You know what? I married that woman.

"I notice Adam eyeing Hazel."

Hazel Scott is now twenty-five years old and has been a star at Cafe Society for all seven years. I was like a father to her. She didn't interest me in any sexual way. Besides, I had a strict rule for myself—never, ever date a woman who works for you. I always abided by it. First of all, it's a good business principle. You don't fool around with your employees. Second, and especially if she was black and how I felt about Negro people. It would be such a grossly unfair advantage for a white-man boss to force himself on a Negro woman, be she housekeeper, performer, whatever. It wouldn't enter my mind to want to do that.

I would warn Hazel about all the men trying to make it with her, the musicians, the drunks, the dope hounds. As for the society guys and Hollywood stars, "These guys are not for marriage; they're for play. You'll only get the worst end of it. Don't get involved." Adam Clayton Powell Jr. would often come to Cafe Society. He was in the process of getting a divorce from Isabelle Washington, who, before her marriage, had been in the chorus line of the Cotton Club and an actress on Broadway.

I notice Adam eyeing Hazel and decide to talk to him. I knew him well from the political end. "Adam, you know what I am to Hazel?" "I think so, Barney." "Are you really interested in Hazel, or are you just screwing around?" That was pretty straightforward I thought. "No, I'm serious." I clapped my hands. "Then I'm the man who can help you." I went upstairs to Hazel's dressing room on the third floor. "Adam says he's serious about you. There's a man for you, the kind of fellow I've been telling you that you should have, who is worthy of you."

From there on the romance blossomed. The time came in 1945 when Adam Clayton Powell proposed to Hazel Scott and she accepted. Adam was living in the Abyssinian Church rectory. He had been divorced only a short time prior to this. Under New York State law at that time you had to wait a certain length of time before you could re-marry after the divorce had been granted. Hazel and Adam were anxious to get married and didn't want to wait for the time limit, so they had to leave New York to get married. It was legal to marry in Connecticut. They decided to go to Stamford for the marriage ceremony in a church there. Since Hazel's father was no longer alive, and I, in a sense, had taken his place, I was elected to give the bride away.

Adam took charge. "Hazel will leave with her mother from White Plains. There's a road to Stamford from there. You, Barney, will leave with me. Charlie Buchanan will be my best man." Charlie was a big-wig in Harlem. "Charlie and you and I and my dad will meet at our church."

Adam Senior was a fine gentleman. He was the son of slaves, born in a log cabin in Virginia. Under his leadership the Abyssinian Baptist Church on West 138th Street was built and went on to house one of the most celebrated black congregations in the world. He was a well-known social advocate. During the depression his church fed thousands of meals to the poor, regardless of color. He had been the church's pastor for thirty years before turning the pastorship over to his son. I went up to Harlem, and we all got into the limousine. Adam put Charlie Buchanan and his father in the back seat. I was put up front with Adam. The chauffeur was behind the wheel. I was in the middle and Adam on the outside.

Before the marriage I had turned everything over to Hazel. I had handled her finances entirely, all of her money, invested it, banked it. I had put a lot of her cash into War Bonds. It was the thing to do. I had all her possessions insured, her jewelry, her furs, so I knew what their value was. I had paid $7,000 for the house in White Plains, a six-room house with a basement which I had finished for a few thousand more. All of this with the money Hazel had earned over the years. She had started with me at $65. By 1943 she had risen to $1,500 a week. I made certain that her money was preserved, not spent foolishly. I never took one cent in any kind of fee.

When I turned over the accounting to Hazel I told her, "You don't need me any longer. You're marrying a man who is quite competent to take care of your affairs. You'll be the wife of a member of the House of Representatives in Washington and the wife of a minister, the rebbetzin, in Yiddish, the rabbi's wife." Hazel understood this because she spoke Yiddish pretty well. She grew up on Intervale Avenue in the Bronx and played with the white kids. She was in and out of their homes all the time and picked up a lot of Yiddish.

"You're not going to work for me anymore. As the wife of a congressman and minister you can't sing in saloons," as I called my cafes. "You'd be criticized for that. You can make all the money you'll need working in films, making theater appearances. Your records sell. I'll arrange a concert tour for you. This is a whole new avenue. Popular artists are going out on these tours, the Andrews Sisters, the Boswell Sisters."

We're on our way to the church in Stamford, driving on the Merritt Parkway, and Adam turns to me, "You know, Barney, I had an insurance man go over the policies you bought for Hazel and the cash surrender for this insurance is worth," and he names a figure. "I had a furrier appraise all her furs," and he names a figure. "I had all of Hazel's jewelry appraised," and he gives me the grand total of their value. "I had a realtor appraise the house," and he tells me its worth. It was already worth much more than what I had paid for it originally.

Adam was not reading any of this from any paper. It was coming right out of his mouth—the jewelry, the furs, the house. Then he went over all the War Bonds in the safe deposit box. He had added those up and gave me their exact total—so many thousands of dollars. Then he gives me the grand total. "You know, Barney, I didn't realize it was so much." Those were his exact words.

Now Adam Powell was a very well-to-do man. He had a Cadillac and chauffeur. He was a Congressman and the pastor of a well-endowed church. His father was a wealthy man, and Adam was his heir. Negro ministers have a different relationship to their churches than white ministers, who usually get a meager salary, a little house adjoining their church, and are paid by their vestry. In the Negro community, ministers control all the money. Any way you looked at it, Adam was not a poor man. When Adam Senior retired in 1937 the church's membership was over fourteen thousand, with assets in the neighborhood of $400,000, a huge sum in those days. And all the way to the church Adam Powell Jr. was counting Hazel Scott's money. I said to myself, "Barney Josephson, Adam Powell is marrying your daughter for her money." I was in shock and disgusted with this man.

We got to the Bethel A.M.E. Church in Stamford, but not before we had a flat tire on the parkway. We were a half-hour late. Hazel looked lovely in a knee-length white dress and carrying a bouquet of roses. It was a simple double-ring ceremony at noon. Pastor Reverend Sims married them. It was fast, and we drove back.

I had promised Hazel, "Kid, when you get married I'm going to throw you the biggest party you ever saw. We'll have the reception at Cafe Society Uptown in the afternoon. I'm not going to invite anybody. You do the inviting, your list of friends and Adam's." I asked my printer to show me a book of wedding invitations, which I turned over to Hazel. "You select what you want and have it printed. I'll pay."

They sent out the invitations. I didn't know or ask how many went out, but they knew exactly how many people Uptown could accommodate. There was a big sign which you couldn't avoid seeing: *Seating not more than 341 people.* Well, they sent out the invitations to everyone way the hell and back, three thousand invitations. I know. I paid the bill.

When we got back from Stamford and approached Cafe Society, 58th Street and Park Avenue were closed off to traffic. You could not go through the block going east. A line of people had formed five and six abreast from 57th Street and Park Avenue at the Hotel Ritz Tower, going down to 58th Street to the entrance of Cafe Society. Another line back to back on 57th Street, going down to Lexington Avenue and up 58th Street, meeting. Two lines converging on Cafe Society, those invited. Police there. I was stunned. I finally got inside.

What we had done in the back room, the one with the high ceiling, was to remove all the chairs. We had many tables pushed together into one long table down the two long sides of the main room. The tables were covered with cloths and flowers, and my chefs in their tall white hats and aprons were serving the food. I had a full staff of waiters, twenty-five of them, all on duty, passing out cocktails and champagne. My manager came running over to me. "Do you see that line out there? What'll I do about the champagne?"

"Look, I asked for it, and I really got it. Let's be sports. Get all the wine from the cellar and let it flow." The next thing I hear someone saying over the microphone, "Ladies and gentlemen, there are thousands of people lined up outside around the block trying to come in. They were also invited. When you have paid your respects to Congressman and Mrs. Powell and you've had your refreshments, please leave so that others can come in." This embarrassed me. It sounded just awful. My place had been taken over.

Alma Scott, lovely lady that she was, had a wedding cake made. It was so big and heavy that it came on an open truck and was brought in on a tablelike platform. The delivery men just set the entire thing down, left, and came back for it the next day. The cake was enormous, must have been thirty-six inches in diameter, with many tiers. On the top tier were the usual bride and groom, Negro figures. The cake was modeled after the White House in Washington. The interior was hollowed out so you could see some of the rooms on the first floor. There in the reception room or whatever stood a white toy grand piano. Seated on the piano bench was a little brown-skinned doll.

I had asked Ivan to write a press release for *Life* magazine, hoping they would cover the reception with pictures as an exclusive. But now, seeing this White House cake, I hoped *Life* wouldn't photograph it and that none of the press would describe it. Even though Alma had ordered the cake, the press would give Adam "credit" for the idea. I'm not at all certain it wasn't. It would not have been Alma's. The cake was not for eating, just for viewing. My baker had prepared little boxes with ribbons, containing slices of cake which each person could take home.

The other photographers had been asked to wait until the *Life* photographers finished. "This arrangement was far from pleasing to the other photographers, who complained that they had no time or inclination to wait and that they had deadlines to meet." Adam and one of the press photographers got into an argument. Adam asked a policeman to eject him. "The argument, the ejection and the walkout followed in that order." *The New York Times* ran the story under the heading "A. C. Powell Jr. Wed with Difficulties."[1] *Life* did take pictures of the couple looking lovingly at each other and ran a full page with six or eight photographs.

Aside from the bill from the printer, Adam had the nerve to send me a bill for the postage as well. I paid for that, too. That was the topper. This horrible man who was so well-off, to pull something like this wedding reception. He had gotten a wife who had money, and he knew her capacity to earn it.

In February 1939 the Daughters of the American Revolution [DAR] had refused the world-renowned contralto Marian Anderson, permission to sing in Constitution Hall in Washington, D.C., because she was Negro. Eleanor

Roosevelt, the First Lady, was so angered that she resigned her membership in the DAR and urged Secretary of the Interior Harold Ickes to arrange for another location for the concert. On Easter Sunday, Miss Anderson sang on the steps of the Lincoln Memorial with the seated statue of Abraham Lincoln behind her and seventy-five thousand people before her, with millions listening on the radio.

As I had promised, I set up a concert tour for Hazel. Six years and five months after the surrender of the Nazis to the Allied forces, the DAR again refused the use of Constitution Hall for a concert to another Negro artist, Hazel Scott. "The D.A.R. in a statement said the decision to restrict the hall to 'white artists only' was adopted in 1932. The rule . . . was in line with the 'prevailing custom in Washington, D.C., regarding schools, auditoriums, theatres, hotels, restaurants, clubs, canteens, playgrounds, etc.'"[2]

Adam sent President Truman a telegram protesting. Truman replied, deploring the action, but said he could not interfere with a private organization. In an editorial, *The New York Times* pointed out that "the D.A.R. is not altogether private. It exists under a Congressional act of incorporation for the purpose, among others cited, of 'securing for all mankind the blessings of liberty.'"[3]

Clare Boothe Luce, who at that time was a Congresswoman from Connecticut, sent a telegram to her local DAR chapter, which found its way into *The New York Times:*

> Like all Daughters of the American Revolution, I am very proud to belong to an organization, the purpose of which is to cherish the memory of our ancestors who fought in the War of Independence. But I hope I have not forgotten why our ancestors fought. They fought to be free from the humiliation and oppression of political inequality. And when they had won their liberty, they founded in liberty's name a nation dedicated to the cardinal principle that all men are equal in the eyes of our Government.[4]

There were no restrictions at Carnegie Hall. On November 26, 1945, Hazel gave a recital there before a large, enthusiastic audience.[5]

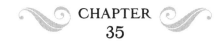
"'Ladies and gentlemen.
This is a zither.'"

I mogene Coca phoned my office one morning. Her father was very ill in the Midwest, and she had to go to him immediately. She was an only child, and they were very close. A few weeks before, Jemy Hammond had called and told me about this sixteen-year-old girl who was a marvelous folk singer, Susie Reed by name. "Jemy, send her down."

Susie Reed: *I used to live in Greenwich Village, and I played the Irish harp and zither for fun and sang old English, Scottish and Irish songs. . . . A neighbor asked me to sing at a birthday party they were giving for Jemy Hammond. . . . She heard me and said, "I want to take you to Barney Josephson." She made an appointment . . . I sang for Barney. . . . He said, "I think we should design a kind of act for you. We'll get you some nice dresses that suit what you're doing. Then in the fall you can open in Cafe Society Downtown."*[1]

Imogene had to leave immediately. I thought of Susie Reed. My secretary called Susie and asked if she could go on that night.

Susie Reed: *I said, "Sure." Then I called my mother, Isadora Bennett, who was the press agent for Ballet Theatre and a very busy mother. She had been the first woman reporter on the* Chicago Tribune. *Charles*

MacArthur was at the desk next to her.[2] I told my mother, "I forgot to tell you, but a few weeks ago I auditioned for a very nice man who has a night club and he wants me to go on tonight." "You what!?"

Ed Hall, the clarinetist in the band, announced, "Tonight Imogene Coca can't be with us." And there was a big "ohhh." "But we have little Susie Reed, who's gonna sing folk songs with a Jews' harp." It was that unprepared. Barney said, "Bring out one of the bar stools for her to sit on. We've got to get her higher than the audience." And that's the way my act went on. I wore a very simple dress. My mother said, "Simple, simple, simple. No jewelry." I had to have my dresses made. I needed a fuller skirt because I had to climb up on that high stool.[3]

"Ladies and gentlemen. This is a zither." When she opened with those words she broke up the house. They just howled. Most of them had never heard of a zither, never seen a zither. She had introduced herself this way when she auditioned, and I told her to keep it in. With her long, red hair, freckled face, unaffected little-girl manner—she looked younger than sixteen—and her pure voice, Susie was an immediate sensation. So I felt comfortable telegraphing Imogene, "Stay as long as you need to. We've got you covered."

Susie Reed: *I just sang the songs I had been singing, the most unusual, the least well-known of the old, old British ones. And I did them just as purely as I could. I didn't adorn them at all. . . . "And now I'm going to sing a song entitled, 'Lord Randall.' His sweetheart fed him poisoned meals. I don't know why but she did."[4]*

Susie had just about completed her first week. Gjon Mili, up front as usual, eating his dinner, never looked at her, just at his plate. "What am I doing wrong?" she wondered. One evening he caught her as she was walking toward the dressing room. "You know, you're not truly a singer." "Oh, really?" Susie didn't know how to respond. "No. You're an actress." This was Gjon's way of complimenting her, but Susie thought it was just an awful thing for him to say.

Susie Reed: *Later I got to know Gjon Mili, and I got to know that his manner was very unlike him. I think he had a very strange other world he lived in, where he really lived. He ended up very badly, in an institution. A lot of* Life *magazine people used to come to Cafe Society and* *sometimes stay afterwards, after it closed, after the 2:15 show was over. Barney would have a big, long table, and they would sit and talk.*

Barney was so good to me. My voice was not very big, and he had no service while I was singing because of the rattling of dishes and glasses. I was once talking with Barney about that. "What a nice thing to do." "Well, it wasn't just for you. I have the waiters go around before you go on and tell the customers, 'Miss Reed is about to sing. If you want to order a drink, there's no service while she's on. So then they would order doubles. It helps me too.'"

Barney was the most loving, quiet, gentle—no phoniness, no show biz honey, darling. He was just the most gentlemanly, civilized—or I'm sure my parents would never have let me do it. I'm sure no other club in the world would have wanted me except his audience. They had learned that if they went to Cafe Society they would hear something different and something new. It was probably the only place in New York that you went to hear the entertainers. You didn't go to take your secretary out or get smashed. You really went to see talent. Those of us who came in later benefited from that reputation.[5]

Jed Harris, the Broadway boy genius producer and director, had become somewhat of an habitué at Downtown. One night he walked in as Susie, who had just been with me a few weeks, was completing her introduction. I greeted him, "Good evening, Jed." He walked right past me, went up the center aisle in front of everybody; didn't care who was sitting there; stood right in the middle, practically on the stage. It would be like walking down the center aisle in a theater and standing at the footlights, blocking the actors. He folded his arms, listened to her, came back to me, snapped, "She's too good for you. She doesn't belong in this place." Well, Jed had this reputation.

Jed's flaying puts me to mind that despite all the accolades bestowed upon me, I had my own share of miscalculations and flops.

"Barney, there's this wonderful singer singing behind a bar in a saloon in Harlem. You should catch her." I always heeded John Hammond. Cabbed up there, had a drink or two at the bar, and listened to the singer. She's making asides, wisecracks, talking out of the side of her mouth. Her patter between numbers bothered me. I thought, "John must be out of his mind. This woman is a bit of a Tom."[6] I was always very careful about presenting black artists who didn't have the proper dignity to reflect their race well. I rejected this singer. I saw her perform, and I went back to the cafe. Before you know it, she's a big hit on Broadway in *St. Louis Woman*. She was Pearl Bailey.

One night a man walked into Uptown, a Ford dealer from Chicago. He was a great jazz buff, flying into New York just to go to jazz joints, mine among them. This night he informs me, "You think you've got such a great thing with Hazel Scott? We have a gal in Chicago who can wipe up the floor with Hazel Scott. She plays rings around Hazel. Her name is Dorothy Donegan."

Next night I'm at the airport on my way to Chicago. I cab to the saloon on the North Side. I don't like her for nothing. She did play better than Hazel. She was a virtuoso at the piano, but she was so vulgar in her performance, her manner, her style. She'd come out onstage with the spotlights on her, wearing a see-through dress, but really see-through. The lights hit her, and she's got no panties on, naked underneath. Why do a thing like that? Heard her, went right back on the next plane to New York. She's done all right but never what she should have gotten.

Carol Channing bombed for me. I fired her, really fired her. She did songs and take-offs of society dowagers and one of Ethel Waters singing "Cabin in the Sky." Now impersonations require exaggerations. When she auditioned and did that bit I explained, "Look, Miss Channing, you're working here with Teddy Wilson, Big Sidney Catlett, and all the other black musicians. They're not going to like this, and I don't either. You can do everything else but please don't do this Ethel Waters bit."

She opened and laid a bomb every show. In view of what had happened at the audition she must have thought I took away her best piece of material and that's why she wasn't doing well. One night after she laid another bomb, she turned to Teddy Wilson and said, "Cabin in the Sky." Without my permission, after telling her not to do it, she does the Waters routine. It was very, very bad. When she came off I didn't waste any words: "I told you not to ever do that piece. Take your two weeks' notice."

CHAPTER
36

"I'm being more temperamental than John Barrymore."

take risks, and like all gambling, you win some, you lose some. Well, I do strange things. I get a letter from a GI in the U.S. Army, stationed in France. He was from New York and had been an ardent fan of Cafe Society Downtown. I didn't know him. He wrote about this wonderful, talented, beautiful gal in Paris who plays the piano and sings. If I think I have something in Hazel Scott, this young lady can wrap rings around her. I asked him to send any recordings she may have made and photographs. I figured if she was really so good, she'd be good for publicity because her name was Moune de Virel, and this had a royalty ring to me.

The GI sent me records and photographs, and she looked and sounded pretty good. I decided to chance it. She would be the first French entertainer to come over since the end of the war. Robert Dana, in the *Herald-Tribune,* was intrigued. "Leave it to Josephson to pull somebody new and different out of a world treasure trove as yet untapped."[1]

When one brings talent from Europe, you pay their passage both ways. Moune arrived December 21, 1945, aboard a French ship, *Le Groix,* which she had booked and which took three weeks to cross a rough Atlantic. She arrived with no clothes other than what was on her back and a small suitcase. She had been part of the French underground during the war, with a diet consisting mainly of beans, potatoes, and black bread, and now was quite impoverished. She was of Guadeloupean descent, the great-granddaughter of a French count who had rebeled against his family's Royalist ideas. He had taken himself off to Guadeloupe and married a native Negro girl. Many of the songs in Moune's repertoire were written by her mother and grandmother. Moune would be in good company at Uptown with Imogene Coca, Mary Lou Williams, Susie Reed, and concert baritone Larry Winters.

Just at this particular time I receive a call from the *March of Time*. In the 1930s and 1940s *Time* magazine had this film division which featured current news and stories. They were planning to do a newsreel feature on nightclubs and would like to do me and Cafe Society. In those days, movie houses would show a short, a cartoon, a *March of Time* newsreel, all on the same bill with a full-length Hollywood movie.

The director of the film came to see me to talk over the filming. He wants to know about my background, experience, everything about me. He told me he used to direct John Barrymore in films in Hollywood. Moune was one of the first imports from Europe after the war. Since she was my new discovery he asked me about this Moune de Virel. "How do you work with talent that they become such big stars? What do you do?" "Well, often I dress them." "What do you mean, you dress them?" "Many women and men starting out in show business don't have a wardrobe. They have no money. If it's a woman I walk her into Bergdorf-Goodman, go to the gown department, tell the saleslady, 'I'd like this woman gowned.' I gowned Moune."

In some instances they were black women. The way the saleswomen would look at me, thinking, Who's this sugar daddy with his young black mistress? They would come out with all their leftover gowns from four years ago, trying to pan them off on me. They didn't know I knew about style from my days in the shoe business. I'd have to tell them, "Don't bring me any of those postmortems. I want *now*."

Rehearsing Moune for the opening, I discovered she didn't know how to walk on and off the stage. She was very awkward. "What did you do?" asks the director. "I showed her how to walk." "Tell me how." "I take a book and put it on her head; tell her to put her shoulders back and to walk balancing the book, not to look at her feet as she walked, how to point her toes."

Next day the cameras come in. There was a hell of a big crew. It was being filmed in the daytime when we weren't open for business. We start to rehearse for the so-called tonight's grand opening. My porter, who helped with our lights, fixed the spotlight on the piano for Moune to play and sing.

The director tells me, "All right, I want you to fix her gown, the way it should flow." The lights come up, and the cameras start rolling. I did as I was directed.

"Now introduce her." I introduce her over the microphone. I ask her to come out. Then I tell her she is not walking properly, all that. "Now what do you do?" he asked.

I had already explained about the book on Moune's head. He made me take a book, put it on my head, and walk back and forth, walking like a girl, sticking out my chest like a bosom. I was a shy guy, and anyone who knows me well enough would know that I would be embarrassed with all of this. But I did it, and he was shooting all the time. Then I was directed to put the book on Moune's head. She has now learned how to walk on and off the stage. He tells me to drape her gown properly. Then he directs me to say, "Moune, you look beautiful. You look gorgeous. Nobody will be able to say you stink tonight."

"Mister, I don't speak that way. I don't use such language." Well, he hit the ceiling. I wasn't taking his direction. I took him aside. "Look, I want you to know something right now. You're shooting me doing things, being myself. Barney Josephson doesn't speak that way. Do you realize what you would have me say to a Negro woman? There are ignorant white people who think Negroes have a smell peculiar to them, which is untrue, and you want me to say that to her? I won't do it."

He was furious. "Goddamn it. I directed John Barrymore in films, and I never had so much trouble directing John Barrymore as I'm having directing you."

How do you like that? Some comparison, eh? I'm being more temperamental than John Barrymore. But when he shouted at me about John Barrymore, who was an idol of mine—I loved that actor, I thought he was the greatest in the world—I told him, "You can call the whole thing off," and I was dying for this publicity. It would be shown all over the country.

"All right. Go ahead. What would you say?" "Moune, you sound marvelous and look beautiful. When you step out tonight you're going to be the new star of New York. Everyone will say how wonderful you are." And then I walked away.

Moune was very pretty, but she had a hairy upper lip and legs. She couldn't speak much English, and I didn't know a word of French. My secretary spoke high school French, and she acted as interpreter. "Tell Moune she's beautiful, but the hairy lip, we have to do something about that." "Non, non, non," she can't. "Why?" she wanted to know. "Explain that here, hair on the lip is considered unsightly and not sexy." "Oh non. Tell monsieur that in Paris a hairy lip is very sexy." About shaving her legs, "Oh non, that is very sexy too."

So I compromised. I would get some pancake makeup, her color, and apply it on the hair above her lip. She agreed to that finally. Earl Wilson, the gossip columnist for the *New York Post,* heard about this brouhaha. Earl was a kind of a lout, and he ran a heading to a paragraph about this story, "Moune with the Moustache," a play on the words *man on the moon.*

Before she opened I had told Gjon Mili about her. He got excited about this new discovery of mine, came to the club, photographed her at the piano, singing. He was such an important photographer for *Life* that he didn't wait for assignments. He just did what he wanted to do. He'd bring in his photos and tell them, "This is what I've got. If you don't want to use it, fine." They usually used his photos because they were so good. Well, he brought in the pictures of Moune, and they went for them. They were going to do a big story on her.

After her opening I saw she was not going to make it.[2] It wasn't there. She was a flop, talentless, really mediocre talent. I thought, "I can't have this story in *Life.* I can't place myself in the situation with *Life* that I gave them a bad steer. I'm going to kill it."

I called the cafe editor and explained the situation. I wanted him to know how I felt about Moune. "I don't think she's worthy of this spread. I don't want to steer you guys wrong. She's a nothing talent." "Thanks Barney. I appreciate what you're telling me, but these photographs are so tremendous we don't care. We're going to run the spread."

Moune had four pages in *Life* magazine. There was one full page of her at the piano, Gjon's photographs were that great. The show biz paper *Variety* had a word, "Josephson, who has one of the most enviable records in modern-day biz as a talent developer, might do well just to write this effort off as a mistake. Moune shows evidence of neither voice nor selling quality."[3]

She lasted her engagement, six weeks, and then I let her go. Not quite. "Tell Monsieur Josephson that I want to go to bed with him," Tibal dutifully reported to me. "You explain to Moune that it's a principle with me. I do not sleep with any of my employees." "Tell Monsieur Josephson that after the last performance of my engagement she expects that I will accommodate her." I didn't.

Even had I wanted to, which I didn't, she already had herself a guy. She was a very smart little lady. Ellis Larkins was just a kid, about eighteen, still studying at Julliard when John Hammond told me about him. I had Ellis playing with a trio Uptown, alternating with Teddy Wilson's sextet. Here was this youngster, and Moune goes after him. She got Ellis to marry her, which allowed her to remain in the United States. She knew exactly what she was doing. This was Ellis's first marriage. They weren't married for too long. She wasn't able to get any gigs here so she went back to Paris.

From Paris, Django Reinhardt, the immortal gypsy jazz guitarist, was in this country, touring as a soloist with Duke Ellington. He had never been here. The war had intervened. Before he went back to France I engaged him to play for a month Uptown.[4]

Django was born in a caravan in Belgium. He never went to school. He thought his parents had picked up his last name traveling around Germany. By the age of fifteen he was already popular in Paris nightclubs. One day the caravan in which he'd been living with his parents caught fire. The two fingers of his left hand were so badly burned that he never regained their use. He practiced without them for over a year. When he was ready, he gave a recital in Paris and was a sensation. He was just nineteen.

Opening night, Nat "King" Cole, Lionel Hampton, Paul Whiteman, Illinois Jacquet, Maxine Andrews, whoever was in town, flocked to hear him, but not my patrons. He was still too unknown: "You still cannot believe that with his handicap, he can make that divine music. . . . His complications of rhythm, magnificent riffs . . . is only the product of real genius."[5] On his return he toured France in his luxurious caravan, visiting every gypsy encampment to play for his people.[6]

(top) Imogene Coca performing her take-off on the I. J. Fox Furriers radio commercial of the 1940s at Cafe Society, 1945. (Marcus Blechman photo, Billy Rose Theatre Division, The New York Public Library for the Performing Arts, Astor, Lenox and Tilden Foundations)

(bottom) Imogene Coca with her trombone, around 1945. (Roman Vishniac photo © Mara Vishniac Kohn, courtesy the International Center of Photography)

(top) The James P. Johnson band, Cafe Society Downtown, 1940. Johnson on piano. Left to right: Mauzie Johnson, drums; Joe Watts, bass; Gene Simon, trombone; Joe Thomas, trumpet; George James, tenor sax. (James P. Johnson Collection, Institute of Jazz Studies, Rutgers University)

(bottom) Pearl Primus in her "African Ceremonial" dance, Cafe Society Downtown, 1943. (Gerta Peterich photo, Jerome Robbins Dance Division, The New York Public Library for the Performing Arts, Astor, Lenox and Tilden Foundations)

(top) Josh White in performance, Cafe Society Downtown, 1944. (Roman Vishniac photo © Mara Vishniac Kohn, courtesy the International Center of Photography)

(bottom) Sarah Vaughan, early 1940s. (Collection of the Institute of Jazz Studies, Rutgers University)

(top) Jack Gilford performing "The Butler Did It" routine, Cafe Society Downtown, 1939. (Courtesy of Madeline Lee Gilford)

(bottom) Susie Reed with her zither; background left, Adolph Dehn mural on wall; Cafe Society Downtown, 1944. (Albert Freeman photo, Barney Josephson Collection)

(top) Barney, front table, seated center, with an unidentified couple, enjoys Mildred Bailey at Cafe Society Downtown, 1942. (Albert Freeman photo, Barney Josephson Collection)

(bottom) The Fletcher Henderson Reunion Band, Cafe Society Downtown, March 30, 1941. Left to right: J. C. Higginbotham, trombone; Buster Bailey, clarinet; Sandy Williams, trombone (partially obscured); Fletcher Henderson, piano; Big Sid Catlett, drums; John Kirby, bass; Henry "Red" Allen, trumpet; Benny Carter and Russell Procope, alto saxophones. (Charles Peterson photo, courtesy of Don Peterson) *(top)* Teddy Wilson in his early thirties, Cafe Society Uptown. (Author's Collection)

(bottom) Art Tatum, nonpareil, Cafe Society Downtown, 1940. (Charles Peterson photo, courtesy of Don Peterson).

(top) Sister Rosetta Tharpe, legendary gospel singer, December 22, 1940, Cafe Society Downtown. (Charles Peterson photo, courtesy of Don Peterson)

(bottom) Zero Mostel as "Senator Polltax Pellagra," Cafe Society Downtown and Uptown, 1942. (Harold Stein photo)

(top) Terry interviewing Ira Tucker of the Dixie Hummingbirds (Jericho Quintet at Cafe Society Downtown), March 12, 2003. (Photo courtesy of Mikie Harris)

(bottom) Django Reinhardt's opening night at Cafe Society Uptown, December 16, 1946. Left to right: Leonard Feather, Roberta Lee, Les Paul, Reinhardt, Lionel Hampton, Nat "King" Cole, Illinois Jacquet. (Photo courtesy of Lorraine Feather)

(top) Eddie Heywood, 1939. (Collection of the Institute of Jazz Studies, Rutgers University)

(bottom) Frankie Newton, early 1940s; old boardinghouse piano at right. (Collection of the Institute of Jazz Studies, Rutgers University)

(top) The Eddie South Trio, Cafe Society Uptown, about 1940. (Collection of the Institute of Jazz Studies, Rutgers University)

(bottom) "The Revuers." Left to right: Judy Tuvim (later, Judy Holiday), Alvin Hammer, Betty Comden, Adolph Green (kneeling), probably late 1940s. (Courtesy of John Cocchi)

Joe Sullivan's band, Cafe Society Downtown, 1939. Joe Sullivan on piano. Left to right: Johnnie Wells, drums; Ed Anderson, trumpet; Edmond Hall, clarinet; Danny Polo, tenor saxophone; Henry Turner, bass. (Collection of the Institute of Jazz Studies, Rutgers University)

(top) Big Joe Turner, the greatest blues singer of them all, early 1940s, Cafe Society Downtown. (Collection of the Institute of Jazz Studies, Rutgers University)

(bottom) Terry and Orlandus Wilson of the Golden Gate Quartet in front of his home, Paris, July 1993. (Author's Collection)

(top Interior of Cafe Society Uptown, 1943. (Herbert Gehr photo)

(bottom) Buck Clayton and John Hammond at Count Basie's funeral, New York, 1984. (Nancy Miller-Elliott photo, Collection of the Institute of Jazz Studies, Rutgers University)

CHAPTER
37

"'She can't sing.'"

I f I liked a performer and had faith in their talent, I didn't care
whether he or she clicked right off or not. I would stay with an
artist. John Hammond had become enthusiastic about a young
singer who had sung with the Earl Hines and Billy Eckstine bands
and arranged an audition for her in early spring 1946. She was kind of awkward, rather dowdily dressed, and had a gap between her front teeth. But
her voice! I had never heard such a voice. John Wilson, the *Times* critic, has
described it as a musical instrument with "soaring highs and incredibly full
lows." Her name was Sarah Vaughan. I hired her then and there. This would
be her first gig working solo.

Susie Reed: *I remember the night Sarah Vaughan tried out. I never*
heard anything like it, and I stayed and listened to her sing. I thought
it was the most wonderful thing I had ever heard because she sang like
an instrument, a clarinet. She did much more then than she did later,
improvising around the melody. When she started singing commercially,
she was much more on the melody of each song. She didn't play the
piano when she worked for Barney. She just came out and sang. She
was skinny, wasn't very attractive looking. I think Barney helped her
to dress. She did not have much presence or charisma. She was really
a diamond in the rough.[1]

Leonard Feather, the renowned jazz critic, lived on the top floor above Cafe Society Downtown, an elevator ride down, which he happily found most convenient.

Leonard Feather: *Right now it looks as though she's [Sarah] finally getting some of the things she had long deserved . . . a fine nightclub spot as a single. . . . Some of the people who listen to her at Cafe Society can't understand what it is that makes others rave about her. It isn't only one thing, but a combination of qualities; the ethereally pure tone, her instrumentlike sense of phrasing . . . the occasional effects she achieves generally toward the end of a song, by spreading one syllable over several notes and suggesting passing chords with these subtle variations on the melody.*[2]

Sarah was not a hit. She sings week after week, month after month. People would complain, "She can't sing and she's not even pretty." They protest my having her. Well, all right. They had a good show with my other acts, Pete Johnson, Cliff Jackson, J. C. Heard and his orchestra. I never had more than one performer who wasn't going over in a big way. And there was the orchestra for dancing. In general, I would say that Cafe Society attracted a rather intellectual crowd, knowledgeable about jazz. But they just didn't understand what Sarah was doing. By this time I had an appreciation. I learned a lot from John. I learn pretty fast.

I would talk to my customers. "Don't you know how this woman is using her throat like a horn?" "I always wanted to imitate the horns, Parker and Gillespie, they were my teachers."[3] When she sang, people were rude enough not to pay attention. One night Paul Robeson was in the audience. In his melodious baritone, which cut through the chatter in the room, and without getting up, he said, "Ladies and gentlemen, I would like to hear this lady. Mr. Josephson considers her to be a great talent. Give her the courtesy of your attention if you please."

Imogene Coca: *My first husband, Robert Burton and I went down to the cafe to see Sarah Vaughan. Bob was a jazz enthusiast and musician. That was the first time I'd heard her, and, oh boy, that was wonderful. There were a couple of tables around us, and they were quite loud. Bob wasn't the kind of person who would start a fight. But he certainly let them know by staring at them and shushing them.*[4]

Sarah had a frightening experience. She had left the cafe about four one early August morning and was walking to the 4th Street subway station on

6th Avenue with George Treadwell and our matron, Naomi Wright. At the entrance, a group of men started to call them names, chased them down the subway stairs, along the passageway toward the platform. Sarah told me, "One of the men swung at Naomi and missed. Then he kicked her in the side and hit her in the eye. Another one of the gang kicked me in the stomach and hit me with his fist on the lip. Then they left."

A few days later a similar incident happened to my band leader J. C. Heard, the great drummer. He had left Downtown about four in the morning and went to the Cube Steak restaurant on 6th Avenue near 3rd Street. He finished and went on his way to the same 6th Avenue subway entrance. A group of men accosted him. One of them knocked his hat off. When he bent down to pick it up, one of the group yelled, "Kick the nigger." He tried to defend himself, but they kept on punching him as they chased him down the subway stairs. Luckily, there were several black men on the platform. His attackers took themselves off fast.[5]

I kept Sarah for six months, hoping she'd catch on. I was determined. She was going to go out of Cafe Society recognized as the newest, greatest, most unusual singer ever since Billie Holiday. It didn't happen. Finally, I gave up. I was beaten. I let her out.

While Sarah was at Cafe Society she was going with George Treadwell, the trumpeter in my band. After she left Cafe Society, George gave up his career as a musician to manage her. Eventually, they got married.[6] Within months he gets her a recording date with a small music company. The record "It's Magic" is released. It's a smash hit on all the jukeboxes. In those days jukeboxes were the rage, and songs played on them could make performers stars. In every joint, young people are dropping in their nickels, listening to Sarah, hearing her voice. It's the number-one record for months on jukeboxes around the country. Disc jockeys pick up the record, play it on the radio, and she becomes famous overnight. Nobody can see her on the record. Today she's glamorous as hell. She looks good—and I haven't seen her since.[7]

CHAPTER
38

"'I just saw a woman singing to chairs on empty tables.'"

We had a large European population in New York, French especially, who had escaped from the Vichy government. By now many of our soldiers had been exposed to some of the European entertainment and culture. That's why I thought it would be smart to bring over foreign talent. I had the idea to bring over Josephine Baker, who, though not French, had been the toast of the Continent during the mid-1920s and 1930s. I knew she was still living in Paris.

I do crazy things. People think I think everything out carefully. Not so. Call it instinct for the right moment. One day I told my secretary, "Get the Paris operator and get me Josephine Baker." Just like that. An hour later I'm talking to Josephine Baker. "Hello, Miss Baker, this is Barney Josephson of Cafe Society in New York."

She never heard of Barney Josephson. Never heard of Cafe Society. I said I would write to her, send her some press clippings so she would better know who I was and what I was doing. Which I did. I got nowhere with her, made no impression.

One evening some months later, a wonderful woman whom I knew, Allene Talmey, one of the editors of *Vogue,* came into Uptown with her husband. We were chatting at the table, and Allene mentioned she was going to

Paris for the magazine the following day on an assignment. I told her about Josephine. "Barney, that's a grand idea." *Vogue* editors were always good to me. My artists always got their photographs in *Vogue*, and photographs in *Vogue* were more important than any written copy. The *Vogue* crowd loved Cafe Society and all the things I did there and were regular habitués. I told Allene I couldn't get to first base with Josephine. She didn't know who I was. "Give me her address, Barney. I'll go to see her for you."

She did. When she saw Josephine, she made her understand who I was, what I'd been doing in my cafes, the kind of places I had, that this milieu would be right for Josephine Baker. Coming from *Vogue* this was very impressive to Miss Baker.

Now I get a letter from Josephine Baker. I'm one of those fellows who doesn't save much, so I don't have the letter. But I do remember everything. Josephine sends me a two-page typewritten letter acknowledging the meeting with Miss Talmey. Now she knows for the first time who I am, the kind of man I am. She understands now that Barney Josephson is a great lover of humanity. "And I, too, am a great lover of humanity. I think we can get together and work something out." There was much repetition of "you love humanity, I love humanity." Then she comes to the point, comes down to business: "I'll be happy to come to perform at your cafe under the following terms and conditions. My wardrobe is absolutely fabulous. I couldn't possibly entrust my wardrobe to any American wardrobe mistress. I have to bring my own. The expense to bring her over and to pay her salary would have to be borne by you." That was condition one.

"I must bring my orchestra conductor, who will lead the orchestra that you have in your cafe." She wants to augment my orchestra with five or six of her musicians, "their salaries to be paid by you," that is, Barney Josephson. Salaries for her musicians she doesn't state. She doesn't know or ask what I have, a sextet or sixteen men. That was only the beginning.

She can't work without her arranger and her secretary, whose salaries I, Barney Josephson, would pay. Continued Miss Baker, "Since you are such a great lover of humanity, Mr. Josephson, and I am too"—again with this humanity thing—"I will cut my salary, and I will work for you for the very reasonable sum of $8,000 a week."

Now $8,000 a week just after the war would be like $160,000 today [1987]. Well, that wasn't for me. Her demands were way out. My place could not sustain such expenses. She hadn't been in this country in years. She must have had grandiose ideas about salaries, which stars could command the high figures. I could not believe it. I wrote back, "Miss Baker, how can you make these demands?" No response, and that ended Josephine Baker for me. I think she would have been a sensation here.

> **Jean-Claude Baker:** *The war had ravaged Europe. Don't forget, Josephine had so many lovers and protectors from 1925 that she had diamonds and jewels stuck everywhere in safe places. So, no, she was not making money in Europe, nowhere in Europe. What do you want? Belgium, France, all were broken. She never got $8,000 a week in her life. Josephine loved to play games. If Barney had been stupid enough, if you are fool enough, why not? You see what I mean? That's why I love Josephine. She's a crook, absolutely a crook all her life. But I give her a standing ovation because there are enough stupid people who get up and give her whatever she wants. So you can't blame her.*[1]

When Josephine Baker turned out to be unattainable I got to thinking, Who else? My eyes, still turned toward Europe, led me to Lucienne Boyer, the French chanteuse. In the mid-1920s, in her late teens she had been brought over here to sing in a musical revue on Broadway, produced by the Shuberts.[2] She was a big smash. Even before she came here she was a big star in Paris. She was much in demand and over the years had sung at a number of nightclubs here, the Rainbow Room at Rockefeller Center, the Versailles.[3] Her signature song, "Parlez-moi d'amour," sold hundreds of thousands of records in this country and abroad.

She hadn't been back in this country for over ten years—World War II. Now no nightclub wanted her. She was washed up. Too old. Pushing forty. But I thought differently. I got in touch with her and made an offer and she accepted. She agreed to come from France. Why did I do a thing like this? My clubs were always jazz-oriented, and here I'm importing a French chanteuse, singing only in French. Well, I felt this was the time. John [Hammond] hadn't been around, having been in the army for three years from early 1943 so I had been on my own. John wanted me to continue with jazz Uptown as well as Downtown, but I'd always had this hankering for a European-type cabaret.

I offered Lucienne $2,500. She accepted. She would bring over her own orchestra conductor, who would also play the violin to accompany her. She wanted to augment my band but on different terms from Josephine. She needed an accordionist. A French chanteuse must have an accordionist. I agreed. Where to find one? John Hammond, "I know a kid at Juilliard who's great. I'll get him for you."

Lucienne arrived the last day of January 1947 on the *S.S. America* with an entourage of six: her husband, Jacques Pils; her five-year-old daughter, Jacqueline; her governess; a personal maid; her orchestra leader; and her manager.[4] She also brought twenty pieces of luggage which included eighty gowns designed by French couturiers. None of this was at my expense.

What she didn't bring, however, were girdles, and she had gotten a bit plump. I sent her to Saks Fifth Avenue. She went there by bus as part of her sightseeing. Before she got off, everyone knew where she was going and why. She had even sung some songs for them. I threw a cocktail party in her honor at Uptown so she could meet the actors appearing in Broadway shows and, of course, the press.

Her first rehearsal was about three in the afternoon at Uptown. The chairs were stacked on top of the tables. The place was dark, with just a spotlight on the dance floor. She walked around the dance floor with a long cord attached to the microphone held in her hand and sang to the tables. I was there alone with the orchestra. She was still rehearsing when I ran up to my third-floor office and told my Gal Friday who handled advertising for me, "Hilda, I want you to prepare an ad to appear in all of the papers the day immediately following Lucienne's opening."

"Aren't you going to wait for the critic's reviews?" "No. I just watched part of Lucienne's rehearsal. I want the heading to read, 'The greatest artist I have ever had the honor to present. Barney Josephson.' A quote from me. I'm not waiting for the critics. Then at the bottom, under our name, in bold type, 'Reservations now being accepted for five weeks in advance.'" I had never done this for anybody.

Hilda protested, "Are you losing your mind?" "No. I just saw a woman singing to chairs on empty tables. This is what she did to me. This is what I want in the ad."

That's what I did. People began reserving five weeks in advance. Settling on $2,500 for Lucienne's salary presented me with a big problem. This sum was usually spread over a couple of acts. My solution. She would have to be the whole show.

"Lucienne, do you think you could stay on for about thirty minutes?" We did have a band for dancing. "Thirty minutes! It takes me forty minutes to warm up." At every show she was on for almost an hour, 9:15 and 12:30. Dinner would be served from 6:30 to 9:00; entrees from $2.75, with a $3.50 minimum.

In the prewar days all of Lucienne's performance gowns were of the same shade of blue, sort of a violet-sapphire blue, "Boyer Blue," a shade created for her by Jean Patou, the French couturier. The tradition went back to the color of the dress her mother had made for her at her debut in a small Parisian music hall, where she had stopped the show.

I staged the show. The lights blacked out. The violin sang the strains of "Parlez-moi d'amour," her theme song. Baby spotlights came up and focused on Lucienne in her Boyer Blue velvet gown, holding a corsage of orchids designed by the florist Irene Hayes, which hid the microphone. She wore no jewelry other than a slender bracelet and an enormous diamond ring. The audience gave her an ovation, which I had anticipated.

George Berkowitz: *Miss Boyer's dramatic entrance was well calculated to heighten the excitement, suspense and anticipation of the blue bloods, many of them from the French Colony, who were there to greet her. She is a beautiful woman with exquisite artistry and showmanship, the glamour of the theater personified. Her most thrilling quality is her voice, which is at various times soft and caressing, breathless, dominant and husky. It is kaleidoscopic in its change to suit the song she is singing.*[5]

She sang only one song in English. "To sing the songs in English I would have to speak slowly and lose so much. You must feel the song and feelings are the same in French or English."

Lucienne's return to New York was triumphant. I had an audience now that I never had before. The foreign crowd packed the place. The diplomats, the politicians, radio commentators, theater and movie stars, all were there. After opening night she told me, "Mon Dieu, I was nervous."

Danton Walker: *The toast of the town . . . her art has grown over the years . . . one of the world's loveliest creatures . . . held a night club audience enthralled for a solid hour.*[6]

Abel Green: *Lucienne Boyer's return to America is big show business news. There's no denying the intrinsic showmanship, basic talent and general appeal of the true artiste. . . . Miss Boyer will be a big Parisian noise in Manhattan in short order.*[7]

Lee Mortimer: *Cafe Society looked like its name. The opening night brought out all the regulars of the mink and diamond tiara set, including the penny-pinching refugees, the wealthy columnists and their wives, the lorgnette-lifters from Morocco, and that great friend of the common man (voter), Rep. Adam Clayton Powell. . . . Importing Mlle. Boyer was one of Barney Josephson's smartest moves. At the same time, he swept out all vestiges of his former policy from the floor show. Lucienne is all.*[8]

The all-male critics could not resist getting in a few wisecracks. Danton Walker: "La Boyer, a trifle older, a trifle plumper"; *Time* magazine: "The baby spotlights focused down on a singer whose face is familiar. It looked a little older now, and the figure—despite the best efforts of Parisian couturiers—was perceptibly heavier"; *The Billboard:* "She no longer is slim and the styling of her gown seemed to emphasize it"; Lee Mortimer: "She's ten years plumper . . . " [he ain't no gent . . .].[9]

I had a pretty good wine cellar, but my regular customers were not largely wine drinkers. They didn't know about years. They drank mostly Scotch and so forth. The Americans, if they ordered a bottle of champagne because they were celebrating an anniversary or a birthday, would ask for Piper-Heidsieck or Mums. Now I was selling this year '31, this year '28, and I was frantically calling my liquor suppliers to send me what they had in French wines, Bordeaux, Burgundy, champagne, whatever they had. I never sold so much wine.

Abel Green: *The Francophiles turned out on a blue Monday in mobs. And were sampling the grape like it was 7-Up. Josephson probably thought this was a misplaced July 4, according to the popping of bottles.*[10]

Ever since the opening of my clubs, no single entertainer had carried the program alone. I cut to two shows from three. I had cards printed for the tables: "No service during Mlle. Boyer's performance."

Lucienne was pleased with our accordionist (whose name I don't remember), so much so that after each show she would bring him down off the bandstand and, in French, say that in all of Paris, "I never had anyone like him." She would hold his hand and squeeze it. This was not just a show biz thing. She actually felt this way about this serious American accordion player. To me, "Monsieur, you aire so cute."

Business was spectacular, so much so that I was able to raise Lucienne's salary to $3,500 a week just a month later. Bringing in Lucienne was a big switch in policy. It had meant taking a big gamble. "For Barney Josephson's Cafe

Society Uptown this . . . marks a curious segue from the Hazel Scott–Jimmy Savo–Zero Mostel style of turn to the Gallic. It gives this bistro a surprisingly effective change of pace, give 'em the attraction and they'll come."[11]

> **John Hammond:** *Barney had a roving eye in those days. Sylvia [Hirsch] was apparently glamorous. She sort of corrupted Barney's taste, I thought. Barney was perfectly willing to buck the tide before, and she tried to make him go with the tide. To a degree, she succeeded. The trouble with Sylvia was that she tried to interfere with the entertainment policy of Cafe Society. She recommended society bands, and she wanted to have a strictly ritzy place. I couldn't stand it. I was in the army during some of the time, so I couldn't assert myself properly. When I came out of the army, I continued to work with Barney. There was nobody else to work with in those days. We had a wonderful relationship together. I still look back with pleasure on it.*[12]

> **Milt Gabler:** *I went Uptown to hear the music. A couple of trips was enough. It wasn't my kind of joint. Too fancy. It was a beautiful room, high ceiling. And he already was putting on a different kind of enter-tainment too.*[13]

Lucienne would throw roses to her audience at the end of each perfor-mance. The night Charlie Chaplin came in with his wife, Oona, Lucienne threw the rose to him as she bowed. Charlie rose from his seat, pantomimed smelling the flower with heavenly pleasure, and clasped it to his heart.

One evening Tallulah Bankhead arrived. After her performance, Luci-enne sat with her at her table. Tallulah spies a columnist, "Come here, I have a story for you. I want you to write that Miss Boyer is such a fine chanteuse that I'm left speechless." The reporter starts to write some notes. "On second thought," Tallulah stops him, "You'd better not put it that way, because if Tal-lulah Bankhead is ever speechless, *that's* a story in itself."

Another night Tallulah excuses herself from her table and begins to work the tables on her way to the powder room. Now every licensed cabaret must have a woman in attendance in the powder room and a man in the men's room. Things could happen in a nightclub if these rooms are unattended, not supervised. We had a nice little old lady in attendance. Whenever anyone left the place was always tidied up. That was her job, and she took care of it. She really did.

Tallulah, finished, descends the stairs in a grand manner, down the last step or two, and calls out to me. This is a distance of about twenty feet from the table where I was sitting. Tallulah, in a room with hundreds of people around, bellows, "Josephson, you communist son of a bitch, I just came out of your ladies' room. If you think I'm going to sit down on your wet toilet seat and catch gonorrhea or syphilis you're crazy." She doesn't stop there. "I haven't slept with a man in two years or with a woman in the last six months, and I'm goddamned if I'm going to sit on your toilet seat and get a disease."

This woman has such a filthy mouth. Now what do you do with her? Her father, William, was speaker of the House of Representatives in Washington, and Uncle John was a United States senator from Alabama.[14] Maybe she had heard some discussions about the Josephsons. Regardless of my political orientation according to Tallulah, she continued to be a patron of Uptown. She would come in with her Gal Friday, who carried her pills and looked after her.

"Oh god, I'm exhausted," she'd complain. So she's exhausted and asks for some sleeping pills. She wouldn't wait until she got home to take them because it takes time for them to take effect. She'd take the pills just as she was leaving. She lived in the country somewhere, and it was a bit of a drive. She had it all figured out. If she took them now, by the time she walked into her house she would be ready to flop into bed, go right off to sleep. She's taken her pills, but before she leaves a party of friends comes in. She doesn't want to go home. She knows, though, that she's going to fall asleep at the table in half an hour. She asks for some Benzedrine. Her secretary has an assortment of all kinds of pills, heroin, cocaine, a variety. She takes the Benzedrine and stays awake. Keeps on drinking. It was enough to kill her, but when she died it was of emphysema. That's the way she was.

Lucienne was the toast of the town, but for me she was even something more. During the war she and Jacques Pils had been part of the French underground, the Maquis, fighting the Nazis. I told her how much I admired her courage. "One did what one could. It was nothing. It was only normal. You can imagine how it was to be a personality in an occupied country. Your telephone was tapped, you couldn't move without being watched. The first time they arrested me, it was for hiding Jewish friends. They told me they knew everything about me—how I slept, how I ate—everything."

Her husband, whom she had married in 1939, had been an officer in the tank corps of the French army and was taken prisoner at the beginning of the shooting war with Germany. He became very ill and was released after a year in prison camp. Lucienne was able to get a pass to southern France, which was under the Vichy government. Their daughter, Jacqueline, was born there. Supposedly, this was unoccupied France, but in reality the Vichy government totally collaborated with the Nazis.

In an interview on the radio program *We the People,* she described how she had been seized by the German police in 1944 while she was singing a patriotic song at a benefit for the children of war prisoners. She had been liberated from the Gestapo headquarters by a woman attendant there. The woman had overheard the Germans planning to send Lucienne to a political prison in Bordeaux. She gave Lucienne to understand that she would leave a certain door open at a certain time. Lucienne escaped, and two days later the Maquis blew up the headquarters. On the air Lucienne appealed to the woman, who was now in the United States, "I must find you. I owe my life to you."

> *Mme. Lucienne Boyer's spring engagement at Cafe Society Uptown was perhaps the greatest single triumph of any café entertainer during the season. She sang, pantomimed and charmed a full house into docile silence twice nightly.*[15]

Business with Lucienne was booming. We closed June 28 for the summer. Lucienne went on tour, San Francisco, St. Louis, and other cities. She would return after Labor Day, September 8, and a salary of $4,000. Performers are paid according to their box office appeal. Lucienne was such a smash that I picked her right up for our fall season. I wasn't going to let anybody come in and grab her away from me.

"She took the check and flipped it back to me."

I did not neglect Downtown. I was in Hollywood in 1947, and Abe Burrows invited me to dinner at Jason's one evening. Jason's was a Lindy's-type restaurant and a popular place where writers, producers, and top actors ate. At dinner Abe mentioned, "There's a little party at Frank Loesser's house. Let's go over after dinner."

Some time during the evening Frank came over to me, "Come with me, Barney." He took me into his music room and put a record on his machine. "Who is that, Frank?" "A woman out here named Nellie Lutcher." "How do I get in touch with her?" "Well, this is a record which hasn't been released yet, made by Capitol out here. I have an advance copy because one of my tunes, 'The Lady's in Love with You,' is on the other side." Nellie wasn't singing his song, the one I was listening to was "Hurry on Down to My House, Baby, There's Nobody Home but Me." "I'll have Dave Dexter at Capitol get her down for you, Barney."

Next day I'm at Capitol Records. While I'm there, Dave played several other recordings of Nellie's, none of which had been released yet. I wanted her for Cafe Society.

Nellie Lutcher: *Dave told Barney he'd have to get in touch with me. At that time I was working in a little spot in Reno, Nevada. Dave called*

me to find out when I'd be home. We met in Dave Dexter's office at
Capitol Records, a little place, used to be here on Vine Street.[1]

Nellie arrives. Since this was a recording studio, they had loads of pianos. Nellie asked, "Do you want to hear me play?" "No, I heard your records. Tell me about yourself."

It seems she had been working in this nightclub. She was the piano act. The club was doing very badly. The Musicians Union knew of this because the owners were always late paying the musicians. They told the management that they would have to pay the musicians nightly so the musicians would only get stuck for one night's pay if they closed on them. That's exactly what happened. The place folded, so Nellie was out of a job.

"Miss Lutcher, what's the best money you've made out here?" "Well, on this job, which was about the best, I was getting $20 a night." So I had some idea of what she was earning. This was early June.

"I don't have an opening now, but I will have the day after Labor Day. I'll draw up a contract now giving you eight weeks at Cafe Society Downtown at $250 a week. We'll go from there. I'll pay your transportation to New York and back to LA. With this contract you don't have to feel you're coming in on speculation for a week or two and then have to go back home on your own." She was delighted. I had visions of making another star.

Nellie Lutcher: *I made the record in March, and it took about three months for the record to come out, which means it came out late June, I guess. So Barney was working fast because he wanted to start promoting. He didn't know if anybody else felt about Nellie Lutcher like he did. When he offered me $250, "That's all I can afford. I know that's not a lot of money," he said. "If you do well, if the business warrants it, I will pay you more. That's all I can promise you right now. You wouldn't go wrong, I can tell you that."*

The other people who had been there [at Downtown] were people already known in the city. All I had to go by was the strength of the records he'd heard. I didn't have a manager at that time, nor did I have an agent. I was just freelancing and working the local spots in Los Angeles. The way Barney had it figured out, I would have been there several months. That's the thing I had to think about because I was divorced and my son was a little guy. My husband wasn't the type to volunteer to do too much, just what the judge told him, something like $5 a week. . . . Finally, Dave Dexter said, "Nellie, you gotta *go while the iron is hot. Barney is calling me every day." So I went to New York and was a big success. If Barney had not been interested, who knows?*[2]

Before Nellie opened the week after Labor Day at Downtown, this one record comes out.[3] A singer is rated by how often their record is played on the jukeboxes. Her record, "Hurry on Down," is a big smash. It's being played on every jukebox in America. It's number one for months. From this hit record, Nellie's in great demand.

Nellie Lutcher: *Before I left Los Angeles, Dave had talked a manager into taking me on, Carlos Gastel, who was also Nat Cole and Peggy Lee and Mel Torme and Stan Kenton's manager. This was after I signed with Barney.*[4]

When Nellie opened, comedian Stanley Prager, Cliff Jackson, dancer Dorothy Jarnac accompanied by singer Hope Foy, and Dave Martin's band were on the program. I didn't have to do a thing to build her up. Nellie is already a big star, and I was paying her only $250 a week. Nothing was said. I had a contract and that was it. Had she not been coming from LA, in all likelihood she would not have had a contract unless she wanted one. *Variety:*

> *It's a safe bet that Josephson's Downtown branch will be doing boom business similar to the time he launched Lena Horne and Hazel Scott among others. Initial night had standees on a week night for the first time in many months, and will likely continue throughout Nellie Lutcher's run.*[5]

Downtown was a small place. My minimum was $1 week nights and $1.50 on Fridays and Saturdays. The seating was only 210. But you never got 210 seating because you would get threes on fours—three customers at a table for four—a single on twos. We did three shows a night, 9, 12, 2, and the late show was never crowded except on Saturdays and sometimes on Fridays. Nellie was selling out every night. The last night of Nellie's gig I called her into my little office and told her how happy I was with everything. I had made out a check for $1,000 as a bonus.

"Nellie, this should be ten times the amount, but this place can't do it. You see what it's like here." She took the check and flipped it back to me over my desk. "I don't want that."

I think she's displeased with it, insulted. So I started to make excuses. She interrupted, "No, no. I'm returning it because when you hired me I didn't have a job. How good was I and the band that was with me, that the club closed up on me and we all got stuck. You took me in, an unknown quantity, gave me more than twice as much pay and transportation both ways. You're entitled to make money off me. Do you know what I'm able to get now?"

"Yes, I know what you're being offered, $3,000 a week."

"Do you think you can extend my salary to $1,000 a week? I'll tell my manager he has to give you ten more weeks next season. Do you know why?"

"Why, Nellie?" "No white man ever gave a Negro anything, money especially, that he didn't have to give a Negro. You're the first one, and that's why I won't take that check now." I insisted.

Nellie Lutcher: *I took the money. I needed the thousand dollars. I didn't expect it. I certainly didn't. I appreciated it very, very much.*[6]

So I got her for another engagement for that money. In my experience, and I've been around a long time, there are not too many artists who have made it big who have such integrity and thoughtfulness. Nellie is an unusual woman, a warm and caring woman.

One week before Nellie's opening Downtown, Lucienne returned, again to glowing notices:

Cafe Society was bursting its seams with well-known personalities, Miss Boyer's loyal followers, newspaper columnists—and even drama critics! In spite of the terrific heat Miss Boyer showed only too plainly how much she loved being back. Call it special tribute to his French star, Monsieur Josephson has switched from his superb American cuisine into an even more superb French one. Indeed everything is very ooh, la, la![7]

Pat Flaherty: *To Americans used to brassy music and high-kicking chorines in their night club entertainment, it is something of a shock to walk into Manhattan's Cafe Society Uptown and find a lone woman of middle years carrying the whole, hour-long floor show. For two seasons now Mademoiselle Boyer has been packing them into Barney Josephson's large room, while other night clubs have been hard hit by the recession in the big money department.*[8]

The postwar was a time of economic and social upheaval for the American people. It was a different world. We were the wealthiest nation on earth, with unmatched international power. Regardless, the average citizen was faced with the highest prices in history for food, clothing, and housing. The free-and-easy spending on entertainment during the war years was over. The division between the haves and the have-nots was growing. The nightclub business reflected the times. *Variety* reported, "New York café business is hitting bottom."[9] We were one of the few exceptions to the dismal nightclub scene: "Since there's currently not enough business to keep all niteries in the black, trade is flowing to cafes which have top attractions. Thus, Lucienne Boyer at Cafe Society Uptown and Carl Brisson at the Versailles are pulling profitable grosses."[10]

Lee Mortimer, nightclub editor of the *Mirror,* a Hearst paper, had picked up a news item about my brother Leon, which he carefully inserted into his review

> *There was good news at Cafe Society Uptown this week. Lucienne Boyer relighted it, with assurance of a packed house and much capitalistic gold for months to come, and the U.S. District Court postponed the trial on contempt of Congress charges of Leon Josephson, brother of the proprietor, until October. La Boyer, every bit as good as last Spring, when she shattered Gotham supper-club records, and with much new material, delighted the enthusiastic customers.*[11]

There were ominous rumblings emanating from Washington, bad trouble brewing, but Uptown and Downtown were doing great business and I was riding the crest.

PART 4

Bloody
but
Unbowed

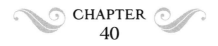

"'Let's have your passport.'"

I t was the year 1935, the first week in February, when a little one-column dispatch about six inches long caught my eye in the newspaper I was reading. The dateline was Copenhagen. The small heading read, "Americans Arrested February 1 for Plotting to Assassinate Adolf Hitler." I read further. "A group of thirty people have been arrested and three Americans are involved. One of the Americans is Leon Josephson, an attorney from Trenton, New Jersey." Leon had begun to make numerous trips to Europe starting about 1930, saying he had clients there.

Franklin Delano Roosevelt had taken office March 4, 1933, with the country in the throes of a catastrophic economic depression. In Germany, Adolf Hitler, using the desperate economic condition the country was in, had seized dictatorial power in January that same year, effectively relegating the nation's reelected president, von Hindenburg, to a figurehead. At the time of Leon's arrest, Denmark still had friendly diplomatic relations with Germany, so a plot to kill a friendly nation's head of state was a crime. It was certainly pretty fast for a person to get involved in the anti-Nazi movement. But that was my brother Leon.

There was no way for me to communicate with him because he was incarcerated in solitary confinement in Copenhagen. He was being held incommunicado and interrogated daily. They were trying to build a case against him. Their system of justice is different from ours. They ask questions to determine if they have a case before taking it to trial.

The United States Ambassador to Denmark, was Mrs. Ruth Bryan Owen, daughter of the "Great Commoner," William Jennings Bryan, so-called because of his unremitting opposition to the special privileges enjoyed by the rich and powerful. Mrs. Owen was a remarkable woman of uncommon parents. Her mother had been admitted to the bar in 1888, pregnant with her second child. Ruth was three. It was common knowledge that Mrs. Bryan worked closely with her husband on all his speeches. In Congress, Mrs. Owen had been the first woman to serve on the Foreign Affairs Committee and to be appointed to a diplomatic post of such high rank in the Foreign Service.[1] She was a friend of President Roosevelt, who was an admirer of her father. Roosevelt had appointed her soon after he took office.

As our ambassador, Mrs. Owen visited Leon in prison since he was an American citizen. She wanted to find out more about the case, to see what she could do to help. Leon told her he had admitted to nothing and that she should not get involved. He asked her not to intercede on his behalf because he hadn't been acting as an agent for the U.S. government. He explained to the interrogating officials that he was only there acting on behalf of a client so they had no concrete evidence that he was actually a part of the assassination plot. Mrs. Owen was astonished. She said she had never heard of an American in trouble in a foreign country who didn't want help from their ambassador.

She was impressed with Leon because he knew a great deal about her father. Leon, who was a voracious reader, could recall, often verbatim, lines from books he'd read. He quoted to the ambassador the "silver-tongued" orator's famous words at the Democratic Convention in 1896, where Bryan had captured the presidential nomination at the age of thirty-six: "You shall not press down on the brow of labor the crown of thorns; you shall not crucify mankind on a cross of gold."

Leon, a student of American history, knew the Great Commoner had been a presidential candidate three times; had campaigned for a graduated income tax, women suffrage, regulation of banks, the direct election of senators. When he was President Wilson's secretary of state he opposed U.S. entry in World War I. Today he is mostly remembered for his fundamentalist defense of the

Bible in the Scopes "monkey trial," opposing the theory of evolution. This has served to obfuscate his then revolutionary calls for social justice for the common man. All this Leon knew. The ambassador and Leon were to become good friends.

How was the supposed assassination plot discovered? The story has an unlikely twist. The Europeans who were arrested were Danish, Swedish, and Norwegian seamen who frequented German ports, carrying fake passports to get people out of Germany whose lives were endangered by the Nazis. The seamen were also taking information in and out of Germany for the underground anti-Nazi movement. Leon told me later that his own connection was with the German communist underground.

One of the other two Americans arrested with Leon was a fellow named George Mink. He got involved with a woman with whom some incident took place. She reported him to the Danish police, who searched his hotel room. They found four passports, only one of which was Mink's. Two of the four passports had Leon's picture on them. In addition, Mink had in his possession detailed information about German naval plans. In the other American's room were plans for installing and operating a secret radio station in Denmark.

After being incarcerated for three months the three were brought to trial on May 11, 1935, charged with espionage. Leon was acquitted May 23 and released May 29. The authorities had nothing on him. The other two Americans were sentenced to eighteen months' imprisonment. All the seamen had previously been released immediately.

Leon was put onboard a freighter, *S.S. Scanyork,* penniless. The captain was sympathetic and nice enough to let him send a wireless to me: "Boat I'm on docking Jersey City Pier D June 3." That meant I should meet him at the dock there. He didn't even have train fare to get from Jersey City to Trenton. I went there and met him. When he disembarked, two gentlemen from the Passport Division of the State Department were there to greet him. As Leon came down off the gangplank, they put out their hands, "Let's have your passport."

Leon's passport was one of the first to be confiscated in this country. From that time on, Leon was never able to secure a passport to travel abroad. He hadn't traveled on a false passport. His passport was in his own name even though he was working with the German communist anti-Nazi underground in Europe. He had nothing to hide.

After Leon was expelled from Denmark, the Communist Party in this country shunned him. He was shunted to the bleachers, dropped like a hot potato. Party members didn't go near him. They would walk on the other side of the street when they saw him. He was a marked man in the world anti-Nazi movement, a premature antifascist so to speak. Leon was his own Marxist theoretician, an intellectual who thought for himself.

In fact, after his experience in Denmark, Leon was never again involved in any kind of political activity. So now he was odd man out. Oh, he had feelings about this, but he also had principles. That's the way it was until he died in February 1966 from a massive heart attack. His wife, Lucy, found him lying on the bathroom floor. At the time of his arrest in Copenhagen, Leon was not yet married to Lucy.

There was one person who appreciated what Leon had tried to do about Hitler—at least I believe she did, judging from her later actions. This is a story I know Leon cherished, and I certainly remember with pride. One day, some years after Leon was released from prison in Copenhagen, I get a phone call from a Mrs. Rhode. She said she had been the ambassador to Denmark and her name at that time was Ruth Bryan Owen. "I often see your name in the press and I was wondering if you were related to Leon Josephson. I've been trying to locate him."

One of the times when she phoned Leon, he told her to take care of what she might say, implying, of course, that his phone was always tapped. She replied, "I know all about your phone. I was visited by some gentlemen from the FBI who asked if I thought it was wise to maintain a friendship with you in these times, suggesting that it might not be wise. Their visit reminded me that I owe you a call. As for the FBI recording this conversation, I want to say that you are one of the finest persons I have ever known. And I think that instead of your being sentenced for contempt of Congress [chapter 42] you should have been given a congressional citation for your work in the anti-Nazi movement. Now then, so much for the recording of this call, the real purpose is to ask when you and your wife can come to have dinner with me."

Leon chose not to continue practicing law because the only law he was interested in was civil rights and labor, but unions would not use him as their lawyer and commercial firms would certainly not hire him. He was never disbarred. So what could he do? He didn't want to go back to Trenton. Our older brother, Lou, the corporation counsel for the city of Trenton, had his own law firm with Leon. The firm's name was Josephson and Josephson, Louis and Leon.

The names were on the door of the office. Lou never removed Leon's name. That was Lou's way. He always defended Leon. For years Leon never walked into that office because he didn't want to hurt his brother Lou's practice.

Leon was so brilliant. He could have been a very, very successful lawyer in any area of law he chose and made lots of money. But he chose to fight for the underprivileged and the oppressed. When Cafe Society opened Leon came to work for me, as it were. I'm now the owner of a popular nightclub and becoming known on my own. Although Leon had given me the where-withal to open the cafe, I was the front man and getting the publicity.

Lee Josephson: *In terms of managing the cafe, as I understood it, Barney was certainly the proprietor in every sense of the word for all legal public documents and for all of the interactions with anything with the public. Leon, if he did anything, would be involved with contracts and other sort of managerial aspects of the business there. Leon had absolutely nothing to do with managing talent. Nothing. Leon didn't know jazz or have any great interest in it. But he would do what he could to keep the business affairs in order. Barney was a more public person by his temperament. He liked the limelight. He was more outgoing. Leon preferred to be in the background and was quite happy that nobody wanted to talk to him about this great business. In addition, I think Leon always knew how controversial he was and always knew that his association with anybody could be trouble for them.*[2]

When Leon would be introduced to people now, he was introduced as Barney Josephson's brother. Leon, who had always been so much of a person on his own, well, I always felt he was smarting a little bit because of the great press notices I was getting. Well, now he's known as Barney Josephson's brother. In our boyhood, whenever I would be introduced to Leon's friends, I was always just Leon Josephson's kid brother. Now the situation is reversed. This upset him tremendously. It knocked him off his backside. He had become my kid brother, in a sense. He couldn't take it. I was aware that he resented me for a time because of this.[3]

How was I aware of his feelings? I was acting independently of Leon. He would suggest what he thought I should or should not do, and I would go ahead and do what I wanted to do. He would be offended. He would sulk. He actually sulked. He wouldn't talk to me for days. He would really carry on.

Once I offended him so much because we didn't agree on something that had to do with Josh White. Josh was a charismatic, sexy as hell folk singer, very popular with my audiences and the press. One of the songs he sang was about the physiological makeup of Negroes and whites. Leon disapproved of some of the lyrics and wanted me to tell Josh not to sing them. I disagreed with Leon and said I would not ask Josh to change the words. And I didn't. Next thing I know, Leon doesn't show up. And he was working for me. At that time he had no means of livelihood, which was just a dreadful thing for him. I went to the house to talk with him. He was in bed, wouldn't talk to me, actually turned his head to the wall. Nothing I could do. I finally left.

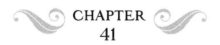

"No one was building
for Negroes."

orld War II was over.[1] During the war, mostly all construction of housing had stopped. Now, there was such a shortage of housing, especially low-cost housing for the working class; at the same time, the population was growing. One day toward the end of the year Leon came to me about a business proposition which he had a chance to be involved with. He knew two men working for the Federal Housing Administration (FHA) in Washington, one an architect and the other an experienced builder. The government itself was building low-cost housing on its own, so the government had such people in its employ. The FHA had been created to finance the building of such housing. These two men had the idea of going into the housing business on their own.

My name was prominent, and when you're prominent everybody thinks you're making a lot of money. The two men from the FHA approached Leon with this wonderful opportunity. They knew how to build low-cost housing. They had been doing it for the government. If Leon had some way of financing this project they would make it a three-way deal. All they needed was money. They had the expertise.

I was very anxious for Leon to go out and do something on his own, to make him feel like a worthy person again without having to make a living from his kid brother's activities. I knew how he felt about that, and it distressed me terribly. We are both very sensitive characters.

I told him, "It sounds like a great idea. You know these people. Go ahead. What's it going to cost? Here's the money." For as long as I can remember it was always even-steven with Leon and me. That's the way we lived. Now I have the money. By this time both cafes were going full blast.

My brother and his two partners formed a corporation, the Dayton Housing Development Corporation of Dayton, Ohio. They chose Dayton because a government commission had reported that of all the industrial areas in the United States, the one needing low-cost housing most was in Dayton. The partners found a site for this project and filed plans with the FHA.

If the FHA approved the plan the builder was obliged to put up 10 percent of the cost of the project and the government would be obligated for the rest. Because of what I had done in the cafes, I was looked upon with great respect, in some areas with a little reverence. So when Leon and his partners drew up plans and presented them to the FHA, they were approved. I had nothing to do with the project except to finance it. I had no share in it. Nothing.

They bought a tract of land. Leon was the president of the corporation because he was the financial man. The other two were officers. The houses would be sold to individuals who qualified. The government would take the mortgage. The purchaser, in essence, would buy the house with a government mortgage and pay back the government over a long period of time. The prices to be charged for the houses had to be approved by the FHA. These prices could not be raised. There was a ceiling on what a family had to have as earnings in order to qualify.

The project had to have a name. It's very interesting to me that Leon never mentioned the name they gave it, nothing except my going into it as a straight business proposition. Leon, without ever discussing anything with me, designated the project the Paul Robeson Park. When I heard about it, I thought Leon's idea to name the project after Paul Robeson was a wonderful idea.

This was going to be the first interracial housing in the United States. Negroes and whites would buy houses together and live in the same community side by side. This had never been done before. There were individual builders building all over the country under these FHA arrangements—for white people. No one was building for Negroes.

Leaders from Negro communities around the country had been going to Washington, protesting to the FHA. They were told to bring a builder to them who would build interracial housing. The FHA would be glad to finance such a project. Nobody came forth. The FHA explained that they couldn't tell builders what to do. There was no law requiring that.

When Leon and his partners came to the FHA with their plan, with its name and the statement that the houses would be offered to all colors, the administration was delighted. They literally threw their share of the financing at them. Now the FHA could say to the Negro community, "See, when a builder wants to build for Negroes, we give the money to them quickly. Here we are financing housing for you in Dayton, Ohio."

Along with Paul Robeson's name, Leon's idea was to have some of the main streets running through the community named after historical Negro figures: [Harriet] Tubman Avenue, [W. E. B.] Du Bois Road, [George Washington] Carver Place, and so forth. The houses were to be private one-family homes, to sell for $5,000 or $6,000.

The way it worked, the FHA, the overall agency, didn't give the builder the financing outright. The government had local agencies which were connected with each project. The FHA money was credited to your account in the local bank. It was done this way to keep unscrupulous builders from absconding with the money. Obviously, building the houses wasn't so easily financed. You needed capital to swing it.

There were FHA administrators in various sections of the country. Each administrator doled out the money as the work progressed. Construction was broken up into three stages. When the first stage of the work had been completed on, say, ten houses, the regional inspector would be called in to check on the work, to make certain, for example, that the proper thickness of cement was poured. He had to make certain that the houses were being constructed according to plan, that the builder was not trying to cut corners. If the inspector approved, he would authorize the local bank to release $10,000, a thousand a house. This $10,000 would be credited to the builder's local bank account. The money was used to pay the electricians, the roofers, the construction workers.

Leon and his partners, with my money, now owned this great big field and were planning to build 250 houses. A lot of preliminary work had to go into such a project—the architecture, laying out the streets, providing for street lighting, plumbing, whatever. Finally they were all set to go. Everything was in place. Construction began. It was the year 1947.

"The Un-American Activities Committee itself was unconstitutional."

In 1945 Rep. John Rankin (D.-Miss.) engineered the creation of the House Committee on Un-American Activities (HUAC). The vote was close, 207 to 186. In fact, this committee was a continuation of another with a similar name, Special Committee to Investigate Un-American Activities but more familiarly known as the Dies Committee, headed by Martin Dies (D.-Tex.). It had been overwhelmingly voted into existence in 1938, the same year Cafe Society saw the light of day.[1] Not everyone then was sanguine about its potential:

> **Rep. Gerald Boileau (Progressive-Wis.):** *If J. Parnell Thomas would be appointed to the Committee, there would likely be an effort to investigate the New Deal, as he claims it to be un-American. . . . If Dies were appointed, Dies would think that those of us who advocated the wage and hour bill are un-American.*[2]

Both Dies and Thomas were appointed, Dies as chairman. In 1944 Dies did not seek reelection to the House. The next year, J. Parnell Thomas was appointed chairman. Leon was subpoenaed to appear before a subcommittee on March 5, 1947. He was forced to respond because if he didn't, that in itself would be contempt of a congressional committee. If you chose not to testify, you answered to your name and address and then took a constitutional amendment.

Leon's premise was that the Un-American Activities Committee itself was unconstitutional. He refused to answer the committee's questions about his political activities and beliefs, citing the First Amendment's guarantee to the right of freedom of speech, thought, and association. Leon was the first to take the First. Thus, he challenged the committee outright:

The Chairman: *Mr. Josephson, will you stand to be sworn?*
Mr. Josephson: *I will not be sworn.*
Mr. Stripling (chief investigator): *Will you stand?*
Mr. Josephson: *I will stand. (Mr. Josephson stands)*
Mr. Stripling: *Do you refuse to be sworn?*
Mr. Josephson: *I refuse to be sworn.*
Mr. Stripling: *You refuse to give testimony before this subcommittee?*
Mr. Josephson: *Until I have had an opportunity to determine through the Courts the legality of this committee.*
The Chairman: *You refuse to be sworn, and you refuse to give testimony before this committee at this hearing today?*
Mr. Josephson: *Yes.*[3]

At Leon's hearing a familiar name was on the committee, Richard Nixon (R.-Calif.). He was quoted in the press describing Leon as a person who "is just as important as [Gerhart] Eisler"—Nixon, even then the master of unproven accusations and bald lies.[4] Leon told me he didn't know Eisler.

Leon was promptly cited for contempt. He knew well before he went to Washington that they would cite him. He was ready, and he was ready to go to the highest court in the land, the Supreme Court, to knock out this committee. He really believed he could do that. Leon had taken what one would call a principled, constitutionally correct position, brilliant student that he was of our Constitution.

"Key Witness Balks at Hearing as Red," *New York Times*, March 6, 1947. When Leon emerged from the committee hearing room the press were all there. He had prepared a typed, mimeographed statement, which he passed out.[5]

He acknowledged that he was a communist. In New York City only the Communist Party newspaper, the *Daily Worker*, printed his statement, but it found its way into the FBI files. Why, one might ask, did Leon, who was ostracized by the American Communist Party, proclaim he was a communist? Well, one can be a Christian and not belong to any church.

> **Lee Josephson:** *Leon always called himself a Marxist. He was an intellectual, not a person who blindly followed an ideology through its secondhand exponents, a Gus Hall or an Earl Browder. He had read Engels and had all the books. He had read Marx—not just read, I mean absorbed. Other thinkers as well. That's where he got his left-wing ideas, directly from his study of these people, the primary thinkers. That also meant, with that as a tool, Leon could decide what he wanted to go along with and what he didn't. Leon viewed anticommunism as substantially a domestic movement. He believed its essential dynamic was internal American. The real reason was to turn back the New Deal, and it was only secondarily a response to an aggressive Soviet Union taking Eastern Europe. It's very clear in his letters, and he said it to me many times. Leon's relationship with the Communist Party was more than complex. He was not a member, Barney told me. He had been in disfavor for a variety of reasons, but he would refuse to be critical of them publicly.*[6]

What was behind Leon's subpoena from the House Un-American Activities Committee? They were attempting to trace the origin of Gerhart Eisler's passport. They wanted to question Leon about his having allegedly procured a false passport for Gerhart Eisler, a German antifascist communist who had fled from the Gestapo with his wife in 1941. Somebody had applied for this passport, but not Leon. Eisler had been subpoenaed by the committee a month before Leon and charged with conspiracy to overthrow our government, income tax evasion, falsification of his passport, and contempt of Congress.

Louis F. Budenz, who had been the managing editor of the *Daily Worker,* had turned informer and given testimony accusing Eisler of being the Comintern representative in the United States, "the real boss of the U.S. Communist Party."[7]

The Un-American Activities Committee had access to the FBI files, which was illegal. At the time that Leon was apprehended in Denmark in 1935 there were antifascists of all persuasions, including communists, who were hiding in Nazi Germany. To escape from the Nazis they were forced to go underground, using various apartments of different people. Always on the run. If they had dared to walk out in the streets they would have been picked up, thrown into a concentration camp, tortured to death. They had to be gotten out of Germany somehow. One of the ways was to arm them with a passport from another country. This was being done in the underground throughout Europe. The seamen who had been arrested with Leon would bring these passports, and whatever else was given to them, to Bremen and other German ports, to be passed along.

The anti-Nazis inside Germany could no longer operate there, but they could continue to fight if they could be gotten out of Germany. With their false passports they could go to a foreign consulate, get a visa, and escape. That's how Gerhart Eisler got out. He came to this country on an American passport as an American citizen, with his picture but someone else's name on the passport, Samuel Liptzen. The subcommittee called Liptzen to testify. He admitted membership in the Communist Party but denied knowing either Eisler or Leon.

When the committee subpoenaed Eisler they had traced, or attempted to, the origin of his passport. Somebody had applied for this passport but not Leon. When you applied for a passport, you needed a witness. Leon's signature, as witness to this application, appeared in the *New York Journal-American,* a William Randolph Hearst publication. It was, as were all Hearst papers, one of the most venomous of all the newspapers in its attacks on anyone even slightly liberal in its eyes.

At the subcommittee hearing Rep. Richard Nixon described the hand-writing expert as the "Treasury Department's chief document examiner."[8] The "expert" testified, that, yes, the signature as shown to him in the *Journal-American* was Leon's handwriting on the passport application. The expert never saw the original passport, only the photo in the newspaper.

When I was a boy in grammar school I loved Leon's penmanship. Any school papers of his that I found around the house that he had no use for I would take and with a pencil write over his writing until I was able to write just like Leon. I mastered it in short order. Today, my writing and his are almost identical. I don't mean to imply that I was the one who had signed the passport application, only that Leon's signature could have been forged easily, especially as it was only shown in the newspaper.

Leon told me how it worked. "I would go to a sympathizer, anyone who was anti-Nazi. I'd tell them we've got people in hiding in Germany, and we've got to get them out. Their lives are in danger. They can't carry on their work inside Germany." He'd ask the person to apply for a passport and give it to him. "If anyone is ever picked up using your passport and you're questioned about it, all you have to say is, yes, this is my passport. I did apply for it. I expected to go to Europe. I put it in my drawer. I wasn't able to go, and I lost it. Nothing can happen to you. Your passport simply got into the wrong hands. What can they do to you?" There were people antifascist enough to do this. All the passports were shipped over to wherever they were needed.

Gerhart Eisler's sojourn in this country ended abruptly two years later. In May 1949 a Polish ship, the *Batory,* arrived in a New York port with passengers and was to return to Poland. Eisler secretly boarded the ship while he was still under indictment, jumping a $23,500 bail provided by the Civil Rights Congress and the American Committee for Protection of Foreign Born. The ship sailed to Southampton, England. The U.S. Justice Department asked Scotland Yard to take Eisler into custody under an Anglo-American extradition treaty. The ship's captain refused to surrender him. Eisler was carried off the ship. It was a big international incident, involving the U.S., Great Britain, and Poland, and headlines for weeks. In the end, the Justice Department was forced to ask the Supreme Court to drop Eisler's conviction for contempt.

Because Leon was the first to challenge the right of the Un-American Activities Committee to exist, headlines appeared nationwide: "Leon Josephson, New Jersey Attorney, Defies the House Un-American Activities Committee; Cited for Contempt." Obviously, no one, even in New York, would know who Leon Josephson was. He was not a celebrity. By the very nature of operating a New York nightclub, presenting new and exciting talent, my name was always in the newspapers and magazines. It was Barney Josephson and Cafe Society Downtown and Cafe Society Uptown.

To better identify Leon, every press dispatch would link Leon with me, who was, I suppose, someone important. "Leon Josephson . . . an admitted Communist . . . an attorney with no film connections, although his brother, Barney Josephson, is more directly in show business as the owner of Cafe Society Uptown and Cafe Society Downtown in New York."[9] I truly don't think any of the press people did that to harm me—at first.

Now the Sword of Damocles is hanging over our heads. Mine because of the snide stories beginning to appear in the right-wing press, and Leon is cited for contempt of Congress, March 24, 1947.[10] Leon's trial, twice postponed, opened in the Federal District Court in New York, October 14. Convicted the same day, he is given the maximum sentence, a $1,000 fine and one year in prison.

Leon appeals. The U.S. Circuit Court of Appeals upholds the contempt conviction in a two-to-one ruling, December 9. Justice Charles E. Clark, former dean of Yale Law School, dissents: "The First Amendment does not speak equivocally. It prohibits any law 'abridging the freedom of speech, or of the press.'"[11] On the basis of the one dissenting opinion by Justice Clark, Leon is able to appeal to the United States Supreme Court.

CHAPTER
43

"'I won't be coming into
the club anymore.'"

L ucienne's triumphant return after the summer was the same day, September 8, 1947, that Leon's trial had been postponed. With his conviction, the attacks on me intensified. Hearst columnists were especially vitriolic: political "experts" Victor Riesel, Westbrook Pegler, George Sokolsky; cabaret editor Lee Mortimer, who was always in my cafes; gossip columnists Dorothy Kilgallen, Cholly Knickerbocker. Walter Winchell had a daily gossip column in Hearst's *Daily Mirror,* which was read by fifty million Americans; even more listened to his weekly Sunday night radio broadcasts.

Dorothy Kilgallen, in the *Journal-American,* wrote about whites and Negroes table-hopping in Cafe Society, Canada Lee dancing with a blond. Canada had burst upon the Broadway scene in 1941, starring as Bigger Thomas in *Native Son,* adapted from Richard Wright's novel. It was voted the greatest American drama of that season.

Canada was always outspoken about racism: "He said he was willing to appear at benefit performances that were sponsored by allegedly Communist groups . . . to talk against racial or religious discrimination . . . to participate in any program designed to make the world a better place to live in, no matter what organization or political party was listed as sponsor."[1] Canada was one more victim of the blacklist. Finally, desperate to get work, he denounced

Paul Robeson at a HUAC hearing in 1952. It didn't help. I heard Canada died penniless.[2]

I was outraged by all of this. The only paper that didn't attack me was *The New York Times*. All the press guys had been my guests in the cafes. They loved what I did, would come around all the time. I got to know them real well, really friendly with them. While Leon was in the courts they would come in and ask, "What's this with your brother? Tell us about him. What's it all about?" It was all new to them. Some of the guys were unfriendly and tried to prompt me into a denunciation of my brother. They wanted me to say, "He's my brother, but I disavow him. He's a communist. He's no good. I will have nothing to do with him. I disagree with him totally."

I made it clear to them: "You'll get no condemnation from me about my brother. I would like you to know that my brother's position is a principled one. He is a lawyer. He knows the law. He knows our Constitution. I can only support a man who takes such a principled position. Furthermore, this is my brother. My brother and I have had differences, but what they have been is nobody's business outside of the Josephson family. That's the way my widowed mother brought us up to behave. She also taught us that no matter what happens in the Josephson family, we help one another, we do for each other."

There were some of the press who were not personally unfriendly, but they worked for unfriendly newspapers. In such a case the reviewer would be called in by his editor if he had given a favorable review, say, to a new artist and told, "Don't you know better than to review Cafe Society? You don't review them unless you can pan them. Otherwise you do not mention their name, only if you can find something dirty." This actually happened to Frank Farrell, who covered nightclubs for the *World Telegram*. He personally told me this story. Bob Dana, a lovely young man, nightclub editor for the *New York Herald-Tribune,* always in my clubs and always writing thoughtful reviews, was placed in a similar situation. "Barney, I won't be coming into the club anymore," and he literally started to cry in his glass of Scotch.

Life had always given me huge spreads of my talent. One of the reporters from *Life* came to me, "Barney, this has been the worst day in my life. One of my editors called me in for an assignment and told me that he understood there was a room in the Uptown Cafe Society where Russian spies passed secret information to one another." His assignment was to get pictures of that room. This was *Life* magazine! They all knew me. How could they have thought such a thing could happen in my club? "Barney, I told him I couldn't do this assignment. I practically live in Cafe Society, and I know such things never take place. I'm sure of it." I guess the editor wanted to believe him because he said, "If you're so sure of this, then my information must be incorrect. Forget the assignment."

There was no let-up for me. His brother is a communist and Barney won't disavow him, so he is one, too. Didn't Barney Josephson open the first interracial nightclub? He brought the niggers—they were still using that language— into his clubs and gave them good seats. They danced on the same floor with white people. Here's a guy who gave Billie Holiday a song like "Strange Fruit" to sing—to bring such a song into entertainment and popularize it. He put Negro and white talent together on the same stage. He gave his place to the antifascists so they could hold fundraising events. It's rumored that he gives money to the Left causes, which I did. I never denied that.

One of the reporters on the *World-Telegram,* an ex-leftist, Frederick Walton, wrote a front-page story with a five-column headline over it: "Cafe Society's Blues Sound a Red Note." Then he goes on to write about this Moscow-line nightclub. I certainly wasn't the only one affected, but I was the only nightclub owner attacked. None of the mobster nightclub owners were. I was blacklisted in the press. My business suffered dreadfully.

I had signed Lucienne for much more money, this big smash that I have. In no time my business dropped 45 percent in five weeks. People stayed away. I thought, "How long is this going to last? It can't go on forever, and I'm certainly not going to close my doors or sell out under pressure. Not Barney. I'm going to see this thing through." So I continue and I continue, and I'm losing all my money waiting for a change. Only the political climate is worsening.

When one presents talent, one must have press. My success was largely in presenting new, young unknowns with talent. The press guys are always looking for new talent to write about. When the clubs uptown would play Joe E. Lewis at the Copacabana or Milton Berle or Sophie Tucker, well, they had already been written up many times. So when a reviewer would go back to a club, what could he say about these performers that hadn't already been said? But when there is new talent just coming up whom you can write about, well, I had given the press that. Two months after Lucienne's joyous return, she's gone. I had to let her out of her contract. The press attacks had taken their toll. My business was shot to hell. The fallout from the attacks hit me in ways I hadn't anticipated. New young talent stopped coming to me. They used to break down my door trying to get an audition with Barney Joseph-son. Now they were staying away. There was this nasty business of guilt by association. If once you worked for Cafe Society, you must be sympathetic to its politics. So new talent was out.

All right, I'll fix them. I'll employ established talent, people who are known, who have big names. I'll pay big money for them. I'll keep this place going. My advertising the papers will not refuse even if they won't review my shows. I'll use quotes from the performers' reviews from their previous engagements. Then I discovered they won't work for me either. They are not going to be la-beled. They'll stay with the mobsters who run the Copacabana, the Versailles. So that idea didn't work.

I had signed the harmonica virtuoso Larry Adler to follow Lucienne, who would be leaving the end of November for a few months. Larry was to be followed in December by Elsa Lanchester, best known as the bride of Frankenstein's monster in that movie. In reality she was a very funny come-dienne. I was also talking to Abe Burrows, at that time a radio comic. This would be his first New York nightclub date. Now I had to fill in Lucienne's untimely departure immediately. Jimmy Savo was gutsy enough to help me out until Larry would come in.

I was fighting, but how long can you fight? Your money runs out. I had been trying to hang on. Events over which I had no control were converg-ing on me, two in particular, neither of which the mobster club owners had to face. They were able to pour money into performers' salaries, even losing money in the process. I was pouring money into Leon's housing project, los-ing money, hoping the government money would come in soon. I had the right-wing press after me. The mobsters had no such press going after them. Cafe Society was hemorrhaging money. I was convicted for associating with my brother. Guilt by kinship. I would not disown him.

Larry Adler did come in Uptown. He didn't last out the gig. I closed two weeks later, December 13, 1947.

Herbert Jacoby and Max Gordon had wanted to buy Cafe Society Up-town, but I was trying to hang on. One day a friend called to tell me a story. He and a prominent lawyer, a close friend of mine who had been a lawyer at the Nuremberg trials in Germany after World War II, were walking along Park Avenue. The caller suggested they drop by Cafe Society, say hello to me and have a drink. The Nuremberg trial lawyer objected. "I'm not going into Cafe Society anymore. I understand the FBI are there taking pictures of everyone who patronizes the club." These were the things close friends of mine were saying and doing. The next day I sold the place.

> *One of the major nitery upsets of the year occurred Saturday (13) when Barney Josephson shuttered his Cafe Society Uptown, N.Y. . . . Josephson will continue his activities at Cafe Society Downtown which he opened in the late '30's. . . . CSU was considered one of the more successful Eastside clubs, hitting an average weekly gross of around $30,000. In the operation of [the] spot, Josephson had also been under attack from columnist Westbrook Pegler because of his brother's activities. Latter had recently been convicted of contempt of Congress for refusing to testify before House Un-American Committee. Whether this contributed to the bad business isn't definite.*[3]

Jacoby and Gordon, who together were operating the Blue Angel club on East 55th Street, bought Uptown for $75,000. Since I owned the building, I tried to salvage something from there. I took my liquor stock to Downtown. I had been informed the new owners were going to take down Ref's murals, destroy them, and put some woven fabric on the walls in their place. They had so little appreciation for art, for anything like this. Simply as businessmen they should have known that they could have cut the murals into sections, sold them off, and made some money. Instead they were going to destroy them. I felt that was simply dreadful. I wanted to preserve them. You just don't destroy an artist's work.

Refregier's assistant Paul Petroff knew Max Gordon. "Paul, I can't go to Gordon to buy the murals. I sold them the place as is. You go up there and see what you can do." So Paul went to Max. "What do you want for these murals? You're going to throw them out anyway." "You want them?" "Yes, Max." "All right. Give me two $250. They're yours." Paul came back, and I gave him the $250. At that time I was trying to preserve my sanity, trying to make a living, trying to keep Downtown from going under.

Ref was in San Francisco, working on a series of murals for the Rincon Post Office. I knew where he was staying because we were always in communication. I sent him a telegram, told him I had to sell Uptown and what I had done about the murals. "As far as I'm concerned, Ref, they're yours. You do what you want with them. I could not allow them to be destroyed. It's up to you."

Ref wired back. "Have Petroff put them on big rollers; ship them out to me. Found two big walls to place them on. They will be preserved." He had found two walls in a building housing the San Francisco Labor School, a left-wing school. He hung the murals on the walls there. The Cafe Society Uptown murals were saved.

Every year *Billboard*, the entertainment publication, puts out a special edition to end the year. They would come around to get ads. They got lots of ads. They gave you a lot of publicity all year long so you always reciprocated. *Billboard* is a large-size publication. I would usually give them half a page. This time when they came around, instead of giving them half a page I gave them a full-page ad, which I could ill afford. I was so full of anger. The copy was centered in the middle of a large expanse of white paper, in small print:

My head is bloody, but unbowed. Barney Josephson

CHAPTER
44

"Two future presidents
were in attendance."

F orced to close Uptown was a terrible blow. I didn't know what hit me. One moment I'm the darling of the press, the next I'm Mr. Anathema. One ray of hope was that the Supreme Court would rule in Leon's favor and the nightmare would be ended. The ruling finally came down in February 1948. In a six-to-three decision, the Court denied certiorari and the next month declined to review Leon's case, thus upholding the lower court's decision. Justices Douglas, Murphy, and Rutledge were in favor of the review. Think of the consequences had the Supreme Court ruled in favor of Leon's First Amendment argument. The House Committee on Un-American Activities could have been knocked out of existence.

There was no further action Leon could take. He surrendered March 18, 1948, and was placed in the Federal Detention House on West Street, New York City. Six weeks later his lovely wife Lucy, pregnant with their second child, and I went to visit Leon. As we arrived he was being led out of the jailhouse—shackled. We couldn't speak to him. He was being transferred to the Federal Correction Institution in Milan, Michigan. There, far away from his family, he was forced to serve out every minute of his one-year sentence. When he applied for parole he was turned down.

During the months we were waiting for the Supreme Court decision, the House Un-American Activities Committee goes to Hollywood. [J. Parnell] Thomas gives as a reason that "the Committee needs to complete certain phases of the Gerhart Eisler case." His brother Hanns Eisler, an internationally renowned German composer, had been writing music for films. He's subpoenaed and is allowed to read a statement:

> For the past five months I have found myself attacked and publicized to a very unusual degree. The reason for this campaign against me is clear. I am accused of being the brother of Gerhart Eisler whom I love and admire. And I have stood by him. I shall continue to do so. . . . I know that when my brother came to the United States, he came as an agent for nobody. He came as a sick man from a concentration camp. I know he wanted to go to Mexico and was held here against his wishes. It would perhaps be better to ask the anti-Nazi underground in Europe for information. They would have more and better information about his activities.[1]

Several months later HUAC is in Washington, D.C. Two future presidents were in attendance: committee member Richard Nixon and friendly witness actor Ronald Reagan, president of the Screen Actors Guild. Hollywood stars Gary Cooper, Robert Taylor, George Murphy, Robert Montgomery; studio heads Walt Disney, Louis B. Mayer, Jack L. Warner are subpoenaed as friendly witnesses.[2]

Hanns Eisler is subpoenaed again. He's attacked by the committee interrogator Robert Stripling as the "Karl Marx of Communism in the music field." The committee is trying to establish a link between Gerhart Eisler, so-called real boss of the U.S. Communist Party, and the Left in Hollywood, with Hanns as the link. Other subpoenas are issued to suspected Hollywood communists. Ten, mostly screenwriters, are called to testify. They refuse to answer the $64 questions, "Are you now, or have you ever been, a member of the Communist Party?" as a matter of principle and their First Amendment rights of freedom of speech "peaceably to assemble, and to petition the Government for a redress of grievances." They are so-called unfriendly witnesses and became known as the Hollywood Ten.[3]

The friendly witnesses tell about the influence of Reds in the motion picture industry and name names. Thomas reports Ginger Rogers's mother had secretly testified that Ginger "had been forced" to speak the subversive line "share and share alike, that's democracy" in the 1943 movie *Tender Comrade*, written by Dalton Trumbo, directed by Edward Dmytryk, two of the Hollywood Ten.[4]

It is no accident that eight of the Ten are among the top screenwriters. The right-wing's agenda is to use these hearings to control what is shown on the screen to the American public. Nine days later [October 31, 1947] J. Parnell suddenly closes the hearings. *Variety*'s headline: "Commie Carnival Closes: An Egg Is Laid." The Hollywood Ten are cited for contempt of Congress, indicted by a grand jury, fined $1,000, sentenced to a year in prison.[5] They appealed and lost.

As the wheel turns, Chairman J. Parnell Thomas, born John Feeney, is charged by the U.S. Justice Department with conspiracy to defraud the government by taking kickbacks from nonworking employees he had placed on his congressional payroll. An ironic twist, Thomas refuses to testify before the federal grand jury on the ground he might incriminate himself. He pleads the Fifth Amendment since the First doesn't apply in his case. He's convicted, sentenced to eighteen months, fined $10,000, and forced to resign from the House of Representatives or be expelled.[6] He's sent to the federal prison in Danbury, Connecticut, where he meets up with fellow prisoners Ring Lardner Jr. and Lester Cole over whose appearances a bullying Thomas had presided.

Leon wrote from prison [on November 29, 1948], "I read a statement by my friend Parnell F. Thomas that he is being persecuted because he is our country's best fighter against all the ISMS, except PATRIOTISM. Now because of his METAMORPHISM from hunter to hunted, this microcephalic MICROCOSM, this embezzling EMBOLISM in the body politic, this vanquished VULGARISM, this atrocious ATAVISM . . . " Leon continued on in this vein.

President Truman had signed his loyalty-oath program in 1947, designed to root out the "infiltration of disloyal persons" in the federal government.[7] Attorney General Tom Clark is charged with drawing up a list of subversive groups so that membership in them would be proof of disloyalty. For the next ten years, under this order the FBI name-checks millions of federal employees and hundreds of thousands of job applicants. The accused are not permitted to confront confidential (paid) informers or to defend themselves. Harry Truman had set the stage for the rise of a junior senator from Wisconsin in 1950, Joseph McCarthy, and for the great wave of anticommunist hysteria that engulfed the entire nation.

What a time to get married. We did, Sylvia and I, after a courtship of over two years, on January 7, 1948. I had waited to tell Leon, we both were going through so much. On Thanksgiving Day 1948 he wrote from prison:

The last paragraph of your letter made me very happy for you and Sylvia. "Love is gratitude for pleasure," said some author. But to be lasting there must be an intellectual affinity which binds the souls together and makes possible a real understanding and appreciation of each other's relationship. I was worried so about Izabel because that affinity didn't and couldn't exist and I was happy when it was over and that is why I have been so happy to read about this in your letter.

While I was the only blacklisted nightclub owner, hundreds of others lost their livelihoods in the entertainment industry. Careers were destroyed—and lives. Zero's pal, actor Phil Loeb, a sweet and funny guy, had gotten a big career break as the patriarch Jake in the popular CBS-TV series *The Goldbergs* [1949]. Gertrude Berg was Mollie, his wife and the show's writer. In 1950 Phil finds himself listed in *Red Channels*. The show's sponsor, General Foods, wants him off the show. Mrs. Berg refuses, appeals to William Paley, big boss at CBS. The long and short, the show is forced off the air in 1951.[8]

Phil had awful years unable to find work. Broke, despondent, with a schizophrenic son who needed expensive special care, it was all too much. Four years later he checked into the Hotel Taft and swallowed enough pills.[9] In Martin Ritt's 1976 movie, *The Front*, written by Walter Bernstein (blacklisted), Zero Mostel (blacklisted) portrays the Phil Loeb character and the tragic circumstances of his suicide. Martin Ritt was also blacklisted.

Red Channels was a book published by three former FBI agents. To keep up to date they put out a weekly sheet, *Counterattack,* which listed "communists," "fellow-travelers," and anyone else.

Jack Gould: *The way the policy operates now is this: the sponsor or advertising agency simply does not hire a person listed in* Red Channels *or does not renew a contract upon its expiration. The individual is not even told in so many words that the* Red Channels *listing is responsible. Any number of perfectly normal excuses—a change of cast, etc.—suffice. The individual is just out of a job. The person named is "controversial" per se, his innocence or guilt is now beside the point so far as many—if not most—prospective employers are concerned. If he speaks up or if he says nothing he still has not lost the tag of being "controversial." His basic and fundamental rights have disappeared into thin air.[10]*

At CBS everyone was required to sign a loyalty oath. Any performer booked on a show had to be cleared by their security office. A lovely young friend, Isobel Gibbs, was married to the comedian Henry Morgan. He was a panelist on a popular CBS radio show *I've Got a Secret* when he found himself in *Red Channels.* Henry protested that he was being persecuted because of his wife's leftist leanings. Proof of his innocence, he explained, was that he was in the process of divorcing her because he detested her politics. Whatever he did, his name soon disappeared from *Red Channels,* and he continued on the show. He had walked out and cut off Isabel with no money. I never did like the guy.[11]

There was terror in the land. People were afraid to keep certain books on their shelves. In the middle of the night people were walking out of their homes. If they didn't have an incinerator they would drop their books in the garbage on the streets. Already people were renouncing their friends. Wives and husbands were fighting or splitting up because one of them belonged to some group labeled communist-front. The Red hysteria affected universities, scientists, teachers, unions, the State Department, the Armed Forces, the press, Civil Service, every aspect of American life into the 1960s.

CHAPTER
45

"'The great
Josephson contradiction.'"

With Leon in prison, he couldn't devote any time to the Dayton Housing Project, which was left up to his two partners, the architect and the builder. Their accountant came to me. "Look, Barney, if we can get some extra capital and throw it in so we don't have to wait for the FHA money to pay the contractors we can push this thing through." The architect and the builder were honorable men, and they concurred. So I did it. I threw in $30,000, then another $20,000, then another $35,000, hoping to push the work to completion. I threw in more.

I had bought the building on 58th Street, and I took out a mortgage. I mortgaged the damn building to send the money out to Dayton, Ohio. I was jeopardizing everything I had for this damn project. At this time I was having plenty of trouble just trying to hold on to Downtown as the attacks mounted.

The houses in the project were already being sold by the Federal Housing Administration (FHA), though not yet completed. Sometimes they were turned over not once, not twice, but three or four times. Why? For a worker to buy a house he had to be in a certain income bracket. He would apply for a house, make a token down payment, wait for the FHA to approve his application, and get the mortgage money from them. He's not supposed to be earning, say, more than $36.20, but he's earning $36.80. The FHA turns down this guy because he's making too much money. So they have to sell the house all over again to somebody else.

Meanwhile, Leon's corporation office in Dayton was being maintained, with office help needed to handle applications, sales, all the paperwork. I had the cost of maintaining the organization, including the architect and builder who were giving full time as officers of the corporation. That wasn't all.

This being Leon's housing project, the FHA found itself financing what they called a "Communist project." To their dismay they discovered they were financing Paul Robeson's name, already anathema to the government. But the FHA had made a firm commitment, signed, sealed, and delivered. They had to go through with their end of the financing, so they tried to figure out, How can we kill this project?

Well, there are ways and ways. Suppose twelve houses are under construction. Leon's housing corporation had completed, let's say, the first stage of the work and were to get $1,000 for each house from the FHA. They call the FHA inspector in Dayton and tell him they're ready for him to see the dozen houses. "All right. I'll be down tomorrow morning." Tomorrow morning comes. The inspector doesn't. The next day he doesn't show up. Ten days pass by, and he can't be reached. They keep calling his office. He isn't in. He's out of town. He's in Washington.

In the meantime, their electrical contractor has forty men working for him. He has to get his money every week to pay his men. The Dayton corporation can't give him his money on time. There was a great demand for workers in the building industry [in] those days. The contractor has offers for jobs all over the lot. He takes twenty men off the Dayton job, sends them to another job where they get paid every week so he can meet his payroll. He has to do it. The same story with the roofers, the plumbers, the other workers.

Finally, after two weeks the inspector arrives. He looks at a joint, two boards coming together at a point. He can see there's one place that's not perfect. "Before I can approve this you'll have to replace it." Leon's partner calls a worker across the way to do this. The inspector says, "Sorry, I haven't got time to wait. I'll be back later." He takes another week to get back. That's the way it went.

In the Dayton Hotel in town, some men are drinking at the bar one night. A friend of Leon's architect is at the bar. He overhears the FHA regional inspector talking to a group of builders, talking about Leon's project. "We'll take care of those communists. They'll never see a nickel out of this project. I'll hamstring them. I'll stretch this thing out. They'll never get a nickel of their investment back."

Finally, the partners corner the FHA guy. He could only hold them up for so long, right? Three more weeks go by, and he releases $16,000, telling the bank to credit this sum to them. The bank could only release the money with his approval. During all this time to keep the corporation from going bankrupt, to keep the project going, I'm dribbling in money little by little.

Sure, the down payment on a house came to us, but it didn't begin to pay for all of my expenses. The inflationary spiral had started and ate up whatever profit there would have been. What with inflation, the electricians, the plumbers, the roofers all were getting more money. This project, which should have taken twelve months to complete, took three years. And I had the awful expense. If the houses had been completed in the period of time in which they should have, my original investment would have been covered.

In prison, Leon was plenty worried, though I tried to keep some of the worst of the news from him. September 10, 1948, he wrote, "Like the bonds by which the population of Lilliput throttled Gulliver . . . so am I tied and thwarted." Leon had such a noble purpose, low-cost integrated housing. May 1, 1948, he wrote, "The great Josephson contradiction is the contradiction between our inner compulsion to do good, to be the 'good guy' and the penalties which capitalism exacts for such conduct."

The ultimate irony? Not one white family would buy a house in this community. When all the houses were sold and everybody was living in them, there was only one non-Negro family who bought a house. This non-Negro family was Japanese. No one would sell a house to a Japanese family in Dayton, Ohio, in the mid-1940s after World War II. This Japanese family had to live with Negro families, which they didn't want to do either.

So it became a housing development for Negroes. The government didn't lose a nickel. They had the mortgages. Everybody got paid. The money I had poured in? Well, I never saw a penny of it. Eventually I lost in the neighborhood of $360,000, a fortune in those days. I had wound up building a monument to Paul Robeson.

In prison, Leon found ways to help the other inmates with their legal appeals. This did not endear him to the prison authorities. One of the times I visited him, the warden took me aside. "Your brother will be down to see you in a little while. We have to give him time to clean up. He's been in solitary confinement for three days. I want to talk to you about your brother. He has an idea that we have political prisoners in this country. Everyone who is in prison in this country is a criminal. Now you get that into your brother's head!" I can never forget his words, and it's been years since I heard them:

"When a person is sent to prison, who sends him to prison? The government, right? So they're sore at the government, and they want to get even. How are they going to get even? They try to perform acts of sabotage. They'll break things, throw something down the toilet, break the plumbing. We have a rule here that when you have food on your plate you must eat everything on it. Leaving food on the plate is another way to sabotage because that's a waste of the government's money. That's what your brother did. He left food on his plate, and we put him in solitary confinement."

When Leon finally came down he told me, "I know the rule about eating all the food on the plate. But when I went through the line they piled my plate so high there was no way I could eat it all. I got to the point that if I took one more bite I would vomit on the table. So I was taken up front of the hall and charged with wasting food. It was a set-up, a way for the warden to get at me because of my argument about political prisoners."

Leon's lawyer Sam Neuberger was with me on this visit. When we returned to New York, Sam must have talked around. The next thing I know, the story appears on the front page of the *Daily Worker*. Westbrook Pegler must have had a subscription to the paper. A day or so later his column in the *New York Journal-American*, "As Pegler Sees It," appears. Now his column is nationally syndicated, carried by some 185 newspapers reaching at least twelve million readers. This particular column was devoted entirely to Leon and me. Pegler was without doubt the most vitriolic of all the columnists.

It's amazing how certain things become engraved in your memory. I'm in my eighties, and I can remember vividly what Pegler wrote. It went pretty much like this:

> *Leon Josephson was placed in solitary confinement in the Michigan Correctional Institution. Everyone in federal prisons is there for dope selling or dope addiction, and some are there for both. Everyone knows that when a person is incarcerated and can't get their drugs they become violent and have to be restrained, so they are put into solitary confinement. Everyone who observed the trial of Leon Josephson noticed that he was very nervous and fidgety on the stand. This is highly unusual behavior for a lawyer who knows his way around the courtroom.*

Practically every sentence began with the word *everyone*. And on the last line of the column I was brought in: "And there is much to be said about his brother, Barney."

(top) High Society mural by Adolph Dehn, Cafe Society Downtown, 1938. (Author's Collection)

(bottom) Patrons at the Bar, mural by Sam Berman; mural above animals, *Dark Clouds* by Christina Malman, Cafe Society Downtown, 1938. (Author's Collection)

(top) Small section of *Jitterbug Dancing,* mural by William Gropper, Cafe Society Downtown, 1938. (Author's Collection)

(bottom) All These Petty Annoyances, mural by Alice Stander, Cafe Society Downtown, 1938. (Author's Collection)

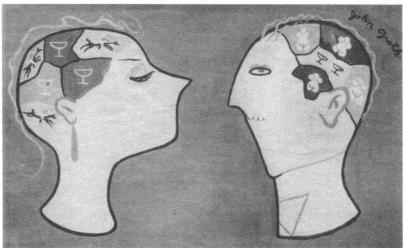

(top) *Speak No Evil. . .* mural by Ad Reinhardt, Cafe Society Downtown, 1938. (Author's Collection)

(bottom) *Her Mind, His Mind,* mural by John Groth, Cafe Society Downtown, 1938. (Author's Collection)

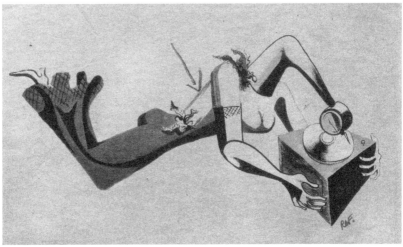

(top) *The Four Seasons,* mural by Abe Birnbaum, Cafe Society Downtown, 1938. (Author's Collection)

(bottom) *Society Gals Never Stop Gossiping,* mural by Anton Refregier, Cafe Society Downtown, 1938. (Author's Collection)

(top) The Social Register, mural by Colin Allen, Cafe Society Downtown, 1938. (Author's Collection)

(bottom) Fan Dance, mural by hoff [Syd Hoff], Cafe Society Downtown, 1938. (Author's Collection)

MADE
NEW YORK, N.Y.
2
SHERIDAN SQUARE
N.Y.C.
The wrong place for the Right people.
DINNER
AFTER THEATRE
SUPPER
WHERE THE
BOOGIE-WOOGIES PLAY
Cafe
Society
PHONE
CHELSEA
2-2737
Colin

Cafe Society Downtown menu cover, Anton Refregier. (Author's Collection)

(opposite) First Cafe Society Downtown matchbook cover—front and back, Colin Allen, 1938. (Author's Collection)

Cafe Society Uptown matchbook cover, 1940. (Author's Collection)

"'They'll set you up.'"

For all that Uptown was loved for its decor and ambience, Jacoby and Gordon were trying to erase anything that smacked of Cafe Society because of the political cloud hanging over it. They changed the name to Le Directoire, for what reason I don't know, only that Jacoby originally came from Paris and named it. It did not become a French restaurant or anything French. The name meant nothing. The entertainment never had anything to do with France or anything from the Continent. They spent about $45,000 to refurbish the room.

Kay Thompson and Andy Williams and his Brothers were on the opening bill for a ten-week engagement. Kay had devised a nightclub act for them, and she certainly had all the credentials as a vocal arranger, great comedian, and singer. She had been with the Arthur Freed Unit at MGM and had coached Lena. On their opening night in April, Dorothy Kilgallen devotes her entire column to them, engraved on my mind: "Last night the beautiful Le Directoire opened on the site of the former Cafe Society, Communist-line night club. No longer will you have to enter these beautiful portals to the strains of the Red Army marching song played by Teddy Wilson." During World War II, when Russia was our ally, there was a Red Army song, "Meadowland." It became very popular to the point that Dr.

Frank Black, Imogene Coca's childhood piano teacher, conducted the famous NBC Symphony Orchestra playing this song over the radio. Now she brings me in. "No longer will you be greeted by Barney Josephson. Instead you will be greeted by the smart, suave and dapper Herbert Jacoby." I'm out of the business. What more does she want?

Le Directoire didn't last long. Our deal had been finalized on December 18. Their lease was for five years, beginning January 1, 1948, with an option for an additional two years. Six months after they opened Jacoby and Gordon handed an empty club back to me. Leon, from prison, December 8, 1949: "Dear Barney: . . . I read about the closing in the papers. In a way I was very glad. For when they opened with a bang you wrote me a very pessimistic letter in which you seemed to think that their 'success' was a reflection on your ability. Now this should prove that you were in no way to blame. And for this demonstration I'm thankful."

I decided then, instead of a nightclub that has to rely on the press for publicity to survive, I would open a good French restaurant, good food, good service, good prices. I redecorated and called it Restaurant Repartie [witty reply]. I hired my chefs, waiters, cashier, everybody. Meanwhile, I applied for my liquor license. I had to surrender the Uptown license when I gave up the cafe. When I applied for a new one I was told, "This isn't a renewal you know. We will have to investigate you." That was standard procedure. Then I was told, "Your place was a hangout for unlawful elements, communists like Paul Robeson. That's an unlawful element." So they procrastinated. "We're not satisfied that we have enough information." I was being killed. I had my staff on payroll, and they were holding me up.

Sylvia's father Emil Friedlander, owner of Dazian's, the legendary theatrical costume house, knew some important people. He tried to help. We were told they were not going to issue a liquor license to me, not if they can help it. I would have to go to court. They couldn't refuse the license, but the lawsuit would be front-page news. I would be ruined by the publicity before I opened. I had planned to keep my name off this restaurant. I was advised, "Barney, the best thing you can do is forget it. Sell the place. Get out of there because they're not going to let you live. They'll set you up. They'll get a kid who's sixteen, looks twenty-one, comes in with a man of forty, and your waiter will serve her a drink. She'll be a plant for the Liquor Authority, and they'll close you up."

I gave up.

I was able to keep Downtown operating for another year. Not content that I was forced to close Uptown, I was being harassed Downtown by various authorities. The Building Department came in and started placing violations. The State Liquor Authority came in. People would be lined up three deep at the bar. They went behind the bar with their testers, checking the bottles. "Let's see this one." Then they would siphon off some whiskey, put some chemicals in a test tube, put the whiskey in, and it would turn colors. People at the bar were watching. There was nothing wrong with my whiskey, but they would come in often, repeating this procedure.

They were going to take care of me. They were not going to let me live. My business was affected more and more. I did not own the building. March 2, 1949, I closed Cafe Society Downtown. I'm now out of the nightclub business.[1]

CHAPTER
47

"She blew her cover."

The fallout from the blacklisting resounded in so many ways. A couple of years after the demise of my cafes I'm in a deli on York Avenue and 63rd Street when I meet an old friend, the well-known comedy writer Abe Burrows. Abe, a big grin, greets me with open arms, "Hello, Barney. What are you doing these days?" "One of the things I'm doing is not talking to you."

Rude? No. When Abe was called before the Un-American Activities Committee in New York he praised the committee for its good work and named friends he had seen at Communist Party meetings.[1] Abe was a regular panelist on the hit ABC program *The Name's the Same.* He was blacklisted anyway and forced off the show. He needn't have worried. His musical *Guys and Dolls* was playing to packed houses on Broadway.

Pearl Primus had been booked for a dance concert at a high school in Greenwich, Connecticut, in 1949. A resident in the area, a Mrs. Mc-Cullough, publicly denounced Pearl as being pro-communist and tried to prevent the concert. When the press went to Pearl for her comment she complained, "I don't know why they're doing this to me. I have been an informer for the FBI all those years I was dancing in Cafe Society." She's being attacked, and she's telling them, "You got me wrong." She blew her cover, pleading to be able to dance. When she worked in the National Maritime

Union office, that's when she must have been informing on the seamen and union officers. Almost the entire Negro professional and intellectual community came to Cafe Society. Pearl met all those wonderful people. I never knew her organizational ties, nor did I care. My artists did their work. I rarely discussed politics with anybody who worked for me. Pearl's friends were from the left wing. By her own admission she was involved with these organizations and giving names to the FBI. Idiotic woman, to come out and tell this.

In 1950 Jack Gilford was engaged by the Broadway writer and stage director Garson Kanin to appear in the Metropolitan Opera production of *Die Fledermaus*, which he was directing.[2] Jack would play the nonspeaking role of Frosch, the drunken jail keeper.

Now it's one thing to have a son who's a stand-up comedian in a nightclub, but to have a son on the Metropolitan Opera stage, this was such a thing for Sophie, Jack's mother. There's a special kind of Jewish mother, a Brooklyn Jewish mother. Sophie was such. She thought I was such a nice boy. Friday night she would bring Jack gefilte fish and wonderful chicken soup with matzoh balls. She always brought me some. She'd scold, "Always eating restaurant food, you get tired from it." Two days before Jack's opening, Madeline Lee, Jack's wife, calls to tell me Sophie has passed away.

The opening of *Die Fledermaus* is a matinee. I attend. I'm sitting by myself, all alone in the mezzanine. Third act, Jack's first entrance, he takes a pratfall, sliding down a whole flight of stairs. The audience roars, and I sit and cry. Jack is handcuffed to his prisoner, the tenor. The prisoner walks in one direction, Frosch in the other. The audience roars. All through the scene they're laughing and I'm crying. Sophie didn't live to see her Jake on the Metropolitan Opera stage. I can't describe how destroyed I was. My mother never lived to see my Cafe Society. She died three years before Downtown opened.

The owner of four supermarkets around Syracuse, a Laurence Johnson, would threaten companies whose products he sold if they sponsored any television program in which "subversives" were involved. He visited TV offices in New York City, phoned and wrote to other supermarket owners, hung signs over "offending" companies' products in his supermarkets. His campaign worked often enough but not always.

Soon after Jack's opening, Rudolph Bing, artistic director of the Metropolitan Opera, calls Jack into his office, tells him that some owner of supermarkets in Syracuse, a Laurence Johnson, has gotten in touch with his office.

He demanded that Bing drop Jack from the cast, called him a Red, threatened to picket the company when they performed in Syracuse. Bing, an Austrian who had fled Hitler's Anschluss, refused point-blank though it might have meant trouble for the company. It didn't.

But there were others who did blacklist Jack just as he was really getting his break in television. Subpoenaed in 1956 in New York, Jack took the Fifth Amendment. Fred Allen is making his TV debut, and Jack is hired to do some sketches on the show. One of the sketches was one he'd done at Cafe Society, where he's sitting in a subway train, desperately trying to keep his eyes open, finally falling asleep. Jack could build a routine from everything he saw. While he's in rehearsal he gets a phone call from his agent at the William Morris office. The producers are sorry but Jack's sketch is dropped. They'll pay him, but they've decided "to go the other way," meaning hiring another actor to do an imitation of Jack's routine.

Years later [1962], Jack and Zero were cast in the Broadway musical *A Funny Thing Happened on the Way to the Forum*. Out-of-town tryouts were not going well. The director, Hal Prince, decided he needed outside help and wanted to bring in the dance choreographer Jerry Robbins. Jerry had been one of the friendly witnesses, naming among others Jack's wife, Madeline Lee. Hal, knowing Jerry was hardly popular with Zero and Jack, asked them if they would mind.

Zero: "If he can help, okay," then, haughtily, "Besides, we of the Left do not blacklist." Jack just wanted to leave the show. Madeline dissuaded him, "Why should we penalize ourselves still further?" Jack stayed.

Josh White disappointed me. He, who had sung songs of Jim Crowism, slums, chain gangs, lynchings, hunger, sang to the House Un-American Activities Committee. They hadn't even called him. He requested the chance to testify "for my own sake and for the sake of many other entertainers who have been used and exploited by people who give allegiance to a foreign power." His "zeal for musical preachment against racial discrimination" had led him into becoming "a sucker." Then he gratuitously denounced Paul Robeson: "He does not speak for my people."[3]

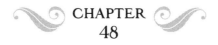

CHAPTER
48

"That's the way she
washed herself."

The one person who caused me more grief than any of my art-ists and friends who had appeared as friendly witnesses was Mrs. Adam Clayton Powell Jr.—Hazel Scott. In 1950 she signs for a show on Dumont Television for a trial run of thirteen weeks. Then it's gone. Nobody bought it. She's listed in *Red Channels*. But she's a congressman's wife. Adam arranges for Hazel to appear before the committee to make a public disavowal. He's promised a hearing. The day before, Adam gives out press releases with excerpts from Hazel's forthcom-ing statement at the HUAC hearing, timed to appear in the papers the day of her testimony.

Comes the day of the hearing, Adam can't get the committee together to sit and listen. This is most embarrassing. Vito Marcantonio, a congressman from New York and a friend, told me the story. Marc said he never saw such a disgraceful performance as that man running around trying to get a com-mittee member to sit and listen to Hazel.

Marc had served in the House of Representatives for fourteen years. He had introduced bills to abolish the poll tax, to make lynching a federal crime, introduced civil rights legislation, fought to protect the gains of organized labor. In 1950 he was defeated by a gang-up of all the parties running a co-alition candidate.

I was proud of his opposition in Congress to the contempt citations of Leon Josephson, the Hollywood Ten, and all the others. "If I have to be alone again in Congress, I will cast my vote against it [fascism] ever happening in the United States of America." Marc was not alone. He was joined by Adam Clayton Powell for the vote on Leon, April 22, 1947.

Marc described the spectacle of Adam pleading with the chairman of the committee John S. Wood of Georgia, a southern racist. Wood talks to another committee member, "If that nigger son-of-a-bitch thinks I'm going to call a meeting so that his wife can get up there and read a statement so she can go out and make more fucking money for him, that nigger's crazy. I won't convene the committee."

Adam's in a spot. It's going to come out in the papers that Hazel read a statement before the committee, but the committee wasn't there to hear it. He grabs another committee congressman, "You can't do this to me," and got an agreement for a hearing in a week.[1] Four of the eight committee members did convene a week later. Chairman Wood opened with a statement to Hazel: "We are making an exception in your case in view of the fact that you are the wife of one of our colleagues."[2]

Hazel testified for twenty minutes. She was quoted in the Washington press: "Barney Josephson was my manager and my employer at Cafe Society. In show business, managers send their talent to appear at various benefits and we go because our managers tell us it builds our audiences. So you don't question, you just do it."[3] That was not true. I always asked Hazel if she wanted to entertain somewhere. I left it up to her. She knew that.

"By 1943, I had heard disturbing talk about the activities of the group [Joint Anti-Fascist Refugee Committee] and when asked to play a joint benefit concert with Paul Robeson, I refused."[4] Hazel was at Cafe Society then, so she obviously did have the option to refuse. It was Barney Josephson who gave her name to organizations for their stationery. I ordered her to make all kinds of appearances.

> **Hazel Scott:** *In October 1943, I entertained at an artists' rally for Benjamin Davis, an avowed Communist running for the New York City Council. [He was elected.] . . . I don't recall exactly how this appearance came about, but I believe it was by direction of Mr. Barney Josephson, my then employer and manager, who often lent my name and time to affairs without consulting me. . . . I had nothing to do with the Civil Rights Congress . . . because in 1946 . . . I, by then, had a man-*

ager who was more interested in furthering my career than in using my talents politically.[5]

Leonard Feather, in his eulogy at her death, wrote, "From the earliest Cafe Society days, Hazel had been deeply conscious of the need to fight for civil rights."[6]

After seven and a half years at Cafe Society she could give such testimony. That's the way she washed herself. Put it on my back. When she gave this testimony, that was the end of Hazel Scott with me. That's the true story.

Leonard Feather: *The second influence (her mother was the other) who provided the crucial turning point in her life, was Barney Josephson. No other club could have provided a springboard for the career of Hazel. She suffered no indignity there when discrimination was rampant.*[7]

Twenty years later, when I was again in the entertainment business and bringing back many of the talents from my Cafe Society days, I would be asked, "How come you don't have Hazel Scott?" That's why.

"'Will Geer, Will Hare, what the hell's the difference?'"

I wondered about Lena. She was never called to testify before the committee. I knew she had been attacked in the right-wing press and had begun to be blacklisted. Then I found out she had met privately with one of the publishers of *Counterattack,* Ted Kirkpatrick, and made her peace—for a fee. That was another one of the "business" sidelines of these great guardians of democracy—blackmail. It's a good thing she never married me. I have little use for stool pigeons. I am reminded of Lillian Hellman's eloquent words she wrote to the committee when she was subpoenaed [in May 1952]: "I will not cut my conscience to fit this year's fashions." The principled stand Lillian and her Dashiell Hammett took left them in bad financial straits.

When Leon was sentenced to prison, Dash signed an appeal to President Truman on March 26, 1948, urging executive clemency. Dash was a lot of things I believed in, so I always wondered how the hell a man like Dashiell Hammett could have been a Pinkerton detective in his youth. The Pinkerton detectives were notorious union strikebreakers in the 1920s and 1930s, cracking not a few heads. Dash was a wonderful man in many, many areas. When we entered World War II he inveigled the U.S. Army Signal Corps to accept him [on September 17, 1942]. I don't know how he did it with his medical history and forty-eight years old. He was a consumptive and had been in sanatoriums for the cure. And he just drank too damn much. Lillian speaks of herself as drinking too heavily also.

Dash was at Uptown one night, and he was loaded. He was always loaded when I saw him. After all, I'm running a saloon, so if a guy is going to be gassed he's going to be gassed in a drinking establishment. Dash, when he was loaded, could get abusive, even to me. This particular night he just be-rated me, thrashed me to the floor without throwing me to it. He thrashed me verbally—"You petty-bourgeois saloon operator. Here you are pretending to be doing the interracial thing and all that, and all you're doing is making a lot of money." Dash was making a lot of money in those days, too, and contributing, I'm sure, to the good causes just as I was. Now he's giving me a hard time, really abusing me. "You're pretending to run a certain kind of operation, but you're just running this operation to make money. You're ex-ploiting these people you're presenting here" and on and on. I finally said to myself, "Fuck you, mister." I got up from the table and walked away. That's the last time I spoke to him.

In 1951 Dash went to prison for six months because he refused to divulge the names of people who had contributed to a fund set up by the Civil Rights Congress to provide bail for defendants arrested for political reasons. Dash was chairman of the fund. He refused because he knew full well that other-wise those contributors would be harassed and blacklisted. When he came out of prison he looked awfully ill. To add to his health problems he was blacklisted in Hollywood, in trouble with the IRS, and broke—but not bro-ken. Dash was an honorable man.

Most assuredly, no honor is due Elia Kazan, who frequented my cafes. Gadge [his nickname], a friendly witness, named his fellow actors from his acting days when he was in the Communist Party [1934–36]. Tony Kraber, the folk singer, now a CBS radio executive, was an unfriendly witness and subsequently fired. He cracked, "Is this the Kazan that signed a Hollywood contract for $500,000 dollars the day he gave names to the committee?" Zero's name for him was Loose Lips. During World War II there were post-ers plastered around the country, cautioning "loose lips sink ships." In all, Gadge named about twenty theater people, among whom was my friend Martin Ritt. Marty had just been appointed to head up the newly formed color television division at CBS, an important career move.

Martin Ritt: *I'd rather not talk about Gadge. He was once my friend, my teacher. I've never been able to look Gadge in the eye, nor he me.*[1]

When the curtain went up for Marty in 1957 he became one of Hollywood's most important film directors. His twenty-five or so films were about subjects and issues he believed in. His movie *The Front* was Marty's tribute to blacklisted writers and actors. On the credits at the end, next to each actor's name is the date he had been blacklisted. One was Johnny Randolph, a fine stage and screen actor, an old friend.

In the early days of Downtown I had the idea to institute a satirical review on Sunday afternoons, modelled on Cabaret TAC.

John Randolph: *David Pressman, an acting teacher, and I had just gotten out of the service, trying to get back in circulation. We went down to Cafe Society because it was like home. Barney came up with the suggestion, "Why don't you guys do something on Sunday afternoons? We don't have anything here." That's how the Sunday matinee* Satirical Revues *came about. Barney opened up something that I had never been involved in, complete faith that two of us could do a job as producers, getting talent. He gave us the place rent free.*[2]

HUAC came to New York in 1955 and 1956 with the intent to "probe alleged Communist infiltration in radio, TV and the legitimate theatre."[3] Hearings were held in the Federal Courthouse on Foley Square. Johnny Randolph and his wife Sarah Cunningham both took the Fifth, and they didn't work again in films for fifteen years.

John Randolph: *There were cases of mistaken identity. The name of a guy, Will Hare, came before the committee. I knew Will Hare was apolitical. I knew him as a lovely, lovely, gentleman. Never got involved. His friend was the vice president of CBS and had brought his name up for the lead in a show. In discussing the casting, one of the vice presidents said, "His name came back politically unacceptable." Will's friend said, "I know he's never been political." "Well, I'm sorry, that's the information I got." His friend went back and told Will. "I don't know what he's talking about. Maybe he got me mixed up with Will Geer." So his friend went back with the information and explained the mix-up. This guy replies, "Will Geer, Will Hare, what the hell's the difference? Sounds the same." And Will Hare was on the blacklist for a long time. Will Geer appeared before HUAC. They never did anything to Will Geer.*[4]

Lionel Stander offered to name names of a group who were trying to undermine the Constitution. The comic Stanley Prager, who had worked in my cafes in 1947, took the Fifth. He was currently starring in *Pajama Game* on Broadway, directed by George Abbott. Stanley was sure he would be fired. Instead, Abbot signed him to a long-term contract. Zero, in Los Angeles, was an unfriendly witness.[5] After his testimony there were a bunch of TV cameras and reporters waiting for him. Surveying the crowd, "They're letting me back on television—first time in years."

Ivan Black came prepared with a copy of the United States Constitution and invoked the First, Fifth, Sixth, Tenth, and Fourteenth Amendments.[6] One of the questions he was asked was whether he had been a press agent for Cafe Society "when Leon Josephson, an admitted communist, was connected with the cafe."[7] Guilt by association.

Imogene Coca: *I don't know the exact year. I don't think it was a long time after I was out of Cafe. I got a call. They wanted me to appear in a brand new nightclub. I think it was called the Papillon. It was an absolutely beautiful club on Sunset Boulevard just as you go into Beverly Hills. I was in the opening show. A couple of nights after we opened the owner said to me, "I know you didn't read your notices, but they're all fine. One of the critics who wrote a very good notice for you is out there. Thank him for the notice."*

So I went out, met the gentleman and said, "Thank you for the notice." He said, "You were lucky." I said, "Pardon me?" He repeated, "You were lucky." I said, "Oh?" He said, "I wrote that notice before I knew all about you." I thought, "Dear god, what is he talking about?" I got cold all over. It scared me. I said, "What do you mean, all about me?" "You worked at Cafe Society." I said, "That's right." "Then you're a communist." I said, "First of all, I'm not a communist. Barney Josephson and I never had conversations. I don't know what food he likes for dinner let alone his politics, and I very much question that idea. Quite frankly, he probably would have given Hitler a job if he had a good act." The man looked at me and went, "Uh." "The man only books you in his room if he thinks you're good. This is a professional. He has a very highly thought of night club, and he's not about to put anybody on that floor he doesn't think is great. I mean, he doesn't care about their politics or what they like for dinner."

I just couldn't get over it. I thought if my mother could hear this, or my father, or my dear friends, or my husband they'd probably start to laugh. Then I said to myself, "Good god, maybe this happens to other people who are equally as far removed from political awareness really as I." This was very frightening, very frightening. I thought too, "He could have given me a devastating notice." I remember I turned cold all over and thought, "Is this really happening to other people? I don't believe this. I'm dreaming." Even talking about it now, and it's so many years.[8]

HUAC was determined to have his own people denounce Paul Robeson, famous names such as Jackie Robinson, who agreed to testify in 1949.[9] His "carefully worded" statement appeared on the front page of *The New York Times.* From that moment on, Paul's public life began a downward spiral. They took away his passport in 1950, one he'd held since 1922, so that he couldn't go abroad to earn a living. They closed concert halls to him here. They removed his record albums from music stores. His income dropped to practically nothing. *Variety* reported on what he had earned in 1946: "Paul Robeson's $141,294, a solo concert mark. Figure represents one of the top earnings in the music biz for strictly concert takes."[10] Paul was subpoenaed in 1956 to appear before HUAC.

Rep. Gordon Scherer: *Why do you not stay in Russia?*
Paul Robeson: *Because my father was a slave, and my people died to build this country, and I am going to stay here and have a part of it just like you. . . . Is that clear?*[11]

Paul passed in 1976, emotionally and physically spent. For his last ten years he lived quietly in his sister's home in Philadelphia. I choose to remember Paul visiting my home. Eddie, my first-born son, wouldn't stop crying. Paul picked him up, cradling him in his arms, softly crooning "My Curly-Headed Baby." Eddie went fast asleep.

We all have deep scars from those years. Leon blamed himself for the loss of the cafes, for the loss of my money. He was devastated. He kept berating himself until finally I told him, "It's not your fault. There's no way in the world anyone could have forecast this terrible period. Don't ever let me hear you say another word. We're going on from here." And I did.

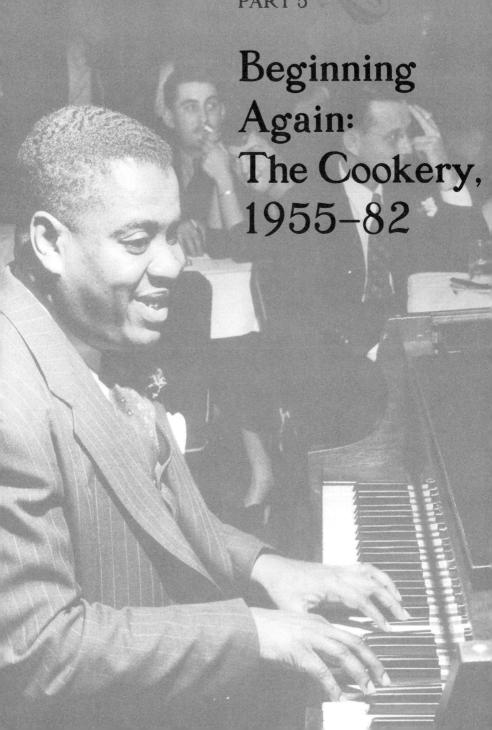

PART 5

Beginning Again: The Cookery, 1955–82

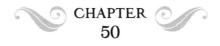

CHAPTER
50

"Mr. Anonymous"

I was walking down Lexington Avenue when I saw an empty store opposite Bloomingdale's. It had a for-rent sign in the window. I said to myself, "This looks like a pretty good location for a hamburger place. I'm going to open in this place." I called the telephone number listed on the window, made an appointment with the dentist who owned the building. I leased the store and called it The Cookery.

I had learned a little about the restaurant business while I had my clubs and had some ideas. I opened a "hamburgerie," a little sandwich place with forty-four chairs. I called in Ref to decorate it. Here I have a place in which I'm selling a few simple sandwiches, ham and eggs, hamburgers, but with Refregier's art on the wall.

He created a whole new thing for me, a very modernistic type of work. He drew designs and then traced them onto panel board. Then with a saw, cut out the designs, painted the panel board. Onto these designs he affixed antique objects, mostly having to do with cooking. Ref lived in Woodstock, New York, and he toured all the old barns and antique places. He picked up old ladles and spoons and cookie cutters and tops of old stoves and little doors from old coal stoves with the old iced glass showing through the design of the door. Then he wired them into the open areas. He was so many years ahead of his time doing this. Picasso has done this kind of thing, too.

I tried to match this in my own crazy way. I bought a lot of oddball china for salad bowls, for ketchup dishes. I sent one young man out to all the antique stores to buy every one he could find of antique shaving mugs with the names on them in gilt and with pictures. I used them for relish bowls on my counters. The counters were table height, with people sitting around them like you now see in Japanese restaurants with the cook in the center. Except I had the cook in the window. I did things like that.

At the same time, I decided that with Ref's artwork and the nice little pieces I was using for service I didn't want coffee-shop waitresses. I met a young man who had contact with dancers, modern and ballet. He would tell me about these dancers, who never had steady work. "Can you bring some of them around for me to see them? I'd like to make waitresses out of them."

Well he brought a dozen of the most stunning young girls you ever saw, eighteen to about twenty-four. I asked them, "Do you want to be waitresses?" I figured for this kind of service, coffee, hamburger, ham and eggs, toasted muffin, and a little salad, anybody can serve that. I put them all to work.

When I first opened the door in 1951 and people walked in, they saw a new kind of restaurant. They were astounded. They had come in for a hamburger and a cup of coffee and saw Refregier's artwork on the wall, the set-up of the place, and these young ladies standing around ready to serve them. They took a look at them and gasped. You could hear it. "Where did you get such waitresses?" They weren't very good at serving a cup of coffee, but they were so beautiful, so unusual for a coffee-shop-type restaurant, together with all the nice little tchotchkes I had around, that the place was a big success from the first day it opened opposite Bloomingdale's main entrance.

The space had been a restaurant, a bar and grill, a little bakery shop, various stores of this nature—one failure after another over a period of years. I came in with Refregier, some beautiful ballerinas to serve coffee, and people just flocked to me. It was the most unusual hamburgerie ever for its menu and its presentation of food. My name was not associated with it in any way. There was no entertainment, no music. I just wanted to keep my name out of the press, Mr. Anonymous. I had found a business where I didn't need reviews, write-ups, to bring people in to my place of operation. So Leon and I were able to continue making a living.

Subsequently, I opened two more Cookerys, one on 52nd Street in the CBS building and then a third one, the longest-lasting, The Cookery on University Place and 8th Street in Greenwich Village, back to where it all began for me. Eventually, I had to close the first Cookery because the building was sold to a bank which wanted the space for itself. The one on 52nd Street was not a great location. After five o'clock everyone went home, so I had to close it. In those days there was very little business in that neighborhood for my type of operation.

The branch on University Place was much larger and grander than my first little shop. Ref's artwork had now become my trademark in a sense, so he had to follow up. He used a similar approach but to suit the greater space. Among others, he made five oblong-shaped panels which are centered over table booths on walls of cypress wood. He cut out the panels, and in the cut-outs are various utensils, old ladles, kitchen strainers, parts of stoves, a cooking grate, an old, battered enamel pot cover, all old stuff. For other panels he used stained glass. He worked in ceramics, objects embedded in cement. He did a whole wall of ceramics. He made duplicates of some of the artwork from the first Cookery. One panel became our trademark. It was a steer, which represented the hamburger motif, a steer's eye, and a strainer. None of these panels were screwed or nailed to the walls. They were affixed to the wall, with a space between the wall and the artwork six or seven inches from the wall, behind which were lights. Thus, the lighting from behind these panels illuminated the panel, the designs, and the objects wired into the panel's cut-out spaces.

For some of the other panels he found wood from an old staircase, the railing coming down a winding staircase, part of the strips holding up the railing from the steps to the top rail, all old, weathered wood. Ref put them in frames as if you were framing a painting. Ninety percent of the objects displayed had to do with food, with utensils used in creating food, serving food. Ref created an oblong panel with a floating figure carrying a tray. Occasionally, he would throw in an old lock, a chair, the spiral piece in a meat grinder, all old, rusted objects, broken, enamel chipped off. No new things. He incorporated old, used objects into the most modern forms. Ref's art is so current. It's the art of today.

From the year I opened on University Place in 1955 and for the next fifteen years The Cookery was conducted as a straight restaurant.[1] Sylvia and

I were divorced in 1951. Actually, those had been such tough years for the both of us, the blacklist and the loss of both my cafes. I was worried about Claudia, Sylvia's daughter. We were so close. I went to a psychiatrist to help me work out what would be best for Claudia. He suggested it would be easier for her if I gradually withdrew from our relationship. A year after opening on University Place I married again, July 26, 1956, to Gloria Agrin.

We were married awfully fast. She lived with her parents in an apartment above The Cookery. The Cookery's windows are glass almost from top to bottom, and I would see her passing by with her briefcase. I knew who she was, that she had worked in the law office of Emanuel Block, the lawyer for Ethel and Julius Rosenberg. The Rosenbergs had been electrocuted, and Block had since died. She was in private practice with Blanche Friedman. Their practice was very small, with Gloria earning a pittance. She always looked so sad, or so I thought. One night as she passed by I went outside and asked her to have a drink with me across the street. We had dinner, and I asked her to marry me—just like that. We saw each other every night for about three weeks. A few weeks later we were married.

She was not, what I would say, physically attractive, but I thought we had a lot in common. She did question why I would want to marry someone like her after all the glamour of my cafe days. I told her I thought we would be good for one another. She was not a woman I ordinarily would have been attracted to, but I had told myself I was through with the glamorous life. I wanted a peaceful one of what was left of it. I was now fifty-four years old, and she was twenty-one years younger. Peaceful? I couldn't have been more wrong. Almost from the very beginning signs of difficulties were there, and I still don't know why I disregarded them.

Not long after our marriage, Gloria suggested we have a child. I had not been thinking along those lines, figuring I was too old to start a family. Then my first son, Edward, was born, and my joy was boundless. Three and a half years later, on August 15, 1961, Louis, named after my brother, Lou, arrived.

Jimmie Josephson: *Barney was a devoted father to those kids. He was so proud of them. He would do anything in the world for them. One time Eddie's and Lucky's [Louis's nickname] school was in some kind of a protest parade along 5th Avenue or Broadway, some sort of social action. Barney didn't want them to go alone, so he walked alongside of the parade on the street. There he was leaving his business, he was that*

protective of them. One of the kids asked Eddie, "Is that your grandfa-
ther?" "No, he's my Dad." Barney laughed when he told me this story.
There was nothing too good for them. They went to the best schools.
He never spared them anything in the way of luxuries. He was always
just glowing when he talked about them. He was so thrilled to have
them. Every little achievement that they had he thought so wonderful.
I thought he spent a lot of time with them. They were always in The
Cookery.[2]

For the next fourteen years The Cookery did well, operated solely as a restaurant. Every so often in the early years I'd spot an FBI guy in the place. One
even approached, wanting to talk with me.[3]

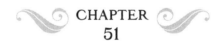

CHAPTER 51

"'We did it, Barney. You and me and the Lord Jesus Christ.'"

J ohn S. Wilson: *Two vital but long-absent contributors to the New York jazz scene have finally returned and they have come back together. One is Barney Josephson and the other is Mary Lou Williams. Her return is a major event in the jazz world and her reunion with Mr. Josephson provides a fitting celebration of the thirty-second anniversary of Cafe Society.*[1]

Mary Lou Williams had come to me practically in tears. It was over twenty-five years since she had played at the cafes. Once in a while she would call me, asking for help for some person, often a musician, never for herself. Now she was telling me, "We jazz musicians can't get work anymore. Nobody wants any jazz. The jazz musicians are starving. Barney, we have to do something about it, and you're the one who can do it. Let me play piano for you." Chuckling in that inimitable fashion of hers, "You know, Barney, the happiest days of my life were with you at Cafe Society." Reminiscing about those days, she told Whitney Balliett, "We were kind of a family there and Barney Josephson thought of us that way."[2]

Mary had come in with a young Jesuit priest, Peter O'Brien. He had phoned me some time previously, asking for an appointment, saying he was a friend of Mary Lou's. He came in a couple of times alone after that but never mentioned what apparently was in their minds. I didn't know then that he was Mary's manager and spiritual mentor.

Mary had become deeply involved in religious work, a Baptist converted to Catholicism. She had been playing in a Paris nightclub in 1953, and one evening she just walked off the bandstand. The music had stopped. She told herself she would never return to music.

> **Peter O'Brien:** *I think part of that retreat in the 1950s could be called a nervous breakdown. I don't know what precipitated it. That's very complex, and I think it's a thirty-year buildup to that. She was working at fourteen. . . . Whatever the profound business was, when she came out the other side of that, whatever the religious construct was that helped her reconstitute herself, this reaching out toward others is part of it. But it always was. That's what's not known.*
>
> *She had lived in a convent in Denmark in 1968 when she had a job in Timmie Rosenkrantz's club. . . . We spent weeks in Newark, New Jersey, she in a convent, me in the rectory; then doing the Masses on a Sunday with the music she had written. She would do concerts, she would do this, she would do that but always on her own terms and always fairly at a distance. She had an idea of maybe getting jobs in Catholic colleges and convents. That's part of what it is before Barney.*
>
> *Barney was very nice, kind of misty-eyed, "Hello Mary. How are you?" He was very warm, very direct, very simple. . . . It is completely true that Mary said, "Why don't you put a piano over there?"*[3]

I walked around the place a couple of times, and I thought it over. Can you imagine, this lady, one of the greatest jazz musicians of all times, composer, arranger, not working? It was all this wild, crazy rock. Well, in the past I would play my hunches. They weren't always successful, but I have a feeling about the moment. This was one of them. I investigated and found out I didn't need a cabaret license in my place if I only had three string instruments.

"Mary, go and rent a piano. Find one you want to play. Send it down here. I only want a rental because I'm not sure. I don't want to buy a piano and invest $1,000. Give me three weeks to publicize that you're coming in. Win or lose, you're going to work four months. If I don't lose any money on this, if I just break even, you can stay forever. If you go over, if it works, we'll buy the piano."

She went out, sent a piano, and I rented it for four months. Within thirty days I called the piano company and bought the piano. I was back in entertainment again.

Art D'Lugoff: *The Cookery came about as far as the music policy because I flubbed, and I'm happy I flubbed. Mary Lou Williams came to me at my place, the Village Gate, and she said, "I'd like a gig at the Gate." I kept putting her off and putting her off. . . . Finally she said, "Well, if you won't hire me, I'll go to Barney." So she went to Barney, and sure enough Barney picked up on it and started once again in the music business. And I'm very happy to have been part of it. I'm glad I turned down that offer.*[4]

Mary's opening on November 20, 1970, was the first night I enjoyed The Cookery business. Mary played from 8 P.M. to 1 A.M. every evening except Sunday. I didn't have a cover charge. I wasn't certain at all how it would go. Sometime after her triumphant return to wonderful reviews, and the crowds pouring in, piano bars started sprouting up all over town. Mary was joyous. "We did it, Barney. You and me and the Lord Jesus Christ."

Peter O'Brien: *What Mary Lou wanted, and what Barney provided for her, was a place to stay in New York. Almost nobody does that now, and certainly nobody was doing that then. The Gate and the Vanguard, I don't know what the policy was absolutely, but my impression is they'd book 'em in for a week. Now, Mary Lou would never have made it that way at that time. There wasn't enough visibility. And she said, "Barney would do that. He would stick with you until it started to pay off."*[5]

Mary, for her first engagement, stayed on the four months. As far as I was concerned she could have remained forever. Actually, the end of January I had sent out a press release that we were extending her gig indefinitely. Now she was getting offers to play from all over the country. She felt she had to take them because it would help her record sales, not for herself but to support the Bel Canto Thrift Shop and Foundation she had established in 1957 to aid alcoholics, narcotic addicts, and other unfortunate folk from the jazz world.

Peter O'Brien: *I'm the one who got her back into a full-time explosion for the last ten years. . . . Just before going to Barney, that summer we were sitting in her Cadillac about three in the morning in front of where I was living at 102nd Street and Riverside Drive, and she said to me, "I'll go out if you'll go with me." When Mary had her own band right before*

Cafe Society, very frequently her niece went with her, sometimes her sister, to take care of the clothes, the correspondence, watch everything, other than the music. . . . She founded a jazz festival with George Wein, got the money for it in Pittsburgh. In the summer of '57 she appears with Dizzy Gillespie at the Newport Jazz Festival. Early in the 1960s she forms a recording company, Mary Records, and her own publishing company, Cecilia Music Publishing. Saint Cecilia is the patron saint of musicians. In 1964 she puts out her first recording, was at the Hickory House, had a profile in the New Yorker. *She really begins to try to put her business affairs in line. It's the way an amateur would do it, and overwhelmed with all sorts of things. She's working steadily from 1957 to 1970, but there's no splash. There's constant accomplishment, constant notice, but no concerted effort and no long presence. There was no ability to make it pay off . . . and that's where Barney comes in.*[6]

Just as in the Cafe Society days when Mary Lou had recorded there, now *Live at The Cookery* was recorded, and a CD was released in 1975 by Chiaroscuro Records with the fine bassist Brian Torff. Mary takes her listeners on a trip through the history of jazz—hymns, blues, stride, swing, bop. Her mission is to reach out not just to the knowledgeable but to the uninitiated, to hear and feel jazz, to understand its roots—to save jazz.

Peter O'Brien: *Mary was a born teacher about music to students and to musicians. We did endless workshops all over the country. . . . She had students in the 1940s and she had students all along. It's kind of like a crusader. We were four years at Duke University.*[7]

Mary Lou was one of the first jazz composers to write sacred music. In November 1975, "Mary Lou's Mass" was sung in St. Patrick's Cathedral, the first jazz Mass ever celebrated there. It made the front pages.

Mary returned to The Cookery each year through 1976 for three-month gigs, always to critical acclaim and crowds. I was saddened to learn in 1979 that she was suffering from cancer, although she did continue to teach at Duke. She passed two years later at her home in Durham, North Carolina. She was seventy-one. We shall not ever meet the likes of Mary Lou Williams in this world.

CHAPTER
52

"'If he liked an idea,
he would do it.'"

Having been out of the music and entertainment business for so long I hadn't kept up. I was not interested in rock. When Mary Lou opened she drew a lot of jazz musicians who came to hear her. One evening I was introduced to the jazz pianist Marian McPartland. I knew her by name, though I'd never heard her play. I knew she had a long-running gig in the 1950s with her trio at the Hickory House, and I knew she was married to the cornetist Jimmy McPartland, who had played with Bix Beiderbecke.

Marian McPartland: *How did Barney come to me? I think I came to him. Mary Lou Williams had been sort of in hiding, and of course I went down to hear her, and that's where I met Barney. Sure I knew of Barney. I heard many people talking about Cafe Society. I knew Mary Lou was there, so it seemed logical to me that he would open The Cookery with somebody he'd had before, like Mary Lou. The nights I was in to hear Mary Lou, Barney would always come over and sit down. "Would you like coffee? Would you like dessert?" Actually, he was always bringing me some kind of dessert, and I was always trying to resist.*[1]

Marian's trio always had a bass player and drummer, but I had no license for anything but string instruments. So Marian accommodated very nicely with a fine young bassist, Jay Leonhart, who was beginning to make a name for himself. She opened to great reviews. My "experiment" was paying off. I could buck the rock and roll with music I wanted. I was turning on the spotlight again to marvelous jazz musicians.

Marian McPartland: *I always think of Barney as somebody that was not weak about doing anything. He would do it regardless. He wouldn't say, "Oh well, this is not a good time." If he liked an idea, he would do it.*[2]

I continued my Cafe Society policy of giving musicians lengthy engagements. Whitney picked up on that in his review of Marian.

Whitney Balliett: *Barney Josephson started his excellent practice of long-term engagements when he had his Cafe Societys. It allows his musicians to grow into the room, to expand and experiment.*[3]

Marian is an elegant and charming Englishwoman, and I always enjoy talking with her. We did have some minor differences. Nothing serious.

Marian McPartland: *I do remember fiddling and fussing with him about where the piano is going to go. I remember spending an afternoon getting the piano set up just right. He wanted it at a certain angle, and I wanted it at another angle. I guess we compromised.*

At times it would be difficult because there was no bandstand. You were right on the floor. Sometimes people would come in who knew me, "Marian!" You'd be right in the middle of a tune. Somebody would want to give me a hug, and I'd be, "I'll see you in a while," giving them an elbow off the bench. I sort of nagged Barney, "Couldn't you just put the bandstand up like a couple of inches?" He would sort of brush it off, "No, we don't need that. You're fine the way you are." People could walk over too easily and sit down on the bench, which they would do.

Boy, they would get noisy as hell sometimes. I never liked that, and I was very snippy about making remarks, trying to keep people quiet. Actually, when you think about it, the room was a very unlikely place for a jazz club, and yet people remember it fondly and talk about it as a fantastic place for music, and, of course, it was.[4]

I wanted to celebrate New Year's Eve 1971 with music. This would be a first for The Cookery, and Marian would be there.

Marian McPartland: *This is the night I persuaded Whitney Balliett to come in and set up drums and play because he was so self-effacing and* *yet loved to play. This may have been the time that Jimmy McPartland came and sat in, too.*[5]

Nancy Balliett: *Whitney played the drums one New Year's Eve.*
Whitney Balliett: *Oh god. . .[embarrassed].*
Nancy Balliett: *I sat at the table with Popsy Whitaker and Tony Hiss and his girlfriend.*
Whitney Balliett: *Popsy Whitaker was a friend of Barney's from the old days, amusement editor at the* New Yorker.
Nancy Balliett: *At the end of the evening, Whitney came back to the table. "It's nice to see you again."*[6]

Marian returned two more times. Then she gets a gig at the Carlyle Hotel. That's uptown and I'm downtown. Marian would not be playing The Cookery anymore.

Marian McPartland: *Barney did get annoyed with me once because he wanted me to come back and I refused. I was ensconced in the Carlyle, and I didn't want to change images. He understood, but I think he felt a little hurt. I just felt it was best for me. I didn't want to make a change because that was such a great job. To rock the boat in any way just didn't seem like the thing for me to do. He did come up to see me quite a few times.*[7]

During my Cafe Society days John Hammond had heard a piano player, Eddie Heywood, at the Three Deuces Club on 52nd Street and asked him if he would like to work for Barney Josephson. Eddie organized a sextet with Vic Dickenson, Doc Cheatham, Lem Davis, Jack Parker, Al Lucas. They opened on a program with Mary Lou, Josh White, and Pearl Primus. That was 1943 at Downtown.[8] On and off for about four years, Eddie played both cafes. Thirty years later, Eddie's at The Cookery. I had persuaded him to come out of retirement.

In the cafe days Eddie was a stutterer. When I didn't have a comedian on the program, my band leaders would substitute as emcees. Eddie didn't want to emcee. He was afraid of being laughed at by the audience. I did a little speech therapy with Eddie. I told him to try, that nobody would laugh and that he'd get rid of his stutter. The first few times he stuttered pretty badly. Nobody laughed. Gradually, over the course of a week he stuttered less and less. By the end of the week it was practically gone. It was to return.

This was draft time, World War II. Eddie had been classified 4F because of his speech impediment. Several weeks into his gig he told me he was due to have another physical, but he wanted his 4F status to continue. Would I allow him to quit emceeing so that his stutter would return? "Okay, but suppose it doesn't return?" He assured me it would, and it did. The army continued his 4F classification, and Eddie resumed emceeing without stuttering. When I was no longer in entertainment Eddie had tried a comeback in the 1950s.

Eddie Heywood: *I got a job at The Embers, but I must say they weren't nice to me at all. I had to open and close, open and close. I decided to quit. The music business was getting bad. Everything was noise. . . . We could live off the royalties. . . . When I opened here at The Cookery the other night, I hadn't gotten used to the instrument, but it was a wonderful feeling when I started on the piano and the audience—young and old—began to applaud.*[9]

Eddie returned for three more gigs and forgot about retirement.

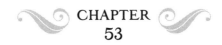

CHAPTER
53

"'I'll tell you, Teddy Wilson, you've just made Barney Josephson cry.'"

I couldn't wait to bring in Teddy Wilson in February 1972. He had played for so many, many years, six or more, at both cafes, starting in 1940. Through all these lean years for jazz Teddy always worked, if not here then in Europe, Japan, in the winter in class resorts in the Caribbean Islands. He taught privately, was on the staff at CBS in the mid-1950s, and reunited with Benny Goodman for recordings and concerts.

Teddy Wilson: *I'm mostly on the road. I've spent more time in Japan in the last three years than I've spent in Boston, where I have an apartment with my son Steven, the drummer. My wife, in New Jersey with the younger children, directs jobs to Boston. It's always New Year's Eve or Saturday night because in every town it's a reunion. Then when I come back it's a reunion with the kids. You're never around anybody long enough to say, well, I want to get away from you. Everywhere you go, you're glad to see the people, when you come home, when you go away. That's the thing about road life that's so good. When you live in hotels, you don't have to wash dishes, you don't have to sweep. You just pay your bill. It's a nice life. But you always have to keep booked, too. You have to fill the calendar. People have to want to pay to see you. You have to keep yourself up. You can't let yourself go to pot.*[1]

John S. Wilson: *There is one thing about Mr. Wilson's appearance at The Cookery that is different. He has found an ideal Teddy Wilson room. . . . To be heard at his best Mr. Wilson needs to be warmed by the atmosphere around him.*[2]

Teddy returned the end of December 1972 for his second gig. He would be here for New Year's Eve, but Teddy had become a drunk. Drunk all the time. He had me in tears one night. He would play ten-, twelve-, fifteen-minute sets. People were walking out. They said they'd come to hear Teddy Wilson. The show was forty on, twenty off, union regulations. People would come and go. So if you came in six or seven minutes after Teddy started his set you only got maybe seven minutes of him. He would go off, lose himself with the people around. Or he would go out to get a drink at one of the bars nearby. He'd be out fifty minutes. Now you've waited an hour for Teddy Wilson to play. He comes back and plays for another fifteen minutes or less.

I talked to him. I had a contract with him to come back again a third time. Teddy's touring schedule was tight, so he needed a contract. I warned him, "I'm going to cancel. You're not going to work for me anymore." He insisted. He had a contract, and he was going to come back and play it.

"Well," I said, "If you insist on playing it, because you do have a contract, you're going to go out there and play forty minutes, take a twenty-minute break, and come back to play forty minutes again, then another twenty-minute break. That's according to our contract. The first time you don't, I'll call Local 802. I'll present charges and cancel you out. You know, Teddy, for all the years we've been together, what you've done to me these last two engagements, it's just unforgivable, unpardonable. Now, if I'm not here one night, and you're sitting with people, and it's time to go on, Moe, my manager, is going to come to you and say, 'Mr. Wilson, it's time.' He'll be keeping time, and if you don't get right up and play, you're out."

When I threatened him with that I started crying. "I'll tell you, Teddy Wilson, you've just made Barney Josephson cry. You'll never make him cry again. Teddy Wilson brought tears to Barney Josephson's eyes when you make me, Barney Josephson, threaten that I'll take you to the union. I never thought I could say that, but I'll do it."

I was crying because for me to have to say that to Teddy Wilson. After all those years with me in both cafes we never had a bad word. I love the guy. I respect Teddy. He was always a gentleman in every way. Now he was always gassed. Finally, all right, he would do what he had to do.

Why did I let this continue? Well, I fought him all the time. After I would have words with him, he'd be all right for one or two nights. But I wasn't there every night. Moe would give me the report on him. He'd go over to the table where Teddy'd be sitting, "Mr. Wilson, it's time." Teddy would snap, "Don't tell Teddy Wilson when to go on. You're not my boss."

Teddy had been through a bunch of wives, and he's had kids with each one of them. He has a lot of alimony to pay all around, so he needs money all the time, but he's a big earner. Teddy called me a couple of months after our last talk about his behavior. "Barney, I have a request to make. The lawyer for one of my former wives hauled me into court. She claims I owe her $12,000 in back alimony. My lawyer told me I was in the clear, but the court ordered me to pay up within a certain limit of time or go to jail. I have a chance to go to Europe to do a gig over there for pretty big money."

But I had signed him for three months for his forthcoming gig.[3] He would like to have the first month off because it would interfere with his European gig. He was asking me for a favor. He had figured it out: "I'll come in a month later and tack that month on the end." I told him no. I didn't want him back after all the aggravation he had caused me. "Teddy, first of all, the month that you want to give me on the end, I already have somebody coming in the day after you go out." That was true; I was always prepared. "I understand you need the money. Take the European gig, but I'll have to cancel you out. I'm not going to stop you from taking the gig, which I could do, but I won't. I know you can always work some place else to make up the money. I'll send you a letter to that effect."

That was the last I saw Teddy Wilson until he came back to play in January of 1983, ten years later. His drinking had gotten so bad that his doctor told him, "You either quit, or you're a dead man." That scared him. I'd heard that he had quit, that he was all right now. When he came back it made us both happy.

Teddy is due back again in July. I receive a note from him [May 12, 1983]: "Barney, please don't use that picture of me playing with a hat on. Someone took that at some rehearsal without my knowledge. . . . That picture is not the image I'm trying to sell for public performance. Please use this pose I'm enclosing. All the best, Teddy." After over fifty years in the public eye he was still meticulous about his image. One evening Teddy and I got to reminiscing at the table:

Barney: *Do you remember when you played Uptown with Carole Channing?*

Teddy: *Jimmy Savo was up there. You had another comedian who used to do that bird routine, the canary would go up his sleeve.*

Barney: *Fred Keating, he was a magician, a big name on Broadway. The canary didn't go up his sleeve. His bird cage was just the wires, no solid bottom. He'd get the bird on the rung, then he'd go one, two, and the cage collapsed with the bird in it. The bird had disappeared. He invited women to come up and search him. I finally found out where it went. The bird was in his crotch. None of the women were going to go down there. Then he'd go right to his dressing room. He killed quite a few canaries.*

Teddy: *Is that true? I know he would get out pretty quick. . . . I met my second wife in Cafe Society. She and some of her classmates used to come in all the time. They lived in Brooklyn.*

Barney [aside]: *He [Teddy] was a charmer.*

Teddy [playfully]: *I've been to Hollywood about fifteen times, and they haven't given me a contract yet. I was there just a few months ago, and they didn't offer me a contract. This has been going on for forty-five years. I think they're giving me the runaround.*

Terry Trilling: *Teddy, how do you keep your music so fresh?*

Teddy: *You never play the same way. Some things are semiarranged. There are little spots in them that are never the same. That's what keeps you going. The piano is a very difficult instrument to play. Some nights you can play it, and other nights it absolutely defies you. You can't play anything significant on it. Some nights it plays itself, and that keeps you interested, too. It's very enjoyable when it's going well. The notes are coming out just like you want them. It's like it's talking. It's saying something. It's hard to figure. You're just at the mercy of it. I played "Body and Soul" earlier tonight. I've been playing it since 1929, but it never plays itself. You never can really rest. It has nothing to do with what you ate. Sometimes when you're tired you play better than when you're rested. Sometimes you're rested, and you play better than when you're tired.*

Barney: *It's time to go on again [leaves to begin Wilson's introduction].*

Teddy: *We didn't talk enough about Barney though. There's not a night-club owner who even talked or thought or acted like Barney. They were different from him. They were crude sort of people. He was a fine person with class. Most of them were street characters. Barney was politically aware. He knew everything that was going on. Nightclub owners in those days, you couldn't even carry on a conversation with them.*[4]

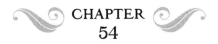

"'He wasn't deceitful about things.'"

Mary Lou Williams had come to me in 1970, pleading to play in The Cookery. She was concerned about all the jazz musicians who could not find work because rock and roll had taken over. Nobody wanted jazz. Another victim of rock and roll was Nellie Lutcher. When I called her she was working full time as an elected official on the board of directors of the Musicians Union in Los Angeles.

Nellie Lutcher: *When Barney contacted me I was thrilled. I really was. He said, "Nellie Lutcher, you know I have a new room now. I have The Cookery, and I'd love to bring you in. People are always asking about you." Barney told me that he would enjoy my performance as much as any patron. That's the truth.*

I had heard about The Cookery. I loved working for Barney. I loved the room. It was a different operation from Cafe Society. That was a very unique spot. It was part of Barney, so I know he was absolutely devastated when he had this problem [being blacklisted]. It was undeserved because he had done so much for musicians and black musicians particularly. There was nowhere hardly for them to work. Barney was a wonderful man to work for. He was just kind and sweet. The thing I loved about him was you knew where you stood with him. He wasn't deceitful about things.[1]

I was happy to welcome back this warm and exuberant lady. Nellie sang her old big hits, the ones she'd written—"Hurry on Down to My House Baby, Ain't Nobody Home but Me," "Real Gone Guy," "Fine Brown Frame"—to great reviews.

Whitney Balliett: *She is an encyclopedia of the black music of fifty years ago. . . . her singing, with its overlay of vocal effects, is full of gospel music. . . . She uses everything in her left hand—stride basses, tenths, offbeat notes and chords, and boogie-woogie basses. . . . She has a robust contralto . . . a master of melisma: she will fill a single syllable with six or seven notes. . . . her singing, like Turner's . . . is easy and seamless.*[2]

Susan Brownmiller: *What else is there to say? You got to haul it on down to The Cookery, sister—Haul it down, drag it down, any way you get down. Ain't nobody home but Nellie Lutcher.*[3]

I had instituted a Jazz by Sunlight program, piano music daily except Mondays from noon to three o'clock and on Saturdays and Sundays until five. A talented young pianist, Chuck Folds, was the third to play this gig and stayed the longest—eventually, just weekends.

Chuck Folds: *That was a pivotal job in my career. I was tired of being always the anonymous jazz band pianist and wanted to develop a solo style and repertoire. That job and Barney's encouragement, made it happen. Whatever success I've had in my seven years now of solo work . . . stems from those weekend afternoons with Barney.*

You don't often hear musicians rave about the nightclub owners they work for. . . . But with Barney Josephson there was much more. He cared deeply about the well-being of his entertainers, as if they were extensions of his family. . . . I stayed five and a half years on that job. There were scarcely any jazz brunches in New York in '73, and Barney took pride in presenting something different. . . . Each afternoon he'd talk with me on any of a hundred topics. . . . Barney was a real charmer—the best storyteller I've ever known.[4]

George Wein phoned. He would like to salute Cafe Society and Barney Josephson for one of his Newport Jazz Festival programs. He would recreate Cafe Society on the stage of Carnegie Hall. As a youngster he had gone to

Cafe Society and had never forgotten. So, on Saturday, June 29, 1974, I found myself seated at a table on the stage of Carnegie Hall with my two boys and Gloria. In my little speech I spoke of the many great artists who had made both Cafe Societys so beloved. "But to one person, not a performer, I must pay tribute above all others. He is John Hammond. . . . He sought out and brought to me the sound of genius that then became the sound of the Cafe Society. If so many of the young talents, who are now acknowledged as our leading jazz performers, think they owe their careers to me, I tell them and I tell you, they owe them first to that marvelous, generous human being, John Hammond."

I was presented with a large, framed, handsome print of a jazz saxophone player by the artist LeRoy Neiman, the official poster for the 1974 Newport Jazz Festival. George Wein added his own very personal touch, an engraved plaque within the frame inscribed with words which are very moving to me: "To Barney Josephson—A creative entrepreneur whose innovative ideas at Cafe Society in the 1930s and 1940s have influenced my life personally, and have served as an inspiration to many program ideas on The Newport Jazz Festival since its inception in 1954. From George Wein, Newport Jazz Festival, N.Y. June 29, 1974."

One of the great singers in jazz history, Helen Humes, had disappeared from the music scene. I hadn't heard of her in years when there she was, singing in George Wein's 1973 Newport Jazz Festival in New York in a tribute to Count Basie. She was working now in a munitions factory, making gunpowder in Louisville, Kentucky, where she was born.

When Billie left Count Basie in 1938, John, who heard Helen at the Renaissance Ballroom in New York, suggested Helen to replace her. I first heard Helen in John's Spirituals to Swing concert. When she left Basie after many years I brought her into Cafe Society as a featured soloist.[5] Now, thirty-three years later, she's back with me. John Wilson remembered her well from those old days: "Her voice is still as sure and flexible as in her Basie days."[6] On the piano accompanying Helen was another of my musicians from the cafe days, Ellis Larkins.

Helen Humes: *It's been such a ball for me, because I haven't been working, and to get here with Barney . . . he gave me my first job when I left Basie. Ohhh, down there at Cafe Society with Meade Lux Lewis, and Tatum, and Joe Turner, Pete Johnson, Albert Ammons, and Teddy*

Wilson, who I just thought was so wonderful, and Leadbelly! . . . Ellis is the greatest. . . . I'm the happiest person in the world just singing.[7]

All kinds of wonderful things were happening for Helen now. John Hammond signed her to a Columbia Records contract. Whitney Balliett profiled her in the *New Yorker*. She was featured in *New York Magazine, Mademoiselle*. From France, Madeleine Hugues-Panassié and the staff of the Hot Club de France sent a plaque, awarding Helen their 1974 Grand Prize in the vocal category. John Wilson wrote, "Jazz singers appear to be staging a comeback in the wake of the great success of Helen Humes."[8]

Helen returned again and again. She was such a joy and so popular. Although we didn't know it at the time, her June 1980 gig would be her last. She was ailing then, receiving treatment for her stomach cancer, singing as well as ever, but a shadow of her former self, always cheerful, never complained. Due to return the summer of '81, she was too ill. Helen was sixty-eight when she passed.[9] Her good friend Nellie Lutcher said, "She was a beautiful person."

I had never completely given up my old idea of a cabaret which presented commentary of the times. Two young ladies, Gretchen Cryer and Nancy Ford, came to audition in 1975. I didn't know anything much about them. They told me they'd written the music and lyrics and performed in two off-Broadway shows, *Now Is the Time for All Good Men* [1967] and *The Last Sweet Days of Isaac* [1970]. Both shows had gotten rave reviews. They sang a number of their songs, and I liked their act. They were young and fresh and had something to say. I made up my mind on the spot to present them.[10]

Gretchen Cryer: *We were probably the only people who ever sang at The Cookery who were not jazz artists, and we were very clearly something else. We were variously called folk, pop, rock, folk-rock, urban-folk, all these labels, but nothing remotely approaching jazz. To me it's really extraordinary that he decided to have us there. What we were doing we called "A Scrapbook of Our Lives" because we started writing songs that were like little snapshots. They were songs about people that we had known. We used their names in the songs. The lyrics, which I wrote, Nancy composed the music, were very much out of my own experience. They were very personal. We had come from the Midwest out of the 1950s, which had a certain set of expectations about what it was to be a woman. This was mid-1970s. The underlying theme always was the changes that women were going through, that we had* *gone through and been witness to. It was kind of the beginning of the women's movement.*

In the middle of a set one night . . . —literally in the middle of singing a song—because of the nature of that material we were doing at The Cookery—the idea came together for writing a show. "I'll make it be about a cabaret singer who's singing songs about her life and I'll call it I'm Getting My Act Together and Taking It on the Road."

Barney was often there. We loved our engagements, had a wonderful time. On the one hand it was very intimate in that people's tables were right up next to where we were singing. But we were also backed up against the omelet bar so that the guy was back there doing his omelet—sizzling. One night a piece of omelet came flipping over onto my keyboard. I started laughing. It's a wonder we didn't have omelet in our hair most of the time.[11]

Big Joe Turner, the greatest of all blues singers, came back to work for me in 1976.[12] Thirty-eight years almost to the month he had opened at Cafe Society Downtown accompanied by his buddy Pete Johnson. This would be his first New York nightclub appearance since the cafe days. The tall, slim Big Joe of those years, still tall, six feet two, was now terribly overweight. He's got a rear end three feet across. I gave him a stool which he engulfed, as one reviewer put it. These days Joe couldn't move around. He had bad trouble with his legs and couldn't stand for very long.

Joe was sixty-five and could still shout the blues as if time stood still. No need for a microphone though he held one in his hand, resting on his knees, the other hand on his cane. Joe dominated the space, all with his voice. These days he was accompanied by an entirely too little known blues pianist, Lloyd Glenn, and a superb guitarist, Wayne Wright. Perhaps only the cognoscenti are aware of Joe's role as a forerunner of rhythm and blues and the rock and roll revolution with his style of singing the blues. Over the years he has sung them all, blues, jazz, rock and roll. They're all the same to him, he has said.

Whitney Balliett: *Turner is probably the greatest of blues singers, stretching from Blind Lemon Jefferson and Big Bill Broonzy through Jimmy Rushing and down to the white English rock singers. Not all his compeers have understood the blues. . . . He sings of every human condition— loneliness, comedy, death, irony, fear, joy, desperation—and he does so in a godlike manner. He hands down his lyrics with his great voice. . . . sometimes he pushes his words together, lopping off the consonants and* *flattening the vowels so that whole lines go past as pure melody, as pure horn playing. . . . On a fast blues, he quickly and repeatedly raises and lowers his voice a tone or a one and a half. . . . On a slow blues, he bends his notes into domes and parabolas, lets them glisten briefly before he cuts them off, pauses, and starts the next line.*[13]

One evening Joe and I were sitting with Whitney Balliett. "Joe, you remember the night I came in Downtown and I kinda looked blue, and you pulled out this little bean?" "Yeah, man, I remember that." "Whatever happened to it?" "I don't have it anymore. Walter Winchell flashed the story on his radio program, and I got hundreds of letters from people all over the country asking me if they could come to me and use the bean on them. I got scared of having so much power. I just threw the bean in the toilet and pulled the chain."

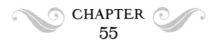

CHAPTER 55

"All I looked at was her mouth."

So many wonderful things happen by accident. I'm a great believer in accidents that shape our lives. People often wonder how it was that someone became this, that, or the other—a singer, actor, writer, criminal. When you delve deeply, it would come out to be something accidental which started them off on such a path.

Sometime early in June 1977 [June 5], Charlie Bourgeois, a good friend and the right hand of George Wein, attended a bon voyage party for Mabel Mercer which Bobby Short threw for her. Mabel was flying to London the following day for an engagement there of a few weeks, her first time back to her native country since World War II. Mabel's mother had been a white English vaudeville headliner, her father a black American. Bobby asked Mabel who she would like him to invite. She mentioned Alberta Hunter, whom she had rarely seen over the years.

Alberta and Mabel were old friends, contemporaries. Both ladies had played with Paul Robeson in *Show Boat* at the Drury Lane in London, which opened in May 1928. Mabel was in the chorus. Alberta was Queenie, Paul's [Joe's] wife, and sang "Can't Help Lovin' Dat Man of Mine." Alberta always admired Mabel's elegant British accent and her way with lyrics. Pictures I've seen of Alberta during her singing days on the Continent show a very chic Alberta wearing elegantly cut English tweeds and couture-designed evening gowns. In the 1920s and 1930s especially, Alberta was a very well-known nightclub and stage singer here and abroad. In Europe, where Negro performers were accorded the respect their talents warranted, where they hobnobbed with the titled fashionables, socialites, writers, artists, Alberta fit right in, this woman born in Memphis, Tennessee, April 1, 1895, of poor but genteel folk.

Alberta received Bobby's formal engraved invitation. She refused to go, grumbling to her good friend since 1925, singer Jimmy Daniels, that she didn't like parties. Mabel learned that Alberta had no intention of going, or maybe Alberta told her. Whatever, Mabel told Bobby, who spoke to Jimmy. It took a lot of talking, but she [Alberta] finally relented although she still maintains she was very angry because Jimmy forced her to go.

At the party, Charlie Bourgeois kept looking at Alberta, intrigued by her manner and her oversized, shoulder-length gold hoop earrings, which have become her signature. Alberta noticed his glances and went over to where he was talking with Alec Wilder. Alec was introduced to Alberta as a writer of songs. Alberta remarked that she'd written a few, too, that she had been a singer and had just retired from a nursing career. Charlie asked her to sing one of her songs, and she softly sang a chorus of her "Downhearted Blues."

Then she told Charlie she was Alberta Hunter, a name with which he was conversant from her old records. He suggested she might try to resume her singing career. She told him outright, "I'm never going to sing again. I don't know if I can. I haven't hummed a tune since I stopped performing." (She neglected to mention that she had made two records with other musicians, one in 1961 and another in 1971. Nothing happened for her then.) "I don't need a job. I'm secure financially. I have all I need for the rest of my days. I don't have a feeling for singing at all. Besides, who'd want an old lady like me?"

Charlie replied, "Why don't you call Barney Josephson? He's the only man I know who would do anything with an old lady singer." That's about the nicest compliment anyone ever paid me. Alberta picked up on Charlie, "I know who Barney Josephson is, but I'm not going to call him." Charlie said, "Ms. Hunter, let me have your telephone number."

The next morning at ten o'clock Charlie called: "Barney, do you remember Alberta Hunter?" "Hell, is she still around?" I hadn't heard her name mentioned in more than thirty years. Personally, I had never liked her voice in the old days. The last time I heard her sing was the early 1940s in a small cafe in New York. I remembered her voice, which at that time was in the soprano range. It didn't quite appeal to me. I like my singers with a warm, sultry kind of voice, sexy, schmaltzy. The soprano was for the opera and that kind of singing. Not for me. But knowing Charlie as I do, she must have looked pretty good to him. "How do I get in touch with her, Charlie?" "I knew you'd ask me that, Barney, so I got her telephone number. Here it is." As soon as we hung up I dialed that number. "Alberta Hunter, this is Barney Josephson."

She didn't seem surprised that I was calling her although she did tell Whitney Balliett, in what was her very first interview, "I was so nervous, I dropped the phone." She's very quick. When Charlie asked her for her phone number she must have known there was going to be a call. With this lady nothing goes by her. She must have given it some thought that night.

"Miss Hunter, I want to see you right away, and I mean right away. Get down here as fast as you can." Within two hours Alberta Hunter was in The Cookery, sitting opposite me at a table.

Why was I in such a rush? Well, Helen Humes would be coming on July 18 and going out three months later. I had engaged Odetta for a five-week period, all she could give me, but she couldn't come in until some time around the last week in November. This gave me a six-week open spread. So if I was going to do anything I had to do it quickly. If it wasn't Alberta it would have to be someone else I'd have to go for. That's why I told Alberta to hurry on down, to quote Nellie Lutcher's song.

As she sat opposite me I looked Alberta, so to speak, in the mouth. My dentist, working on my teeth, mentioned that as we age there's a great deal of bone shrinkage in the gums. When one gets older and may require dentures, there's always difficulty in getting them to hold because there's not enough bone structure for the denture plate to hold on to. That's why you get the whistle and the clicking. So all I looked at was her mouth.

Gerald Cook: *Barney said, "Open your mouth." Amazed, Alberta did as she was told. "Are those your teeth? Are they real?" "Of course," she replied, "Everybody else would have theirs too if they brushed daily with Arm and Hammer baking soda."*[1]

I saw a mouthful of healthy teeth. It looked to me like there was never a dentist in that mouth. While they were not pearly white, they were healthy, solid, good teeth and all her own. And now in her speaking voice I hear something else, not the soprano but a warm, contralto voice. All this played a part in my engaging her. I told myself, "Barney, you haven't a thing to worry about."

"Miss Hunter, you are going to be singing again, here in The Cookery, for me. You have four months to get ready. Helen Humes is going out on the eighth of October, and you're opening on the tenth." To make the story more provocative, I always tell the media she had only three weeks to get ready.

She didn't resist too strongly although she did protest that she wasn't sure that she wanted to sing again, didn't know if she could. "Miss Hunter, I don't want to hear any nonsense that you don't know whether you can sing, whether you have a voice for singing, that you have to think about it. You're singing again. If you don't know an accompanist whom you want to start working with, I'll get you someone." "No. I know somebody." I knew it was all right when she said that. She'd already been thinking ahead. This is a woman who has no hardening of the arteries in her head. She probably had it all worked out by the time she arrived at The Cookery.

How could I have taken this chance without hearing her sing? Well, if one has a hunch to bring in an eighty-two-year-old woman to sing, you can't say to her—not if you're human, although I suppose there are most who would—I could not say to her, "Miss Hunter, I have this job for you, but I'd like to hear what you sound like now." Most artists would not think that to be an unusual request. But I don't know how you ask an eighty-two-year-old artist whom you're urging to come back to singing again on condition she sounds all right. This was a woman who was a very competent singer, an actress, a composer, someone a long time in this business. After all, she was coming to me at my request, and then I say, "I want to hear you sing"? I couldn't do that.

I wasn't hiring her for the voice I knew in the 1940s. I have a sense of timing. You may do the right thing at the wrong time and then it doesn't happen. Seven years ago I started back into this field of jazz with Mary Lou Williams. Her success had been important to a revival of jazz and blues and everything that had to do with this music which had begun to come back. This was the time for me to bring back a really old-timer, a contemporary of the legendary Bessie Smith. No one else could do this. As a so-called saloon impresario (if I may use that term), I love it when people say that because I'm not more than that. It's the way I view myself. In this business if you're an "impresario," I say that with quotation marks around the word, you have a feeling. You hear something, and you say, "This is it!" You go ahead and you do it. You don't analyze. You have to follow your hunches. I've always been instinctive about my discoveries.

Alberta was honest. "Mr. Josephson, I can tell you that you're taking an awful chance with an old lady who hasn't heard herself sing, not even hum in a bathtub in twenty years." "Well Miss Hunter, that's my business. Those are the chances I take. You'll have six weeks. I can't give you more because I have Odetta under contract. That's the way she wanted it. I have to honor it. When Odetta goes out, if you're a smash, as I think you will be, I'll bring you back five weeks later. This is the deal."

Alberta must have known I had managed other performers during my Cafe Society days. So first interview she informs me, "If I am going to do this, if I come in, if anything good should happen to me I want to tell you now I don't want to be bothered with those agents and personal managers hovering around, coming after me. I will come in only if you will promise that you'll take care of me, if you will look after my affairs." I wasn't looking for this kind of work, but I said, "Okay, I'll look after you." That's how we started.

Before Alberta is launched I begin to worry. "Well, Barney, you've committed yourself to this little old lady for six weeks. What makes you think she'll last for six weeks? What makes you think her voice will hold up for six weeks? This lady is going to be doing three shows a night, six nights a week. That's a long engagement singing in a cafe to not fall apart. That's the way you set it up." I'm concerned. All this after I had already committed myself.

I continue my soliloquy, "Now, Josephson, if she lasts six weeks, fine. But here you are going to open her, and you haven't heard her sing. You don't know what's going to happen. You're inviting the press. They'll be here. If she comes off, great. They'll say, 'That Barney Josephson, he did it again. He did it with Billie Holiday. He did it with Zero Mostel, Jack Gilford, Lena Horne, Josh White, and so on. His touch is still there.' If she doesn't go over and she can't really sing, and if she appears like a tired little old lady out there, the press are going to say, 'Barney muffed it this time. For all he did, now he has reached the point where he's scraping the bottom of the barrel for his talent. For all that he brought back Mary Lou Williams, Helen Humes, Big Joe Turner, Nellie Lutcher, Teddy Wilson, still, comes the day when you've lost your touch.' This will finish me off. That about washes me up for the moment." All this went through my mind.

"Miss Hunter, as soon as you have some songs worked up, call me and come in some morning when there are few people here and feel the room." What I had in mind was to help her "routine" her program. Many artists who perform beautifully do not know how to routine their show. They'll sing all blues or all rhythm songs, whatever. They don't know how to mix them up, how to make their program interesting. As it turned out I never had to do it for Alberta. This lady is so on top. She knows just how to program. She never went on without working out with Gerald Cook, her long-time accompanist, at their table what songs she would sing for each set. Gerald would write each program in his notebook.

About three weeks after our meeting Alberta called, "I'm coming tomorrow morning at nine o'clock to rehearse." I was surprised when she came in with Gerald Cook, who had played for me long years ago in Cafe Society Downtown—Bonds and Cook. John Hammond had sent them to me:

> **Gerald Cook:** *I came to New York with my childhood piano teacher Margaret Bonds. The range of our repertoire was largely classical music through splashy romanticism. Barney auditioned us and, amazingly, engaged us. Both of us thought, "My god, Downtown Cafe Society. Wow!" We often played, in addition to pop music, theater music, occasionally spirituals. I was nervous about our out-of-place musical venue, being under the watchful eyes of those fabulous musicians working there. With us, Barney remained supportive, encouraging, and he helped nurture, certainly in me, a sense of self-confidence to do a variety of things that brought me into the world of jazz.*[2]

I found out later that Alberta didn't have any of her music. "It caught a rare disease in the Philippines and decomposed." She needed someone with Gerald's conservatory training, a student of Nadia Boulanger, to organize and arrange her songs. Like me, Alberta can't read or write music.

Magazines are put to bed two weeks in advance of publication. Whitney Balliett at the *New Yorker* finds himself at a disadvantage; the magazine is published once a week. The newspaper critics can come in opening night, and their reviews can appear the next day. Whitney had asked, "Barney, if you ever have anything that looks awfully good, let me know. I would like to come to a rehearsal so that I can start writing my piece, get it in, and not be the last one with it." I had done this for Helen Humes, rented rehearsal space at Steinway Hall and Whitney came there.

I called him about Alberta Hunter. She was only a name to him from old records. I'd not yet heard her myself. When I told him she was coming in at nine in the morning, a first rehearsal, Whitney was in my Cookery at nine, sitting at a table near the piano. There was no one else in the place except some waitresses setting up the room for lunch. No introduction. I didn't tell Alberta, didn't want to make her nervous. I sat with Whitney, and he and I heard her for the first time.

Whitney didn't take notes. He just listened. She pleased me, but I didn't know how Whitney was taking her. Whitney, when he listens, is very stone-faced. I'm told I am, too. Alberta has now sung for an hour and a quarter. Whitney said, "Well, Barney, I've had it. I've heard her." I didn't know how to take that line "I've had it," the way he said it, straight. Then, "Barney, I would like to talk to her." When he said that I knew that he liked her.

They went over to the far side of the room, where there was less activity. He sat with her until about a quarter to four that afternoon, taking notes. I heard her singing to him without the piano. They were discussing music. I made myself scarce. When he was finished he came over to me. "You know, Barney, this little lady can not only still sing like hell, she swings like mad and has all her marbles. She remembers it all. She hasn't forgotten a thing. She reminded me about a few things that I was mixed up about, who wrote this and who did the lyrics." He walked out. I knew I had Mr. Balliett for her. He wrote her profile in the *New Yorker* in their issue of October 31, and she had opened on the tenth. That was pretty fast.

After her next rehearsal I suggested getting the brilliant jazz pianist Jimmy Rowles, who had previously played in The Cookery, to accompany her. She knew Jimmy's reputation. He had worked and recorded with Billie Holiday, Ella Fitzgerald, Sarah Vaughan, Peggy Lee, Tony Bennett, played in the bands of Benny Goodman, Lee and Lester Young, Woody Herman. I knew he was a superb accompanist and could give her the backing I thought she needed. She began to rehearse with Jimmy at the same time that she was climbing up three long flights of stairs to Gerald's fourth-floor apartment on West 23rd Street to work with him on her arrangements.

Opening night, October 10, 1977, all the critics were there, every one. I don't remember when before all the critics would come on opening night to a cabaret. Word must have gotten around. Maybe I let drop a few hints. A man like the estimable *New York Times* critic John Wilson is very considerate.

Unless a performer is coming in for only a night or two or three and he wants to review them, he will not come opening night. In my case he knows I keep artists for rather lengthy engagements. He believes it's fairer not to be in the club on opening night, to give the artist a chance to warm up, get used to the room, find his or her way. That's a commendable way to review and a lovely thing to do. For Alberta's opening night, however, John was there. He knew her from way back. When she finished her second show that night I wasn't worried about whether she was going to hold up.

The critics, all of them, raved about her. Such acclaim! Just imagine if Alberta had not gone to Bobby Short's party. That's what I mean by accidents shaping our lives. Some call it fate. Alberta calls it "God's hand."

> **Whitney Balliett:** *Rowles parallels her melodic lines, echoes them, cushions them. He gives her rhythmic nudges when her time falters, and he plays rich and dense chords behind her. But he uses this complexity sparingly, and it sets off the purity and simpleness of her voice—a jungle framing a smooth clearing.*[3]

Jimmy Rowles was wonderful but drunk all the time. I have strict rules: no smoking, no drinking while performing. The first night Jimmy came in for his solo gig with me, before Alberta, he asked for an ashtray. Okay, at least he was a gentleman. Then came the vodka and tonics. He'd drink as he played. I was going to speak to him, but his music was so good that I told him, "I don't allow this sort of thing but keep it in." So the vodka and tonics just flowed. But with Alberta that didn't work too well, and I had to call in Gerald Cook. Al Hall, a fine bassist, came in with Gerald. Al, also drunk all the time, stayed on for a year.

Alberta took a bus to work, disguising herself in old clothes, carrying her gold hoop earrings and money in well-worn paper napkins in an old cloth handbag. This had worried me, so I offered to pay for a taxi both ways. Gerald had a car, and then he began bringing Alberta to work. Even so, she continued to collect her taxi fare from my manager every evening. Gerald, gentleman that he is, told me she never offered to pay for gas or toward the upkeep of the car. Her old friend Bricktop, famed as a cabaret hostess and singer in Europe in the 1920s and 1930s, knew Alberta well from those days: "Alberta squeezes a nickel until the buffalo cries."

CHAPTER
56

"'You don't need a contract
with Barney Josephson.'"

Alberta became a celebrity overnight. Requests for interviews from newspapers, television shows, magazines, radio programs poured in. She pretty much tells them all the same story, a story of remarkable persistence. It goes like this: She knew she could sing, singing in the church choir. Her teachers said she had a nice voice. She had overheard a friend of her mother saying that her daughter in Chicago wrote that singers were making $10 a week in nightclubs there. She put this in her mind.

One day her mother sent her to the store to buy a loaf of bread. On the way she met her schoolteacher, Miss Florida Cummings, who was going to Chicago that night. Alberta asked if she could go with her. Miss Florida had a child's pass and said she would need her mother's permission to go. Alberta, not one to let an opportunity pass, hid between some houses for awhile, went back to Miss Florida, said her mother gave her permission. Her mother never would have, but Albert figured her mother wouldn't be worried because she often spent the night with a friend.

When they arrived in Chicago they took a streetcar. This is pretty much the story Alberta tells the media: suddenly she got off the streetcar and went accross the street. She walked into a building and asked a lady who was washing clothes if she knew a girl named Ellen Winston. "No, but a girl by the name of Helen Winston lives here." She never fails to add, "God's hand, all my life God's hand has guided me."

When Ellen came home, there was Alberta. "What are you doing here, Pig?" Alberta says she was always dirty as a little girl. Ellen had a job working in a boardinghouse as a cook and got Alberta a job there, peeling potatoes for room and board. She had a little bed in the basement with the other hired help. At night she'd sneak out, go to the places where the girls were singing, and beg for work. She'd be kicked out but kept going back.

One day the pianist at one of the places where she hung out, Dago Frank's, asked the owner, Roy, to give her a chance. She learned a new song every night from a player-piano roll in Ellen's building. She sang at Dago Frank's for a year and ten months exactly. It was, of course, a brothel. Alberta always adds, "But it was classy. The girls used to give me money to buy dresses so I would look nice. Those sporting women were very tenderhearted." Then the police came after Roy, and he was forced to close the place. That was Alberta's training ground.

Miss Laura, Alberta's mother, passed in 1954 at the age of seventy-seven. Alberta's story to the press is that the music went out of her and she quit show business. She was very close to her mother and had supported her ever since she had run off to Chicago. But closer to the truth was that she wasn't getting any work in the clubs. Actually, Alberta's glory days had come to an end by the late 1930s. During the 1930s she was back and forth with gigs on both sides of the Atlantic. In 1934 she'd replaced Josephine Baker at the Casino de Paris. Then had an engagement [1934–35] at the luxury Dorchester Hotel in Mayfair, London, where the Prince of Wales stood in front of her as she sang "Time on My Hands" to him. 1938, and Alberta, along with American black performers working in Europe, were gradually returning. Hitler was in power. Alberta, always a keen observer of the world around her, knew full well what the racist Nazi government meant for Negroes. Already Jews and gypsies and communists were being incarcerated in prison camps.

World War II and Alberta joined a USO troupe. Segregation was in full force in the U.S. armed forces, so Alberta was forced to join an all-Negro unit, the first sent out to entertain black soldiers overseas. In her way, Alberta had fought discrimination as far back as the early 1920s. She had refused to work the Negro vaudeville circuit because black women were required to wear Aunt Jemima–type outfits.

At the war's end she joined another USO unit, touring the V.A. hospitals in the United States, entertaining the wounded soldiers. Came the Korean War in 1950, and Alberta enlisted again with a USO troupe. The war ground to a halt, and Alberta was at liberty. Finding work in the clubs was impossible in the mid-1950s for singers like Alberta. Elvis Presley and rock were all the rage. Alberta faced the fact that her career in the entertainment world had wound down. Besides, she was past sixty.

Alberta likes to tell the press how she came upon her next profession. One day she was walking along 137th Street in Harlem when she saw a poster on the YWCA building advertising a nursing program. "God's hand had guided me to the Y." It was not quite that way. Alberta was always sharp about dramatizing her life's story. The true story: She had been doing volunteer work for about a year at the Hospital for Joint Diseases in Harlem and had liked it so well that she wanted to continue hospital work. She knew she would need to learn more about nursing, so she applied at the YWCA school. She was turned down. Too old. Never one to give up, she persisted and finally was able to persuade the woman director of the Y to admit her. She was enrolled; passed all her courses, putting in long, hard hours of study; did an internship; and in 1957 received her degree—LPN—licensed practical nurse.

The woman director had put back Alberta's age twelve years so that Alberta could be admitted into the nursing program. As it was, she worried that Alberta was too old at age fifty. So at her real age of sixty-two Alberta embarked on a totally new career which was to last twenty years at Goldwater Hospital on Roosevelt Island. When the hospital forced her to retire at age seventy Alberta was actually eighty-two. It never ceases to amaze me that this woman was able to carry on such back-breaking work all those years at her age, but she loved it and was good at it. Her patients loved her. She was a kind and dedicated nurse. Opening night at The Cookery, a group of her co-workers from Goldwater Hospital were in the audience, cheering.

In interview after interview on television, in newspapers, magazines, Alberta explains that she knew she would work for Barney Josephson after three minutes. "Not longer than three minutes. I was convinced I wanted to work for him. He's a fine man. He's too good a man to be in this business. Too honest. Oh, I adore that man, child."[1] She was quick with the witticisms: "Businessmen would steal your eyelashes if they could." She tells them that she hadn't sung for twenty years: "I didn't know what was going to come out of my mouth." And [she] always adds, "Am I glad that Barney

Josephson takes chances on people. Now who else would have hired me at age eighty-two!"[2]

I had been handling Alberta's outside bookings on television and tours as I had promised. "Barney, you have to take a manager's percentage for what you're doing for me." "Alberta Hunter, let me tell you something. I handled Hazel Scott for seven and a half years. I managed Zero Mostel. I handled others. Yes, I had manager's contracts with them that I could deduct 10 percent for my efforts, but I never took it. I could not take it, and I'm not starting now with an eighty-two-year-old lady. I won't talk about it. That's the way it's been and that's the way it will be."

Actually, there are two separate aspects to this problem. As the owner of a business you are an exploiter of labor. Profit is only made if you make a profit from the work of people you're employing. They produce $10 worth of labor for you, and you pay them $9. You have $1 left. That's your profit. I understand this economic system. Somehow when you sell a sandwich or a drink I think it's not as direct exploitation as when it's a person whom you're managing, whom you sell for $100 a week, let's say, and you take $10 as your commission. Where an artist is performing in my club and then I'm managing that person, how can I take a commission from a person who's working for me, on work that I get money for? On all the programs she's on, she talks about me and will deliberately put in, "Child, I have no contract with Barney Josephson. This man's word is his bond. You don't need a contract with Barney Josephson." You see, I'm well repaid for what I do.

Alberta understood something else about her meteoric success, what it meant for other artists, the older ones considered washed up. "The side effect of Barney's bringing me back is that he gave a lot of people jobs because of me. Look at all these singers coming out of the woodwork who are getting jobs all over town because everybody wants another Alberta Hunter. They may not know it, but they owe their working today to him. He opened up a new avenue."

The Cookery was not set up originally for entertainment, so we don't have a dressing room. The artists have to use my little office downstairs. The night after Alberta's opening before her performance, I went down to the "dressing room." "You know, Alberta, when one has lived a lifetime, and you've lived a long time and I'm not that far behind you, there comes a time for us to go. It is just wonderful when we can go out of this world in a blaze of glory. When you leave this world, believe me that's what's going to happen. And Barney

Josephson will be standing beside you to feel the heat of that blaze." I can't recount those words without tearing up. That's why I talk so long when I introduce her. I guess I'm just a sentimental fellow.

She didn't forget. Four years after her opening, Alberta reminded me, "Barney, do you remember the second night of my engagement when you came down here and said to me about going out in a blaze of glory?" She had just come off the floor to a standing ovation. "What you said has come true. This old lady is going out in a true blaze of glory. I'm the happiest woman alive." She knew. "I never imagined that I would meet with so much success, that I could be so lucky all over again. I've been successful, but never as much as now. I'm having a convention."[3]

What more is there to be able to accomplish than that? I don't need contracts. I'm satisfied. That very first night Alberta Hunter was reborn a greater star than she was in her young days. Never has a vocalist, after twenty years away from singing, at age eighty-two, come back to such stardom. And she sings better now than she did at thirty. "She was a popular singer ten years before Franklin Roosevelt became president."[4]

She is great copy for the press, knows exactly the kind of quotes to give them. "I knew I could still sing because I always took good care of the old pipes." After a few years of constant press and television interviews she became more selective about granting them. "They don't do their homework, Barney." Her mail is tremendous; requests from all over the country, the world, for personal appearances.

In 1981 a German television crew came in to film a show with Alberta. I negotiated and got them to agree to $10,000 in cash for her. When I received the cash, I handed it all to her, didn't keep any of it for filming rights. She stashed it in her bosom. A friend who was with her worried that it might fall out. Winking, "Baby, nothing ever fell out of there unless I wanted it to."

Did she know her audiences! Who else could get away in a cabaret with the sermons she delivers nightly, with variations on the theme. "Children, don't let anybody tell you can't make it in this life. I made it with 15 cents in my pocket. Eight years old when I ran away from home [sometimes she was eleven, sometimes fifteen]. And here I am. I've been all over the world. You can make it. It's a hard road. Just have will power. Never become discouraged. Keep faith in God, children. He's powerful. Faith in God and confidence in yourself and you'll never stop. There is nothing you can't do." She tells them to keep in touch with their parents: "If they were good parents, call them. If they were not such good parents, call them anyway. Then your conscience will be clear. And on Saturdays, Sundays, and holidays you can call for practically nothing." Roars of laughter.[5]

Her timing is impeccable. They heed her words. They call, often enough from The Cookery. I don't know another entertainer in the world who could speak to the audience as she does and not be hissed off the floor. They return over and over again, never get enough of her. There's something that comes out of this woman. They bring her flowers. After a performance they come to her table in the corner of the room where she sits, wanting to kiss her. She hates to be touched. Tells them, "I have such a cold, baby. I was a nurse so I know about spreading germs."

She's gracious about signing autographs, responding to their stories. A young man, "I enjoyed you so much. I came all the way from England"; Alberta, "What part?" young man, "London"; Alberta, "London's all right with me. I played *Show Boat* with Paul Robeson at the Drury Lane Theater in 1928." One night an attractive woman in her mid-forties approached Alberta's table. She said she was from Dallastown, Pennsylvania. "Miss Hunter, you saved my life." Alberta, now used to almost anything, didn't lose her cool. "How, baby?" "Well, I didn't want to live anymore, and one morning I was about to take my life when I saw you on a morning television show. You talked about yourself and your life and your faith in the Almighty and how we shouldn't give up. Your words reached me, and here I am to tell you my story."[6]

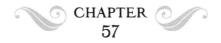

CHAPTER
57

"She and I know the secret
of staying young."

I was living single again. I had walked out of my marriage of twenty years when my youngest son, Louis, left to enter Tufts University in 1978. He was on his own now. I had been concerned about how my boys would take it. My oldest son, Eddie, took it in his stride. Having graduated from Harvard at the age of sixteen, Eddie was attending New York University Law School, just as his Uncle Leon had done. He had been admitted to Harvard Law School but chose NYU instead. Harvard was too elitist for him, he said. I was always a strong believer in not propagandizing my own children, but Eddie became an activist radical [in the 1980s]. When I told Lucky [Louis], he surprised me, "Dad, now you are a man."

This marriage caused me such untold grief. I am very, very sorry about it. Now I must say that I did not always behave in the best manner toward some of the women I've known. I could not ever really behave in a bastardly manner toward any woman in my life. This is going on record; I want to clear myself. I know of no time, even from any woman I might have wronged or treated poorly, no woman has ever said one bad word about me. I've met them since. None of them. The only one is the woman of my second marriage, who has maligned me so dreadfully.

I had suffered enough anguish and humiliation in this marriage, and I vowed I wanted no more relationships. I had The Cookery which, with Alberta, was doing good business.

One evening early June 1979, a young lady, Terry Trilling, whom I knew casually in the early 1950s walked into The Cookery with her lovely daughter to join a party. I knew she was coming. I was waiting for her. The hostess of the party, Augusta Yelin Cherry, was an old friend and an initial investor in The Cookery. Terry was the last to arrive. She greeted me warmly with a big hug. I looked at her. I had a feeling. This was it. And I wasn't looking for anyone at this time. I had desperately needed to find some peace.

I escorted them to their table and left. Terry sat at the end of the table on the aisle and crossed her legs, talking to someone across the aisle. I saw those gams and I kept looking at them and watching her listening, speaking, her manner, her facial expressions. That feeling hasn't stopped since.

The very next day I called Augusta and asked whether Terry was involved with any man. I knew she was divorced. Augusta didn't think so. I hung up and phoned Terry for a date. We went out to one of my favorite French restaurants, came back in time for me to introduce Alberta for her last show, then left. I asked Terry if she would care to see my new apartment a half block away. When I had walked out on my marriage I left that apartment just as it was. Leon's wife Lucy, now a widow, kind and generous, had suggested that I stay with her until I could find another apartment.

Until Terry entered my life there had been no woman who had attracted me, although I must say, immodestly, not for want of approaches by a few. My wife had become increasingly impossible as the years went by, and I had years of celibacy. Now I wasn't sure of my abilities although I certainly felt young and eager. I explained to Terry. It was an enchanting evening.

I have never been interested in women my own age. I've always hated the term *senior citizen* and disdain using the discounts. "Keep me away from the old people," Alberta's words, old in spirit she means. She and I know the secret of staying young, to work until we "shuffle off this mortal coil," to be involved in trying to make the world just a little better than when we entered it. What else do you live for? My life continues to open up because I continue to walk into it. No bitterness. Oh, I've felt plenty frustrated and despondent when I was out of the entertainment business for twenty years, but you can't be a complainer. You only make it worse for yourself.

My mother was wise, "Son, you've got to keep doing, keep turning, like a corkscrew." "But Ma, you can also bore yourself into the ground." "Son, sometimes you can turn yourself up to heaven." She impressed upon all of us that we mustn't feel too proud to do menial work and to do it the best we can but never to be content with it. Always look to better yourselves. You have to have principles to live by. If I didn't I would grieve.

It was not more than two weeks after our first evening together, and there were others, I phoned Terry. "This is Barney. I don't want you to say a word. I love you." I hung up before she could respond. Another week passed, and I asked her to marry me. I wasn't divorced, but I thought there would be no difficulty obtaining one. I couldn't have been more wrong. I totally miscalculated Gloria's hostility, especially when she found out I wanted to marry Terry.

Terry Trilling: *Barney was exuberant about Alberta. When we met Barney had not made a secret of his age, but I must have misheard him. I thought he was ten years younger than his seventy-seven years. His step was lively and quick, and he never seemed to tire, irrepressible in his enthusiasms. I did wonder though, why, when reminiscing, he never referred to himself as I but always Barney Josephson, as if speaking of another person, as if he had separated his two lives. Then one day I suddenly became aware that he was talking about I. I had noticed that his name never appeared in The Cookery newspaper ads or on the table cards. After all, his was a famous name. I asked him. From then on, "Barney Josephson presents" appeared on the cards and in the ads.*

Some months into our relationship Barney had left for work before I had awakened. When I walked into the bathroom, scrawled across the entire width of the double medicine cabinet mirror in heavy red magic marker, "Thank you for coming into my life." Barney was a very early riser. At the breakfast table would be a plate of colorful tropical fruit, cut into a variety of erotic designs. He was like a young man.

Alberta was invited to do a concert at Vassar College in 1979. On our way up we were in the car, talking, Alberta, Gerald Cook, and bassist Aaron Bell. Alberta said, "Barney, you look so well. I see you're happy, and I'm so glad. I know it's time you experienced some pleasure in your life." Alberta detested Gloria, referring to her sarcastically as "Madam" because of her imperious ways. Gloria had been most unpleasant to Alberta. This may sound crazy, but she was jealous of my relationship with this eighty-two-year-old woman. If she saw me spending time with Alberta, or a friend, or a woman customer she would rush over, call me away on some pretext, always rudely.

Alberta saw all this. When she spoke of my looking so well, she got me onto my lady, Terry. "Well, Alberta, I have something to tell you. Just last night I said to Terry that I was such a lucky man, a man at this time in my life, to meet a woman who could say, 'I love you, Barney.' She said, 'Yes, you are a lucky man. You have two women who love you. Alberta Hunter loves you and I love you.'" It was a very touching thing for me to hear. I thought Alberta should know. She was just delighted to hear that my Terry could say that.

Terry Trilling: *Alberta was not always friendly to me. When Barney and I first dated he would seat me at Alberta's table with Gerald while he took care of the room. Alberta totally ignored me. I didn't exist. I felt very uncomfortable, but I had just met Barney and was reluctant to say anything to him. Gerald, at the table, too, warm and gracious, made it easier for me.*

One night Barney and Alberta had an altercation. She remained downstairs in the dressing room. Barney, upstairs, was refusing to talk to her. There was a good possibility she would not go on. Gerald suggested I try to talk to them. I went downstairs to Alberta, spoke to her, ameliorated her hurt feelings with Barney; went back upstairs, soothed Barney. Finally he went downstairs. They made up. The ice was broken for me with Alberta. From then on I was her "angel" and we were friends.

We reached Vassar and were met by Herbert Schultz, a vice president of the college. Backstage, he worked out the program with us. "Mr. Josephson, I'll introduce Miss Hunter. After the intermission, I'll talk about you, and then I'd appreciate it if you would speak about Miss Hunter and yourself." Then he showed Alberta an old shellac record. It was the original recording of her song "Downhearted Blues," which Alberta had made for Paramount Records. Mr. Schultz asked if she had the record. "I had it once. I showed it to somebody, and somehow it disappeared." He said, "I'm going to show this record while I introduce you, and before you leave I'd like you to have it." At the end of the evening he did just that. Alberta asked him to autograph it for her; a classy gesture. Alberta opened with her theme song: "My Castle's Rockin'":

Come on up some night, my castle's rockin',
You can blow your top 'cause everything's free.
On the top floor, the third door to the rear,
That's where you'll always find me.

Alberta: "This is a song I wrote before you children were born. The title is 'Downhearted Blues.' I recorded it for Paramount in 1923. Many records were sold. Then came the world's greatest blues singer, that awful Bessie Smith. She recorded it for Columbia. Millions were sold—and I'm still collecting royalties!" That line never failed to get a big laugh.

> Gee but it's hard to love someone
> When that someone don't love you [to audience: "it's a mess"]
> I'm so disgusted, heart-broken too
> I've got the downhearted blues.

Alberta explains her next song: "As I sing, the words of this song will tell you what's in the envelope."

> I may be brown as a berry
> That's only secondary
> Cause you cain't tell the difference after dark.

She sang another song she wrote.

> When I come home some morning all dressed up like Astor's horse,
> I want him to grab me and tear off all my clothes,
> Just to let me know who's boss . . .
> I want a two-fisted, double-jointed (aaah) rough and ready man.

She sang "Handy Man." The kids were screaming. There were well over six hundred students. Such cheering and shouting. Such a spontaneous outburst. I never heard anything like it, and I've been around a long time and I know audiences. I'm easily moved to tears. Well, I was crying all the time. I was so proud. When I read items in the papers such as "since 1977, under Josephson's management, her legend has grown steadily" or I'm described as "the man who changed her life," I'm indescribably delighted.

Herbert Schultz introduced me. He spoke of when he was a student at Princeton he would come in to New York at least twice, sometime three times a week, taking the milk train back. He told about dating Mrs. Schultz, herself a Vassar graduate. They would meet in New York to go to Cafe Society Downtown.

From the beginning, when I would introduce Alberta I always said she had worked as a scrub nurse at Goldwater Hospital. One evening almost three years after her opening she quietly asked Terry to explain to me that she was a practical nurse with a diploma. She had never corrected me all that time.

Terry Trilling: *Barney's introductions were notoriously lengthy. Alberta would stand behind the column, patiently waiting to go on. I was often with her to help her walk, arthritis, from her table to that point. Once I mentioned that sometimes Barney's introductions are too long. Alberta smiled affectionately, "He likes to talk about me, Terry."*

"'Several times Rosalynn Carter shaped her mouth into O's of amazement.'"

Somehow, bringing Alberta back to singing again opened doors that I thought were forever closed, nor was I looking for them to ever open. But such happened. I walked into the White House with Alberta. Anybody named Josephson couldn't have taken a piss within ten blocks of the White House not so many years past. And here I go into the White House and meet President and Mrs. Carter. Alberta had been invited to attend a reception at the White House which the president was giving for about five hundred people and then to sing on a program that evening at the Kennedy Center Opera House.

For the occasion Alberta went to Henri Bendel, bought herself a full-length black mink coat, one inch off the floor, a beautiful coat. She paid something like $6,250 and I never saw it again. She put it in storage. At the White House we walked into an oval-shaped foyer, not the Oval Room, where there was a cloakroom. I wanted to take her new mink coat and give it to the cloakroom attendant. "No, no, no. I'm wearing it." Here there are several hundred of the most gorgeously attired women in the height of fashion, in their evening gowns, because they were going from the reception at 5:30 in the afternoon to the program at the Opera House. I'm sure they all had their minks and sables checked. Not Alberta; she's wearing hers.

As we came up the receiving line, Alberta, her coat slung over her shoulders, casual-like, and I are introduced to President Jimmy Carter and Mrs. Carter. There was a plush rope with all the cameramen and newsmen standing behind it. The cameras were going. Three days after the event a large envelope arrives from the White House with photographs of us with the Carters.

The occasion, the "Kennedy Center Honors Gala," December 3, 1978, was to honor five artists for their contributions to the arts in the United States: Marian Anderson, Arthur Rubinstein, Fred Astaire, Richard Rodgers, and George Balanchine. Marian Anderson was an old, old friend of Alberta. They had lived in the same house in London in the late 1920s when Marian was studying abroad and struggling to be heard. A black classical singer in those days, unheard of.

Well, Alberta stole the show, the only one permitted an encore.[1] She was such a success, and the Carters had such a good time, that they invited her back two and a half months later [February 27, 1979] to be the sole entertainer after dinner in the East Room at a gathering of United States governors. Introducing Alberta, Pres. Carter said he began "an instant love affair with Alberta" when she performed at the Kennedy Center awards program. Then Alberta "laid it" on the guests.

Several times Rosalynn Carter shaped her mouth into O's of amazement as Alberta sang "Handy Man." Alfred Kahn, the president's inflation adviser, sat on the edge of his chair.[2]

Alberta sang:
  He shakes my ashes,
  Greases my griddle,
  Churns my butter,
  Strokes my fiddle.

As Hunter tapped her black T-strap shoes, she sang about "Get yourself a workingman," and the President roared with laughter.[3]

Alberta sang:
  I don't want no hipster lover
  They've got larceny in their eyes
  Got a handful of gimme
  And a mouthful of much obliged.

For last night's black-tie audience, the raunchier the lyrics, the greater

*the response. "The spice was just what the people wanted," Alberta said
with a gleam in her eye afterwards. . . . For all the Baptists' straitlaced-
ness, the Carters clearly adore Alberta Hunter.*[4]

Thursday I get called to the phone. White House calling. Mrs. Mondale
wants to speak to Barney Josephson. I get on the phone. "How are you, Mr.
Josephson?" Long-lost friends. I never met the lady. The election campaign
has commenced. This is the Second Lady. "I want to know if Alberta Hunter
would endorse the Carter-Mondale ticket. It's very important to us. Would
she come to Washington? There's going to be a conference of the most prominent women in America who are supporting us. Would she take part in this
conference?" "Well, Mrs. Mondale, that I can't be sure about because Miss
Hunter has commitments here. I will, of course, ask her and let you know."
"Please call me tomorrow, Mr. Josephson."

I spoke to Alberta that night. "What do you think, Barney?" "Well, this is
only for the nomination. If you wish to do this, and if Ted Kennedy should
get the nomination, you can still support him. You're not harming the Democratic Party that you love." "Whatever you think, Barney." "You love the
president. I would endorse him, Alberta. You're not going to support any
Republican candidate." "Oh God, no!"

I was supposed to call Mrs. Mondale the next day but didn't get around
to it. A call from the White House. "This is Mrs. Mondale. Do you have any
good news for me?" "Miss Hunter gives her unqualified support for the re-
nomination of her president and vice president, but she cannot attend the
conference. She's eighty-four years old, and energetic as she is, working here,
appearing on television shows, it's just not possible. You may say whatever you
wish and send it along. She'll be happy to sign it." Well, you never heard such
effusiveness on the phone. You would have thought they had gotten Frank
Sinatra's support. But this is what this lady has generated. She has become a
national figure.

She has been on Gene Shalit's *Today* TV show six times. No artist has ever
received that many invitations on that show. When she's on such a program
she's reaching twenty-five to thirty million viewers each time. She has been on
the *Dick Cavett Show* three times, on Merv Griffin and Mike Douglas shows,
on Brazilian television, London television, Italian, French, Japanese, adulated
all over the world. So an endorsement from her became important.

When she refers to Jimmy Carter, she calls him "my president" and has taken to dedicating a song to him with a little speech: "This song is for one of the finest presidents we ever had. He remembered the old people, the poor people, the young. They said he was weak. He wasn't weak. He was misunderstood because he has a heart. You know whom I'm talking about" and sings "Georgia on My Mind."

Alberta was having a grand ball, and I was dancing with her. As her manager I was fielding all sorts of requests for personal appearances throughout this country and other countries, arranging press interviews, appearances on the television programs, *Sixty Minutes, Good Morning America, To Tell the Truth*—all shows which reach vast audiences. TV crews came from the world over just to film her at The Cookery.

During the summer of 1979, when she was on vacation from The Cookery, I arranged appearances for her in Denver, Minneapolis, Omaha, Memphis, Detroit, Ann Arbor, Berkeley, Virginia, the Smithsonian Institution. I set her fee at $7,500 per concert, more than what the top opera singers at the Metropolitan Opera were getting, plus air fare and first-class hotels for her and her two musicians. She was responsible for their salaries.

I gave a great deal of time to handling Alberta's affairs, as I had promised. I had booked her into a club, George's, in Chicago in 1980 for an unusual engagement of two weeks, to open June 10. The contract I drew up provided for her to perform six nights a week, twice a night, $5,200 a week, out of which she would pay her two musicians and her own hotel room. She opened to an enthusiastic reception.

The next day I get a phone call. Alberta is in the Michael Reese Hospital with a fractured hip and wrist. She had fallen while getting out of a car, shopping for food. She didn't want to pay for a hotel room and had persuaded Gerald Cook to arrange for her to stay at his sister's apartment during her gig. Now she was saving money on meals, and she doesn't even like to cook. I called my nephew, Chuck Feldstein, whose firm handles fundraising for the hospital, to make certain that Alberta would get the best care possible. I was plenty worried, what with Alberta's age and arthritis.

I was able to get Bricktop, so-called because she dyed her hair orange, to take over for Alberta. Bricktop had owned nightclubs in Paris and Biarritz in the 1920s which drew royalty, famous artists, all manner of celebrities. Mabel Mercer was a singer in her club on the Rue Pigalle. I canceled the rest of Alberta's summer engagements. Alberta, on the phone from her hospital bed, "Barney, I never felt better."

She returned, mid-September, chipper as ever. Her doctors were amazed at this old lady's recovery. I ran an ad in the *New York Times* announcing her return. The Cookery's address was inadvertently omitted, only our phone number was printed. A friend called, asked if I thought we were so famous we didn't need an address. It seems we were. We sold out.

CHAPTER
59

"'When the inspiration of God is missing, I just rely on talent.'"

Some time back John Hammond had spoken of the magnificent gospel singer Marion Williams. That had brought back memories of the exciting Golden Gate Quartet. For the past five years I had been trying to get Marion Williams. She would have none of singing in a nightclub. I tried again. To entice her I made the point to her manager that the people she's singing to in churches are already there. If she wants to bring God's word to people she should be singing in clubs and getting folks out of there into church.

I don't know whether that was what finally convinced her, but to my surprise and delight she agreed to come in from July 14 to September 13, 1980, to sing in what gospel singers call a saloon. This would be the first time she had sung in a jazz cabaret although as she has said, "Jazz started out in the church." Marion had been the lead singer of the greatest gospel group in the 1940s and 1950s, the Clara Ward Singers. Typically, before then she worked as a maid and laundress.

I tried to get an appearance for her on Bob Sherman's *Listening Room* on radio station WQXR, but he was all booked. At the last minute he had a cancellation and called Marion's manager. She had to decline, explaining that Marion was too tired after a long trip from overseas. That one radio exposure on that particular program would have been worth reams of newspaper print.

I needed to be able to reach out to another audience. Here I was, presenting one of the greatest gospel singers of all times in an unusual setting for these times—a nightclub.

One of Marion's concerns about singing in a club was that alcohol was served. I explained to her the bar would not be in her line of vision while she was singing.

> **Marion Williams:** *At first the drinking bothered me. But I think I need to be out in the field. I'm on a field mission into the highway and hedges. When I'm singing I get inspired by God. I call it "the anointing."... When the inspiration of God is missing, I just rely on talent. . . . I couldn't tell you how I sing because I don't know when I'm going to hit a high note or when I'm going to growl.*[1]

> **John S. Wilson:** *With magnificent timing... Miss Williams rolls a song out somewhat like a holler ... and with a sense of involvement that holds her audience in absolute silence. It is a breathtaking display of subtly controlled artistry that provides a sublime contrast to the lighter side that she shows singing.*[2]

Marion had a sense of humor about my audience. They didn't know how to clap. "They're always off; one side clapping one way and the other side clapping another way."

When I had started with entertainment in The Cookery my idea was to build it up as a place where the legends of classical jazz could find work again. A good measure of my success in the Cafe Society days had been presenting and developing great but little- or unknown talent. I wanted to repeat that formula for The Cookery. One such talented but unknown artist was the singer Susannah McCorkle. She had come to my attention when she subbed in 1979 for Dardanelle, a delightful pianist-singer who had Sunday and Monday nights.[3] I liked Susannah's way of interpreting the lyrics of the songs she was singing, unique and warm and intelligent. I engaged her for five months of Sundays and Mondays.[4]

> **Susannah McCorkle:** *Barney sat me down in a booth after my first show. He felt I was doing too many obscure songs and should do more things that everybody knew. I had built my small reputation on doing unusual songs, so I was reluctant to go with very well known ones. Still, I had a lot of respect for Barney, so I listened to him and did what he asked,* but *to keep myself satisfied artistically I did verses and alter-*

nate choruses to standards, and tried always to work out arrangements that were fresh and brought out the lyrics in a new light. Then I found that I really enjoyed doing that. From that time on I have also become known for my singing of standards. I really credit Barney for giving me a push in that direction. He was right, I was doing too many obscure songs. By doing a mixture of well-known songs and lesser-known ones I was able to build a new audience and still feel I was doing something worthwhile artistically.

The Cookery had a special feeling for me since so many of the greats of jazz had played there. I was bothered though by the noise of frying hamburgers on the grill. It was very difficult to be in the middle of a lovely quiet song with everyone listening and suddenly have the spell broken by the sound and smell of frying meat! Still all these experiences go into your training.

I was so glad and grateful to have that long booking, and it really jump-started my career in the U.S. I'd been singing for five years in London, where I started my career, and wasn't known in the U.S. till The Cookery booking.

I have to admit I was afraid of Barney. I felt very intimidated by him. He didn't often come in on Sundays. When he did, I was honored and yet apprehensive. He was such a towering figure in the world of music clubs to me, he'd made such an important contribution by giving long runs to people like Billie Holiday and Sarah Vaughan, and I wanted him to like me so much.[5]

Stephen Holden: *With a repertory of more than three thousand songs and with seventeen albums . . . Ms. McCorkle was more than a nightclub singer. She was a passionate, intrepid scholar of twentieth-century pop. And her cabaret shows, which she wrote herself, featured rich anecdotal histories of the songwriters whose work she performed.*[6]

Susannah was fifty-five years old when she died.

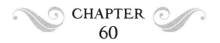

CHAPTER
60

"Her name meant nothing to me."

A Friday evening [February 17, 1981], Terry and I had gone out for dinner after I introduced Alberta. On our way home we stopped by for a few moments. It was quite late, but there were still people inside. Moe, my manager, rushed over, pushing a wheelchair. "What are you doing with that?" "Alberta fell. She's okay. She couldn't walk so I got this chair from St. Vincent's Hospital so she could do her last show." She had fainted and collapsed onto the floor, but nothing could keep this lady from taking care of her audience. She insisted on doing her eleven o'clock show in the wheelchair. Then she was taken to the hospital, where the doctors set a fractured knee and implanted a pacemaker.

While she was recuperating, her eighty-sixth birthday rolled around [April 1, 1981]. I bought a birthday cake, and Terry and I visited her in her apartment on Roosevelt Island. She also owned a co-op apartment on Riverside Drive and 139th Street, which she shared with her friend of over sixty years Harry Watkins, whom she called her brother. Alberta greeted us in an old pair of pajamas. She must have been resting in her bed, a couch placed against one wall in a large, sunny living room. The blanket was old, and the pillowcase was torn. The room itself was clean, nicely but sparsely furnished. She looked frail, and I wasn't sure she was eating properly.

"Alberta, do you have enough food?" "Come here, Barney." She took us into a small kitchen and opened the refrigerator door. "Everybody's bringing me food. It's too much. I can't eat it all. It'll probably spoil." She was not a big eater. At The Cookery she picked at her food even though my staff tried so hard to please her, to get her to eat more. We went back to the living room. Alberta must have noticed Terry glancing at her unmade bed. "Terry, go over to that closet door and open it." She pointed to the top shelf. "See those packages? Those are bed sheets and pillowcases which I've never opened. They're brand new." There were several packages stacked on top of each other in their original brown wrapping paper. Who knows how long she had them.

Alberta, recovered from her second episode, returned, raring to go, this time Wednesdays to Saturdays.[1] If anything bothered her she never let on. "Barney, I feel like a million dollars." Then she took off for the summer out-of-town bookings I had set up before she fell.

Helen Humes, due to come in July 1981, was very ill, cancer. I needed a replacement for her—fast. I put out the word and was told about a rhythm-and-blues singer, Ruth Brown, who would be available immediately. She had been one of the big stars in the 1950s. Her name meant nothing to me. I was out of the entertainment business in those years. Ruth couldn't come down for an audition because she was in the midst of recording an album. I went to her recording session. She opened her mouth, sang the first few notes, and I hired her then and there.

The veteran jazz booker and saloon owner, Barney Josephson, has rediscovered the red hot R&B mama Ruth Brown, who recorded for Atlantic even before Aretha arrived. Salty, Spicy. Very warm and tasty.[2]

Even after World War II recordings of black artists were still called "race records." The beginning of some kind of breakthrough began in the 1950s when the designation "race records" was replaced by "rhythm and blues" to signify recordings by black musicians.

Ruth Brown: *Black musicians worked under all kinds of hurtful conditions. So when we got up on stage to sing, the rhythm, the beat, covered up the blues we were feeling inside. I come from gospel. Church was something you did regardless of what else. Gospel is very definitely the underlying factor to everything I do. The tambourine I use, that's to the church, too. I'm working a little differently now. I always work with an* *organ because it gives me a spiritual undertone that comes out of the church. There's something about the organ that's basically gospel.*

My mother's people were from North Carolina. Every year when school was out June 15, by June 16 we were on the train or bus to Warren County, North Carolina, to work on my grandmother's farm, not always for her but sometimes for neighboring farms. I worked as a sharecropper. It was our salvation, really. I had to pick a hundred pounds of cotton a day. When I was seven I could work behind a single plow with a mule. I worked that until I was old enough to be responsible for going to the house, preparing the meals and bringing them to the low ground for everybody that was working there. I was up before sun up to do break-fast, milk the cow, bring in the eggs. I had an uncle and cousins, all who sang. I could hear them down in the low ground, singing to keep yourself physically and mentally alert.

During the month of August, it was revival meeting. I remember having to sit on the mourners' bench for twelve days and twelve nights while they preached continuously. Old people marching around sing-ing "Sit down sinner, you can't sit down." We had no piano, no organ, nothing. Everything was a cappella with the hands.[3]

My eightieth birthday arrived February 1, 1982. Terry gave a small surprise party for my family and a few close friends. When we walked into the apart-ment, there was Alberta sitting next to Esmé and John Hammond, dressed in her offstage outfit, a plaid flannel shirt and pants. With my birthday cake, Terry played a prerecorded Alberta singing "Happy Birthday *My* Barney"— her own personal touch. Terry told me later that when she had invited Alberta and Gerald, Alberta wouldn't give her a definite answer; probably wanted to surprise me.

Alberta was eighty-seven April 1, 1982. I sent an invitation to President and Mrs. Carter to join with other celebrities to honor the occasion. They were unable to attend but sent cordial greetings. Lena Horne sent balloons with warm words. A delegation from ASCAP presented Alberta with a lovely bouquet of roses. We had two birthday cakes, one for each performance. And old friend, ninety-nine-year-old Eubie Blake, sitting in front of her, tall and erect, beamed as she sang his song "Memories of You" to him. Then he polished off a huge portion of ice cream.

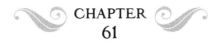

CHAPTER
61

"'Fame hasn't changed me.'"

I 've known Sylvia Syms a long time. She had never worked for me. Always wrong timing. Now she could come in for the month of July 1982. Over the years she had developed into a fine interpreter of songs.

Sylvia Syms: *I used to listen to the remote broadcasts on the radio and that's how I got to know about Cafe Society. I came there all by myself at fifteen. I'd wait until my mother and father went to bed, and then I'd hop out of the bedroom window and get on the BMT subway from Brooklyn. In those days the subway only cost a nickel each way. That was my allowance every day.*

I had pains, pangs of hunger, that were necessary to satisfy. There were two clubs on that street. Here was Number 1 Sheridan Square and here was El Chico. Cafe Society had a long flight of stairs down. It was summertime, and the doors were wide open. I appeared at the top of the stairs and this guy, the maitre d', looked at me. I said, "Can I come in and listen?" "How old are you?" "Fifteen." "No, you can't." I begged, "Oh please." Barney was gracious and let me in. They used to put me in the coat room. Then Mildred Bailey became my friend. She used to tell everybody I was her little sister.

My impressions of Barney are the same as my impressions of Florenz

Ziegfeld would have been for similar reasons. This is a man who knew. This was a man who was sophisticated. This was a man who could convey to people like me the proper things to be and do because he was elegant and articulate. He was a very dapper, very handsome gentleman. I really thought he was a knock-out. Well, he was the darling of Cafe Society.

Barney is a very special man unto me. He cared about human beings of all kinds. It had to be Barney's intelligence, his understanding of talent, to have the gift to present these people. Performers wanted to be able to say in their bios that they had played Cafe Society, and that was when Barney was no longer presenting entertainment. There was no other place like it in the world. . . . Through these years Barney kept saying, "Come and work for me." But the truth of the matter was, you arrive at a time in your life when there is a certain kind of decorum and a certain amount of money is required, and Barney couldn't afford me. I know that you do favors for people, but there are certain things you have to do for yourself. I told Barney, and I made it come to pass, "Barney, if you want me to come and work for you, I will, for a week. Just pay me my expenses. In the back of my head I always thought that this was my way of giving my gift back to Barney."[1]

Alberta returned for six weeks and then in early November 1982, took herself off to Paris, Berlin, and Zurich, where the audiences applauded her wildly. I wasn't keen at all on her going, worrying about her health and, if truth be told, for the financial health of The Cookery. I fully appreciated her desire to return to the scene of her youthful glory days, returning a far bigger star than she was in the late 1920s and 1930s.

She was back in The Cookery mid-November. Then, on December 3, what I had feared, happened. In the middle of a song Alberta keeled over. She was carried to her table. A woman doctor in the audience rushed over and kept Alberta conscious, talking to her, getting her to respond until the ambulance arrived. For the third time in as many years Alberta was in the hospital. For ten days she refused to have surgery, "All those doctors want to do is use the knife. I know them." Without the operation, the doctors told her, she wouldn't survive the internal bleeding. She finally consented. A gangrenous small intestine and right colon were removed. She survived.

While Alberta was in St. Vincent's Hospital, Terry and I visited her often. On one of our visits we came in rather late in the evening. Alberta was just settling down for the night. Her face glistened with cream. Even there she was concerned with keeping her skin fresh and unlined.

Alberta, out of the hospital after major surgery at eighty-eight, needed time to regain her strength. I needed her for the well-being of The Cookery. No matter the talent I brought in, no one could fill the place night after night as Alberta did. With Alberta incapacitated for who knows how long I tried to cope, to fill in. Not easy. Artists make their commitments well in advance if they're in demand.

Before Alberta's operation she'd been splitting the week with composer-pianist Arthur Siegel. He was a find. I gave him the Tuesday-through-Saturday slot until Alberta could return.

> **Mel Gussow:** *Arthur Siegel's specialty is the forgotten song, the tune that was cut on the road, slighted in production. He is a musical sleuth on trail of the lost lyric, and his discoveries make his act fresh and unfamiliar. As he profusely demonstrates, he is also a very entertaining performer as pianist and singer. On his opening night, I stayed for two shows and they were entirely different and equally enjoyable, infused with the same cheerful spirit and spontaneity. He offers an evening that thaws the wintry chill and also removes the pall that has fallen over the Broadway musical that, as Mr. Siegel reminds us, was once glittering with song.*[2]

Arthur titled his program "A Loving Salute to Show Tunes." He was a marvelous composer in his own right. He wrote all the songs for *New Faces of 1952*, from which came "Love Is a Simple Thing," "He Takes Me Off His Income Tax," Eartha Kitt's "Monotonous." He wrote some two dozen off-Broadway musicals and revues over the years. I kept Arthur on for a long time, expecting good things to happen for him with all the great reviews he was getting. But I couldn't advertise Arthur properly. I didn't have the financial resources.[3] Arthur had invited us to an off-Broadway musical, *Tallulah*, about you know who. He had written the score, and it was just wonderful. Frank Rich's damaging review of the score was inexplicable. We sent a note to Arthur, and he wrote back:

November 8, 1983

Dear Barney and Terry,

Thank you for your beautiful letter! You sure know how to make a fella feel good! At least Clive Barnes gave us a rave in the Post *and there were other good reviews, so maybe we can ride over Frank Rich. But thanks for the lovely things you said about my score, and I know you know better than Frank Rich.*

Love, Arthur[4]

The balladeer Oscar Brand was starring in an off-Broadway cabaret review, *It's a Jungle Out There*, a satire on current events. I had visions of my old dream, and I brought him in. Surely, this was the time. Oscar sang songs of trouble in the streets, of nuclear disarmament, Three Mile Island, Ronald Reagan, and called his little revue *The Unturned Cheek*.

John S. Wilson: *Facing a world in which idiocy and disaster run rampant, Mr. Brand sings with great good humor in a big easy voice . . . Mr. Brand and his friends [Jonathan Segal on piano and Vic Colucci on electric bass] are rekindling a spirit that has been missing from Greenwich Village for quite a while.*[5]

Oscar's repertoire of songs, I discovered, is legendary. "I despair of singing half my repertoire before I die. You've heard some of the new songs I've been singing here that I wrote while I was here. I find I have trouble remembering them. One of the reasons is that I keep changing the lines. Some of the songs I have five different versions. Sometimes I don't know which version I'm going to sing, neither does Jonathan [Segal]."[6]

Dan Barry: *There are not many singers who would dare to sing in a single set a 1968 Nixon campaign chant, a homosexual liberation song, a couple of bawdy ballads, a mock fundamentalist hymn.*[7]

Oscar goes back a long way. His weekly radio program *Folksong Festival* began in 1945 when Fiorello LaGuardia was mayor. In the early days, Woody Guthrie, Pete Seegar, Burl Ives, Huddie Leadbetter; later Bob Dylan, Judy Collins, Harry Belafonte, Joan Baez were among the many who found their way into Oscar's studio.[8] I was happy with Oscar. But for this kind of program to succeed I needed money to advertise—and time—time to develop an audience for Oscar's witty topical cabaret program. The Cookery's financial situation did not permit it.

For his 1983 Newport Jazz Festival, George Wein presented some real old-timers, among whom was Adelaide Hall, here from England. I liked her exuberance, her elegance, her warm voice. I engaged her for a month, with Ronny Whyte on piano and Frank Tate on bass. Opening night, before a packed house of celebrities, she and Honi Coles, the legendary tap dancer, performed a little tap routine. She and Josephine Baker had hoofed in the chorus line of a 1925 revue, *Chocolate Kiddies,* "with Josephine at one end of the line and me at the other," Adelaide recalled. John Wilson wrote, "[Her program] was dotted with memories of her career . . . Mr. Josephson has brought in another glowing representative of autumnal life . . . Miss Hall is a bright and warming memory of the past who still has the resources and the talent to give it a contemporary presence."[9]

What was happening in the music world? Ever since my success in 1970 with Mary Lou Williams the cabaret world had been changing and growing. I had plenty of competition now. There were over forty clubs in Manhattan, hotel rooms and restaurants offering music, some presenting top jazz musicians and singers. I had a situation which few of these venues encountered. I was restricted to what I could present musically. I could not bring in more than three string instrumentalists, no drums, brass, or wind.

And something else had transpired which I never anticipated. In the public's eye The Cookery and Alberta were *one.* With her many continuous years at The Cookery I had inadvertently made The Cookery synonymous with Alberta Hunter. It is true, few cabaret performers, anywhere, could bring in the crowds year after year as Alberta did. She was a once-in-a-lifetime phenomenon. Without Alberta my business was way off, regardless of the fine talent I was bringing in. I had lost the audience I had before her. And I didn't have the wherewithal for the kind of publicity and public relations needed to change the image.

Six months after her third hospitalization Alberta returned, frailer, her spirit not one whit diminished. She stayed a month, returning again the end of August. But age and hospitalizations took their toll. Instead of five nights I had her performing four, and two shows rather than the three she'd been doing Fridays and Saturdays. No way to keep that lady down. Performing was what kept her alive.

Then she stunned me, announcing that she had decided to accept a three-week gig in São Paulo, Brazil, first week in October 1983.[10] I didn't think she could survive the ten-hour plane trip. I strongly opposed her going, I needed her. She went. She returned happy with her rave notices and audience reception—so happy that she went back in May 1984. Years ago John Hammond had suggested a music copyright lawyer, Bill Krasilovsky, to help register Alberta's music and collect royalties. Bill, now her lawyer, had taken over, handling her Brazilian and other bookings.

My insistence on no contracts had come home to roost. Alberta was deciding when she would perform at The Cookery and which outside gigs she would accept. With no contract she had this freedom.

> **John Hammond:** *It would have been better for Barney if he had a contract with Alberta. It's very hard with someone who has been a star in her earlier days, retires for twenty years and then comes back to tremendous acclaim, it's very hard to keep your perspective.*
>
> **Terry Trilling-Josephson:** *You know, John, Alberta boasted to me, "Fame hasn't changed me."*
>
> **John Hammond:** *Well, it did.*[11]

CHAPTER
62

"In effect, this stripped me
of my business."

At the beginning of our relationship I would tell Terry "I'm a poor man" without explaining. For one thing, I didn't own The Cookery. When my youngest son was born I was almost sixty years old. I had another son, age three, a young family, of great concern to me. Would I be around long enough to provide for my sons' schooling? My current lawyer, David Friedman, the husband of Gloria's former law partner, advised me to transfer my majority corporation stock to Gloria in an irrevocable trust to avoid inheritance taxes. My sons' mother would act as trustee for the children until they each reached twenty-one. They would then assume control of the stock. This seemed to be a good way to ensure their well-being.

So six months after the birth of Louis I signed the irrevocable trust. In effect, this stripped me of my business, my only substantial asset. Having assigned Gloria as trustee for the boys, she was in control of The Cookery. She had given up her meager law practice with Blanche Friedman to work full time in the place. I did not anticipate the consequences of this transfer of my assets. As time went on, with literally total control of The Cookery, Gloria became more imperious and high-handed.

Jimmie Josephson (David's wife): *She walked around with a big air and antagonized the help and the customers. Barney liked to pick up the check for people who came from Trenton. She raised hell about it in front of the people. I wasn't there. I heard about it. She swaggered around the place. She was boss-lady. There was something bitter about Gloria. I know Lucy, Leon's wife, wouldn't go in when she was there.*

Barney said to me some weeks ago [early December 1983], "Well, I don't have a family anymore." It was a terrible thing to say. I would never have suspected that they [his sons] would treat him now the way they do. As a matter of fact, I always thought they were closer to him than to her. When he turned over everything to the boys in an irrevocable trust, why you don't do that. What was he trying to show? That he was a good father?[1]

I had locked myself into an untenable position. I thought of leaving her. I couldn't. The business was all Leon and I had. And I wouldn't leave my young sons fatherless.

Lee Josephson (Leon's son): *Leon worked in The Cookery from when they founded it in '53 'til he retired in '62 at the age of sixty-four. The main reason, the overriding reason, was that he couldn't stand Gloria, plus he was old.*[2]

When I married Gloria she was living with her parents in the same apartment house as The Cookery. She moved into my apartment, also in that building. We didn't have to buy a thing. My apartment was well furnished with my collection of original art, antiques, silver, rare books, jazz collection—a ready-made household. When I walked out the summer of 1978 I took only my clothes and a few personal belongings. The boys were still living there; it was their home. Gloria had the apartment and everything in it. More to the point, she controlled The Cookery.

We drew up a separation agreement. It was agreed that I would assume sole managerial operation of the place. The Cookery could not exist without me. Gloria knew that, and I was adamant that I would not stay on unless she was off the premises. I had one asset out of her control—Alberta Hunter, who would go with me wherever I would go.

Edgar (Ted) Coons: *I started coming into The Cookery in 1965. Literally, the restaurant was practically my dining room and the place where*

I interviewed my students. It was my office away from my office, and it was almost my home away from home. So I got to see lots of what went on in The Cookery. Finally, Barney came over to me. "You seem to be a regular here. Come over to this table. Let me buy you a drink and I'll find out a little bit of who you are."

That's how we started. I began to see that he was a very kind, gentle man. I had become aware of his importance to the field of jazz.

It's a funny thing, I would start to talk to him about music, thinking that this would be something he would glom into. Actually, it seemed as if his eyes would glaze over. It was sort of inexplicable to me because he was normally very involved. But this was one thing where he backed off and actually seemed to hide inside himself. Then I understood it later when he began to work again in the jazz field with Mary Lou Williams. It began to change. He started to blossom. He seemed to take pride, as if knowing that once again he was doing what his true love was in life, that it wasn't a painful thing, and his stories began to come out.

In some sense it's a conjecture on my part, but as a psychologist I'll give it a little more credit. When the big hit came, which was Alberta, then he really blossomed. As he blossomed, and the more he came out of his shell, the more mean and vindictive Gloria got to him. It's my sense of two things. His sons were over what you call the critical stages of maturing, and the fact that he had come into his own, that he could finally take the action that I suspect he had been wanting to take for a long time, of cutting the ties with Gloria.

He felt like he was once more a whole person in some sense. I felt it was that he had gotten back in touch with the important mission in his life. I know Barney felt he was really performing an invaluable service in terms of taking a new generation and letting them know what their heritage had been, introducing to them what had been the era of jazz and making it live again. That was the thing that pleased him basically more than anything else. And it was in this sense, in the greatest sense of the word, that he was a fabulous teacher. He was an educator.

Looked at another way, he just did a great favor to all the people that he loved dearly. He made work for them at a time when a lot of them needed work and were getting old. I talked to Alberta on several occasions, and she said, "I will always be in Barney's debt because he's made me proud in my old age. He's made my old age the best part of my life."[3]

My son Eddie had turned twenty-one the end of 1978. I spoke to him about his shares. "Of course, Dad, The Cookery is yours, no one else's." Without consulting his mother he assigned his shares back to me just before Thanksgiving Day, November 26, 1979. Eddie later reported that Gloria was enraged when she found out. Nonetheless, I still did not have control of the majority of the stock. Louis, my youngest, would not come of age until August 1982 but promised his shares to me, too. He did not keep his promise. Gloria owned some shares herself, which gave her majority control together with Louis's shares.

In 1980 the New York State Legislature passed a new divorce law and with it the prospect for me to regain at least half of my assets, including a house on Fire Island. I sued for divorce. Gloria had been continually siphoning off large sums of money from the business, which I was powerless to halt. This created the serious financial crisis for The Cookery I'd been facing over the years. As stated in my divorce action, filed August 25, 1981, before the New York State Supreme Court, "The current payments [to Gloria] seriously jeopardize the soundness of the financial structure of the business."

Gloria fought the divorce, requesting one postponement after another. Finally, it went on the court calendar late 1982. Judge Cahn of Albany heard the case, my testimony. He tried to effect a settlement. After speaking to each of us separately in his chambers he told me that Gloria would never agree to a divorce. All she wanted was for me to die. That's what she told him, that's what she was waiting for, that she would appeal any court decisions. Judge Cahn explained, "That could take three years or more."[4]

The judge was to hand down his decision on Monday, January 17, 1983. I had been concerned about my sons, knowing that Gloria was talking to them:

Terry Trilling: *The evening of Friday, January 14, 1983, Barney told me he'd had a phone call at The Cookery during the day from Louis. He was calling from his apartment at Tufts University. The court's decision was due in three days. Barney was white and shaken as he related Louis's diatribe. He'd never heard such words from his sons, he said. Louis berated him, telling him he didn't know how to run a business, that he was no father to him, that he could live on his Social Security, that Eddie felt the same way. It must be said here that Barney had been paying for Louis's tuition at Tufts.*

Barney asked me, "How did Lucky [Louis] know the court's decision was due on Monday if Gloria hadn't been talking to him?" Barney said she was well aware that Judge Cahn had made it quite clear he was prepared to grant Barney's petition for equitable distribution of all the assets

After Louis's phone call, Barney reacted as Gloria figured he would: "If that's the way the boys feel, to hell with it, let them have it all. I'm not going to fight. All I want is the divorce [for our marriage] and The Cookery, whatever it's worth now."

Barney called his attorney, Norma Hack, to tell her to withdraw his suit for the equitable distribution of all marital property and the return of his premarital separate property. Norma strongly opposed his decision and explained its consequences for his financial situation. Barney could not be talked out of it. The divorce action was subsequently "transferred to the uncontested calendar." Barney had his divorce. The Cookery was returned to him in severe financial straits.

Whitney Balliett: *The last time we saw Barney we had a long chat with him. He was very upset.*

Nancy Balliett: *He said he had lost everything. He was very emotional. He wept freely without being embarrassed about it. He said he just couldn't believe the change, how he'd lost the children completely. That was shocking. He was so proud and had such a good sense of humor about what they used to do.*[5]

Alberta, more and more frail, was able to manage one show a night at 9:30, four nights a week for a six-week stretch. The restrooms and the dressing room were in the basement and required negotiating a steep flight of stairs. Impossible for Alberta. On the ninth of January 1984 Alberta gave her last performance at The Cookery. The lyrics to one of the songs she wrote, "I'm Having a Good Time Living My Life Today," tell her story:

I'm playing it cool while I'm living
Cause tomorrow I may die.
That's why I'm having a ball today
And I ain't passing nothing by.

Nine months after her final appearance at The Cookery, October 17, 1984, Gerald Cook found her in her Roosevelt Island apartment, sitting in an armchair, her head resting on her arm. She never quite made it to ninety.

As I predicted, Alberta went out in a blaze of glory. On October 21, the *New York Times* honored Alberta in an editorial. I chuckled because the editor wrote she had worked as a "scrub nurse," which was how I would introduce her until I was corrected. She was honored for her dedication to her nursing profession. The activities building at Goldwater Memorial Hospital was renamed the Alberta Hunter Memorial Building.

Alberta

A gardener's adage holds that the oldest trees yield the sweetest fruit. Before her death at eighty-nine, Alberta Hunter showed how that can apply to singers, too. One of the last of the classic blues singers, Miss Hunter returned to the stage in 1977 after a twenty-year absence. All the time, she had worked as a scrub nurse in Goldwater Memorial Hospital on New York's Roosevelt Island.

But she hadn't lost the voice that gave her a reputation rivaling Bessie Smith's. So the owner of a Village cabaret, Barney Josephson, took a chance by arranging her comeback at the Cookery, where she became a fixture after her "debut" at eighty-two. Audiences who knew nothing of her legend succumbed afresh when she sang her old songs, intermingled with impudent asides about life and love.

Miss Hunter chose silence and nursing in 1954 after her mother's death. She decided that she ought to do something for others. Having paid her dues, she sang again, thereby disproving another adage—that there are no second acts in American lives. Hers had three glorious ones.[6]

I had wanted to re-do The Cookery for many years, to give it a new face, a new name, to reflect what it had become since I'd brought in entertainment. I envisioned installing a large, circular bar on the University Place side to replace the present open kitchen. The sizzling sound of hamburgers and other food cooking on the open grill were so very bothersome to my artists and audience. The grill would be dispensed with. The bar would then open up the room to young people who could come in, drink without dining, and listen to the entertainment for a small cover charge.

The performance area I was using was never meant to be one. I wanted to create an efficient, attractive theatrical space. The outdoor cafe on University Place needed to be enclosed for the winter months with glass doors which could slide open during the warm weather. It was wasted space otherwise. But, and there was a big but, I didn't control The Cookery.

Now, with control of the place, I wanted to renovate. I went so far as to enlist an architect friend to draw up plans. Additional capital was needed to get The Cookery back on solid footing, to give it the image I envisioned. Several likely proposals involving other partners almost came to pass. Each time the landlord threatened to sue anybody I took in. No one wanted to engage in a lawsuit—except one.

Years past, a Japanese woman, Hisae Vilca, had worked as a waitress in The Cookery for over five years. She had married a man who started out as a dishwasher with me and graduated to chef. Hisae left to open her own restaurant and became a well-known restaurateur. I thought of her. Hisae was now a partner in a successful barbecue chicken-and-ribs chain and agreed to take over the location but with her own kind of restaurant. She told me, "Mr. J., I learned from you. I watched you very much." The landlord did go to court. Hisae fought. The case was thrown out. Overnight, a barbecue restaurant emerged. The Cookery vanished. I would stay on as consultant until the liquor license expired.

On May 6, 1984, The Cookery closed its doors forever after thirty-one years of continuous operation. In this business that's a record.

(top) Jack Gilford kidding around with Barney at The Cookery, January 1981. (Author's Collection, courtesy of Madeline Lee Gilford)

(bottom) Barney leading Alberta Hunter onstage at The Cookery, 1978. (Author's Collection)

(top) Barney and Alberta Hunter in discussion at The Cookery, December 1977. (Photo courtesy of Susan Kuklin)

(bottom) White House reception, December 1978. Left to right: Rosalynn Carter, President Jimmy Carter, Alberta Hunter, Barney. (White House photo, Author's Collection)

(top) Alberta Hunter in performance at The Cookery, 1977. (Photo courtesy of Diana Jo Davies)

(bottom) Alberta Hunter and accompanist Gerald Cook, The Cookery, 1977. (Photo courtesy of Anton J. Mikovsky)

(top) Jack Gilford as Frosch in
Die Fledermaus, Metropolitan
Opera, 1950. (Photo courtesy
of Madeline Lee Gilford)

(bottom) R&B legend Ruth
Brown at The Cookery, 1981.
(Photo courtesy of Stephanie
Chernikowski)

(top) Cabaret chanteuse Susannah McCorkle around 1990. (Photo courtesy of Theadora Lurie)

(bottom) Marian McPartland with Rick Petrone on bass, The Cookery, 1971. (Courtesy of Marian McPartland, Author's Collection)

(top) Mabel Mercer visiting her old friend Adelaide Hall (left) at Hall's opening at The Cookery, April 1983. (David Gould photo)

(bottom) Nellie Lutcher at The Cookery, 1973. (Raymond Ross photo)

(top) Helen Humes, autographed to Barney, 1980. (Author's Collection)

(bottom) Milt Gabler at home with his Commodore Records collection, May 8, 2000. (Photo courtesy of Mikie Harris)

(top) Gretchen Cryer at the mike; Nancy
Ford at the piano; The Cookery, 1976. (Photo
courtesy of Gretchen Cryer)

(bottom) Gospel singer Marion Williams, studio
shot around 1980. (Music Division, The New
York Public Library for the Performing Arts,
Astor, Lenox and Tilden Foundations)

Interior of Barney's first Cookery; Anton Refregier collage on the wall.
(Author's Collection)

(top) Agnes de Mille, Gayle Young, and Sallie Wilson in *A Rose for Miss Emily,* choreographed by de Mille, American Ballet Theatre premiere, October 1970. (Jerome Robbins Dance Division, The New York Public Library for the Performing Arts, Astor, Lenox and Tilden Foundations)

(bottom) Barney and Terry Josephson. (Jean Germain photo, Author's Collection)

Postlude

Terry Trilling-Josephson

"I'm in business," Barney announced one day, just like that. He was eighty-five years old and, incredibly, eager to start afresh. His fervor for doing what he loved most remained unabated. He had embarked on a search for a new location. "This is the time," he reasoned, "for a return to cheek-to-cheek dancing in a cabaret offering good food and featuring young unknown jazz musicians and entertainers. I know they're out there. I've spoken to John Hammond. It will be like old times."

> **Don Nelson:** *When veteran impresario Barney Josephson opens a new jazz room shortly, he will be reaffirming what seems an obvious though oft forgotten truth—that jazz is a continuum with remarkable resilience. Its popularity over the decades may rise, fall and rise again, yet its residual strength as America's indigenous music is never diluted. . . . . In this case, Josephson's in luck. He'll present Barbara Lea with the Mike Abene trio backing her up. Depending on Abene's availability, Josephson will open Oct. 14 or 21.*[1]

Hisae Vilca owned the Backstage Restaurant on West 45th Street, and this is where Barney would open. He would not be involved in the restaurant. The cabaret would be a separate operation in another room. But it was not to be. Less than three weeks before the opening the proprietor of the dining room, not Hisae, reneged on the original agreement. Barney canceled. He paid off the musicians. Barbara Lea, who was to be the featured singer, graciously refused to accept payment, telling him, "There'll be another time."

There would not be another time. Rents were exorbitant. Time was not on his side, and John Hammond was gone July 10, 1987. A year later Barney, too, was gone on September 29, 1988, a day before his lease on The Cookery would expire.

A brilliantly hued hibiscus was delivered to our apartment with a note: "Dear, dear Barney, This street is sadder and meaner since yesterday. Love, Agnes de Mille Prude." Barney loved the fresh flowers that were always artfully arranged on the coffee table. Although Agnes de Mille never worked for Barney, she and her husband, Walter Prude, lived around the corner from The Cookery on East 9th Street and were regulars for Sunday brunch.

On November 16, 1988, a memorial service was held for Barney at St. Peter's Church, with the Rev. John Garcia Gensel, the "Jazz Priest," presiding. The following tributes are from that service, although not in the order given:

Art D'Lugoff, owner of the Village Gate: *I guess we all owe a great debt to Barney, the life we live today, the music, the ideas, the thoughts. His was not just a jazz club. I learned from him very early. It was jazz, it was comedy, it was folk, it was ethnic, it was people, it was taste. Barney had a great ear and a great eye and he was one of my heroes. And he is my lineal father . . . I think Barney and his story should be made into a movie . . . I think Cafe Society should be the story that should be told about our century. . . . Just about a year or two ago, Barney said to me, "You know, Art, I'd really like to start up a new club. I've got some great ideas. Do you know anything about a new location?" So Barney, wherever you are up there, I hope you found that new location and you still continue to do the same thing that you've been doing and make everybody happy, both Uptown and Downtown.*

Betty Comden: *I have very happy memories of Barney—and I was an employee. . . . I mean he was a very nice boss, nice to work for. . . . I was part of this loosely hurled together group which came to be known as The Revuers. With me was Judy Holiday and Adolph Green and two other very gifted men, Alvin Hammer and John Frank. Barney was so wonderful to be with. He'd sort of put his head to one side and sit out front, and he'd laugh a lot. That's very important when you're trying to do comedy. He was a good audience and a fine boss, and he took good care of us. . . . Part of the contract with the musicians who played there was that they had to play for us. . . . The first orchestra that we had was Frankie Newton and a stellar group of musicians—absolutely stunning. Then shortly after that Teddy Wilson and the immortal Edmond Hall the clarinetist and Benny Morton the trombonist—just incredible. And later the band that came in was Lee and Lester Young.*

They were great musicians. And there they had our pitiful little orchestrations. One of the numbers in it was the finale of the Tchaikovsky Fourth Symphony. There were three shows. So the first show they played for us was absolutely on the nose. The second show got a little more improvisational, let us say, a "leetle" wilder. By the third show it was just an incredible riffing going on. I didn't know why that was going on. I didn't know anything in those days.

Then later we did move up to Cafe Uptown. And how elegant that was, all kind of dark and black, little lights and sparkling. We played both places twice I believe. . . . My husband Steve was in the army. Between the first and second show I asked Barney if it was all right if I went over to the Stage Door Canteen. He said, "Yes, but don't get carried away and be sure you get back here for the twelve o'clock show." I would go over there and dance or serve coffee, then we'd do the second show.

Doing the shows, they were extraordinary audiences. In those days, and in those clubs particularly, the audience really came to pay attention and listen. . . . I remember one night between shows S. J. Perlman brought Robert Benchley there. These were some of the things which were so thrilling to us. We had the best time. And all through it, Barney was being very supportive, very genial, this lovely quiet voice and smile, and I don't remember, ever, any kinds of altercations or any trouble. . . .

Years and years later, my husband and I would go down to The Cookery and sit around and talk to Barney. We'd reminisce about those days when we'd finish up at Cafe Society at—what—three o'clock in the morning and then maybe go down the block to Reuben's and stay up another couple of hours. Even so, I'd go home by subway by myself and not worry. Those were fascinating times, and they were really good times, and there were good people around like Barney.

St. Peter's Church was packed to overflowing, people sitting in the aisles. The doors were closed; no more could be accommodated. The program was underway. Out of the corner of my eye I caught sight of an elderly black woman slowly making her way with a walker across the horizontal length of the aisle that separated the orchestra from the balcony. She was wearing an undistinguished cloth coat and a cloche-type hat. I wondered who was coming in so late and why she was crossing the width of the room instead of sitting near the entrance. A while into the program Reverend Gensel announced, "Rose Murphy," and there at the piano was a glamorous youngish looking woman in a lovely turquoise beaded dress—the woman with the walker.

Rose "Chi-Chi" Murphy: *I listened to all these wonderful people saying such nice things about Barney Josephson, and it's all so true. He was a good man. He made you feel like you were worthwhile—if you didn't do anything but "chi-chi." The thing is, he made you think everything was wonderful.*

Then she turned to the piano and exuberantly sang "I Can't Give You Anything but . . . Chi-Chi," and the audience responded with appreciative laughter. Rose spiced her singing "with twitterings, chirrups and occasionally the sound 'chi chi' which provided her nickname." She then sang "Does Your Mother Know You're Out?" accompanied by Morris Edwards on bass and to prolonged applause. "Thank you so much. It really seems like Barney Josephson is here."[2]

Jack Gilford was shooting a movie in Hollywood, so his son, Joe, read from the letters Jack sent to Barney every anniversary day over the years. The Reverend Gensel read a telegram Nellie Lutcher sent from Los Angeles: "I can't be present, but I recall with much pride . . . Barney's foresight and confidence in bringing me to New York. . . . With much love and deepest sympathy."

I had asked Imogene Coca to speak. She said yes and was listed on the program. Then she changed her mind. A week later I received a note from her:

Dear Mrs. Josephson—

I am so very sorry I did not come to Barney's Celebration. I fully intended to be there and had I not been expected to make a speech—I'd have been there. I become so nervous at the thought of "speaking"—I—well—I couldn't go—. . . I respected Barney and loved working for him—I, as he knew, am a rather shy person and when it comes to making a speech—I freeze—Please accept my apology and understand—I am being totally honest with you—I hear it was a lovely tribute and I wish I had been there just to hear the beautiful things that were said about Barney—If you ever need me for anything other than a speech—. . . I hope you understand.

Sincerely,

Imogene (Coca)

Gail Lumet Buckley, Lena Horne's daughter, telephoned to say they would not be able to attend because they had to be in Washington, D.C. I had spoken to Gail weeks earlier, asking Lena to speak. At that time, Gail explained, Lena was ambivalent about speaking, but they were planning to be there.

Dick Hyman, the brilliant musician of multiple talents, had played solo piano Sunday nights for many, many years at The Cookery whenever he would be available. I was grateful to Dick when he graciously volunteered to give of his time and expertise to organize the musical portion of the program. The Reverend Gensel persuaded Dick to play his composition "Something for Barney."[3]

A touching surprise was the presentation of a posthumous award, an illuminated scroll, read to the audience by New York University Associate Dean Jerrold Ross:

> *Gentleman, foster father to people of talent . . . friend to all academicians, Barney Josephson for fifty years epitomized the very reasons for art to exist, as his artistic vision both reflected and led not only Cafe Society, but society at large. New York University's School of Education, Health, Nursing and Arts Professions posthumously bestows on our friend, neighbor, and musical guide its Creative Leadership Award in the Arts Professions.*

Agnes de Mille spoke from her wheelchair:

> *We today, occasionally, come upon a still point, where there is courtesy, where there is quiet, where there is a place or a moment where we can put ourselves to order, in order, and be kind to one another and be courteous—courtesy is kindness—and appreciate what we have to say; where we can be human in the best sense of the word. And that is what Barney Josephson brought to 8th and University Place. . . . And there was Barney with his extraordinary courtesy, very quiet, attentive, and careful of your well-being, your accommodation. I couldn't go in after a while, it was not possible.[4] But I'd knock on the glass, and he'd come out, and we'd converse in the street. And the last time he kissed me and then talked about how my husband was . . . and he told me about a long correspondence he'd had with Sean O'Casey. . . . I don't suppose you knew he moved in a circle like that. But he did. And it was just lovely. And we'd have these long conversations. . . . Well, Barney isn't there now. And you've been talking about how much that you feel Barney's here with you now. But I feel that Barney's there at the corner of Eighth and University forever. And I feel that his presence had made the street gentle . . . I think this is what a good life means. It spreads grace every-*

where. Every life he touched is kinder, more interested, more alert. . . .
I think we can be very thankful we were blessed to know Barney for so
long and have him with us.

Terry Trilling-Josephson: *Barney loved words, and he especially loved*
the words of Shakespeare. During what was to be his last week in the
hospital, and just to while away the time, I asked him if he would quote
a few lines from Shakespeare, as he would often do. He thought for a
moment, shook his head, "It would have been the occasion which would
clue the quotation." Then he thought another moment, cocked his head,
looked at me, and smiled slightly:

> Age, I do abhor thee, youth, I do adore thee;
> O! my love, my love is young:
> Age, I do defy thee: O! sweet shepherd, hie thee,
> For methinks thou stay'st too long.[5]

Notes

CHAPTER 1: "'Take my advice, go back to Trenton and open a shoe store that sells health shoes.'"

1. Syd Hoff, telephone interview with TTJ from Miami Beach, Fla., Aug. 25, 1999.
2. Jack Gilford, interview with TTJ at his home, New York City, Dec. 14, 1989.
3. Colin Allen, telephone interview with TTJ from Detroit, Mich., Aug. 31, 1999.
4. Colin Allen telephone interview, Aug. 31, 1999.

CHAPTER 2: "'I've got Billie Holiday. . . .' 'Who is she?' I asked."

1. John Hammond, *John Hammond on Record: An Autobiography with Irving Townsend* (New York: Ridge Press, 1977), 199, 200.
2. Mary Lou Williams in *Melody Maker,* April–June 1954 (twelve installments).
3. Hammond, *John Hammond on Record,* 203.
4. The first Holiday-Goodman recording was made on November 27, 1933; the second session, on Columbia's Brunswick label, was recorded July 2, 1935.
5. Hammond, *John Hammond on Record,* 67.

CHAPTER 3: "I saw Gypsy Rose Lee do a political striptease."

1. The ban was issued by President Franklin Roosevelt on January 6, 1937.
2. "News of Night Clubs," *New York Times,* Nov. 27, 1938.
3. Jack Gilford, interview with TTJ at his home, New York City, Dec. 14, 1989.

CHAPTER 4: "'Tell your friend to call it Cafe Society.'"

1. Handwritten letter from Syd Hoff to TTJ from Miami Beach, Fla., Aug. 13, 1999; Syd Hoff, telephone interview with TTJ from Miami Beach, Aug. 25, 1999.

2. Syd Hoff telephone interview, Aug. 25, 1999.

3. Abe Birnbaum was sixty-seven when he died on June 19, 1966.

4. Syd Hoff telephone interview, Aug. 25, 1999. Hoff died on May 12, 2004, at ninety-one.

5. John Groth was eighty when he died in June 1988.

6. Colin Allen, telephone interview with TTJ from Detroit, Mich., Aug. 31, 1999.

7. Syd Hoff telephone interview, Aug. 25, 1999. Irving Hoffman often supplied Walter Winchell with gossip for his column and at times wrote the column when Winchell wanted time off.

8. Colin Allen telephone interview, Aug. 31, 1999. Sam Shaw, eighty-seven, died April 5, 1999. The opening paragraph in his *New York Times* obituary mentions that he was famous for his photograph of Marilyn Monroe standing over a subway grate. In the 1950s and 1960s he was renowned for his covers for *Life* and *Look*. In Hollywood he became a top sound editor whose work included *Star Wars* (1977).

9. *New York Times,* Nov. 11, 1938, 1.

10. Colin Allen telephone interview, Aug. 31, 1999.

CHAPTER 5: "There we were, occupying six windows of the elegant Bergdorf-Goodman."

1. All of Jack Gilford's and Zero Mostel's routines in this book are given as Barney Josephson recounted them.

2. "Brenda Frazier Bows to Society," *New York Times,* Dec. 28, 1938.

3. Colin Allen, telephone interview with TTJ from Detroit, Mich., Aug. 31, 1999.

CHAPTER 6: "'What he should have is six goils and one guy.'"

1. John Hammond, *John Hammond on Record: An Autobiography with Irving Townsend* (New York: Ridge Press, 1977), 92.

2. Holiday toured with Count Basie from March 13, 1937, to February 1938, and with Artie Shaw from March 9, 1938, to November 19, 1938. The quotation is from Ted Yates, *New York Amsterdam News,* Dec. 7, 1935.

3. Billie Holiday interview with Dave Dexter, *DownBeat* (Nov. 1939).

4. Bill Chase interview, *New York Amsterdam News,* Jan. 21, 1939.

5. Holiday left Shaw's band on November 19, 1938.

6. *New York Times,* Jan. 8, 1939.

7. Hans J. Mauerer, *The Pete Johnson Story* (Bremen, Germany: n.p., 1965).

CHAPTER 7: "'You'll be a big star.'"

1. Jack Gilford, interview with TTJ at his home, New York City, Dec. 14, 1989.

2. Ibid.

3. Ibid.

CHAPTER 8: "Billie looked at me. 'What do you want me to do with that, man?'"

1. The Fifteenth Amendment was ratified on February 3, 1870.

2. Between 1882, when lynchings began to be recorded systematically, and 1968, it was estimated that 4,742 persons died at the hands of lynch mobs; 90 percent were African American (figures from the Charles Chestnut Digital Archive, Tuskeegee University).

3. John Hammond, *John Hammond on Record: An Autobiography with Irving Townsend* (New York: Ridge Press, 1977), 209.

4. Milton Gabler, interview with TTJ at his home, New Rochelle, N.Y., Sept. 22, 1999.

5. Ibid.

6. "Strange Fruit" was recorded April 20, 1939, with Frankie Newton (tp), Tab Smith (as), Kenneth Hollon and Stanley Payne (ts), Sonny White (p), Jimmy McLin (g), John Williams (b), and Eddie Dougherty (d).

7. Ibid.

8. Ibid.

9. *New Amsterdam News,* Dec. 7, 1938.

10. Hammond, *John Hammond on Record,* 209.

11. Billie Holiday interview with Dave Dexter, *DownBeat* (Nov. 1939).

12. Milton Gabler interview, Sept. 22, 1999.

13. Billie Holiday with William Dufty, *Lady Sings the Blues* (1956, repr. New York: Penguin Books, 1984), 85; quotations from the 1984 edition.

14. *Melody Maker,* Aug. 8, 1959, 5. John Hammond died on September 5, 1987.

15. Teddy Wilson, interview with TTJ and Barney Josephson, The Cookery, Jan. 27, 1983.

CHAPTER 9: "You don't keep anybody working for you under contract. That's slavery."

1. Stuart Nicholson, *Billie Holiday* (Boston: Northeastern University Press, 1995), 117.

2. John Chilton, *Billie's Blues: The Billie Holiday Story, 1933–1959* (New York: Da Capo Press, 1975), 65.

3. Colin Allen, telephone interview with TTJ from Detroit, Mich., Aug. 31, 1999.

4. Ibid.

5. Chilton, *Billie's Blues,* 68.

6. Joe Glaser died June 4, 1969.

7. Louis Armstrong, *Satchmo: My Life in New Orleans* (New York: New American, 1954).

8. The Theatre Owners Booking Agency (TOBA), a venue below the Mason-Dixie Line, offered all-black programs, including music, dance, minstrel shows, and comedy, for all-black audiences across the South and Midwest.

9. *Variety,* Nov. 1, 1939, 33.

10. John Hammond, *John Hammond on Record: An Autobiography with Irving Townsend* (New York: Ridge Press, 1977), 231.

11. "Table for Two," *The New Yorker,* May 4, 1940.

12. Hammond, *John Hammond on Record,* 231.

13. Teddy Wilson, interview with TTJ and Barney Josephson, The Cookery, Jan. 27, 1983.

CHAPTER 10: "'Never borrow a week's salary from the M.C. to pay other bills.'"

1. John Hammond, interview with TTJ at his office, New Yoork City, Jan. 10, 1986.

2. Ibid.

3. John Hammond, *John Hammond on Record: An Autobiography with Irving Townsend* (New York: Ridge Press, 1977), 207.

4. Jack Gilford, interview with TTJ at his home, New York City, Dec. 14, 1989.

5. John Hammond interview, Jan. 10, 1986.

CHAPTER 11: "'There will be no craps-shooting Negroes in my place.'"

1. The Golden Gate Jubilee Quartet first appeared on April 22, 1940.

2. Orlandus Wilson, interview with TTJ at recording studio in his home, Paris, France, July 3, 1993.

3. John Hammond, interview with TTJ at his office, New York City, Jan. 10, 1986.

4. Ibid.

5. Ira Tucker of the Dixie Hummingbirds, interview with TTJ, Philadelphia, March 12, 2003. Tucker died on June 24, 2008, at age eighty-three.

6. Orlandus Wilson interview, July 3, 1993.

7. I (TTJ) explained to Ira that Barney and I were not married in those days. I didn't know Barney then.

8. Ira Tucker interview, March 12, 2003.

9. Mollie Moon at memorial for Barney Josephson, Nov. 16, 1988. Moon, the founder and president of the National Urban League Guild for fifty years, was seventy-eight when she died on June 24, 1990.

10. Herbert L. Schultz, April 10, 1979. Schultz was vice president of Vassar College,

and the Princeton University student in the photo with Ammons, Johnson, and Turner (see page 9 of photo section B).

11. Henry Lee Moon was publicity director of the NAACP; Billy Rowe became the deputy police commissioner of New York; Ernest Johnson was a journalist; and the de Passes were the parents of entertainment executive Suzanne de Passe.

12. Fredi Washington interview courtesy of Jean-Claude Baker, Dec. 17, 1983. Washington was an African American actress, writer, dancer, and singer whose sister, Isabelle, had been married to Adam Clayton Powell.

CHAPTER 12: "Always hand-me-downs like that, but I had beautiful clothes."

1. The word *gaon* was from the phrase "rosh yeshivat ge'on Ya'kov" (the pride of Jacob, one who is brilliantly versed in Talmudic knowledge).

CHAPTER 13: "'She was a remarkable woman, way ahead of her time.'"

1. Jimmie Josephson (married to David Josephson), interview with TTJ at Josephson's home, East Orange, N.J., Jan. 24, 1984.
2. Jimmie Josephson interview, Jan. 24, 1984.

CHAPTER 14: "As natural to me as drinking a glass of milk."

1. Jimmie Josephson, interview with TTJ at Josephson's home, East Orange, N.J., Jan. 24, 1984.

CHAPTER 15: "Leon set up that kind of thing, share and share alike."

1. Interview with Ethel Barrymore, *New York Times*, Aug. 24, 1919.

CHAPTER 17: "The workers sleeps in a old straw bed and shivers from the cold."

1. "All Seven Convicted at Gastonia Trial: Four Get Twenty Years," *New York Times*, Oct. 22, 1929. The seven were released on bail provided by the International Labor Defense, which filed notice of appeal to the highest courts.
2. "The Big Fat Boss," *The Nation*, Oct. 9, 1929.
3. "The Mill Mothers' Song," *The Nation*, Oct. 9, 1929.
4. "Gastonia Frees Nine in Wiggins Case," *New York Times*, Oct. 25, 1929.
5. Jimmie Josephson, interview with TTJ at Josephson's home, East Orange, N.J., Jan. 24, 1984.

CHAPTER 18: "I'm the right man in the wrong place."

1. Malcolm Johnson, *New York Sun*, Oct. 12, 1940.
2. "Goings On about Town," *The New Yorker*, Nov. 2, 1940.
3. Paul Petroff, assistant to Anton Refregier, interview with TTJ, Brooklyn Heights, N.Y., March 20, 1991.
4. Johnson, *New York Sun*, Oct. 12, 1940.

CHAPTER 19: "'A Rockefeller can afford to wear such a coat.'"

1. "Goings On about Town," *The New Yorker*, Oct. 19, 1940.
2. Malcolm Johnson, *New York Sun*, Nov. 12, 1940; emphasis added.
3. Malcolm Johnson, *New York Sun*, Oct. 12, 1940.
4. Malcolm Johnson, *New York Sun*, Feb. 26, 1941.
5. Robert Dana, *New York Herald-Tribune*, March 15, 1941.
6. "Goings On about Town," *The New Yorker*, Oct. 5, 1940.
7. Malcolm Johnson, *New York Sun*, Oct. 5, 1940.
8. John Hammond, *John Hammond on Record: An Autobiography with Irving Townsend* (New York: Ridge Press, 1977), 203.
9. Anthony Heilbut, *Gospel Sound: Good News and Bad Times* (New York: Simon and Schuster, 1971).
10. Whitney Balliett, *The New Yorker* jazz critic, interview with TTJ at his home, New York, Sept. 29, 1989.

CHAPTER 20: "Everybody was making a big fuss over me."

1. Billie Holiday with William Dufty, *Lady Sings the Blues* (1956, repr. New York: Doubleday, 1984), 83; quotation from the 1984 edition.

CHAPTER 21: "'Lena, what do you think a song is?'"

1. The Paramount Theater closed in August 1965.
2. From a tape-recording of Lena's Broadway stage show *The Lady and Her Music*, 1981.
3. Ibid.
4. *New York Daily News*, Oct. 24, 1935.
5. Charlie Barnet with Stanley Dance, *Those Swinging Years: The Autobiography of Charlie Barnet* (Baton Rouge: Louisiana State University Press, 1984).
6. Teddy Wilson, interview with TTJ and Barney Josephson, The Cookery, Jan. 27, 1983.

7. Lena Horne as told to Audreen Buffalo, "Lena!" *Essence* (May 1985): 150.

8. Teddy Wilson interview, Jan. 27, 1983.

9. From *The Lady and Her Music*.

10. John S. Wilson, *PM*, June 8, 1941.

CHAPTER 22: "Truth to tell, I was falling."

1. Joe Louis with Edna and Art Rust Jr., *Joe Louis: My Life* (New York: Harcourt Brace Jovanovich, 1978), 187.

2. One of these photos is included in Gail Lumet Buckley's biography *The Hornes: An American Family* (New York: Alfred A. Knopf, 1986).

3. Robert Wahls, "Stormy Weather Is Behind Her," *Sunday News*, Oct. 27, 1974, 1.

4. From Lena Horne's speech honoring Barney at the National Urban League Guild's Beaux Arts Ball, Grand Ballroom of the Waldorf-Astoria Hotel, New York, Feb. 26, 1982.

CHAPTER 23: "Nine months later she dropped a bomb on me."

1. Count Basie as told to Albert Murray, *Good Morning Blues: The Autobiography of Count Basie* (New York: Random House, 1985), 250.

2. John Hammond, interview with TTJ at his office, Jan. 10, 1986.

3. Jack Gilford, interview with TTJ at his home, New York City, Dec. 14, 1989.

4. Robert Wahls, "Stormy Weather Is Behind Her," *Sunday News*, Oct. 27, 1974.

5. Lena Horne and Richard Schickel, *Lena* (Garden City: Doubleday, 1965), 140.

CHAPTER 24: "'You have to be her trustee.'"

1. Dixie Tighe, *New York World-Telegram*, Dec. 14, 1940.

2. Jack Gilford, interview with TTJ at his home, New York City, Dec. 14, 1989.

CHAPTER 25: "'I'm nobody's fat black mammy, but that's how I make my money.'"

1. Among the Freed Unit films are *The Wizard of Oz, Meet Me in St. Louis, Gigi, Show Boat, Singin' in the Rain, On the Town, Cabin in the Sky, The Geat Ziegfeld,* and *American in Paris.* Along the way, the Freed Unit collected twenty-one Academy Awards.

2. Whitney Balliett, *Dinosaurs in the Morning: Forty-one Pieces on Jazz* (Philadephia: J. B. Lippincott, 1962), 149.

3. John Hammond, *John Hammond on Record: An Autobiography with Irving Townsend* (New York: Ridge Press, 1977), 104.

4. Jessie Carney Smith, ed., *Notable Black American Women* (Detroit: Gale Research, 1996), 3: 704, 705.

CHAPTER 26: "'Why don't you call him Zero? He's starting from nothing.'"

1. Himan Brown, telephone interview with TTJ, New York, Feb. 1, 1999.

2. Mary Lou Williams in *Melody Maker,* April–June 1954 (twelve installments).

3. Paul Petroff, interview with TTJ, Brooklyn Heights, N.Y., March 20, 1991.

4. *Variety,* Feb. 1942.

5. Roger Butterfield, "Zero Mostel," *Life,* Jan. 18, 1943.

6. Kyle Chrichton, "Podden the Expression," *Collier's,* Sept. 19, 1942.

7. *Keem 'Em Laughing* opened April 24, 1942.

8. George Freedley, *New York Morning Telegraph,* April 27, 1942.

CHAPTER 27: "No Zero."

1. Zero died on September 8, 1977, at the age of sixty-two.

CHAPTER 28: "We are on the same beam together,
Barney and Mildred."

1. Mildred Bailey and Red Norvo split in 1939.

2. John Hammond, *John Hammond on Record: An Autobiography with Irving Townsend* (New York: Ridge Press, 1977), 343.

3. Mildred Bailey died on December 12, 1951.

CHAPTER 29: "'He'll never come back.'"

1. Savo opened Uptown on May 10, 1943.

2. Burton Rascoe, "A Drama Critic Goes of All Things . . . Pub-Crawling!" *New York World-Telegram,* May 21, 1943.

3. Whitney Balliett, "Jazz: Big Sid," *The New Yorker,* March 8, 1976, 105.

4. The Revuers played Downtown again in January 1943.

CHAPTER 30: "She took one leap."

1. Virginia Forbes, *New York Sun,* May 11, 1943.

2. Teddy Wilson, interview with TTJ and Barney Josephson, The Cookery, Jan. 27, 1983.

3. Primus opened Downtown on April 24, 1943.

4. John Martin, "The Dance: Allies in the Arts," *New York Times,* June 13, 1943.

5. John Martin, "The Dance: Laurels—Award No. 2," *New York Times,* Aug. 1, 1943, 2.

6. Josh White opened on August 28, 1943.

7. From "One Meat Ball" by Hy Zaret and Louis Singer.

8. Pearl Primus opened on April 24, 1944.

9. Gene Knight, *New York Journal-American,* May 15, 1944.

10. Primus died on October 29, 1994, at the age of seventy-four. Her *New York Times* obituary written by Jennifer Dunning appeared on October 31, 1994. In it, Dunning observed, "Miss Primus played a role similar to that of Katherine Dunham in establishing dance by and about blacks as an important part of American culture. . . . But Miss Primus was equally celebrated for her depiction of American life and the injustices inflicted on black Americans."

CHAPTER 31: "When Mary Lou plays it all looks so easy."

1. Mary Lou Williams opened at Cafe Society Downtown on July 17, 1943.

2. John Williams died November 24, 1996, at age ninety-one. Transcribed from tape of Oct. 24, 1994, interview with Williams, Columbus, Ohio, Jazz Oral History Program, National Museum of American History, Smithsonian Institution, Washington, D.C.

3. Mary Lou Williams in *Melody Maker,* April–June 1954 (twelve installments).

4. Ibid.

5. Whitney Balliett, "Out Here Again," *The New Yorker,* May 2, 1964.

6. "Cafe Society Downtown," *Variety,* Dec. 6, 1944.

7. Mary Lou Williams in *Melody Maker.*

8. Susie Reed, interview with TTJ, Brooklyn Heights, N.Y., Dec. 29, 1991. Reed was a sixteen-year-old folk singer when she and Williams shared a dressing room.

9. Whitney Balliett, "Out Here Again," *The New Yorker,* May 2, 1964.

10. Susie Reed interview, Dec. 29, 1991.

11. Paul Bowles, *New York Herald-Tribune,* Dec. 31, 1945.

12. Abel Green, "Night Clubs Reviews," *Variety,* July 12, 1944.

13. Bob Dana, *New York Herald-Tribune,* Dec. 1, 1945.

14. Leonard Feather and Jane Feather, interview with TTJ at their home, Sherman Oaks, Calif., April 24, 1991. Leonard Feather was an important figure in the jazz world, writing about it, critiquing it, composing, and producing records. He died on September 22, 1994; Jane Feather died a year later.

15. "Ivan Black, Seventy-five, a Publicity Agent," obituary, *New York Times,* March 27, 1979.

CHAPTER 32: "'I am, believe it or not, usually pretty shy.'"

1. Imogene Coca opened at Cafe Society Uptown on February 21, 1945.
2. Imogene Coca, interview with TTJ in Coca's apartment, New York City, Jan. 31, 1991.
3. Coca opened at Cafe Society Downtown on April 23, 1945.
4. Imogene Coca interview, Jan. 31, 1991.
5. Ibid.
6. Buck Clayton and Nancy Miller Elliott, *Buck Clayton's, Jazz World* (New York: Oxford University Press, 1989), 165, 166.
7. Imogene Coca interview, Jan. 31, 1991. Frank Black was a highly respected orchestra conductor on radio during the 1930s and 1940s.
8. Buck Clayton and Nancy Miller Elliott, interview with TTJ at their apartment, New York, March 8, 1991.
9. Imogene Coca interview, Jan. 31, 1991.
10. Susie Reed, interview with TTJ, Brooklyn Heights, N.Y., Dec. 29, 1991.
11. Imogene Coca interview, Jan. 31, 1991.
12. Buck Clayton and Nancy Miller Elliott interview, March 8, 1991.
13. Imogene Coca interview, Jan. 31, 1991.

CHAPTER 33: "'Mr. Josephson, you are asexual.'"

1. The curfew began on February 25, 1945.

CHAPTER 34: "I notice Adam eyeing Hazel."

1. "A. C. Powell Jr. Wed with Difficulties," *New York Times,* Aug. 2, 1945.
2. *New York Times,* Oct. 12, 1945, 25.
3. *New York Times,* Oct. 13, 1945.
4. *New York Times,* Oct. 14, 1945.
5. She was reviewed: "Whatever may be said about Miss Scott's performance of the standard piano repertoire . . . she plays the popular kind better than any of the other pianists identified with this type of music." R.L., "Hazel Scott, Pianist, in Varied Program," *New York Times,* Nov. 27, 18.

CHAPTER 35: "'Ladies and gentlemen. This is a zither.'"

1. Susie Reed, interview with TTJ, Brooklyn Heights, N.Y., Dec. 29, 1991.
2. With Ben Hecht, MacArthur wrote the 1929 hit play *The Front Page,* which was based on his time on the newspaper.

3. Susie Reed interview, Dec. 29, 1991. Reed opened at Cafe Society Downtown on September 3, 1945.

4. Ibid.

5. Ibid.

6. The term *Tom* refers to an African American whose behavior is servile toward or who fawns upon white people, derived from the character Tom in Harriet Beecher Stowe's *Uncle Tom's Cabin.*

CHAPTER 36: "I'm being more temperamental
than John Barrymore."

1. Robert Dana, *New York Herald-Tribune,* Jan. 1946.

2. Moune de Virel opened on January 22, 1946.

3. *Variety,* Jan. 1946.

4. Django Reinhardt appeared from December 16, 1946, through January 11, 1947.

5. *New York Morning Telegraph,* Dec. 28, 1946.

6. On May 17, 1953, Reinhardt, forty-three, had a fatal hemorrhage.

CHAPTER 37: "'She can't sing.'"

1. Susie Reed, interview with TTJ, Brooklyn Heights, N.Y., Dec. 29, 1991.

2. Leonard Feather, quoted from an unidentified article, 1946, TTJ's files.

3. Jessie Carney Smith, ed., *Notable Black American Women* (Detroit: Gale Research, 1996), 2: 1168.

4. Imogene Coca, interview with TTJ in Coca's apartment, New York City, Jan. 31, 1991.

5. Both incidents occurred during the middle of August 1946.

6. The couple married in September 1947.

7. Paris Vaughan, her daughter, quoted Sarah as saying, "I come onstage looking like Lena Horne, and I leave looking like Sarah Vaughan." *The Divine One* on *American Masters,* PBS-TV, July 29, 1991. Sarah Vaughan died on April 1990.

CHAPTER 38: "'I just saw a woman singing to chairs on empty tables.'"

1. Jean-Claude Baker, interview with TTJ, New York, Nov. 21, 1993. Baker is the author of the well-received *Josephine: The Hungry Heart.* His New York restaurant Chez Josephine is his tribute to his "second mother."

2. The show, produced in 1926, was *A Night in Paris.*

3. Lucienne Boyer appeared at The Versailles in 1936.

4. Years later, Pils married Edith Piaf.

5. George Berkowitz, "Cafe Society Uptown, New York," *The Billboard*, Feb. 22, 1947.

6. Danton Walker, "Broadway," *New York Daily News*, Feb. 12, 1947.

7. Abel Green, *Variety*, Feb. 12, 1947.

8. Lee Mortimer, "Mlle. Boyer Grand at Cafe Society," *New York Daily Mirror*, Feb. 13, 1947.

9. Walker, "Broadway"; *Time*, Feb. 24, 1947; *The Billboard*, Feb. 22, 1947; Lee Mortimer, *New York Daily Mirror*, Feb. 18, 1947.

10. Abel Green, *Variety*, Feb. 12, 1947.

11. Ibid.

12. John Hammond, interview with TTJ at his office, New York City, Jan. 10, 1986. Sylvia Friedlander Hirsch, Barney's lady friend, was later his wife. Hammond was in the army from 1943 until January 20, 1946.

13. Milton Gabler, interview with TTJ at his home, New Rochelle, N.Y., Sept. 22, 1999.

14. William Bankhead (Dem.-Ala.), served from 1917 to 1940; John Bankhead served from March 4, 1931, until his death on June 12, 1946.

15. *Cue Magazine*, May 24, 1947.

CHAPTER 39: "She took the check and flipped it back to me."

1. Nellie Lutcher, interview with TTJ, Local 47 Musicians Union headquarters, Los Angeles, May 3, 1991.

2. Ibid.

3. Lutcher opened at Cafe Society Downtown on September 16, 1947.

4. Nellie Lutcher interview, May 3, 1991.

5. *Variety*, Sept. 14, 1947.

6. Nellie Lutcher interview, May 3, 1991.

7. *Gotham Guide*, September 20, 1947.

8. Pat Flaherty, quoted in unidentified newspaper clipping, TTJ's files.

9. *Variety*, March 19, 1947.

10. *Variety*, April 2, 1947.

11. "Nightlife," *Sunday Mirror*, Sept. 14, 1947.

CHAPTER 40: "'Let's have your passport.'"

1. Ruth Bryan Owen's official title was U.S. minister to Denmark. She was appointed in April 1933.

2. Lee Josephson, son of Leon Josephson, interview with TTJ, Brooklyn Heights, N.Y., April 28, 1996.

3. A sampling of reviews: "Cafe Society today is one of the most successful joints

of its type in New York"; "Mr. Josephson, giving in to the Park Avenue gentry who mob his place, is opening Cafe Society Uptown between Park and Madison Avenues" (*New York World-Telegram*, July 19, 1940.3); "Boniface Barney Josephson is now applying his magic touch along new channels, that of rediscovering erstwhile topnotchers. It's to Josephson's credit that he's come up with a show that's just about tops any way you look at it" (Abel Green, *Variety*, May 19, 1943.4); "He [Barney] can talk as expertly about Byron as he can about Boogie-Woogie; he takes his reading seriously" (Candide, "Only Human" column, *New York Daily News*, Jan. 22, 1942); and, "Jutting head and shoulders above all others is the polished entertainment that Barney Josephson always manages to assemble for the amusement of his patrons" (Gene Knight, *New York Journal-American*, Aug. 10, 1943.6).

CHAPTER 41: "No one was building for Negroes."

1. Germany surrendered on May 7, 1945; the Japanese signed terms of surrender on September 2, 1945.

CHAPTER 42: "The Un-American Activities Committee itself was unconstitutonal."

1. The vote on May 26, 1939, was 181 to 41.
2. William Gellerman, *Martin Dies* (1944, repr. New York: Da Capo Press, 1972), 64, citation from the Da Capo Press edition.
3. Hearings before the Committee on Un-American Activities—House of Representatives—Eightieth Congress, March 5, 1947, FBI Files, 27.
4. "Key Witness Balks at Hearing as Red," *New York Times*, March 6, 1947, 14.
5. Leon Josephson's statement to the press, March 6, 1947:

> *I am an American. I believe in democracy, in government of the people, by the people and for the people, which to me means government that stands for the greatest good for the greatest number, even if that greatest good can only be obtained at the expense of a few.*
>
> *The Constitution of the United States guarantees to me the freedom to advocate changes in our constitutional form of government and changes in our economic system, using the procedure set forth in that Constitution for effectuating such changes. That freedom of expression, I have freely exercised, and shall continue to do so.*
>
> *I am a Communist. Like all Communists, and like most Americans, I am also anti-Fascist. In the early years of Nazism, I saw clearly what this committee does not see even now, that Fascism leads directly to war. It leads to the extermination*

of my people—the Jewish people—as well as to the extermination of all that is good in our society. It leads to the end of the democracy in which I believe, and to the end of the civilization we all know.

As a Communist and an anti-Fascist, I took an active part in the fight against Hitler long before most Americans felt that fight was necessary.

I went to Europe and worked with the underground in Germany. I did not hesitate to risk my life in this work, and I spent four months in solitary confinement in a Danish dungeon, charged with "attempting to assassinate Hitler."

In the course of my anti-Fascist work, I helped some people to get into Germany so that they could better fight Hitler, and I helped others to escape from Germany so that they would live to carry on the fight against Fascism elsewhere.

I know that during these years, I freely violated the laws of Nazi Germany. It has been charged that I was also guilty of a technical violation of the laws of this country. If I ever did violate a law of this country, I certainly harmed no one, and did what I did in an honest effort to help save humanity from its greatest enemy. Working in an underground movement is a dangerous business and often involves such risks. Everything I did, I did consciously and with full knowledge of all the dangers involved. I am not ashamed of what I did; on the contrary, I am proud of it.

I cannot be shocked at the thought that my activities may have violated some law or other, and I can claim the best of historical precedents for my actions. Samuel Adams, Patrick Henry, and George Washington, violated laws too, and our independence was won by their efforts.

The abolitionists, in 1850, violated laws by smuggling Negroes out of slavery into the free North, and slavery was destroyed through their efforts.

In more recent times, over 3,500 American heroes went to Spain to fight Fascism. If any of them did violate any law, a higher morality motivated them when they defied our State Department to fight Hitler and Mussolini.

Had more people been so motivated, the last war might have been avoided.

The role of this un-American Committee is clear to anyone familiar with the American political scene. For nearly ten years, it has smeared the New Deal and every progressive group in the country.

Now, because of a change in political fortunes, it is attempting to assassinate politically, by scare headlines and red-baiting the remnants of the New Deal.

By creating a hysteria over Communism, it is trying to scare every progressive into acquiescence to reaction, to destroy the progressive trade unions, and to wipe out the broad social gains achieved under Roosevelt.

I do not believe that this committee is activated by ignorance, but rather by a well-planned program to create a national psychological basis for a domestic brand of Fascism.

I have been advised by counsel that the proceedings of this committee are repugnant to the provisions of our Constitution, and I feel it my duty to challenge its legality in the Courts. I am confident that I will ultimately be sustained.

6. Lee Josephson, son of Leon Josephson, interview with TTJ, Brooklyn Heights, N.Y., April 28, 1996.

7. The Comintern was the international organization of communist parties founded by Lenin in March 1919 to promote revolution worldwide. In 1943 Joseph Stalin ordered the body's dissolution to reassure his American and British wartime allies.

8. "Key Witness Balks at Hearing as Red," 14.

9. *Variety,* Dec. 10, 1947.

10. The House of Representatives voted to uphold the committee's citation on April 22, 1947; the Federal Grand Jury in Washington, D.C., indicted Leon on April 30; bail was granted on May 2; and the Court denied his motion to dismiss contempt citation on June 13.

11. "Argued November 6, 1947. Decided December 9, 1947. United States of America, Appellee, against Leon Josephson, Defendant-Appellant. Before: Swan, Chase and Clark, Circuit Judges," FBI Files, 343.

CHAPTER 43: "'I won't be coming into the club anymore.'"

1. Canada Lee interview, *New York Times,* July 7, 1949, 31.

2. Canada Lee, forty-five, suffered a fatal heart attack on May 9, 1952.

3. *Variety,* Dec. 17, 1947.

CHAPTER 44: "Two future presidents were in attendance."

1. Hanns Eisler, May 12, 1947, Los Angeles, FBI Files, released under the Freedom of Information Act. This was the first interrogation. Eisler's second interrogation by the HUAC was in September 1947 in Washington, D.C. He was not allowed to read another prepared statement; it was published by the *Daily Worker* on October 14, 1947.

2. The HUAC convened for the second time on October 20, 1947. Thirty-eight years later, Ronald Reagan was identified as a secret FBI informer to the committee. *New York Times,* Aug. 26, 1985. A friendly witness was anyone who "named names," that is, informed on friends, co-workers, or even family about membership in the Communist Party, past or present, or who had sponsored or belonged to any organization the committee deemed a front for the Communist Party.

3. The Hollywood Ten were the screenwriters Dalton Trumbo, Ring Lardner Jr., Lester Cole, Herbert Biberman, Alvah Bessie, Albert Maltz, Samuel Ornitz, and John Howard Lawson; the director Edward Dmytryk; and producer Adrian Scott.

4. Lela Rogers (mother of Ginger) testified secretly in May 1947.

5. "The word 'comrade' was not propaganda; 'tender comrade' was Robert Louis Stevenson's words for his beloved wife." Patrick McGilligan and Paul Buhle, *Tender*

Comrades: A Backstory of the Hollywood Blacklist (New York: St. Martin's Press, 1997), xiv.

6. A grand jury in Washinton, D.C., indicted the Hollywood Ten for contempt of Congress on December 5, 1947; they were arraigned and pleaded not guility on January 9, 1948.

7. J. Parnell Thomas pleaded the Fifth Amendment on November 4, 1948; was convicted, sentenced, and fined on November 28, 1949; and resigned from the House on January 1, 1950.

8. The Federal Employee Loyalty Program was established by Executive Order 9835 on March 21, 1947, Harry Truman, president.

9. The right-wing pamphlet *Red Channels* was published June 22, 1950. As Harriet Berg Schwartz recalled, "My mother . . . appealed to influential people . . . among them David Sarnoff of NBC and Frank Stanton and William Paley of CBS. All pleaded that they saw she was right, but could not do a thing about fighting advertisers or viewers or politicians." Schwartz letter to *New York Times,* Nov. 11, 1990.

10. Phil Loeb, sixty-three, died September 1, 1955.

11. Jack Gould, "Conspiracy of Silence," *New York Times,* April 22, 1951.

12. "I went Downtown to ask Barney to lend me some money for food. Barney said, 'The one thing you don't have to worry about is money.'" Isobel Gibbs letter to TTJ, Nov. 14, 1988.

CHAPTER 46: "'They'll set you up.'"

1. Barney never explained the detail of Downtown's closing. Years later, I (TTJ) found an unattributed, two-sentence article dated March 9, 1949: "Lewis I. Louis and Max Mansch have taken over operation of Cafe Society Downtown (N.Y.). Spot was sold by Barney Josephson, owner, subject to transfer of liquor license, which was approved March 2." Barney was no longer involved in any way. The particulars of the deal have created confusion over the years for jazz aficionados and writers because the name and ambience remained the same. *Variety* reported that "although Cafe Society Downtown has undergone a change of management, the entertainment policy . . . is being continued. The marquee lure currently is Dorothy Donegan" (March 30, 1949). Barney never presented Donegan; he did not like her as a performer. Two months later, on May 2, 1949, Gordon Allison reported in the *New York Herald-Tribune* that "the current proceedings . . . are under the guidance of Juanita Hall, Irwin Corey and George Shearing." Those artists, however, never appeared in Barney's Downtown or Uptown cafes. A story appeared in *Variety*, December 10, 1952, reporting that "Cafe Society Downtown, N.Y., was forced to suspend last week when the State Liquor Authority revoked

its license. . . . Cafe had been operating as the L&M Corp., an outfit now defunct and adjudged a bankrupt." Barney had been out of his Cafe Society Downtown since March 2, 1949.

CHAPTER 47: "She blew her cover."

1. Abe Burrows testimony in *New York Times Index*, Nov. 13, 1952. Burrows, seventy-four, died on May 1, 1985.
2. The production of *Die Fledermaus* opened September 1, 1950.
3. Josh White, *New York Times*, Sept. 2, 1950, 6. White was sixty-one when he died on September 5, 1969.

CHAPTER 48: "That's the way she washed herself."

1. "Chairman John S. Wood (D., Georgia) said she [Scott] would have to testify later because his other Congressional duties were too pressing at the moment." "Hazel Scott Denies Any Red Sympathies," *New York Times*, Sept. 16, 1950.
2. *New York Times*, Sept. 22, 1950.
3. Testimony of Hazel Scott Powell, Hearing before the Committee on Un-American Activities House of Representatives—Eighty-first Congress, Sept. 22, 1950.
4. The Joint Anti-Fascist Refugee Committee was established to collect money to feed and clothe refugees from the Spanish Civil War.
5. Testimony of Hazel Scott Powell.
6. Leonard Feather, "Hazel Scott: Her Era Never Came, a Dream Was Denied," *Calendar Magazine*, Oct. 11, 1981, 5. Scott died on October 2, 1981; Feather died on September 22, 1994.
7. Ibid.

CHAPTER 49: "'Will Geer, Will Hare, what the hell's the difference?'"

1. Patrick McGilligan and Paul Buhle, *Tender Comrades: A Backstory of the Hollywood Blacklist* (New York: St. Martin's Press, 1997), 564.
2. John Randolph, interview with TTJ, Sardi's Restaurant, New York City, March 7, 1991.
3. The HUAC held hearings in New York from August 15 to 18, 1955, and in July 1956. *New York Times Index*, 1955, 1172.
4. John Randolph inverview with TTJ.
5. Zero Mostel testified before the HUAC on October 14, 1955.
6. The Sixth Amendment involves trial rights, the Eighth bars cruel and unusual punishment, and the Fourteenth concerns rights of citizenship.

7. Black testified before the HUAC on August 19, 1955.

8. Imogene Coca, interview with TTJ in Coca's apartment, New York City, Jan. 31, 1991.

9. Jackie Robinson testified before the HUAC on July 18, 1949.

10. *Variety*, Dec. 18, 1946.

11. Paul Robeson testimony before the HUAC, June 1956.

CHAPTER 50: "Mr. Anonymous"

1. The lease was signed May 23, 1955, and the corporation was organized August 11, 1955, with $100,000 in shares.

2. Jimmie Josephson (married to David Josephson), interview with TTJ at Josephson's home, East Orange, N.J., Jan. 24, 1984.

3. According to a letter to the director in the FBI Files, "An Anonymous source of the Los Angeles Field Division stated that the name BARNEY JOSEPHSON appeared in the address book in the possession of [blacked out] when the latter was in Fresno, California, on March 3, 1945. The informant stated that [blacked out] was then a key figure in the [most of the page blacked out]. On May 8, 1953, the subject refused to be interviewed by Bureau Agents."

CHAPTER 51: "'We did it, Barney. You and me and the Lord Jesus Christ.'"

1. John S. Wilson, "Jazz Finds Home at The Cookery," *New York Times*, Nov. 27, 1970.

2. Whitney Balliet, "Out Here Again," *The New Yorker*, May 2, 1964.

3. Peter O'Brien, interview with TTJ, St. Malachy Church, New York City, Aug. 26, 1996.

4. Art D'Lugoff, owner of the Village Gate, at memorial for Barney Josephson, Nov. 16, 1988. The Village Gate was a famous jazz club in Greenwich Village from 1955 to 1993.

5. Peter O'Brien interview, Aug. 26, 1996.

6. Ibid.

7. Mary Lou Williams was artist-in-residence at Duke University, beginning in 1977.

CHAPTER 52: "'If he liked an idea, he would do it.'"

1. Marian McPartland, interview with TTJ at McPartland's home, Port Washington, N.Y., Aug. 3, 1994.

2. Ibid.

3. Whitney Balliett, *The New Yorker*, March 4, 1972.

4. Marian McPartland interview, Aug. 3, 1994.

5. Ibid.

6. Nancy Balliett and Whitney Balliett, interview with TTJ, Balliett home, New York, Sept. 24, 1989.

7. Marian McPartland interview, Aug. 3, 1994.

8. The opening was on August 28, 1943.

9. Interview in Stanley Dance, *The World of Swing* (New York: Scribner's Sons, 1974), 324. In the 1940s, Heywood made a lot of money recording, arranging, and playing in Hollywood films. He opened at The Cookery on April 3, 1972. Heywood died on January 2, 1989; he was seventy-three.

CHAPTER 53: "'I'll tell you, Teddy Wilson, you've just made Barney Josephson cry.'"

1. Teddy Wilson, interview with TTJ and Barney Josephson, The Cookery, Jan. 27, 1983.

2. John S. Wilson, *New York Times,* Feb. 12, 1972.

3. Wilson was signed from December 8, 1972, to March 1, 1973.

4. Teddy Wilson interview, Jan. 27, 1983.

CHAPTER 54: "'He wasn't deceitful about things.'"

1. Nellie Lutcher, interview with TTJ, President's Room of the Musicians Union Local 47, Los Angeles, May 3, 1991.

2. Whitney Balliett, "Our Local Correspondents," *The New Yorker,* April 7, 1980, 120. Nellie Lutcher, ninety-four, died on June 15, 2007.

3. Susan Brownmiller, "Back at Last—Nellie Lutcher; Hurry on Down!" *Village Voice,* May 17, 1973, 72.

4. Chuck Folds to TTJ, Oct. 25, 1989; Chuck Folds, unpublished article.

5. Helen Humes was with Count Basie from 1938 to 1942.

6. John Wilson, *New York Times,* Jan. 21, 1975.

7. Gary Giddins, "The Joy of Helen," *New York Magazine,* Feb 17, 1975, 60.

8. John Wilson, *New York Times,* Jan. 21, 1975.

9. Helen Humes died on September 13, 1981.

10. Cryer and Ford opened at The Cookery on July 14, 1975, and returned again in September 1975 and then in 1976. Their first engagement was July 14–30, 1975; they were back again from September 15–30, 1975, and from April 5 to May 21 in 1976.

11. Gretchen Cryer, interview with TTJ, Cryer's home, New York, Aug. 13, 1999. The show, which opened off Broadway in 1978, ran for three years.

12. Big Joe Turner appeared at The Cookery from November 8, 1976, to December 4, 1976, and returned March 10, 1977, to May 7, 1977.
13. Whitney Balliett, "Majesty, Joe Turner," *The New Yorker,* Nov. 29, 1976.

CHAPTER 55: "All I looked at was her mouth."

1. Gerald Cook at memorial for Barney Josephson, Nov. 16, 1988.
2. Ibid. Margaret Bonds (1913–72) was an accomplished pianist and teacher and famous as an African American composer of orchestral, choral, chamber music, art, and popular songs.
3. Whitney Balliett, *The New Yorker,* Oct. 31, 1977.

Chapter 56: "'You don't need a contract with Barney Josephson.'"

1. Barbara Kantrowitz, "Alberta Hunter Delivers the Blues—and a Message," *Philadelphia Inquirer,* Jan. 31, 1980, 1C.
2. Lolly Golt, "Comeback at Eighty-two," *Montreal Star,* Nov. 19, 1977.
3. Bill Hunter, "Alberta Hunter in Silver and Blue," *Players,* n.d., 53.
4. Robert Fulford, "At Eighty-seven, Alberta Hunter Is Still Belting the Blues," *Toronto Star,* May 28, 1982.
5. Taped by TTJ at The Cookery.
6. TTJ was at the table and heard both stories.

CHAPTER 58: "'Several times Rosalynn Carter shaped her mouth into O's of amazement.'"

1. Among the artists and other notables on the program were Harry Belafonte, Tony Bennett, Leonard Bernstein, Grace Bumbry, Douglas Fairbanks Jr., Suzanne Farrell, Jose Ferrer, Aretha Franklin, Rosemary Harris, the Howard University Choir, Alberta Hunter, Edward Kennedy, Mary Martin, Peter Martins, Charles Percy, Itzhak Perlman, John Raitt, Mstislav Rostropovich, John Rubinstein, Julius Rudel, Isaac Stern, Edward Villella, and the dancers from *A Chorus Line.*
2. "Opera House, the Kennedy Center Honors Gala," *Washington Star,* Dec. 3, 1978.
3. Ibid.
4. Joy Billington, "Governors' Gathering," *Washington Star,* Feb. 28, 1979, C3.

CHAPTER 59: "'When the inspiration of God is missing, I just rely on talent.'"

1. Ken Emerson, "Marian Williams Is Carrying Her Gospel Mission into a 'Saloon,'" *New York Times,* July 18, 1980.
2. John S. Wilson, "If a Child Don't Favor His Father Some Way, It's a Dead Cat on the Line," *New York Times,* July 20, 1980.

3. When Barney and I stopped in one evening Dardanelle introduced one of her songs as "All the Things You Are, Mr. Josephson" in tribute.

4. Susannah McCorkle opened at The Cookery on November 3, 1980.

5. Susannah McCorkle to TTJ, Feb. 28, 1991. McCorkle passed away on May 19, 2001, ten years after she wrote to me. I (TTJ) understand she had a long history of clinical depression as well as serious health issues and a career at a stand-still. "I just can't keep fighting myself and my own biochemistry any longer" she wrote in her farewell note. Robin Pogrebin, "A Brave Singer Who Finally Ran out of Silver Linings," *New York Times,* May 24, 2001.

6. Stephen Holden, "Susannah McCorkle, Fifty-five, Pop-Jazz Singer," *New York Times,* May 21, 2001.

CHAPTER 60: "Her name meant nothing to me."

1. Alberta Hunter appeared from May 5 to June 13, 1981, at The Cookery.

2. "Tonight in Manhattan," *New York Daily News,* July 13, 1981.

3. Ruth Brown, interview with TTJ, The Cookery, July 18, 1981.

CHAPTER 61: "'Fame hasn't changed me.'"

1. Sylvia Syms, interview with TTJ, The Cookery, July 31, 1982.

2. Mel Gussow radio program, Station WQXR, Dec. 22, 1981.

3. Arthur Siegel's gig was from December 21, 1981, to April 13, 1982. He died September 1994 at the age of seventy.

4. Frank Rich was then the chief theater critic for *The New York Times.*

5. John S. Wilson, "Folk Music: Oscar Brand," *New York Times,* March 6, 1983.

6. Oscar Brand, interview with TTJ, The Cookery, March 31, 1983.

7. Dan Barry, "A Little Brand-Name Music," *New York Daily News,* March 18, 1983.

8. On December 10, 2006, *Folksong Festival* celebrated its sixtieth anniversary and continues to broadcast every Saturday morning from 10 to 11 on radio station WNYC in New York City.

9. John S. Wilson, *New York Times,* April 8, 1983.

10. The engagement was to begin on October 6, 1983.

11. John Hammond, interview with TTJ at his office, Jan. 10, 1986.

CHAPTER 62: "In effect, this stripped me of my business."

1. Jimmie Josephson (wife of David Josephson), interview with TTJ at Josephson's home, East Orange, N.J., Jan. 24, 1984.

2. Lee Josephson, son of Leon Josephson, interview with TTJ, Brooklyn Heights, N.Y., April 28, 1996.

3. Edgar E. (Ted) Coons Jr., professor of psychology and neuroscience, New York University, interview with TTJ, Brooklyn Heights, N.Y., Nov. 11, 1989.

4. Gloria Josephson died three months before Barney, on June 20, 1988.

5. Nancy Balliett and Whitney Balliett, interview with TTJ, Balliett home, New York, Sept. 24, 1989.

6. "Alberta," *New York Times*, Oct. 21, 1984.

POSTLUDE

1. Don Nelson, *New York Daily News*, Sept. 12, 1986.

2. Obituary, *New York Times*, Nov. 23, 1989, 18:6. Rose Murphy was seventy-six when she died.

3. The musicians and performers on the program were Oscar Brand, Doc Cheatham, Ellis Larkins, Sammy Price, Ram Ramirez, Carrie Smith, Dick Sudhalter, Brian Torff, Chuck Wayne, and Johnny Williams Jr. Whitney Balliett spoke, as did Joseph Kline, son of Barney's sister, Ethel, who reminisced about his uncle's childhood. Mollie Moon's and Gerald Cook's reminiscences are quoted elsewhere in the narrative.

4. Agnes de Mille had suffered a second stroke and was confined to a wheelchair.

5. William Shakespeare, "The Passionate Pilgrim," Sonnet XII.

Index

Page numbers of photos appear in italics and indicate one of the five sections where photos appear. Photo section A follows page 44, section B follows page 102, section C follows page 202, section D follows page 252, and section E follows page 336.

Barney Josephson (1902–88) was a nightclub impresario in New York City.

Terry Trilling-Josephson is a former actress, off-Broadway theater producer, and speech-language pathologist. She is professor emerita of communications and performing arts, The City University of New York.

Dan Morgenstern is the director of the Institute of Jazz Studies at Rutgers University and has written widely about jazz.

Music in American Life

The Hank Snow Story—*Hank Snow, with Jack Ownbey and Bob Burris*
Milton Brown and the Founding of Western Swing—*Cary Ginell, with special assistance from Roy Lee Brown*
Santiago de Murcia's "Códice Saldívar No. 4": A Treasury of Secular Guitar Music from Baroque Mexico—*Craig H. Russell*
The Sound of the Dove: Singing in Appalachian Primitive Baptist Churches—*Beverly Bush Patterson*
Heartland Excursions: Ethnomusicological Reflections on Schools of Music—*Bruno Nettl*
Doowop: The Chicago Scene—*Robert Pruter*
Blue Rhythms: Six Lives in Rhythm and Blues—*Chip Deffaa*
Shoshone Ghost Dance Religion: Poetry Songs and Great Basin Context—*Judith Vander*
Go Cat Go! Rockabilly Music and Its Makers—*Craig Morrison*
'Twas Only an Irishman's Dream: The Image of Ireland and the Irish in American Popular Song Lyrics, 1800–1920—*William H. A. Williams*
Democracy at the Opera: Music, Theater, and Culture in New York City, 1815–60—*Karen Ahlquist*
Fred Waring and the Pennsylvanians—*Virginia Waring*
Woody, Cisco, and Me: Seamen Three in the Merchant Marine—*Jim Longhi*
Behind the Burnt Cork Mask: Early Blackface Minstrelsy and Antebellum American Popular Culture—*William J. Mahar*
Going to Cincinnati: A History of the Blues in the Queen City—*Steven C. Tracy*
Pistol Packin' Mama: Aunt Molly Jackson and the Politics of Folksong—*Shelly Romalis*
Sixties Rock: Garage, Psychedelic, and Other Satisfactions—*Michael Hicks*
The Late Great Johnny Ace and the Transition from R&B to Rock 'n' Roll—*James M. Salem*
Tito Puente and the Making of Latin Music—*Steven Loza*
Juilliard: A History—*Andrea Olmstead*
Understanding Charles Seeger, Pioneer in American Musicology—*Edited by Bell Yung and Helen Rees*
Mountains of Music: West Virginia Traditional Music from *Goldenseal*—*Edited by John Lilly*
Alice Tully: An Intimate Portrait—*Albert Fuller*
A Blues Life—*Henry Townsend, as told to Bill Greensmith*
Long Steel Rail: The Railroad in American Folksong (2d ed.)—*Norm Cohen*
The Golden Age of Gospel—*Text by Horace Clarence Boyer; photography by Lloyd Yearwood*
Aaron Copland: The Life and Work of an Uncommon Man—*Howard Pollack*
Louis Moreau Gottschalk—*S. Frederick Starr*
Race, Rock, and Elvis—*Michael T. Bertrand*
Theremin: Ether Music and Espionage—*Albert Glinsky*
Poetry and Violence: The Ballad Tradition of Mexico's Costa Chica—*John H. McDowell*
The Bill Monroe Reader—*Edited by Tom Ewing*
Music in Lubavitcher Life—*Ellen Koskoff*

The University of Illinois Press
is a founding member of the
Association of American University Presses.

———————————————————————————

Composed in 10.5/14 Minion Pro Regular
with P22 Parrish display, and Type Embellishments
Two LET ornaments
by Celia Shapland
at the University of Illinois Press
Manufactured by Sheridan Books, Inc.

University of Illinois Press
1325 South Oak Street
Champaign, IL 61820-6903
www.press.uillinois.edu